TREATISES OF
THE SUPERVISOR
AND GUARDIAN
of the Cinnamon Sea

TREATISES OF
THE SUPERVISOR AND GUARDIAN

of the Cinnamon Sea

THE NATURAL WORLD AND MATERIAL CULTURE
OF 12TH CENTURY SOUTH CHINA

Fan Chengda (1126–1193)

TRANSLATION AND INTRODUCTION
by *James M. Hargett*

A CHINA PROGRAM BOOK

UNIVERSITY OF WASHINGTON PRESS
Seattle & London

This book was supported in part by the China Studies Program,
a division of the Henry M. Jackson School of International Studies
at the University of Washington.

© 2010 by the University of Washington Press
Printed in the United States of America
Design by Thomas Eykemans
Composed in Minion, designed by Robert Slimbach
Display type set in Gotham, designed by Tobias Frere-Jones and Jesse Ragan
15 14 13 12 11   5 4 3 2 1

UNIVERSITY OF WASHINGTON PRESS
P.O. Box 50096, Seattle, WA 98145 U.S.A.
www.washington.edu/uwpress

LIBRARY OF CONGRESS CATALOGING-IN-PUBLICATION DATA
Fan, Chengda, 1126–1193.
[Gui hai yu heng zhi. English]
Treatises of the supervisor and guardian of the Cinnamon Sea =
Guihai yuheng zhi / by Fan Chengda;
translated, with an introduction and annotations, by James M. Hargett.
p. cm.
Includes bibliographical references and index.
ISBN 978-0-295-99078-1 (hardback : alk. paper)
ISBN 978-0-295-99079-8 (pbk. : alk. paper)
1. Natural resourses—China—Guangxi Zhuangzu Zizhiqu.
2. Guangxi Zhuangzu Zizhiqu (China)—Description and travel.
3. Fan, Chengda, 1126–1193—Diaries.
4. Fan, Chengda, Song dynasty, 960–1279.
I. Hargett, James M. (James Morris)
II. Title.
HC428.K88F3613 2010   333:70951'2809021—dc22   2010024932

For Kermit L. Hall (1944–2006)

a man of vision, a true leader, a swell guy

卓有遠見, 造福眾人, 鞠躬盡瘁, 永駐人心.

Contents

TREATISES OF THE SUPERVISOR AND
GUARDIAN OF THE CINNAMON SEA
Author's Preface   *3*

5   IMPLEMENTS

6   BIRDS

Lichees

Longan

Steamed-Bun Mandarin Oranges

Kumquats

Soft Plums

Stone Chestnuts

Sweet-Sword Almonds

Dragon Lichees

Woody Bamboo Fruit

Winter Peaches

Luowang Fruit

Human Face Fruit

Black Olives

Square Olives

Coconut-Palm Fruit

Banana Fruit

Fowl Banana Fruit

Bud Bananas

Red-and-Salty Cardamom

Star Anise

Indian Gooseberry Fruit

Carambola Fruit

Wild Lemon Fruit

Jackfruit

Pomelos

Lugu Fruit

Rubbing-and-Scratching Nuts

Earthworm Fruit

Fiery-Red Pomelos

Fiery Charcoal Nuts

Wild Rambutan

Wild Longan

Soapberry Fruit

Mulai Fruit

Nian Fruit

Thousand-Year Fruit

Fiery-Red Jujubes

Creeping Rambutan Fruit

Gumi Fruit

Qiao Fruit

Creeping He Fruit

Woody Lotus Fruit

Luomeng Fruit

Mao Chestnuts

Tenai Nuts

Buna Fruit

Goat-Droppings Fruit

Ritou Fruit

Bishop Tree Fruit

Wampee Fruit

Zhuyuan Fruit

Oblate Peaches

Fen'gu Fruit

Tagu Fruit

Yellow Belly Fruit

Acknowledgments

I HAVE BEEN STUDYING CHINESE FOR A VERY LONG TIME. ONE aspect of the language I still enjoy is learning proverbs. One proverb that comes to mind when I think about how this book came to be published is *wu qiao bu cheng shu* 無巧不成書, which means something like "without coincidence there is no good story." Well, the "coincidence" here is that (1) Charles Hartman, my friend and colleague at the University at Albany, suggested I consider the University of Washington Press as a possible publication venue for the manuscript that eventually became this book; and (2) another friend and colleague in the field, Patricia Buckley Ebrey (University of Washington, Seattle), put me in touch with Lorri Hagman at the University Washington Press. After Lorri received my initial email query, she wrote back immediately and described my book proposal and timing as "serendipitous," for she had just finished up with one translation project and was now looking for a new one. Therein lies the "coincidence" in my "story."

Now some background. Much of the material I have published in my career has concerned one author: Fan Chengda (1126–1193), a well-known government official and writer who lived during the Southern Song dynasty (1127–1279) in China. My main interest all along has been Fan's four major prose works, which include his three travel diaries, *Diary of Grasping the Carriage Reins* (Lanpei lu), *Diary of Mounting a Simurgh* (Canluan lu), and *Diary of a Boat Trip to Wu* (Wuchuan lu), along with his valuable miscellany on southwest China titled *Treatises of the Supervisor and Guardian of the Cinnamon Sea* (Guihai yuheng zhi). Annotated translations of the first two diaries are included in my *On the Road in Twelfth Century China* (1989), while a study and English version of the third appears in my more recent *Riding the River Home* (2008). In this book I provide the first complete and annotated translation of Fan Chengda's *Treatises* published in any language. Thus, my initial goal to provide English readers with translations of Fan Chengda's four major prose works has now been realized, and I thank Lorri Hagman and her colleagues at the University of Washington Press for publishing this final installment of my almost lifelong "Fan Chengda project." It has indeed been a long journey and many colleagues, students, and friends have helped me along the way.

First and foremost, I extend profound thanks to my good friend Professor Xu Yongming of Zhejiang University, who on numerous occasions responded enthusiastically to my questions about the text. Without Yongming's help and support I could never have finished this book.

Others who helped me along the way include Charles Hartman, Peter Lorge, Meng Yuanyao, Zhou Nanzhao, and Song Tiesha. I also extend warm thanks to Mr. Zhou Wenye and his students at Capital Normal University (Beijing), who prepared the useful map that includes most of the places mentioned by Fan Chengda in *Treatises* (map 1), and to Josh Sisskind, who helped me get this map ready for publication. I also want to thank Nicole Novak, who prepared the revised version of the late Southern Song dynasty "Map of Jingjiang Municipality with Walls and Moats" (map 2).

To Bill Pyszczymuka and Joe Katz, who helped with many computer-related problems, I owe a tremendous debt of gratitude.

I also to send thanks to the two anonymous readers of my manuscript, both of whom made numerous useful suggestions for improvement.

I only recently learned that my old friend and fellow China traveler, Gary Flint (a.k.a. "Dongbo"), passed away in August of 2009. He will be missed by many. Two of Gary's beautiful photographs grace the pages of this book (figs. 1 and 3). No doubt, Dongbo is in heaven now, chatting and singing songs with his hero, Su Dongpo (or Su Shi, 1037–1101).

Finally, I respectfully dedicate this book to my former university president and good friend, Kermit L. Hall. We spent a lot of time "on the road" together in China. He left us much too early.

Guilderland, New York
November 2010

Translator's Note

THIS BOOK IS FULL OF PERSONAL NAMES, PLACE-NAMES, technical terms, and other specialized vocabulary. The Chinese characters for these names and terms can be found in the Glossary-Index. As a general rule, I have included Chinese characters (for names and terms) in the body of the text and footnote apparatus only when possible confusion begs clarification.

Complete references for sources cited in the footnotes are included in the Bibliography. Titles of sources cited frequently in the footnotes are given in abbreviated form (for example, *WXTK* for *Wenxian tong-kao*). For the complete titles of these sources, see Abbreviations Used in the Notes and Bibliography.

Readers with a special interest in technical matters such as scientific nomenclatures, various units of measurement, office titles, Song dynasty administrative terminology, and so on, may want to read through the section of the Introduction titled "Terminology, Measurements, and Dates" before turning to the translation.

On some occasions Chinese characters will appear in brackets, as in the following example: Fubo Yan 伏[洑]波巖. This indicates that the character in brackets is an alternate and, on some occasions, more correct, written form of this particular name. In the example just given, the commonly used character for *fu* is 伏, though strictly speaking the correct character is written 洑.

Map 1 includes most of the Southern Song (ca. 1175) place-names mentioned in *Treatises*. Some of these toponyms have more than one written form in Chinese, for which readers may consult the Glossary-Index. On several occasions in the text, different names are used to refer to the same place. On Map 1, the official name is given first, followed by the alternate name (or names) in parentheses: for example, Jingjiang (Gui, Guilin, Guizhou).

Introduction

THIS BOOK PRESENTS, FOR THE FIRST TIME IN ENGLISH, A complete and annotated translation of *Treatises of the Supervisor and Guardian of the Cinnamon Sea* (Guihai yuheng zhi; hereafter called *Treatises*). Most scholars of traditional China, especially those whose research interest concerns the Song dynasty (960–1279), are familiar with this work, and for good reason: it contains a wealth of geographical, historical, cultural, and other types of information about southwest China—mainly, Guangxi—in the twelfth century, with special reference to the various non-Chinese Man[1] peoples who inhabited that general region and lands immediately beyond, including Hainan (map 1). Fan Chengda (1126–1193), the author of *Treatises*, completed the text in 1175, just after he had served for twenty-two months as civil and military governor of Guangxi.

Treatises is important because it provides the earliest and most detailed written account on China's southwestern frontier and the non-Chinese peoples and cultures active there in the premodern period. Although Guangxi and Hainan were under nominal Chinese control during the Song, most tribes of the region were in fact untouched by Chinese influence. This political reality coupled with China's desire to control the south sometimes resulted in turbulent and bloody encounters along the border. *Treatises* reveals how China

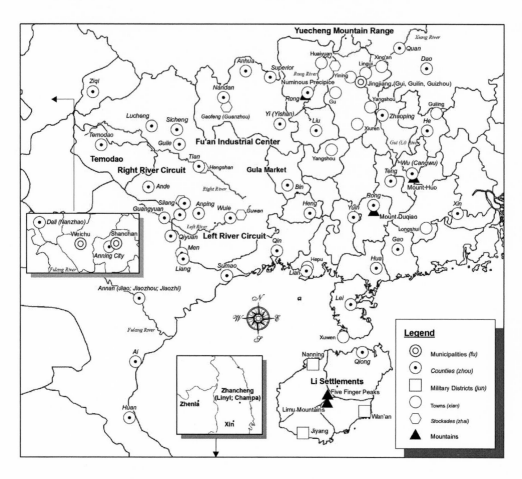

Yuecheng Mountain Range

MAP 1
Southern Song Place-Names Mentioned in the *Treatises of the Supervisor and Guardian of the Cinnamon Sea*. My thanks to Mr. Zhou Wenye and his students at Capital Normal University (Beijing) for preparing this map.

sought to maximize its control in the south while minimizing military conflict. What actually happened in southwest China during the Song, however, is fascinating because it deviates from the "usual" scenario, seen often in later Chinese history, whereby the "core" or "inner" culture (that is, China) dominates—militarily and politically—an "outer" or "alien" people on its periphery. In this scenario the border people are either marginalized to mountain regions or else "absorbed" into Chinese culture. *Treatises* tells a very different story.

HISTORICAL, ADMINISTRATIVE,
AND GEOGRAPHICAL BACKGROUND

Treatises concerns an administrative district known during the Song dynasty as the Guangnan West Circuit (Guangnan *xilu*).[2] This circuit was large and included most of modern Guangxi (known officially today as the Guangxi Zhuang Autonomous Region), a portion of Guangdong, the island of Hainan, and a small slice of modern Vietnam. While "Guangxi" is not widely known outside of China, its best-known tourist attraction, the modern city of Guilin (lit., "Cinnamon Grove"), is renowned throughout the world. Droves of domestic and foreign tourists flock there annually, mainly to glimpse the picturesque limestone spires that thrust upward from Guilin's otherwise flat and lush landscape. Many of these sightseers do so while plying a slow-moving catamaran down the scenic Li River, which flows directly through the city (fig. 1).

The history of Guangxi, like most places in China, is long and complex. Human activity in the region extends back to the Paleolithic era (ca. 12,000–7,000 B.C.E.), while carbon 14 testing of artifacts discovered at the Zengpi Yan archaeological site near Guilin, discovered in 1956, date to ca. 10,000 B.C.E.[3] During the Spring and Autumn period (722–481 B.C.E.) the area around Guilin shared a common boundary with the ancient states of Chu and Yue (or Nan-Yue). But later, during the Warring States period (475–221 B.C.E.), the region fell under sole control of Chu.

One major factor that has influenced the history of Guangxi is the large population of non-Chinese people, many originally of Tai stock, who inhabit the region. The largest group among these indigenous people is now called Zhuang. A smaller ethnic group, the Li, populates the coast of the Leizhou peninsula and parts of Hainan. Later migrations brought in other tribespeople, such as the Yao. Modern scholars often present the history of Guangxi in the context of how these and other non-Chinese peoples living in the region interacted with Chinese administrators, military forces, and colonists who began arriving from the north during the Qin dynasty (221–206 B.C.E.). This marked the beginning of Chinese expansion in the region, a trend that continued throughout the dynastic period. Essentially, the Chi-

FIGURE 1
Li River and Karst Formations, Guilin. Photograph courtesy
of Dongbo of www.mountainsongs.net.

nese sought to colonize and control Guangxi, as they did with other
areas in the south, because it is a land of abundant natural resources
and unique local products. Moreover, beginning in the Qin period the
region was also regarded as a security or buffer zone between China
and various alien states to the south and west.

Following the conquest of its six major rival states in 221 B.C.E.,
the Qin mounted military campaigns to the north and to the south
to extend its borders and acquire colonies. The southern campaign
ordered some half a million soldiers to Lingnan, the territory south
of the Southern Ranges (Nanling), sometimes also called the Five
Ranges (Wuling).[4] Lingnan for the most part corresponds to the modern provinces of Guangxi and Guangdong. One portion of the Qin
military force sent to the south marched across the Southern Ranges

and into Guangxi from Hunan via the so-called Xiang-Gui corridor—the key land route that connected the heart of Chinese civilization in the Central Plains (Zhongyuan) in the north with Lingnan.[5] After about three years of intense and bloody fighting between the Qin and forces of the Yue (or Viet) people in the south, the Lingnan region was finally pacified in 214 B.C.E. Thereafter the Qin created three administrative commanderies (*jun*) to oversee its interests in the region: Guilin Commandery, in roughly what is now Guangxi; Nanhai Commandery, most of which was in Guangdong; and Xiang Commandery, located in the central and northern parts of Vietnam. These fertile and well-watered territories were of great economic and social importance, mainly because one key strategy of the Qin was to control and consolidate its new land acquisitions in the south by transplanting into the region Chinese settlers, who would then follow and spread a northern Chinese agrarian lifestyle. Our main interest is Guilin Commandery.[6] At about the same time this commandery was established (that is, in 214 B.C.E.), the First Emperor of Qin dispatched one of his best engineers, Shi Lu (also known as Censor Lu), to Guangxi in order to construct a canal that would connect the Xiang River, which flows from northern Guangxi into the Changjiang (or Yangzi River) drainage system, with the West River and its major tributaries in Guangxi. This water link was designed to provide a means to transport food and supplies to support Qin military campaigns in the south. Known as the Numinous Canal (Lingqu), it passed in close proximity to where the city of Guilin would later be built. With just a few interruptions, the canal has remained in use until the present day.[7]

The history of Guilin Commandery is a short one. Most of the south was lost to Chinese control in the turmoil that followed the collapse of the Qin in 206 B.C.E. The appearance of the formally organized Nanyue kingdom in 203 B.C.E., headed by an independent king who in fact was a Chinese from the north named Zhao Tuo (d. 137 B.C.E.), hindered efforts by rulers of the Han dynasty (206 B.C.E.–220 C.E.) to regain some control of the south. In 112 B.C.E. a renegade prime minister of the Yue kingdom named Lü Jia incited a rebellion in Panyu (modern Guangzhou), which required that a suppression force of 100,000 troops be sent to the south by Emperor Wu of Han

(r. 141–87 B.C.E.). The rebellion ended in the following year when Han military forces reached Panyu and forced it to surrender. Afterwards, Emperor Wu divided the three original commanderies of Lingnan into nine smaller ones, one of which was called Lingling. Under this commandery a number of towns (*xian*) were established, including one named Shian.[8] Some modern scholars believe this Han dynasty town was located on or very near the site of modern Guilin.[9]

During the Han period the Chinese presence in Guangxi expanded greatly. Most of the new arrivals from the north settled in the hill regions around Guilin in the northeast and Hepu (near modern Beihai) in the south. Ceramic, bronze, and iron relics unearthed in tombs in these areas indicate a sophisticated level of economy and (Chinese) culture during the Later (or Eastern) Han (25–220).[10] While the Guilin and Hepu regions seem to have been under firm Chinese control, other parts of Guangxi—in particular, the areas around the Left River (Zuojiang) and Right River (Youjiang) in the southwest,[11] where a large concentration of tribal people lived—remained largely free of Chinese influence. During the Later Han, however, the increased incursions of Chinese colonists, who began to appropriate the rich alluvial soil along these and other major rivers in the region, increasingly drove some of the non-Chinese population to retreat into the mountains. At the same time, the increased presence of these new settlers stimulated resistance on the local level. The result was often tribal uprisings and armed conflict. A large-scale local revolt took place in 40 C.E. that led to the formation of yet another major Han military campaign in the south. The man chosen to lead this expedition was the famous general Ma Yuan (14 B.C.E.– 49 C.E.). It took Ma Yuan and his troops three long and difficult years to complete their suppression of the revolt.

In 265, during the Three Kingdoms period (220–280) that followed the Han, a new commandery was created in the region. This new commandery, established by Sun Hao (242–284), the fourth and last emperor of the state of Wu (222–280), reorganized the southern part of Lingling Commandery, which included most of the northeastern portion of modern Guangxi, into Shian Commandery. The administrative seat of Shian was located on the site of modern Guilin. From this time forward, Shian (or Guilin) became the central transportation hub linking north China and points south in Lingnan. Its location on the Xiang-Gui corridor and close proximity to the Numinous Canal meant that during times of peace Shian could function as an important economic center, while in times of unrest it was always a focus of contention.

Throughout the remainder of the Six Dynasties era (220–589) the name of Shian Commandery was changed several times. This reflects the unstable political situation throughout China at the time, which led many people from the north to flee to Guangxi and other parts of the south. During the Liu-Song dynasty (420–479), the well-known writer Yan Yanzhi (384–456) was appointed protector (*shou*) of Shian and wrote many poems and essays praising the beauty of Guilin. Yan's famous Reading Cave (Dushu Yan) is described in Fan Chengda's "Treatise on Precipice-Grottoes." An administrative reorganization of Shian Commandery in 507 led to the adoption of a new name: Gui County (Guizhou). Then, in 540, the Gui County seat was moved to the former site of "old" Shian Town during the Han dynasty. It was about this time that people began calling the city and surrounding area "Guilin."

Given the strategic location of Gui County and its importance in consolidating the southern frontier, it comes as no surprise that the rulers of the Sui (581–618) and Tang (618–907) dynasties over time enhanced its civil and military functions. Guilin's first city wall, built in a perfect square measuring three *li* in circumference (roughly one mile), and standing one *zhang*, two *chi* in height (roughly 14 feet), was built in 621 by the Tang official and military commander Li Jing (571–649).[12] The city and wall were both enlarged in the ninth century and again during the Song.[13] In 624 the entire area was put under the control of a military governor and called the Gui County Commanding General's Headquarters (Guizhou Dudu Fu). Then, in 681, Gui County was enlarged and reorganized into the Gui Administration (Guiguan), headed by a managing and organizing commissioner (*jinglue shi;* functionally, military governor). Finally, at the end of the Tang (specifically, in the year 900), the name Gui Administration was dropped for yet another new name: Jingjiang Military District for Order and Rule (Jingjiang Jun Jiedu). But afterwards, during the Five Dynasties (907–960) and Ten Kingdoms (902–979) eras, the former name Gui County was reinstated.

Throughout the Northern Song dynasty (960–1127), Gui was one of twenty-five counties under the jurisdiction of the Guangnan West Circuit. Then, in 1133, after the Jin invasions forced the remnants of the Song court to flee to the south, Gui County was elevated to the status of a *fu,* or municipality, and bestowed with a new name, Jingjiang.[14] A surviving map dated 1272, "Map of Jingjiang Municipality with Walls and Moats" (Jingjiang fu chengchi tu), suggests that the size of Jingjiang in the late Song was much larger in size than Gui County during the Tang. The Jingjiang that Fan Chengda knew when he served as governor there from 1173 to 1175 was probably not very different from the city we see outlined on this map (map 2).

In order to enhance administrative control of areas in Guangxi with heavy concentrations of tribespeople and only limited Chinese influence, the Song followed a practice of managing what were called "bridle and halter" (*jimi*) political-administrative units in its frontier provinces. In Guangxi these existed on three levels: county, town, and settlement (*dong*).[15] In the twelfth century some of these units were continuations of the bridle and halter administrations established under the Tang; most, however, were new ones created by the Song. The majority of these administrative centers were concentrated along the Left River and Right River valleys, where most non-Chinese inhabitants of the region resided. The largest number of bridle and halter units fell under the jurisdiction of Yong County (Yongzhou; modern Nanning, Guangxi). Yong County was in turn divided into two *dao,* or circuits: the Left River and the Right River. Each of these circuits was further subdivided into bridle and halter counties, towns, and settlements.[16] The expression "bridle and halter" suggests the idea of "loose rein." In other words, willing or submissive local people were organized by the Song into a Chinese administrative hierarchy, usually headed by hereditary local chiefs who had near-absolute control over land distribution but who were subordinate to Chinese civil and military authority in the region. This approach to organizing local people into administrative units reflects a long-standing Chinese policy of "using barbarians to control barbarians" (*yi yi zhi yi*). Again, the purpose of this policy was to achieve and maintain some level of Chinese political control over border regions without engaging in costly military campaigns against the local people. At the same

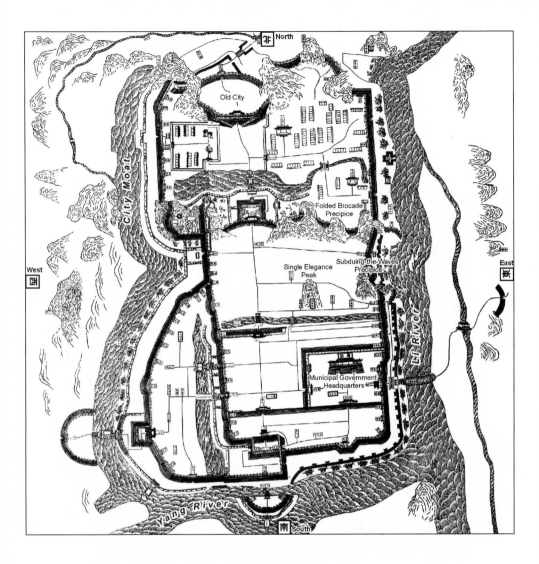

MAP 2
Redrawn version of "Map of Jingjiang Municipality with Walls and
Moats" (Jingjiang fu chengchi tu) (1272), prepared by Guilin shi diming
weiyuanhui bangongshi (1983). My thanks to Ms. Song Tiesha for
providing me with a copy of this map. Nicole Novak prepared the final,
published version.

time, the Chinese hoped this system would also "convert" or "Confu-
cianize" the various border peoples to a "cultured" Chinese lifestyle.[17]
Following the Jin invasions in the 1120s and their later occupation of

north China, and during the Song-Jin treaty negotiations that took place in the decades that followed, the Song had neither the interest nor the resources to mount a costly military campaign in the south.

Guangxi hosts a rugged terrain that is overwhelmingly mountainous. Spectacular limestone spires, formed by erosion, are found in about one-third of Guangxi's territory. The region's mountainous terrain has always made land travel there especially difficult. However, Guangxi is also home to thousands of lakes and waterways, the latter of which form an extensive and navigable river system. Since early imperial times, the West River and its tributaries have facilitated the movement of people and goods back and forth between Guangxi and various regions to the north. The construction of the Numinous Canal was undertaken by the Qin for the purpose of enhancing this movement.

Throughout the traditional period, beginning with the First Emperor of Qin's colonization efforts, there always existed a tension between the centralizing state (that is, China) and the local population. Successive dynasties sought to extend their influence in the south by establishing administrative and military hierarchies there. Yet, according to the modern historian Leo K. Shin, Guangxi did not come under firm control of China's central government until 1949.[18]

Fan Chengda would have found himself in a remote and backwater border region when he arrived in Guangxi in 1173. The Yuan dynasty (1279–1368) editors of Fan's official biography in the *History of the Song* (Songshi) describe Guangxi as a "destitute and impoverished" (*jiongkui*) land.[19] While Fan expressed some positive and optimistic thoughts about Guangxi, both before and after his residence in Guilin (see the discussion below and the remarks in Fan's Preface), this attitude was an exception among the Chinese elite. Most Chinese officials dispatched to the region harbored great fear, not only because of Guangxi's remote, border-region location, but also because it was thought to be infested by miasmas and malaria, populated by spear-wielding, tattooed, and aggressive "barbarian" peoples, and home to dense forests infested with savage beasts, venomous snakes, and leeches detachable from the body only by fire.

When Fan Chengda was at home at his country estate at Rocky Lake (Shihu) outside Suzhou preparing for his journey south to Guilin, he sought to gather information on the region from the works of earlier writers. It appears, however, that all he was able to find were a few general descriptions in poems by the Tang writers Du Fu (712–770) and Han Yu (768–824), neither of whom had ever been to Guilin, as well as a few lines from the writings of Liu Zongyuan (773–819) and Huang Tingjian (1045–1105), both of whom had spent periods of exile in the south.[20] Liu Zongyuan passed the last four years of his life (815–819) in Liu County (Liuzhou), Guangxi, not far from Guilin (or Guizhou, as it was called in the Tang). During this period, most of Liu Zongyuan's literary efforts concerned Liu County and the surrounding region. As a result, his *Works* say next to nothing about Guilin. Other, less famous visitors did leave written accounts about the region, some even about Guilin, but it seems that many of these texts were either unknown to Fan Chengda or unavailable to him.[21] With just a few notable exceptions (*Treatises* being one of them), little information about Guangxi appeared in Chinese literary and historical writings before the Ming dynasty (1368–1644), when the first gazetteers for the region were compiled and published.[22]

When Fan Chengda arrived in Guangxi in the 1170s, the sparse population of the region was overwhelmingly non-Chinese (his thirteenth and final treatise describes these tribal peoples in some detail).[23] Most of the native Chinese in the region were either government officials like Fan Chengda; merchants who dealt in silver, handicrafts (especially brocades), hardwoods,[24] aromatics, herbs, furs, pelts, and other southern commodities; or settlers who farmed the flat, fertile areas in the narrow valleys along its rivers. So, although the Southern Song (1127–1279) government held control of Jingjiang Municipality and the various counties and towns under its jurisdiction, beyond these Chinese administrative areas were lands controlled by tribal peoples. Those among them who lived in bridle and halter counties, towns, and settlements were considered by the Chinese to have been "sinicized." But many others lived in remote or mountainous areas and had not been assimilated into the cultural orbit of Chinese civilization. When Fan Chengda arrived in Guangxi in 1173, he found himself in a strange, alien land. And despite his high office and considerable local power, prestige, and influence, he was an outsider there.

FAN CHENGDA

The author of *Treatises*, Fan Chengda, is known in literary history as an outstanding poet and writer. Several book-length studies of his life and literary works have been published, with his *shi* poetry commanding the most attention.[25] Fan's seasonal sequence in verse about rural farm life in Suzhou, "Random and Impromptu Fields and Garden Poems on the Four Seasons" (Sishi tianyuan zaxing), has received particular praise in this regard.[26] Fan Chengda was also a gifted prose writer. Several of his most distinguished contemporaries, including Hong Kuo (1117–1184), Lou Yue (1137–1213), Zhou Bida (1126–1204) and Yang Wanli (1127–1206), all praise his prose compositions.[27] Six of Fan's major works have survived. The most important of these texts are his three travel diaries—*Diary of Grasping the Carriage Reins* (Lanpei lu), *Diary of Mounting a Simurgh* (Canluan lu), and *Diary of a Boat Trip to Wu* (Wuchuan lu)—and *Treatises*.[28]

Fan Chengda's career as a public official spanned about three decades, roughly from the mid-1150s until the mid-1180s. While he did serve occasionally in the Southern Song capital at Lin'an (modern Hangzhou), he spent most of his career as an official in the provinces. Some of these postings, specifically those undertaken in the 1170s, took him to distant places. In 1170 he traveled north to Dadu (modern Beijing) as Song ambassador to the state of Jin. His *Diary of Grasping the Carriage Reins* describes his experiences on this trip.[29] Fan's second travel account, *Diary of Mounting a Simurgh*, describes his late 1172 and early 1173 journey south to Jingjiang Municipality (or Guilin), where he served until 1175.[30] Finally, in 1175 he was transferred to Chengdu (modern Sichuan). Fan spent about two years there, after which time he returned to Rocky Lake. *The Diary of a Boat Trip to Wu* chronicles his journey home, which was undertaken by boat on the Min River and the Changjiang.[31] Three points related to these journeys and Fan's travel diaries merit mention. First, Fan Chengda was not only an experienced traveler, but a keen observer. The travel diaries reveal him to be especially interested in reporting on local customs and affairs, and he goes out of his way to distinguish between facts (what he has seen or verified personally) and second-hand reports (that is, information derived from informants). Second, during his terms of office in Jingjiang and Chengdu, Fan Chengda served as the chief civilian and military officer of those administrative areas. Thus, his job required that he be well informed about almost every aspect of regional affairs. The detailed information Fan provides in the "Treatise on the Man" concerning the history and current state of Song military relations with tribes in the region (to cite just one example) reveals this was indeed the case. And finally, although Guangxi, Guangdong, and Hainan served for many officials during the Tang and Song as destinations of demotion and political exile,[32] Fan Chengda was surprisingly enthusiastic about his new assignment in Guilin. After reading some favorable descriptions of Guilin's scenery in the poetry of Du Fu and Han Yu, he draws the following conclusion: "So, as for the best places I might travel to as an official, could there possibly be any better destination [than Guilin]?"[33] This positive attitude notwithstanding, Fan Chengda had no idea what he would find there.

GAZETTEER? ETHNOGRAPHY? NATURAL HISTORY? MISCELLANY?

Into what category of prose writing does *Treatises* fall? Is it a gazetteer? An ethnography? A natural history? A miscellany? The short answer is that it can be classified in any or all of these generic categories and perhaps some others not mentioned here.

Written texts whose subject matter is limited to a specific geographic region and whose purpose is to provide information about the history, administration, topography, religious institutions, social customs, and local products of that region, often in a topically arranged, chapter-by-chapter format, are common throughout the world. The great value of these works is that they are often based on firsthand observation, thus offering readers a means by which to observe vicariously the essentials or inner workings of a particular place and how people lived there. Such texts often reflect a government-administrative orientation or emphasize the enumeration of the cultural attributes of a particular place, although these two approaches are not always mutually exclusive. One well-known example of the first of these categories is the gazetteers or handbooks prepared by British colonial administrators in nineteenth- and early-twentieth-century India, which typically include geographic and demographic data as well as the historical background of a particular district. In addition, they record notable events such as natural disasters and famines. In contrast, works that stress the importance of observing and chronicling a living culture in situ are often called ethnographies.[34] One prominent example is Diego de Landa's (1524–1579) famous account of the Yucatán (Mexico), in which he chronicles the living habits, social customs, religious practices, and spoken and written languages of the Mayan people. These reports were based on his own observations and discussions with local informants. The Franciscan priest's notes helped later scholars to decipher much of the previously inaccesible written language of the Mayans.[35]

As for ethnographic writing in traditional China (that is, roughly before 1900), if one defines "ethnography" as the sorts of descriptions (penned by Chinese writers) of non-Chinese peoples one finds in local and regional gazetteers and sometimes in private accounts (that is, works not sponsored by the government) dealing with border areas and peoples, based on "direct observation as opposed to reliance on historical sources alone,"[36] then one could say that China has produced its fair share of ethnographic writing. Early examples range from the accounts of foreign lands and peoples in Sima Qian's (ca. 145–90 B.C.E.) *Records of the Historian* (Shiji) to Fan Chuo's monograph *Book on the Man* (Manshu). The latter work, written in the ninth century, describes the customs, products, and living conditions of the "Southern Man" people in what is now western Yunnan.[37] Many similar works survive, bearing the title "such-and-such-place *fengtu ji*," or "account of the local customs of such and such place."

The gazetteer first appeared in China, in rudimentary form, during the Han and Six Dynasties, developed in the Tang and Song, and flourished during the Ming and the Qing (1644–1911) eras. Traditional bibliographies, especially those found in the dynastic histories, often list gazetteers either under the "geography subcategory" (*dili lei*) or the "biography subcategory" (*zhuanji lei*), both of which fell under the more general "history category" (*shilei*). Titles subsumed under these headings, especially before the Ming period, included works with widely varying contents, related only in that they were concerned, in a very broad sense, with places and/or travel.

The history and development of the gazetteer in China from its embryonic form in the Han to full maturity in the Ming and Qing is much too long to consider here in any detail.[38] But some background concerning the development of gazetteers in China is necessary if *Treatises* is to be understood in generic and historical context. In other words, how does Fan Chengda's text relate to other works produced in traditional China that are classified as "gazetteers," and how did *Treatises* influence other, similar works produced during the Southern Song and thereafter?

One important early forerunner of the gazetteer in China is Chang Qu's (fourth century) *Gazetteer of the State South of [Mount] Hua* (Huayang guo zhi). The focus of this text is the political administration of a particular region, in this case, the ancient state of Shu (roughly the area of modern Sichuan). Chang Qu's gazetteer also deals with territorial boundaries, mountains, rivers, local products, ancient historical sites, and customs, but in a peripheral way. Its underlying purpose is to legitimize ancient Shu's place in the larger Chinese body politic.[39] The information provided in the *Gazetteer of the State South of [Mount] Hua* and similar works of the Six Dynasties was for the most part general and summary in nature, though some specialized texts or monographs provide detailed information on the geography and customs of a given locale or some special feature of a particular city. Two well-known examples of the latter are Ji Han's (263–306) invaluable botanical study of the southern regions, written in 304 and titled *Descriptions of the Herbaceous Plants and Trees in the Southern Quarter* (Nanfang caomu zhuang),[40] and Yang Xuanzhi's (sixth century) famous reminiscence *Record of the Buddhist Monasteries of Luoyang* (Luoyang qielan ji).[41]

Several important innovations in gazetteer writing took place during the subsequent Sui, Tang, and Northern Song periods. Gazetteers during this period were usually called *tujing*. This name reflects the two main components of these works: maps/illustrations (*tu*) and text (*jing*). By the early seventh century the textual portion of *tujing* had become primary as a direct result of imperial policy. For example, the following mandate appears in the dynastic history of the Sui: "In the

Daye reign [605–617] of the Sui it was decreed that all commanderies throughout the empire prepare accounts of their customs and products, with accompanying maps, and submit them to the Department of State Affairs."[42] With information on local administrative institutions, roads, customs, legends, and products, as well as up-to-date maps from virtually every corner in the empire, the Sui was better prepared to maintain control of and provide security to all local areas.

The practice of submitting *tujing* to the central government continued during the Tang, when the chief administrators (or "prefects") of counties (*zhou*) were required to submit revised and up-to-date *tujing* every three (later five) years. The collection and updating of *tujing* expanded in the Northern Song, no doubt in part because the need for such data became more vital as the Song economy grew and the size of the bureaucracy burgeoned. Northern Song *tujing* assumed the overall form and thematic breadth of the variety of writing that would later be classified as *fangzhi*, or local gazetteers, providing information on practically every aspect of a local government district, including administrative history, physical geography, and religious institutions; reports on local buildings, landmarks, and roads; and information on taxes, population, and so on. These works were written by and for government officials and were designed to serve the needs of both the central government and local administrators (especially new arrivals unfamiliar with local conditions).

Although the term *fangzhi*, or local gazetteer, appears as early as the fifth century,[43] and use of the word *zhi* in the titles of local administrative works increased in the Southern Song (as use of the term *tujing* in titles correspondingly diminished), *zhi* was not used consistently in the titles of administrative gazetteers until the Ming dynasty. Some texts circulated during the eleventh century that carried *zhi* in their titles, meaning something like "account" or "monograph," and were not designed mainly to serve government administrative needs. Perhaps the best surviving example is Song Minqiu's (1019–1079) *Account of Chang'an* (Chang'an zhi) in twenty chapters (*juan*). What is significant about this work is that the author's main concerns were scholarly and historical, and his primary goal was to be comprehensive, to present virtually everything that was known at the time about the history of Chang'an. National-level gazetteers of the Northern Song, such as Yue Shi's (930–1007) *Records Encompassing the Universe from the Taiping [Reign]* (Taiping huanyu ji), also reflect this same concern with detail and completeness. Virtually all Song authors who were writing about places, whether for administrative, geographic, historical, or private purposes, shared the same concern with presenting "all there is to know" about a given place.

Local gazetteer production increased in the twelfth and thirteenth centuries. Surely one reason for this development was the continuing need on the part of government officials for reliable information on local conditions. Another factor, pointed out long ago by Aoyama Sadao, is that literate persons in Southern Song China displayed a strong interest in local conditions in general and historical monuments and antiquities in particular.[44] This interest had a profound influence on the development of gazetteer writing and production during the Southern Song as well as subsequent historical-geographical writing. Local-, regional-, and national-level gazetteers were now designed not only to provide information to government administrators, but also to serve scholarly purposes and even accommodate local interests. Compilers of gazetteers now expressed a strong desire to verify, whenever possible, the information on local conditions that went into their compilations by a personal inspection of the place in question or by quoting passages from (reliable) written sources to supplement their reports. Learned persons of the Song valued and promoted the production and systemization of new knowledge with an unprecedented zeal and enthusiasm.[45] The methodological approach and contents of *Treatises* show Fan Chengda to be an avid practitioner of this scholarly trend.[46]

FAN CHENGDA'S *TREATISES*: BACKGROUND AND PURPOSE

It was not unusual for Chinese officials sent to remote areas in the south to develop a sentimental attachment to those locales. Su Shi's (1037–1101) exile to Hainan, where he spent three years (1097–1100), comes to mind as just one example.[47] But Fan Chengda's fondness for Guilin, which he expresses on several occasions, goes beyond mere nostalgic attachment. After leaving Guangxi for his new assignment in Chengdu, he would remark (referring to *Treatises*): "I remain deeply attached to Guilin, so much so that I have compiled and edited this [collection of] minutia and trivia."[48] His affection for Guilin seems to be traceable to the "wondrous" qualities of its sublime scenery. Thus, in the opening lines of his preface to the "Treatise on Precipice-Grottoes," Fan remarks: "I once assessed the wondrous nature of the hills in Guilin and found them worthy to be rated first in the world. Scholar-officials sent down to the south are few, and so oftentimes they are unaware [of Guilin's magnificent spires], while those who hear about them likewise cannot believe it." Later in his preface Fan mentions that his two years in Guilin were a time when he found "peace of mind" (*xin'an*). So, on one level, *Treatises* can be viewed as a personal memoir of Fan's happy and restful days in Guilin. However, the textual result of his testimonial is not merely a nostalgic recollection. Quite the contrary, it is a serious and detailed scholarly study, the ultimate purpose of which was to enhance the body of empirical knowledge on Guangxi.

The circumstances under which Fan Chengda came to write *Treatises* are explained in his preface:

> While I was on the road, there were no official matters [to occupy me], and so from time to time I thought about my former travels [in Guilin]. Because of this I recalled from memory Guangxi's scenic places as well as its local goods [*fengwu*] and natural products [*tuyi*][49]—the kinds of information not generally found in local gazetteers—and collected them together to make this one book.[50]

These words were written in 1175, while Fan was traveling from Guilin to Chengdu, a difficult river and land journey that took him six months to complete. Thus, he had ample time to finish at least a draft of *Treatises* while on the road, and apparently he did so: the preface is dated "second year of the Chunxi reign [1175], Summer Solstice Day," which predates his arrival in Chengdu.[51] Fan also mentions that he relied on memory to compose the text. Given the large amount of specialized and detailed local information and technical terminology in *Treatises*, however, it seems likely that Fan may have had "field notes" of some sort to draw upon. In fact, on one occasion he does mention relying on notes.[52]

As for the title of Fan's treatises, *Guihai yuheng zhi*, three components require explanation. The first is *guihai*, which translates literally as "Cinnamon Sea." This is an ancient name for Guilin and, by extension, for the entire southern region, long known for producing the cassia, or true cinnamon tree (*Cinnamomum cassia*). Fan may have adopted this expression from a verse by Jiang Yan (444–505), a well-known poet of the Six Dynasties era.[53] The term *yuheng* is a Zhou dynasty (ca. 1027–256 B.C.E.) office title. It designates local officials who served as "supervisors" (*yu*) and "guardians" (*heng*) of the "mountains, waterways, marshes, and forests."[54] Fan Chengda uses this ancient office title to refer to his own tenure in office as the "supervisor and guardian of the Cinnamon Sea." As for the word *zhi*, typically, the final character (or characters) in the title of an ancient Chinese prose work indicates the form or generic category under which it falls. Such genre, or subgenre, names are often general in nature and do not specifically define the form and content of the work. When used in titles that date from the Song and before, *zhi* can indicate many different varieties of prose texts, including geographic works of a more general nature, monographs on places, gazetteers, and even travel works. Although we know that Fan Chengda classified his collection of "minutia and trivia" as a "*zhi*," without scanning the contents of *Treatises*, there is no way to know what *zhi* specifically indicates in this case. I have chosen to translate *zhi* as "treatise" to preserve the ambiguity suggested by *zhi* in the original title.[55] Furthermore, all thirteen individual divisions or chapters of Fan's collection also carry *zhi* in their titles, but here—with two exceptions[56]—*zhi* appears as the initial word in the chapter title and is used as a verb, meaning "treatise on."

Fan's chapter titles and entries reflect the broad topical scope of the text. Indeed, his description of Guangxi in the twelfth century is extensive and touches on multiple aspects of society and culture. Although some earlier Tang and Song works contain reports about the south that include particulars about the unique aspects of the Guilin region, these texts in their extant forms are short on details. Moreover, they say next to nothing about the non-Chinese people of the region. In the words of two modern scholars, they are a "blank, white space" when compared with the rich contents of Fan Chengda's *Treatises*.[57]

With the exception of Tan Cui's (1725–1801) *Treatises of the Supervisor and Guardian of the Yunnan Sea* (Dianhai yuheng zhi), which was modeled directly after *Treatises*, I know of no other surviving prose work in China whose content and form compare closely with Fan's text.[58] While the use of *zhi* in the individual chapter titles of *Treatises* does suggest some affinity with the monograph or treatise sections in the dynastic histories (called *shu* in earlier dynastic histories, *zhi* in later ones), especially those dealing with non-Chinese peoples (these accounts often appear in the *liezhuan*, or "grouped biographies," section), the similarity ends there. *Zhi* in the dynastic histories emphasize the historical evolution of institutions such as the calendar, music, and astronomy. Fan Chengda's accounts are concerned with relating, in a methodical way, his personal observations and his knowledge of the south. Using a systematic approach to organize information into topical categories is one characteristic of *leishu* (lit., "classified digests," sometimes translated into English as "encyclopedias"), which are collections comprising quotations from various works on specific topics. Unlike *Treatises*, however, *leishu* as a general rule contain no original writing. As a prose form, *leishu* reached maturity during the Song, when several massive and highly influential collections appeared, most notably the *Imperially Reviewed Encyclopedia of the Taiping Era* (Taiping yulan) of 984 and the *Outstanding Models from the Storehouse of Literature* (Cefu yuangui) of 1013. These and subsequent *leishu* digests embody one quality that is apparent in the organizational structure of *Treatises*: subdividing individual chapters into specialized headings or categories. A glance at the contents pages of *Treatises* reveals that Fan Chengda followed this pattern of organization. But the similarity between *Treatises* and *leishu* collections goes no farther. Fan Chengda's text is almost completely original and contains only a few quotations from earlier works.

In one sense, *Treatises* resembles a gazetteer: it is concerned with relating local information about a specific geographic region. While including some information that typically appears in gazetteers ("local products" would be one example), the text more often than not concerns products, phenomena, and people unique to Guangxi and the surrounding region. In fact, Fan Chengda mentions specifically in his preface that he does not want to include information in the treatises that usually appears in gazetteers. Furthermore, *Treatises* was not compiled for political-administrative purposes, though Fan mentions that he hopes it might help local government officials when they prepare maps of the region,[59] and it was not intended as a government document destined for the imperial archives. In every respect it is a private work.

Portions of Fan's text, especially the final chapter on the Man people of the south, can be regarded as "ethnographic," in that they are based largely on firsthand observation (by Fan Chengda) of "foreign peoples" in their native culture and environment. However, the ethnographic portion of Fan's text also includes a copious amount of information on the material culture of the Man peoples and the various "exotic" products (aromatics, textiles, weapons, and so on) they produced. The descriptions of these products tell us much about economic, scientific, medical, and technological developments in Guangxi in the twelfth century. At the same time, Fan's reports on the flora and fauna of Guangxi (fruits, plants, and so on) read like a natural history of the region. In the final analysis, then, the multifaceted content of *Treatises* makes it impossible to classify the work under a distinct generic category of prose writing. Since *Treatises* defies specific classification, perhaps we should call it, as do many bibliographies and collectanea, a "miscellany" or an example of Song dynasty *biji* writing.[60]

FAN'S *TREATISES* IN LATER TEXTUAL HISTORY AND SCHOLARSHIP

One measure of the usefulness of a written text is how often it is cited or extracted in contemporary or subsequent works. On this account the value of Fan's *Treatises* is undeniable, for its rich contents have been mined by numerous scholars, both traditional and modern. If one were to attempt to cite all the quotations from *Treatises* that appear in works written during and after Fan Chengda's lifetime, such a list would comprise hundreds, perhaps thousands of citations. Most of these would be quotations in local and regional gazetteers on Guangxi. But since no gazetteers for Guangxi have survived that predate the Ming, Fan Chengda's *Treatises* represents a virtual gold mine of unique information on Guangxi and Hainan during the Southern Song.

However, scholars began drawing on the contents of the treatises long before the Ming. Contemporaries of Fan Chengda during the Southern Song turned to Fan's miscellany when preparing studies on topics related to the south. First and foremost among these authors was Zhou Qufei (1135–1189).[61] Zhou, a native of Yongjia (modern Wenzhou, Zhejiang), passed his *jinshi* examination in 1163. One of his fellow graduates and close friends was the writer Lou Yue. Although details about Zhou Qufei's career as a government official are scanty, we know that he spent about six years in Guangxi serving in various minor posts. For one or two of those six years, he was police official in Jingjiang under the command of Fan Chengda. Since Fan has left a parting poem dedicated to Zhou, we can be sure that the two men were acquainted.[62]

Zhou Qufei has only left only one prose work to posterity, *Vicarious Replies from Beyond the Ranges* (Lingwai daida), in ten chapters. The contents of this valuable work are based mainly on two sources: (1) information and data that Zhou collected while serving as an official in Fujian and Guangxi, and (2) the contents of Fan's *Treatises*. In his preface Zhou Qufei mentions specifically that he acquired a copy of *Treatises*.[63] Although he says it reached him "late" (that is, after he began to revise and ready his manuscript for distribution), he made good use of Fan's text, copying numerous passages and entries, often verbatim and in their entirety, directly into *Vicarious Replies*. Yang Wuquan, an authority on *Vicarious Replies from Beyond the Ranges*, notes that Zhou Qufei's biggest weakness as a scholar is his indiscriminate copying of large portions of Fan Chengda's original text into the work. Using modern standards of scholarship, one can certainly make this argument. But Yang's criticism misses an important point: compilers of gazetteers, geographic monographs, and ethnographic texts in ancient China routinely drew on and copied passages from earlier works, often without citing their sources. Zhou Qufei extracted large portions of *Treatises* mainly because he viewed Fan Chengda's reports and descriptions as accurate and reliable. Zhou's own experiences in Guangxi provided him with the knowledge to make such a determination. Fan was also a famous government official and one of the most renowned writers and poets of his day as well as Zhou Qufei's former supervisor. No doubt, this inspired Zhou to quote liberally from *Treatises* as well.

That a substantial portion of Zhou Qufei's text was copied from *Treatises* was never an issue with later scholars. Among these subsequent writers, Zhao Rukuo (1170–1231) merits special mention. Zhao's well-known *Treatises on Various Foreign Peoples* (Zhufan zhi), which is the most important surviving source from the Song concerning foreign peoples "beyond the seas" (with whom China had direct or indirect contact), quotes generously (again without citation) from *Vicarious Replies*. One wonders, however, if Zhao Rukuo was aware that many of the passages he appropriated from Zhou Qufei's work had their origin in Fan Chengda's *Treatises*.[64] I strongly suspect that Zhao Rukuo knew this, and it was simply not a matter of concern. Like Zhou Qufei, Zhao copied information he thought was coming from a reliable source or sources. My point here is that numerous passages from Fan's *Treatises* have been copied and recopied in other works ever since the twelfth century.

In addition to historical works, such as Li Xinchuan's (1166–1243) *Register of Essential Matters during the Successive Years since the Jianyan Reign* (Jianyan yilai xinian yaolu),[65] and *biji*, such as Zhou Mi's (1232–1308) *Rustic Words from East of Qi* (Qidong yeyu),[66] lengthy passages from *Treatises* are quoted in two important and influential works of the Southern Song and early Yuan: Huang Zhen's (1213–1280) *Mr. Huang's Daily Transcriptions* (Huangshi richao) and Ma Duanlin's (1254–ca. 1325) *Comprehensive Investigation of Texts and Viewpoints* (Wenxian tongkao). *Mr. Huang's Daily Transcriptions* includes quoted passages from various texts along with Huang Zhen's reading notes or commentaries about those passages. Chapter 67 cites lengthy quotations from Fan's *Treatises*. It is almost certain that Huang was quoting from the original, "complete," version of the treatises, now lost (more on this matter presently). As for Ma Duanlin's massive encyclopedia, it also includes large portions of Fan's text (in ten separate quotations) that appear nowhere in surviving versions of the treatises. For example, the "Treatise on the Man" in surviving editions of *Treatises* runs just over one thousand Chinese characters in length, whereas the extended passage from Fan's "Treatise on the

Man" quoted in the *Comprehensive Investigation of Texts and View-points* has more than ten thousand characters. The lengthy passages of text from *Treatises* quoted in *Mr. Huang's Daily Transcriptions* and *Comprehensive Investigation of Texts and Viewpoints* were instrumental in the textual reconstruction of the treatises after large portions of the original version were lost during the textual transmission from the Southern Song to the Ming. The received editions of Fan's miscellany, which date from the middle or late Ming, are abridged versions of a much longer exemplar text that is now lost. When one collates and joins the passages from *Treatises* preserved in *Mr. Huang's Daily Transcriptions* and *Comprehensive Investigation of Texts and Viewpoints* with the surviving abridged version, as some modern scholars have done,[67] the result is a text that is much closer to Fan Chengda's original manuscript. All of the lost passages preserved in the works of Huang Zhen, Ma Duanlin, and others, are translated in this book.

During the Ming period several well-known authors quoted passages and entries from *Treatises*, including Li Shizhen (1518–1593) in his *Compendium of Basic Pharmacopeia* (Bencao gangmu), Huang Zuo (1490–1566) in *Comprehensive Gazetteer for Guangxi* (Guangxi tongzhi), Wei Jun (*jinshi* 1604) in *Trivial Notes on Jiaonan* (Jiaonan suoji), and Kuang Lu (1604–ca.1650) in *Chiya*. We also know that during the Ming some passages from the original version of *Treatises* were copied into the massive encyclopedia *Great Compendium of the Yongle Reign* (Yongle dadian), completed in 1408.[68] And during the Qing dynasty the eminent scholar Gu Yanwu (1613–1682) often quotes from *Treatises* in his *Book on the Strengths and Weaknesses of the Commanderies and States in the World* (Tianxia junguo libing shu; preface dated 1662).

The Qing period produced two works patterned directly after *Treatises*. The first of these was composed by Wang Shixing (1547–1598), one of the most prolific travel writers of the traditional era and one of only a few persons known to have climbed all of China's Five Cardinal Mountains (Wuyue). After visiting several of Guilin's best-known limestone cliffs and caverns, all of which Fan Chengda describes in the first of his treatises, Wang Shixing wrote an account of his travels titled *Continuation of the Treatises of the Cinnamon Sea* (Guihai zhi xu). This work contains sixteenth-century updates on the limestone mountains, spires, and caverns that Fan Chengda wrote about three hundred years earlier. Another Qing work worth noting is Tan Cui's *Treatises of the Supervisor and Guardian of the Yunnan Sea*. Tan not only modeled the title of his study of Yunnan after that of his Song predecessor, but also divided his text into thirteen separate treatises with individual titles exactly the same as those used by Fan Chengda.

As for modern scholars, in both China and the West who have tapped the treatises' resources in their research and writing, space only allows mention of the following: Bertold Laufer in his *Sino-Iranica*; Wolfram Eberhard in his *Local Cultures of South and East China*; R. H. Van Gulick in his *Gibbon in China*; Joseph Needham in various volumes of his *Science and Civilisation in China*;[69] Edward H. Schafer in his *Vermilion Bird*, *Golden Peaches of Samarkand*, and *Shore of Pearls*; Almut Netolitzky in her German translation of *Vicarious Replies*; Charles Hartman in his study of a type of artistic expression called "stomping songs" (*tage*);[70] Leo K. Shin in his monograph on Guangxi borderlands during the Ming; and Yang Wuquan in his notes and collations to *Vicarious Replies*.

HISTORY AND TRANSMISSION OF THE TEXT

Before his death in 1193, Fan Chengda spent several years personally editing his collected works, which, when completed, totaled 136 *juan*.[71] This collection is listed in Fan's necrology as *Rocky Lake's Collection* (Shihu ji), while in the *History of the Song* it appears under the title *Rocky Lake's Great Complete Collection* (Shihu da quanji).[72] Although these sources cite different titles, they no doubt refer to the same collection. This compilation, which included both verse and prose, was printed and published by Fan Chengda's sons, Fan Xin and Fan Zi. In their postface to the collection, dated early 1204,[73] the two sons mention that the collection consisted of "poetry and prose in 130 *juan*." There is a difference, then, in the size of the collections reported by Zhou Bida and the *History of the Song* (136 *juan*), on the one hand, and that described by Fan Xin and Fan Zi (130 *juan*) in their postface, on the other. I suspect, as do some modern scholars of Fan Chengda's works, that different versions of *Complete Collection* were in circulation in the early thirteenth century.[74] It seems quite possible, even likely, that the 136-*juan* version included Fan's six longer prose works, while the 130-*juan* version did not. If this was the case, then it is reasonable to assume that Fan's three travel diaries, his two flower manuals, and *Treatises* were the six works not included in the 130-*juan* version of Fan Chengda's oeuvre. They may have been omitted because these prose texts were already in independent circulation in the thirteenth century, which is certain.[75] For example, a line in a poem by Fan Chengda's contemporary and friend Li Shi (1108–1181) confirms that *Treatises* was in circulation during Fan's lifetime.[76]

For reasons unknown, the original, complete collection, edited by Fan Chengda himself, was not reprinted in the Southern Song or Yuan periods. By the late Ming or early Qing it was lost.[77] What survives today is titled *Rocky Lake's Poetry Collection* (Shihu shiji), sometimes also called *The Layman from Rocky Lake's Poetry Collection* (Shihu jushi shiji), and comprises only thirty-four *juan*. This collection, published by the Zhonghua Shuju in Beijing in 1962 under the title *Fan Shihu ji* (with numerous reprints since), is based on the 1688 edition of Gu Sili (1669–1722). Most of this collection is *shi* poetry. It includes none of Fan Chengda's prose works.

Fan Chengda's six surviving major prose works are scattered throughout various collectanea (*congshu*) and other sources dating from the Ming, Qing, and Republican periods as well as some modern collections.[78] It has already been mentioned that the version of *Treatises* that survives in these collections is incomplete; portions of the original work were lost by the middle or late Ming.[79] According to Kong Fanli, the surviving, abridged version has about 14,000 characters, whereas the complete version probably included more than 100,000 characters.[80]

Although parts of *Treatises* were lost, the current thirteen-treatise division of the text reflects the original layout and treatise headings of Fan Chengda's text. We know this because it is almost certain that Huang Zhen had access to an original, complete copy of *Treatises*. As Huang read the text and made his reading notes, he copied out passages, many of them quite long, from the original. With just two exceptions,[81] the names and organizational outline of the treatise headings copied out by Huang Zhen are the same as those in surviving abridged versions of the text.

As for the number of *juan* that comprised the original version of *Treatises*, Zhou Bida states that the work comprised one *juan*.[82] Since Zhou was a close friend of Fan Chengda and wrote his epitaph shortly after Fan's death, his report is credible and authoritative. In other words, the version of *Treatises* he was familiar with was not apportioned into *juan* divisions. Chen Zhensun's (fl. ca. 1250) well-known bibliography *Explanatory Abstracts of Books and Texts in the Upright Studio* (Zhizhai shulu jieti) says, however, that the text is divided into two *juan*.[83] To complicate matters further, Zhao Xibian (fl. late thirteenth century) in his "Supplement" (Fuzhi) to Chao Gongwu's (*jinshi* 1132; d. 1171) *Essays on Reading the Books in the Commandery Studio* (Junzhai dushu zhi), lists Fan Chengda's *Treatises* as comprising three *juan*.[84] This is repeated in the "Bibliography" section of the *History of the Song* and in the late eighteenth century by the editors of the *Abstracts in the General Catalog of the Complete Library of the Four Treasuries* (Siku quanshu zongmu tiyao), who say the original text was in three *juan*, but since much of it was lost, only one *juan* survives in abridged form.[85]

We should remember that the apportionment of texts into *juan*, especially of monographs, was sometimes executed by editors in arbitrary fashion. This seems to have been especially the case with compilers and editors of collectanea. I suspect that the question of *juan* divisions in *Treatises*, despite the efforts of several modern scholars,[86] will never be resolved. It seems reasonable to assume, however, that the textual content of the treatises that circulated in the late Song and early Yuan (the so-called complete version), in whatever *juan* division it followed, was probably the same.

The earliest collectanea to include the shorter, surviving version of *Treatises* is *Sea of Talks, Ancient and Modern* (Gujin shuohai), a popular anthology of short stories and miscellaneous works compiled by Lu Ji (1515–1552). The preface to Lu Ji's collection is dated 1544. Modern editors and commentators on the treatises often refer to this and other abridged versions of the text (reprinted in subsequent collections) as the "modern version" (*jinben*), as opposed to original, complete edition, which they call the "old version" (*jiuben*). It is not known whether only this "modern version" was available to Lu Ji and his team of collators when they decided to anthologize the treatises in *Sea of Talks* or whether they were working with a more complete version of the text, which they (for reasons unknown) excised. We can be sure, however, that at least some copies of the "old version" were still in circulation in the mid-sixteenth century since passages cited by Li Shizhen in the *Compendium of Basic Pharmacopeia* seem to come from the "old version" or some other unknown edition. The same holds true for some *Treatises* passages cited in the *Miscellaneous Sources on Western Yue* (Yuexi congzai), an important collection of materials on Guangxi compiled by Wang Sen (1653–1726) that dates from around 1704. By the time *Abstracts in the General Catalog of the Complete Library of the Four Treasuries* was completed in the late eighteenth century, however, the "old version" seems to have been lost.

Following publication of *Sea of Talks* in the mid-sixteenth century, *Treatises* was reprinted in many other collections, the most important of which are listed in the Appendix.

LANGUAGE AND CONTENT OF THE TEXT

Like Fan Chengda's three surviving travel diaries, *Treatises* is written in a direct, unadorned, and allusion-free register of classical Chinese prose (*guwen*). This language style is appropriate to the treatises' purpose: to convey information in a straightforward, systematic, and informative way. The clear and direct prose style used in *Treatises*, which the editors of the *Complete Library of the Four Treasuries* praise as "simple and elegant" (*jianya*),[87] is representative of a type of classical Chinese that gained popularity in the Song and is found in a number of prose genres, especially informal writings and travel diaries.

Fan Chengda's three surviving travel diaries contain two general types of language: narrative (that is, details about the actual journey itself, distances covered, places visited, and so on, related in diary format) and descriptive (descriptions of the places Fan saw or visited on the trip, which may either be objective or subjective, as when he gives his personal impressions or reactions to the place in question).[88] The treatises, however, overwhelmingly contain what might be called reportorial-descriptive language. Fan reports information and relates facts to his readers about matters of which they probably knew little or nothing. He accomplishes this through orderly, detailed descriptions.

As an example, consider his entry on betel nuts (*binlang*), the mildly intoxicating fruit of the betel nut palm tree:

> Betel nuts grow in the settlements of the Li people [on Hainan]. Those gathered at the time of Ascendant Spring are made into soft betel nuts. Those gathered in summer and fall and dried are made into rice betel nuts. The smaller and pointy ones are made into chicken-heart betel nuts. Oblate ones are made into big bellies. All of these can give off an [identifiable] odor. Those preserved in a salty solution are made into salty betel nuts. The Qiong County administration collects taxes on betel nuts, which accounts for half of its annual budget. Guang County also collects several tens of thousands strings of cash in taxes. From Min [Fujian] to Guang betel nuts are chewed with lime powder and betel vine leaves. Only after one spits out the fiery red liquid, which resembles blood, can one swallow the remaining juice. In Guang County they add cloves, cinnamon flowers, and ginger to make "aromatic-medicinal betel nuts."[89]

This passage is a good example of Fan Chengda's reportorial-descriptive style of language. Note that the author's personal views or experiences regarding betel nuts play no role in his report. In this case, Fan's purpose is to (1) identify the place of origin of the betel nuts he is about to describe; (2) mention when the nuts are harvested; (3) enumerate and describe the different varieties of betel nuts he knows about; (4) explain how taxes on betel nuts subsidize the county budgets in Qiongzhou (Hainan) and Guang County; (5) relate how the nuts are chewed and when can one spit out the excess "fiery red liquid"; and (6) inform readers about a particular betel nut medicinal recipe used in Guang County.

In addition to entries of the sort we have just seen, each of the thirteen individual treatises includes a preface or introduction (I call these "opening remarks") in which Fan Chengda provides background information about himself and personal experiences as they relate to the entries that follow. It is precisely Fan Chengda's "authorial presence" in the prefaces (and occasionally in individual treatise entries) that distinguishes *Treatises* from the common gazetteer in China.[90] The length of these introductions and their content can vary greatly, but all of them reveal Fan's scholarly intentions. To cite just three examples, the preface to the "Treatise on Precipice-Grottoes" is quite long and contains autobiographical information regarding Fan's numerous travels across the empire and how various famous scenic mountain environments throughout China compare with the unique features of Guilin's karst landscape. The introductory remarks to the "Treatise on Metals and Stones," however, are confined to just a few short lines explaining that the author will "concentrate on those [minerals] necessary for making prescription medicines." And finally, on a few occasions, Fan uses the "opening remarks" to correct previous misunderstandings. In his "Treatise on Aromatics," for instance, he addresses the common northern (or "Chinese") view that aromatics are produced in Guangxi and Guangdong. Fan is quick to point out, however, that in Southern Song times aromatics in Guangdong were shipped there from other places, mainly Hainan, via oceangoing junks.

As for the criteria Fan Chengda used to select material for *Treatises*, it will be recalled that in the Preface he mentions "recalling from memory" his experiences in Guangxi and his desire to include in *Treatises* "the kinds of information not generally found in local gazetteers." In fact, the contents of *Treatises* are not simply items "recalled from memory." Rather, the text is based, at least in part, on notes the author kept in Guilin. In the opening remarks to the "Treatise on Insects and Fishes," we find additional information on Fan's criteria for selecting material: "I will list only a minuscule number of those [insects and fishes] that, by chance, I have seen or heard about." As for the fruits of Guangxi, Fan remarks: "Here I will list those I know about that are edible, which number fifty-seven varieties." Clearly, then, Fan Chengda was seeking to make an original contribution to scholarship and did not want to repeat the sorts of information one commonly finds in local gazetteers, and he was careful to delineate the limits of his knowledge and experience. His rigorous approach to selecting material—firsthand observation, sometimes based on field notes—attests to his integrity as a scholar. Finally, as noted by Deborah Marie Rudolph,[91] within the text of *Treatises* Fan reveals yet another criterion for selecting material: he would only include items that are "unique to the region." Note the following comment in this regard, which appears in the introduction to the "Treatise on Flowers": "Here I will describe only those [flowers] uniquely suited to local conditions. As a general rule, none of those found in the Northern Counties [China] will be noted." It is precisely this selectivity that makes the contents of the treatises so valuable, especially to later scholars, for much of the information found in them is simply not available anywhere else. On a few occasions Fan Chengda even reminds his readers of this fact. For example, in the "Treatise on Birds," after informing his readers of the southern practice of using parrot and peacock flesh to make condiments and dried meat, he remarks: "These two matters have not yet been chronicled in historical sources. I am the very first to do so."

The reportorial-descriptive language of *Treatises* makes exsensive use of expressions from specific lexical classes. At the simplest and most basic level, a select group of monosyllables appear repeatedly throughout the treatises that function grammatically as stative verbs (that is, verbs that also include an adjectival function). These are common fare in classical Chinese and are often used to describe scenic environments. Four of Fan Chengda's favorites, glossed with their English meanings as used in the treatises, are *guai* (fantastic; surprising; strange); *jue* (unsurpassed; superlative); *qi* (wondrous; wondrous nature; singular); and *xiu* (elegant).

A second general category of Fan Chengda's descriptive language is two-character expressions, sometimes call binomes. Fan employs several different types or classes of binomes in *Treatises*:

Coordinate combinations may be nominal, verbal, or stative-verbal.[92] Consider the following illustrative example, taken from the "Treatise on the Man." This passage describes the indigenous people of Guangxi who lived outside the influence of Chinese civilization and culture. Note that in this brief report Fan Chengda uses six different coordinate expressions, italicized here:

> Their manner is *fierce and ferocious* [*guanghan*]; their *customs and habits* [*fengsu*] are *preposterous and strange* [*huangguai*]. It is not possible to completely *rein in and rule* [*shengzhi*] them by means of the *teachings and laws* [*jiaofa*] of the Middle Kingdom [China], so for now all we can do is to *bridle and halter* [*jimi*] them.

Alliterative combinations appear frequently. Examples are *guiguai* (surprising and strange) and *jinjiao* (sinews and adhesives).

Rhyming combinations are extremely common. They may include elements that are opposites, but more often than not they are composed of synonyms or near synonyms. Examples are *dili* (to drip and drop) and *xiongyong* (to rush and gush).

Reduplicative combinations, such as *diandian* (spots and specks), *paipai* (flapping and fluttering), and *wanwan* (curved and crooked).

Similes are the most frequently used figure of speech. A common trope in classical Chinese, similes are usually executed by using one of three words, *ru, ruo,* or *si,* all of which essentially carry the same meaning: "look like," "similar to," "resemble," and so on. In *Treatises* these expressions appear most often in chapters describing flora and fauna and inanimate objects. Fan Chengda knew that many of his northern readers would be unfamiliar with the material culture and exotic phenomena of the south, so he often uses similes comparing the size, shape, and color of his subjects to some generally known northern referent. Examples are "Cockatoos [*bai yingwu*] are the size of a small goose [*xiao e*]" and "Winter peaches [*dongtao*] are shaped like dates [*zao*]." When Fan can establish an exact match, we find descriptions such as "There is another variety [of southern sheep] that is dark brown, with a black back and white spots, which looks exactly like a deer." On many occasions, however, he cannot find a suitable simile and instead employs a rough approximation, using a sentence pattern such as "X is sort of like such and such item[s] in the category Y" (X *ru* Y *zhi lei*). The following example attempts to describe the "pure and gentle" smell of Hainan aromatics: "As a general rule, the smell of all Hainan aromatics is pure and gentle, sort of like the smell of lotus flowers [*lianhua*], mei-flowers [*meiying*], goose pears [*eli*], and bee's nests [*mipi*]."

A special category of language used by Fan Chengda is the terminology he employs when referring to the non-Chinese people of Guangxi and Hainan. Several of these terms require explanation.

MAN. It is general knowledge that the Chinese regarded all foreign people, including members of indigenous tribes within China itself, as racially and culturally inferior. Fan Chengda was no exception. In the introduction to his "Treatise on the Man," Fan distinguishes five different tribes (*zhong*) of non-Chinese people who lived in the bridle and halter areas: Yao, Lao, Man, Li , and Dan. He then immediately notes, however, that "they are collectively referred to as Man." Man, then, was a general term used in the sense of "southern tribes."[93] From the Chinese perspective, it carried with it the pejorative connotation of "barbarian." Fan Chengda further distinguishes the Man people who lived outside (or beyond) the areas of Chinese administrative control as either "Outer Man" (Wai Man) or "Petty Man" (Xiao Man) and clearly regarded them as a potential threat to Chinese administrative and political control in Guangxi. These "Outer Man" were also known as the "Raw [or Uncooked] Man" (Sheng Man), as opposed to the "Cooked Man" (Shu Man) in the bridle and halter areas who had submitted to China and begun to follow Chinese cultural practices.

FAN. After the Southern Song exile court was established in Hangzhou in the 1130s, the word *fan* was used increasingly to mean "southern barbarian," and this usage continued to the Qing.[94] Fan Chengda, however, uses *fan* consistently in a more neutral sense to mean "foreign." On one occasion, he employs the term "Fan Man" to refer to the Man people who lived in northeastern Guangxi.

DONG.[95] The character *dong* appears numerous times in the treatises and is used consistently as the name of a territorial administrative unit. Fan makes this clear in his "Treatise on the Man": "When [the Song government] demarcated their [Man] tribal areas, the larger ones were made into counties [*zhou*], the smaller ones into towns [*xian*], and the still smaller ones into settlements [*dong*]." Various editions of *Treatises* as well as modern secondary literature on the text interchangeably use the two characters *dong* 洞 and *dong* 峒 (and less frequently, the character 峝) to indicate this administrative unit. Most Song dynasty sources, including the *History of the Song, Comprehensive Investigation of Texts and Viewpoints,* and *Vicarious Replies from Beyond the Range,* prefer the 峒 form of the character. Scholars in the field agree that this Chinese character was devised to reflect the meaning of a native Man word. They disagree, however, about the source and original meaning of that non-Chinese term. Sung-shih Hsü, an authority on the Zhuang language, defines *dong* as "a large village."[96] This gloss tallies with the explanation in the *Chiya,* an authoritative Ming miscellany on the south: "When Zhuang people band together and form into a village, it is a *dong*."⁹⁷ This explanation seems consistent with the way *dong* functions in *Treatises*. Since Fan Chengda also uses the expressions "county settlement" (*zhoudong*) and "village settlement" (*cundong*), it is clear that *dong* functioned as a subunit of both counties (*zhou*) and villages (*cun*). To distinguish *dong* from these other administrative designations, I translate it as "settlement."

MIN. In traditional Chinese texts *min* usually refers to the *simin*, or four "approved" social classes—scholars (*shi*), farmers (*nong*), craftsmen (*gong*), and merchants (*shang*)—that together constituted the free imperial subjects of the realm. Although Chinese officials did not usually refer to border tribespeople as *min*, Fan Chengda does so in *Treatises* but adds ethnic components. For example, "As a result of the present dynasty's expansion efforts and increased presence [in the south], there are more than fifty such counties, towns, and settlements. Those individuals who are imposing and senior [*xiongzhang*] are selected to be leaders [*shouling*]; their people [*min*] are registered as able-bodied men [*zhuangding*]." This comment reveals that Fan regarded the registered "able-bodied men" of the bridle and halter areas as he did free Chinese subjects, presumably because the "able-bodied men" of Guangxi were registered as tax-paying residents who could be called up to serve in the local militia as needed. Fan also uses the expression "civilian households" (*minhu*) to refer to non-Chinese families who have agreed to convert to Chinese cultural practices: "Strong and sturdy males from civilian households [*minhu*] who can be persuaded to [Chinese ways] through teaching are referred to as field sentinels [*tianzi jia*]." As a general rule, Fan uses the expression "civilian households" only when he is referring to persons expected to pay taxes and provide occasional state labor and military service.

DI AND JIE. On many occasions we encounter the related terms "government land" (*shengdi*) and "government borders" (*shengjie*). These expressions indicate land (*di*) and border areas (*jie*) under the nominal control of the Chinese Command Headquarters (Shuaifu) in Guangxi, in other words, all territory that fell under jurisdiction of Jingjiang Municipality. Residents of these areas, many of whom were of Chinese descent, are called "government subjects" (*shengmin*).

TRANSLATION AND ANNOTATION

Although I have described the language of *Treatises* as direct and unadorned, translating it into smooth and readable English presents formidable challenges, particularly in handling local terms and technical vocabulary specific to Guangxi and Hainan in the twelfth century. Terms such as Man, *dong* (settlement), and *min* ("people" or "civilian"), discussed in the previous section, are examples of such vocabulary. Other examples are abundant throughout the treatises: terms such as "steamed-bun mandarin orange" (*mantou gan*), which, as far as I know, appears nowhere in Chinese letters before *Treatises;* Luowang fruit (*luowang zi*), for which multiple authorities on ancient Chinese botany confidently offer very different explanations; and "celestial shrimp" (*tianxia*), an unusual variety of insect in Guangxi that in shape resembles a large flying ant (*feiyi*), about which reference books say nothing at all.

Fortunately, my translation work has been aided greatly by three separate studies of *Treatises*, all of which were published in China in the 1980s. These are Qi Zhiping, *Treatises of the Supervisor and Guardian of the Cinnamon Sea, with Collations and Emendations* (Guihai yuheng zhi jiaobu); Yan Pei, *Treatises of the Supervisor and Guardian of the Cinnamon Sea, with Collations and Annotations* (Guihai yuheng zhi jiaozhu); and Hu Qiwang and Tan Guangguang, *Treatises of the Supervisor and Guardian of the Cinnamon Sea, Including Lost Passages, with Collations and Annotations* (Guihai yuheng zhi jiyi jiaozhu). While all three of these works are useful, each has strengths and weaknesses. The collations and emendations of Qi Zhiping are useful but quite brief when compared with those of Yan Pei and the team of Hu Qiwang and Tan Guangguang. Yan Pei's volume is especially helpful in identifying textual variants and omissions, which are numerous. Hu and Tan also identify and attempt to resolve textual issues but spend more time providing lengthy footnotes that explain technical terms, local vocabulary, and historical issues as they relate to the contents of *Treatises*. Both Yan Pei and the Hu-Tan team are extremely knowledgeable about the history of Guangxi, especially in the twelfth century.

I have also benefited tremendously from the publication of Kong

Fanli's *Six Examples of Fan Chengda's Informal Writings* (Fan Chengda biji liuzhong) in 2002. This is, without a doubt, the most authoritative modern edition of Fan Chengda's six surviving prose works, including *Treatises*. Kong uses the 1927 *Shuofu* edition as his base text but collates it with other editions. While I do not always agree with Kong's punctuation and there are some minor printing errors in his text, overall this version of the text has proven to be extremely useful. I have also benefited from Kong's collation notes, which do not always match up with those of Yan Pei and the team of Hu Qiwang and Tan Guangguang.

The only complete translation of *Treatises* I have seen is appended to M. IU. Ul'ianova's Russian rendition of Zhou Qufei's *Vicarious Replies*, published under the title *Za khrebtami, vmesto otvetov: Lin vai dai da*. The *Treatises* translation appears without notes. I have also benefited from Jennifer Took's annotated translation of Fan Chengda's "Treatise on the Man," which appeared in her undergraduate honor's thesis at the University of Melbourne. Her annotations, based mainly on those of Qi Zhiping, are quite useful, and I have drawn on them often.

In my own attempt to render the text of *Treatises* into readable English, I have followed the so-called literal approach to translation. This means preserving, whenever possible, the word order and precise diction of the original, although the requirements of English sometimes necessitate the insertion of subjects, conjunctions, prepositions, and so on, when they do not appear in the original text. I have avoided adding or embellishing my translation with images not found in *Treatises*. At the same time, I have made every attempt to preserve the tone of Fan Chengda's prose. Most of the time Fan maintains his descriptive-reportorial language and tone, which to some readers may seem lacking in literary flavor and appeal but in my view is never boring. On a few occasions he adopts a lively or even jocular tone, which I have attempted to convey in English.

As for the many technical terms and historical references that appear in *Treatises*, there is only one way to explain these to the modern reader: through annotation. I am well aware that an extensive footnote apparatus, stuffed with explanations and references, is cumbersome and distracting. Fan Chengda's intended audience—the scholar-official class of twelfth century China, would have required no glosses or explanations because they shared his educational background and knowledge. For the modern reader, however, even the trained sinologist, such an apparatus is necessary. I have tried to keep footnote content to a minimum, but I have not skimped on providing full explanations and references describing where readers can find additional information. At times, the terse nature of Fan's prose demands interpolation in order to make the English meaning and sentence complete. These insertions appear in square brackets. Supplementary information, such as transliterations of official titles, place-names, and so on, as well as occasional clarification is provided in brackets as well.

This translation is based on the text of *Treatises* in Kong Fanli's *Six Examples of Fan Chengda's Informal Writings,* although, as my annotation reveals, I consult and follow readings in other editions.

TERMINOLOGY, MEASUREMENTS, AND DATES

Botanical, Zoological, and Other Scientific Terms

The precise identification of ancient botanical, zoological, and other scientific terms is often difficult and sometimes almost impossible. Frequently there are several Chinese names for the same plant or animal, and sometimes the same names are used for other plants or animals as well. Furthermore, these names and their referents change over time. Modern botanical terminology also introduces challenges. An example is the *mei* tree, the flowers (*meihua*) of which are usually translated into English as "plum blossoms." Strictly speaking, this is not a "plum tree" but a variety of apricot (*Prunus mume*). For a variety of reasons, however, in North America the *mei* tree, its fruit, and its blossoms are generally known by a Japanese name, *ume.* To distinguish the *mei* from the common Chinese plum (*li*; *Prunus salicina*), throughout this book I will render *mei* as "mei-flower," "mei-fruit," "mei-tree," and so on, depending on context.

Chinese Characters

Chinese characters for names, official titles, places, and other terms are provided in the Glossary-Index. Full-form (or traditional) Chinese characters (*fanti zi*) are used.

Date Conversion
Chinese lunar calendar dates have been converted to Western dates based on the tables in *A Sino-Western Calendar for Two Thousand Years* (Liangqian nian Zhong-Xi li duizhao biao).

Names of Tribal People
Although traditional Chinese writers often designated all the tribal people in the south as Man, some authors distinguished the individual tribes by name. As mentioned earlier, Fan Chengda notes five of these (Yao, Lao, Man, Li, and Dan). The Chinese characters used to identify these tribes have changed over time, which in some ways reflects changes in official or government attitudes toward the southern tribes. To cite one example, depending on which source is consulted, the Chinese character for the "Yao" people can be written in three or four different ways: 徭 (this form, or its variant *moyao* 莫徭, was used from the late sixth or early seventh century through the Song; sometimes it is alternately written as 傜); 猺 (this derogatory form, with the "dog classifier" *quan* 犭 on the left side, was used often during the Ming and Qing dynasties and appears in all extant editions of *Treatises* dating from those periods); and 瑤 (this is the modern form of the character, stripped of negative implications and literally meaning "precious jade" or a "beautiful, jadelike stone"). When Fan Chengda was writing in the twelfth century, he used the second of these forms, which Kong Fanli (for the most part) has restored in his modern recension of *Treatises*. In my notes and in entries in the Glossary-Index, I will also use the "original" forms of characters designating the Yao, Lao, Man, Li, and Dan people, as did Fan Chengda.

Linear, Area, and Weight Measures
Song dynasty linear measures mentioned in this book are listed below. My main source for metric equivalents is Wenren Jun and James M. Hargett, "The Measures *Li* and *Mou* during the Song, Liao, and Jin Dynasties," *Bulletin of Sung-Yuan Studies* 21 (1989): 8–30.

Linear Measures
    cun: 1 *cun* (inch) = 3.1 cm = 1.2 in
    chi: 1 *chi* (foot) = 31.6 cm = 12.6 in

bu: 1 *bu* (double-pace) = 5 *chi* = 158 cm = 6.3 ft

li: 1 *li* (mile) = 360 *bu* = 568.9 m = 1,877.6 ft

pi: 1 *pi* (bolt [of cloth]) = 4 *zhang* = 48 ft

zhang: 1 *zhang* = 10 *chi* = 316.1 cm = 126.4 in = 12.0 ft

xunzhang: *xunzhang* is an imprecise measure of distance or height, ranging from roughly 8 *chi* to 1 *zhang*

cheng (stage): an imprecise measure of distance, usually referring to the distance that a traveler could reasonably cover in one day. On average, this was between 45 and 60 *li* (15 to 20 miles), but it could vary with local conditions.

Area

mou: 1 *mou* = 240 sq *bu* = 453.4 sq m = 1,373.9 sq ft

Weight and Capacity

dan: 1 *dan* = 120 *jin* = 71.616 kilograms = 157.884 pounds[98]

liang: 1 *liang* = 24 *shu* = 37.3 grams = 1.315 ounces

sheng: 1 *sheng* = 0.6641 liter

OFFICE AND GOVERNMENT AGENCY TITLES

English translations generally follow those given in Charles O. Hucker's *A Dictionary of Official Titles in Imperial China*.

Place-names

Traditional and modern place-names are given in Hanyu Pinyin. Modern equivalents or approximations for traditional place-names are identified on first occurrence.

Pronunciation

Modern pronunciation of Chinese characters and words generally follows *Hanyu da cidian*.

Romanization

The Hanyu Pinyin system of phonetic transliteration is used throughout this volume.

Song Dynasty Government Administrative Units
  lu: circuit
  fu: municipality
  zhou: county
  xian: town
  jian: industrial complex
  jun: military district
  zhai: stockade
  zhen: market town
  xiang: village

Supplementary Text
I have sometimes added to individual entries translations of supplementary or lost passages gathered from *Mr. Huang's Daily Transcriptions, Comprehensive Investigation of Texts and Viewpoints*, and other sources. On some occasions lost *entries* are added as well. As a general rule, I have not repeated lines in the supplementary text passage that are already translated in the entry proper. In addition to providing the source of the supplementary text or entry, I also provide the page reference from Kong Fanli's *Six Examples of Fan Chengda's Informal Writings*. Most of these supplementary passages and entries are also reproduced in the Yan Pei and Hu Qiwang/Tan Guangguang texts, but I do not provide page citations to those works.

Translations from the Chinese
All translations from the Chinese are mine unless otherwise noted. In the bibliography, a Chinese publication's official English title appears in parentheses in italics with title capitalization.

Variant Readings
Although my translation is based on Kong Fanli's text of *Treatises*, on occasion I have made emendations based on other editions. While I always cite the source of the variant reading I am following, I have avoided lengthy explanation of the philological reasons for my adoption.

NOTES TO INTRODUCTION

1 The Chinese term Man 蠻, used throughout the translation and notes, should not be confused with the English word "man."

2 The modern province name "Guangxi" is a shortened version of this circuit name. In the early Song there was just one Guangnan Circuit (Guangnan *lu*), but in 997 it was split into two new political-administrative jurisdictions: the Guangnan East Circuit and the Guangnan West Circuit. *Songshi*, 85.2094.

3 A useful English abstract of the many fascinating discoveries made at Zengpi Yan since the 1970s appears in *Guilin Zengpi yan*, 680–703.

4 This east-west alignment of mountains runs between latitudes 25° and 26° north. For additional information on the term "Lingnan" and its various geo-political implications, see Marks, *Tigers, Rice, Silk, and Silt*, esp. 22–25.

5 The key hub of this corridor is Dongting Lake (Dongting *hu*), which connects with the Changjiang (or Yangzi River). From Dongting Lake one could travel south on the Xiang River (Xiangjiang) to the northern part of Guangxi, and then from there down to Guilin and other points south.

6 The administrative history of Guilin Commandery and its subsequent development, outlined on the pages below, is based mainly on the following sources: Gu Zuyu, comp., *Dushi fangyu jiyao*, 107.4814–15; Deng Minjie, *Guangxi lishi dili tongkao*, 130–36; Huang Tirong, *Guangxi lishi dili*, 89–108; and Tan Yan-huan and Liao Guoyi, *Guangxi shigao*, 84–89.

7 For additional details on the Numinous Canal, see the "Miscellaneous Items Treatise."

8 *Hanshu*, 28*shang*.1569, lists Shian as one of four towns under the jurisdiction of Lingling Commandery.

9 For instance, see Deng Minjie, *Guangxi lishi dili tongkao*, 130. Others, however, disagree and argue that the old Han town was some 80 *li* northeast of modern Guilin. See Zeng Duhong et al., *Guilin jianshi*, 14.

10 Good examples are some of the sophisticated ceramics found in these tombs. An excellent source on these ceramics, with informative descriptions and color plates, is *Guangxi bowuguan gu taoci jingcui*, esp. pls. 13, 14, 20, 25, and 29.

11 From its source in Yunnan (west of modern Guangnan *xian*), the Right River flows a southeasterly course into western Guangxi. When it reaches modern Hejiang *zhen* in Yongning *xian* it merges with the Left River. During the Song dynasty, the Right River and the various towns along it fell under the jurisdiction of Yong County (Yongzhou).

12 Mo Xiufu, *Guilin fengtu ji*, 14a.

13 These later modifications to the city wall are described in Gu Zuyu, comp., *Dushi fangyu jiyao*, 107.4814.

14 *Songshi*, 90.2239. Jingjiang was adopted from the name of the former Tang military district mentioned in the previous paragraph.

15 On translating *dong* as "settlement," see below.

16 A useful discussion and list of these various administrative units is provided in Richard David Cushman's dissertation on the Yao people, "Rebel Haunts and Lotus Huts," 157–73 (see esp. the remarks on 157–60). For additional information on the *zhoumi* system under the Song, see also Wiens, *China's March*

toward the Tropics, 211–14. As the modern scholar Su Guanchang has demonstrated, there were surely many more "bridle and halter" administrative units under the Song than those listed in the *Songshi* and other works. See the remarks in his "Tang Song Yuan Ming Qing Guangxi jimi zhouxian," esp. 36–37.

17   At least this seems to have been the general thinking on the issue. On the so-called Chinese cultural takeover of south China, see Hisayuki Miyakawa's essay "The Confucianization of South China." But cf. also the comments in Cushman, "Rebel Haunts and Lotus Huts," 168 and 169 (table 4). Cushman observes that some of these "tribal leaders" were actually Chinese from the north who were awarded hereditary positions as "tribal leaders," because of their distinguished military service on behalf of the Song. To say the least, such appointments diverge from the policy of "using barbarians to control barbarians."

18   Shin, *The Making of the Chinese State*, 10.

19   *Songshi*, 386.11869. This expression is probably taken from Fan's obituary, written by his friend Zhou Bida, which describes Guangxi as a place that is "desolate and removed, destitute and impoverished" (*huangyuan jiongkui*). See Zhou Bida, "Xianzheng dian daxueshi zeng yinqing guanglu dafu Fangong Chengda Shendao bei" (hereafter cited as "Shendao bei"), 116.

20   On the lines from Du Fu and Han Yu, see the Author's Preface, this volume; on those by Liu Zongyuan and Huang Tingjian, see the opening remarks to the "Treatise on Precipice-Grottoes."

21   Unfortunately, only a handful of these works, such as *Guilin fengtu ji, Lingbiao luyi*, and *Beihu lu*, have survived. There is no indication that Fan Chengda knew about any of these texts. WXTK 205.1703 (repeated in Lü Mingzhong et al. eds., *Nanfang minzu gushi shulu*, 77–78) lists a work titled *Guilin zhi* by Jiang Wenshu, who served as a minor official in Jingjiang in the late 1160s. Fan Chengda probably knew about this work but makes no mention of it anywhere in the *Treatises* or his other writings.

22   The first comprehensive gazetteer for Guangxi, the *Guangxi tongzhi* in sixty *juan*, edited by Huang Zuo, was published in 1532. The earliest extant local gazetteer for Guilin (which survives only in fragments) is the *Guilin junzhi*, edited by Chen Lian. This text dates from 1450 and is extant but has not been available to me.

23   I have not been able to find any reliable information on the population ratio of Man to Chinese residents in Guangxi during the Song. Barlow estimates the non-Chinese population in the Song "had to have been sixty to seventy percent" ("The Zhuang Minority Peoples," 258, n. 60). Population figures for Jingjiang Municipality are equally scanty. *Songshi*, 90.2239, lists 46,343 households (*hu*) for Jingjiang during the Yuanfeng reign (1078–1086) of the Northern Song. If we figure an average of five persons per household, this would mean the entire municipality had a population of just over 230,000 people in the late eleventh century. This figure probably refers only to registered, tax-paying residents the region. *Songshi*, 90.2239, says the population for the entire Guangnan West Circuit in 1152, less than a century later, was 1,341,572 persons (*kou*). The

population increase indicated by this figure is probably the result of migrations south into Guangxi after the Jin invasions.

24 Coffins made of hardwood from Liu County, for instance, were shipped throughout the Chinese empire during the Song.

25 The most complete study of Fan Chengda's poetry in any language is J. D. Schmidt's *Stone Lake: The Poetry of Fan Chengda (1126–1193)*.

26 Some of these poems are translated and discussed in Schmidt, *Stone Lake*, 80–86. For a complete translation of the entire sixty-poem sequence, see Hargett, "Boulder Lake Poems."

27 Hong Kuo describes Fan Chengda as follows: "His erudition is admirable, while his prose is elegant." See *Panzhou wenji*, 22.10a. Lou Yue is more generous, exclaiming that "[Fan's] prose is so very magnificent!" *Gongkui ji*, 38.12b. Zhou Bida, Fan Chengda's good friend and author of his necrology, remarks: "Heaven endowed him with talent and intelligence, which is supplemented by extensive knowledge. His prose compositions are admirable and lovely, clear and effortless." "Shendao bei," 121.

28 Aside from the four texts mentioned here, Fan's two remaining major prose works are his *Mei-Flowers Manual* (Meipu) and his *Chrysanthemum Manual* (Jupu). Fan's six surviving prose works are conveniently assembled in *Fan Chengda biji liuzhong*.

29 For additional information on this embassy, see my "Fan Ch'eng-ta's *Lan-p'ei lu*."

30 The *Lanpei lu* and the *Canluan lu* are both translated and discussed in my *On the Road*.

31 For a complete and annotated translation of the *Wuchuan lu*, see my *Riding the River Home*.

32 The most famous Tang exiles in the south were Han Yu and Liu Zongyuan. But many other Tang writers also visited Guilin under various circumstances. These include Song Zhiwen, Zhang Yue, Zhang Jiuling (a native of Guangdong), Yuan Jie, Li Bo 李渤 (not to be confused with Li Bo 李白, the famous Tang dynasty poet), Li Deyu, and Li Shangyin. The Guilin connections of these writers are summarized in Zeng Duhong et al., *Guilin jianshi*, 28–37. None of them wrote extensively about Guilin. It should be added, however, that three important Tang literary figures were native to the greater Guilin region: Cao Tang, Cao Ye, and Zhao Guanwen. See *Guilin jianshi*, 38–41.

33 See his Preface.

34 Ethnography is a multidisciplinary field that is simply too broad and diverse to characterize within a given set of strictly defined parameters. See the remarks in Paul Atkinson et al., eds. *Handbook of Ethnography* (London: Sage Publications, 2001), esp. the comments in the Editorial Introduction, 1–7. Cf. also the following observation in Martyn Hammersley and Paul Atkinson, *Ethnography: Principles in Practice* (London and New York: Tavistock Publications, 1983), 2: "The ethnographer participates, overtly or covertly, in people's daily lives for an extended period of time, watching what happens, listening to what is said, asking questions; in fact collecting whatever data are available to throw light on the issues with which he or she is concerned." For the discussion here

we need only keep in mind that ethnographic research is based on fieldwork of the sort described by Hammersley and Atkinson that results in a textual product. Such works are different from government-sponsored gazetteers, described below, whose main purpose is political administration.

35   Diego de Landa's original manuscript, written in Spain (after he left Mexico) around 1566 and titled *Relación de las Cosas de Yucatán*, is lost. What survives is an abridged version, discovered by the French cleric Charles Étienne Brasseur de Bourbourg (1814–1874) in 1862 and published later in a bilingual French-Spanish edition, under the title *Relation des choses de Yucatán de Diego de Landa*.

36   Laura Hostetler, *Qing Colonial Enterprise: Ethnography and Cartography in Early Modern China* (Chicago and London: University of Chicago Press, 2001), 81. See also her useful article "Qing Connections to the Early Modern World: Ethnography and Cartography in Eighteenth-Century China," *Modern Asian Studies* 34.3 (July 2000): 623–62.

37   Fan Chuo's monograph has been translated into English by Gordon H. Luce. See Bibliography.

38   The brief discussion that follows concerning the development of the gazetteer in China draws heavily from my article "Song Dynasty Local Gazetteers and Their Place in the History of *Difangzhi* Writing." Readers interested in local history and gazetteer production during the Song dynasty should also consult Peter K. Bol, "The Rise of Local History: History, Geography, and Culture in Southern Song and Yuan Wuzhou," *Harvard Journal of Asiatic Studies* 61.1 (June 2001): 37–76.

39   Steven F. Sage discusses this in his *Ancient Sichuan and the Unification of China* (Albany: SUNY Press, 1992), esp. 10–13.

40   Hui-lin Li has published a translation and study of Ji Han's text. See Bibliography. Although attributed to Ji Han, who flourished in the early fourth century, this text is probably a twelfth-century compilation based only in part on Ji Han's original work. Ma Tai-loi comments on this issue in his article "The Authenticity of the *Nan-fang ts'ao-mu chuang*."

41   The *Luoyang qielan ji* has been translated twice into English: Yi-t'ung Wang, *A Record of the Buddhist Monasteries of Lo-yang* (Princeton: Princeton University Press, 1984); and W. J. F. Jenner, *Memories of Loyang: Yang Hsüan-chih and the Lost Capital, 493–534* (New York: Clarendon Press of Oxford University, 1981).

42   *Suishu*, 33.988.

43   *Hou Hanshu*, 88.2931.

44   Aoyama Sadao, *Tō Sō jidai no kōtsū to chishi chizu no kenkyū*, 490.

45   This intellectual or scholarly approach, which stressed the collection, verification, and classification of new knowledge, was part of an intense and competitive intellectual culture that developed during the Song dynasty. New and exacting standards for writing history, which stressed comprehensiveness, accuracy, and verification, influenced gazetteer production in a major way. For additional information, see the discussion and references in my "Song Dynasty Gazetteers," especially the remarks in the "context" section, 428–36. Two more

recent publications that discuss the collection of empirical evidence during the Song are Alistair D. Inglis, *Hong Mai's "Record of the Listener" and Its Song Dynasty Context* (Albany: SUNY Press, 2006), and Hilde de Weert, *Competition Over Content: Negotiating Standards for the Civil Service Examinations in Imperial China (1127–1279)* (Cambridge: Harvard University Press, 2007).

46   In addition to *Treatises,* Fan Chengda's surviving manuals (*pu*) on the chrysanthemum (*juhua*) and mei-flower (*meihua*)—factual studies of natural objects, precisely classified—are also good examples of this trend in Song scholarship.

47   I discuss Su's fondness for Hainan in my article "Clearing the Apertures and Getting in Tune."

48   See the Author's Preface.

49   On translating *tuyi* as "natural product," see Author's Preface, note 16.

50   In fact, local scenic areas, historical antiquities, customs, people, and products are the kinds of topics one does commonly find in local gazetteers, especially those of the Ming and Qing periods. I suspect that here Fan wants to distinguish the varied contents of *Treatises,* which often describe "unusual" products and phenomena unique to Guangxi and the south, from the administrative reports and lists of population figures, households, taxes, water projects, and so on, one usually finds in government-sponsored gazetteers.

51   We know that Fan Chengda arrived in Chengdu on the seventh day of the sixth lunar month (or 26 June 1175). See Yue Ke, *Baozhen zhai shufa zan,* 26.13b. "Summer solstice" day in 1175 fell on the twenty-sixth day of the *fifth* lunar month (or 16 May 1175). Thus, we can be sure that Fan Chengda completed at least a draft of the *Treatises* and his Preface *before* he reached Chengdu. See also the remarks on dating Fan's arrival in Chengdu in Liu Kongfu, "*Guihai yuheng zhi* chengshu qingkuang ji juanshu kaobian," 91.

52   For instance, see the opening remarks to his "Treatise on Birds."

53   The poem in question, "Yuan taiwei," is found in Xiao Tong, comp., *Wenxuan,* 31.707. A complete English translation of this verse is included in John Marney, *Chiang Yen* (Boston: Twayne Publishers, 1981), 121.

54   The origins and functions of this office are explained in the *Zhouli.* See *Zhouli zhushu,* 2/9/647.

55   I use the word "treatise" here in the very general sense of a "book or writing which treats of some particular subject." *The Compact Oxford Dictionary* (second ed.; Oxford: Clarendon Press, 1989), 2104.3.

56   The most important exception is the twelfth chapter, "Za zhi," or "Miscellaneous Items Treatise," where *zhi* in all surviving editions of *Treatises* comes at the end of the chapter title and functions as a noun ("treatise"). I strongly suspect that "Za zhi" in surviving editions of *Treatises* should instead read "Zhi za" (Treatise on Miscellaneous Items), thus following the "*zhi* (verb) + topic" pattern used for chapter titles throughout Fan Chengda's text. It seems that during the textual transmission process "Zhi za" was reversed to "Za zhi." Strong evidence in support of the "Zhi za" reading is preserved in Huang Zhen's *Huangshi richao,* 67.58b, where quotations from Fan's "miscellaneous items" chapter are preceded by the title "Zhi za." On the other exception among Fan's chapter titles, see note 81 below.

57   Hu Qiwang and Tan Guangguang, in *Guihai yuheng zhi jiyi jiaozhu* (*Hu-Tan*), 4.

58   The closest match is probably Duan Gonglu's *Beihu lu*, but this work differs from *Treatises* in two notable ways. First, Duan's work is not specific to a particular geographic or administrative area; rather, it deals with the entire "south." And second, his various entries on flora, fauna, and local products are not presented in any systematic way, but instead are randomly arranged throughout three *juan*. Another Tang work that deserves mention here is Duan Chengshi's *Youyang zazu*. This work comprises about 1,300 entries organized into twenty *juan* with a ten-*juan* sequel. Its content, however, is so varied—including tales of romance and intrigue as well as stories about bloodthirsty vampires—that it almost defies description or classification. See the remarks in Carrie E. Reed, "Motivation and Meaning of a 'Hodge-Podge': Duan Chengshi's *Youyang zazu*," *Journal of the American Oriental Society* 123.1 (2003): 121–45. Moreover, some of the titles of Duan's entries are so cryptic they seem beyond understanding. But Duan does devote a full seven *juan* to flora and fauna, and, like Fan Chengda's entries, Duan's text seems to be based in large part on personal observation. One aspect of the *Youyang zazu* that might have influenced Fan Chengda is Duan's chapter prefaces, in which he often speaks in the first person and says he wants to correct mistakes or misunderstandings in earlier works. Fan also includes short prefaces (or "opening remarks") to each of his thirteen treatises that at times serve the same purpose.

59   See Author's Preface.

60   The title of Kong Fanli's 2002 recension of Fan Chengda's major surviving prose works—*Fan Chengda biji liuzhong*—suggests that Kong believes these six texts to be a form of *biji* (sometimes translated as "note literature"), a popular style of prose writing during the Tang and especially the Song. Kong does not explain why he considers *Treatises* and Fan's other major prose works to be *biji*. I suspect he considers *biji* in this context to mean something like "private, informal writings," as opposed to prose pieces composed for more formal occasions or for government-administrative purposes. Unfortunately, Kong's classification is only useful in the most general terms, for *biji* (and related forms of prose writing during the Song such as *suibi* and *zhaji*) cannot be defined as a literary genre in precise terms. The structure and contents of *biji* literature are so varied that as a genre it defies classification.

61   The biographical information on Zhou Qufei that follows, including his birth and death dates, is drawn from Yang Wuquan's excellent critical essay "Zhou Qufei yu *Lingwai daida*," in *LWDD*, 1–18.

62   This poem survives. See *FSHJ*, 14.174 ("Song Zhou Zhifu jiaoshou gui Yongjia").

63   *LWDD*, preface, 1.

64   One could cite numerous examples. Here are just three: compare the entry on "giant clams" from *Zhufan zhi jiaoshi* (*chequ*; *ZFZ*, 2.206 [*Chau Ju-Kua*, 231]) with Fan's entry on the same subject in his "Treatise on Insects and Fishes"; compare Zhao Rukuo's report on "betel nuts" (*binlang*; *ZFZ*, 2.186 [*Chau Ju-Kua*, 213]) and his description of kapok (*jibei*; *ZFZ*, 2.192 [*Chau Ju-Kua*, 217]) with the entries on those topics in the "Treatise on Herbaceous Plants and Trees."

65   According to FCDBJ, 6, Li Xinchuan quotes from *Treatises* on twelve occasions.

66   For an example, see Zhou Mi, *Qidong yeyu*, 20.372.

67   I refer here mainly to Yan Pei, Hu Qiwang and Tan Guangguang, and Kong Fanli. Their various contributions to the textual history of *Treatises* are discussed below.

68   These passages have all been retrieved by Kong Fanli and are reprinted in his *Fan Chengda biji liuzhong*.

69   In *Science and Civilisation in China*, 6-1.1, 461, for instance, Needham and his colleagues praise Fan Chengda's "analytical approach" in describing southern camellias and red cardamoms (for which see the "Treatise on Flowers").

70   See his "Stomping Songs: Word and Image," 4.

71   In his preface to Fan Chengda's *Rocky Lake's Great Complete Collection* (Shihu da quanji), which survives, Yang Wanli mentions that Fan worked "day and night [in his final years] editing his verse and prose, and it took him several years to complete the collection." The preface is reprinted in FSHJ, 502–3 (Yang's comments about Fan's editing of the collection appear on 502).

72   Zhou Bida, "Shendao bei," 121; *Songshi*, 208.5382.

73   The postface is reprinted in FSHJ, 505.

74   See, for instance, the remarks on this in Zhu Shangshu, *Songren bieji xulu*, esp. 2:979–80.

75   Fan Chengda's biography in the *Songshi*, 386.11870, says specifically that *Treatises* was "in general circulation"; Zhou Bida's "Shendao bei," 122, identifies *Treatises* as a "separate work" (*biezhu*) from his complete collection.

76   This verse, titled "Song Fan Zhineng zhizhi," is included in Li Shi's collected works. See *Fangzhou ji*, 1.20b. The ultimate line of the poem indicates that Li Shi had a copy of *Treatises* in his possession before he died in 1181.

77   Judging from the *Treatises* excerpts quoted in the surviving portions of the *Yongle dadian*, Fan's complete collection was still extant when the *Yongle dadian* was compiled in the early Ming. Also, some of Li Shizhen's quotations from *Treatises* in the *Compendium of Basic Pharmacopeia* seem to be drawn from an earlier, more complete edition, different from the one that survives today.

78   The most important and useful of the modern collections is Kong Fanli's *Fan Chengda biji liuzhong*. Many of Fan's other surviving prose works, mostly shorter pieces culled from various encyclopedias and collectanea, are assembled in *Fan Chengda yizhu jicun*, also compiled by Kong Fanli.

79   Perhaps "excised" is a better word than "lost." For reasons unexplained, it appears that portions of all of Fan Chengda's six major prose works were excised by unknown Ming dynasty editors. Cf. *Qi Zhiping*, 99, which says the text of *Treatises* was already in poor condition by the Ming period, and thus the incomplete nature of the surviving text is not the result of excisions made by editors of that period. Regarding the surviving, abridged condition of Fan's three travel diaries, see my comments in *On the Road*, 137–38.

80   FCDBJ, 73.

81   In *Mr. Huang's Daily Transcriptions* the title of Fan's first chapter is "Treatise on Hills" (Zhishan), whereas in the received edition it is "Treatise on Precipice-

Grottoes" (Zhi yandong). The second exception concerns the title of the chapter on "Miscellaneous Items." See note 56 above.

82   Zhou Bida, "Shendao bei," 122.

83   Chen Zhensun, *Zhizhai shulu jieti*, 8.259.

84   Chao Gongwu, *Junzhai dushu zhi*, 5shang.570.

85   *Songshi*, 204.5158; *Heyin Siku quanshu zongmu tiyao*, 14.101 (2:1525).

86   See, for instance, Liu Kongfu, "*Guihai yuheng zhi* chengshu qingkuang ji juanshu kaobian," 91 and 101; *Hu-Tan*, 8–9; *Qi Zhiping*, 99; and Wan Yingmin, "*Guihai yuheng zhi* wenxian xue yanjiu," 8.

87   *Heyin Siku quanshu zongmu tiyao*, 14.102 (2:1526).

88   For additional information on the language used in Song dynasty travel diaries, see my "Some Preliminary Remarks on the Travel Records of the Song Dynasty."

89   For explanatory notes on the various names and terms that appear in this passage, see the "Treatise on Herbaceous Plants and Trees."

90   That authorial presence is also a major characteristic of Fan's three travel diaries explains why *Treatises* is often considered part of traditional Chinese travel and landscape literature. For more on this see the useful discussion in Deborah Marie Rudolph, "Literary Innovation and Aesthetic Tradition in Travel Writing of the Southern Sung," 26–29.

91   Ibid., 24.

92   My understanding and translation of these coordinate expressions is based on (1) their individual and relational (if any) meanings; (2) how they are used in other Song texts, if relevant; and (3) how Fan Chengda uses them in *Treatises*.

93   The term "Man" probably derives from the word for "people" or "I" in one of the Miao-Yao languages of the southwest. See Liang and Zhang, *Dong Tai yuzu gailun*, 10–12.

94   Endymion Wilkinson, comp., *Chinese History: A Manual*, 724.

95   In modern Chinese 峒 is usually read *dong* (though in some place-names it is read *tong*), but in the native languages of the Zhuang and other non-Chinese tribes in the south, it is usually read *tong* (IPA: tuŋ). Tan Xiaohang, *Lingnan gu Yueren mingcheng wenhua tanyuan*, 70. Throughout this book I will follow the modern Chinese pronunciation (*dong*).

96   Sung-shih Hsü, "The Chuang People of South China," in Drake, ed., *Symposium on Historical Archaeological and Linguistic Studies on Southern China, South-East Asia and the Hong Kong Region*, 116. Cf. Hirth and Rockhill, *Chau Ju-Kua*, 179, where *dong* is translated as "village"; Wiens, *China's March toward the Tropics*, 209, where *dong* are called "protectorates"; Hucker, no. 571, which calls them "subordinated prefectures"; and Barlow, "The Zhuang Minority Peoples," 253, which defines *dong* as "valleys."

97   Kuang Lu, *Chiya kaoshi*, 24. The modern scholar Lan Hong'en adds the following commentary to this line: "When Zhuang people level an area in a place surrounded on all four sides by mountains, they call it a *dong*" (24).

98   My source for this figure is Chang and Smythe, trans., *South China in the Twelfth Century*, 25.

TREATISES OF
THE SUPERVISOR
AND GUARDIAN
of the Cinnamon Sea

Author's Preface

ARLIER, AFTER I LEFT THE PURPLE MYRTLE WALL [ZIWEI Yuan][1] and was about to go out and serve as commandant [*shuai*] of Guangyou,[2] some in-laws and old friends held a farewell drinking party for me in a tent by the Pine River [Songjiang].[3] All of them were concerned about the scorching heat and desolate local conditions [I would find in the south]. I looked up some poems by Tang authors and checked on the geography of Guilin. Shaoling referred to it as "suitable to man";[4] Letian referred to it as "free of miasma";[5] Tuizhi went so far as to regard [gazing at] the rivers and mountains south of the Xiang River as superior to mounting a simurgh and riding off to the land of immortals.[6] So, as for the best places I might travel to as an official, could there possibly be any better destination [than Guilin]? After parting with relatives and friends, I set out on my journey.

When I reached the commandery [Guilin] in the third month of the ninth year of the Qiandao reign [1173],[7] the weather was clear and fair—just as I had heard it would be. But the wondrous and unsurpassed nature of the cliff-caverns, the richness and antiquity of local customs and practices, and the grandness and superiority of the municipal government seat far exceeded what I had heard before. Since I refrained from "looking down on the [local] people,"[8] they in turn forgave my ignorance and trusted in my sincerity. We made an agreement never to deceive one another. As one year followed the next, there were good harvests, and in the field office[9] there were few official documents [to occupy my time]. I stayed for two years and found peace of mind there.

When I received an imperial order to take up a new government post overseeing the entire frontier in Shu [Sichuan], I promptly sent up a memorial, politely insisting on my inability [to hold such a post]. I remained in Guilin for another month, but my plea failed to produce [the desired change in] orders. And so I parted with the people of Guilin, who presented me, now the traveler, with a goblet of wine by the roadside.[10] After passing through the outer city wall, I was detained for two more days [by the local people] before I was able to depart. I traveled by boat on the Xiao and Xiang Rivers,[11] crossed Dongting Lake, proceeded upstream past the Yanyu Heap [Yanyu Dui],[12] galloped[13] through the Two Chuan [Liang Chuan],[14] and after half a year reached Chengdu.[15] While I was on the road, there were no official matters [to occupy me], and so from time to time I thought about my former travels [in Guilin]. Because of this I recalled from memory Guangxi's scenic places as well as its local goods [*fengwu*] and natural products [*tuyi*][16]—the kinds of information not generally found in local gazetteers—and collected them together to make this one book. Information worth noting on the Man people in remote areas was added as well for the purpose of providing information for the maps of local informants.[17] Alas! Although Brocade City [Jincheng][18] is known throughout the world as a "famous capital and joyful land" [*mingdu leguo*] and I am fortunate to have reached it, at the same time I remain deeply attached to Guilin, so much so that I have compiled and edited[19] this [collection of] minutia and trivia, which proves that I did not look down on the people there. Although I am now far away from them in a "famous capital and joyful land," still I will never forget them! Second year of the Chunxi reign [1175], Summer Solstice Day,[20] written by Fan Chengda, *zi* Zhineng, of Wu Commandery [Wujun].

NOTES TO AUTHOR'S PREFACE

1   The Purple Myrtle Wall, also known as the Purple Myrtle Palace (Ziwei Gong), is a circumpolar constellation composed largely of the stars of Ursa Major. For

additional details see Schafer, *Pacing the Void*, 47, and *Yan Pei*, 2, n. 1. The term "Purple Myrtle Wall" also refers to a central government administrative unit—the Secretariat (Zhongshu Sheng)—the name of which was officially changed in the eighth century to Purple Myrtle Department (Ziwei Sheng). *Hucker*, no. 7545. Fan Chengda had previously served as a drafter in the Secretariat (Zhongshu Sheren), so here he refers to that government agency by the name "Purple Myrtle Wall."

2   Geographic references and place-names in China that include the words "left" (*zuo*) or "right" (*you*) are given from a south-facing perspective. In other words, "left" indicates east and "right" indicates west. Guangxi is thus rendered "Guangyou."

3   The source of the Pine River, also known as the Wusong River (Wusong Jiang), is Tai Lake (Taihu) in modern Jiangsu. From there it flows a zigzag, easterly course through Jiangsu to modern Shanghai (today it is called Suzhou He), where it joins with the Huangpu River (Huangpu Jiang). The "drinking party" to which Fan Chengda refers here was a gathering with relatives and friends that took place on 31 December 1172 at the Rainbow Bridge (Chuihong Qiao). See *Canluan lu*, 41; Hargett, *On the Road*, 180. Constructed in 1048, this famous bridge spanned Pine River at a point just east of Wujiang Town (Wujiang *xian*; modern Jiangsu). Fan Chengda, *Wujun zhi*, 17.155.

4   Shaoling is the nickname (*hao*) of the Tang poet Du Fu. The poem in question here is his "Ji Yangwu Guizhou tan," which includes the lines "The Five Ranges are all scorching and hot; / Only Guilin is suitable to man" (Cao Yin et al., eds., *Quan Tangshi*, 226.2435–36).

5   Letian is the courtesy name (*zi*) of the Tang poet Bo (or Bai) Juyi. His verse "Song Yan dafu fu Guizhou" includes the line "Guilin is free of miasmic vapors" (Cao Yin et al., *Quan Tangshi*, 442.4944).

6   The reference here is to Han Yu's (*zi* Tuizhi) verse "Song Guizhou Yan Daifu; tongyong 'nan' zi." This poem closes with the following lines: "This far surpasses an ascent to the land of immortals; / So why take the time to mount a flying simurgh?" (Cao Yin et al., *Quan Tangshi*, 344.3864). The simurgh (*luan*) is an exalted member of China's pantheon of fabulous birds and often associated with Daoist immortals sauntering through the heavens. Han Yu's entire poem is translated in Schafer, *Vermilion Bird*, 26, and in my *On the Road*, 102.

7   FCDBJ, 81, following the 1927 *Shuofu* ed. (*Shuofu sanzhong*, 50.792), reads "third month of the eighth year of the Qiandao reign" (that is, 1172). This is wrong. Fan Chengda reached Guilin on the tenth day, third month, of the *ninth* year of the Qiandao reign (23 April 1173), as is confirmed in several sources. See, for instance, Kong Fanli, *Fan Chengda nianpu*, 238; Yu Beishan, *Fan Chengda nianpu*, 168.

8   The expression "not look down on its local people" (*bu biyi qi min*) is drawn from Han Yu's temple stele inscription "Liuzhou Luochi miao bei." See Han Yu, *Changli xiansheng ji*, 31.5b.

9   The expression *mufu* (lit., "tent office") usually denotes the field headquarters of a military commander on campaign. *Hucker*, no. 4052. Fan Chengda uses this term because one of the official posts he held in Guangxi was that of pacification and comfort commissioner for regulation and order (*anfu zhizhi shi*),

which in effect made him military commissioner of the region.

10 That is, they gave him a farewell banquet. Fan Chengda's fellow officials in Guilin no doubt also prepared a banquet for him. In the preface of a poem in *Fan Shihu ji*, 15.189 ("Xing'an rudong"), Fan mentions that twenty-one of his colleagues from Guilin accompanied him north as far as the border at Xing'an Town (Xing'an *xian*).

11 The Xiang River originates in Lingchuan *xian* in Guangxi, from where it flows north into Hunan and merges with the Xiao River (Xiaoshui).

12 Yanyu Heap is a rocky promontory in the Changjiang just east of the Kui County seat (in eastern Sichuan) and is regarded as the most dangerous place in the Three Gorges (Sanxia). It marks the entranceway into Qutang Gorge (Qutang Xia). Fan Chengda describes his passage through Yanyu Heap in 1177 in the *Wuchuan lu*, 217 (Hargett, *Riding the River Home*, 134).

13 "Galloped" (*chiqu*) indicates that Fan Chengda traveled on horseback. More specifically, when he reached Wuning Town (Wuning *xian*) in Wan County (Wanzhou; modern Chongqing) Fan abandoned his boat and traveled overland instead. By this route he reached Chengdu in fewer than twenty days, whereas with further boat travel on the Changjiang and Min Rivers it would have taken him about one hundred days to reach Chengdu. See *Wuchuan lu*, 216 (Hargett, *Riding the River Home*, 132).

14 Liangchuan refers to Sichuan. During the Tang dynasty the Jiannan Circuit (Jiannan *dao*) was divided into two parts: Eastern Chuan (Dongchuan) and Western Chuan (Xichuan).

15 One reason it took Fan Chengda six months to reach Chengdu was that a good portion of the journey was undertaken upstream on the Changjiang.

16 The expression *tuyi*, rendered loosely here as "natural products," is difficult to translate. Literally this expression means something like "suitability (*yi*) to the [local] soil (*tu*)." The idea here is that everything that is unique to a particular place—its people, products, flora, fauna, and so on—all develop as a result of their response and adaptability to the unique local conditions (specifically, the soil of that region). See the gloss in *Yan Pei*, 4, n. 16. See also Rudolph, "Literary Innovation and Aesthetic Tradition in Travel Writing of the Southern Sung," 21, where *tuyi* is rendered as "local resources and industries."

17 During the Zhou dynasty, the term *tuxun* (rendered here literally as "local informants") denoted members of the Ministry of Education, called Diguan, who prepared maps to brief the emperor on areas through which he planned to travel. Cf. Hucker, no. 7348, where *tuxun* is translated "Royal Scouts." Fan Chengda is probably using *tuxun* to refer to local government officials ("local informants") in Guilin, who were obligated periodically to revise and update the local gazetteer and maps of that region.

18 Brocade City is another name for Chengdu.

19 Reading *zhuiji* 綴輯 (compile and edit) as a variant for 綴緝.

20 The sĸQs ed., Preface, 2a, provides a more complete date for the preface: "Second year of the Chunxi reign, Yiwei Year, Summer Solstice Day." The reference *yiwei* 乙未 indicates the second year of the Chunxi reign, or 1175. Summer solstice day in 1175 fell on 16 May.

1

PRECIPICE-GROTTOES
(Zhi yandong)

I ONCE ASSESSED THE WONDROUS NATURE OF THE HILLS IN Guilin[1] and found them worthy to be rated first in the world.[2] Scholar-officials sent down[3] to the south are few, and so oftentimes they are unaware [of Guilin's magnificent spires], while those who hear about them likewise cannot believe it.

TRANSLATOR'S NOTE: The Guilin region of Guangxi hosts a karst topography, where erosion of the limestone over millions of years has produced solitary precipices (or pinnacles), odd-looking fissures, sinkholes, spacious caverns, picturesque hills, and subterranean streams. In his "Treatise on Precipice-Grottoes," Fan Chengda often refers to Guilin's magnificent spires as *yan*, the primary meaning of which is "precipice" or "steep cliff." On other occasions he simply calls them *shan*, or "hills." As for the caves inside these precipices, Fan usually designates them *dong* (grottoes), although in the title of this chapter he refers to them as *yandong* (lit., "precipice-grottoes").

1   Although Guishan, translated here as "the hills in Guilin," is an ancient name for Folded Brocade Precipice (see below), here I understand the expression in a more general sense, referring collectively to all the limestone precipices in and around Guilin.

2   Some modern scholars believe this sentence to be the source of the now famous descriptive line "Guilin's scenery is the best in the world" (Guilin shanshui jia tianxia). See, for instance, the remarks in Su Hongji and Deng Zhuren, "*Guihai yuheng zhi*—Nan Song shiqi Guilin de lüyou baike quanshu," 109.

3   Reading *luo* 落 in the sense of *liuluo* 留落, which means something like "to have the unfortunate experience of being sent or exiled to an out-of-the-way place."

I was born in Eastern Wu[4] but in the north served in You and Ji,[5] in the south resided in Jiao and Guang,[6] and in the west held office below the Min Mountains and Mount Emei.[7] I traveled 10,000 *li* in all three of these directions, and wherever I went there was no scenic site that I failed to ascend and survey. Taihang,[8] Changshan,[9] Hengyue,[10] and Lufu[11] are all venerated and lofty, noble, and grand. And while each has various named peaks, these peaks are actually imposing, huge mountains themselves. Those who have spoken of [described] these peaks have probably been forced to give them [individual] names. As for those mountains best known for their wondrous quality and elegance, none are better than Jiuhua in Chi,[12] Mount Huang (Huang-

---

4   "Eastern Wu" is an ancient name for the general area in and around modern Suzhou, Jiangsu. Fan Chengda was a native of nearby Wu Town (Wu *xian*).

5   "Served in You and Ji" refers to Fan Chengda's ambassadorial mission to the state of Jin in 1170. The Jin capital at Zhongdu (modern Beijing) was located in ancient You County (Youzhou), which included modern Beijing, northern Hebei, and part of Liaoning. During the Former Han dynasty (206 B.C.E.–8 C.E.) the You County seat was in Ji Town (Ji *xian*), located southwest of modern Beijing.

6   "Jiao" here refers Jiaozhi, an ancient Chinese administrative name for what is now the northern and central part of Vietnam. "Guang" indicates the Guang-nan West Circuit.

7   Fan Chengda held office in Sichuan (or "below the Min Mountains and Mount Emei") from 1175 until 1177. While there he served in essentially the same posts he had previously held in Guangxi.

8   The Taihang Mountain Range (Taihang Shanling) extends between Shanxi and Hebei.

9   Fan Chengda's reference here is Mount Heng (Hengshan) in Hebei, which among China's Five Cardinal Mountains served as the Northern Cardinal Mount (Beiyue). Since Heng was the given name of the Northern Song dynasty emperor Zhenzong (Zhao Heng, r. 997–1022), Fan Chengda could not use this taboo character in his reference to the mountain. He instead employs the name Changshan (lit., "Constant Mountain"), an alternate designation for Mount Heng. See the remarks in Li Deqing, *Zhongguo lishi diming bihui kao*, 133–34.

10   "Hengyue" is the Nanyue, or "Southern Cardinal Mount," in Hunan, one of China's most venerated mountains.

11   "Lufu" refers to Mount Lu (Lushan) in northern Jiangxi.

12   Mount Jiuhua (Jiuhua Shan) is southwest of modern Qingyang *xian*, Anhui. During the Tang dynasty it fell under the jurisdiction of Chi County (Chizhou).

shan) in She,[13] Xiandu in Gua,[14] Yandang in Wen,[15] and Wu Gorge [Wuxia] in Kui.[16] These are jointly praised throughout the world, yet they are all limited to a few [praiseworthy] peaks and nothing more. Furthermore, they are located in desolate and remote out-of-the-way border regions and not accessible to members of the senior generation.[17] Moreover, mountains that are able to stand far above the crowd[18] must certainly do so because of the contours of their folded crests and layered ridges, which twist and extend as they rise, and approach naturally from their place of origin.

As for the thousand peaks of Guilin, none extend outwardly to their flanks. They all rise prominently from flat ground and stand independently. Like jade bamboo shoots and jasper hairpins, forests of them extend without limit. Their fantastic features are all pretty much as described here. Truly, they deserve to be rated first in the world. Han Tuizhi's [Han Yu's] poem reads: "The river forms

---

13   Mount Huang, or Yellow Mountain, is in southern Anhui. "She" indicates She County (Shezhou), an administrative district established near Mount Huang during the Sui dynasty. In the twelfth century, the government administrative area around Yellow Mountain was known as Hui County. Fan Chengda's first appointment as a government official was to the post adjutant households inspector (*sihu canjun*) in Hui County. He served there from early 1156 until late 1160.

14   Mount Xiandu (Xiandu Shan; also known as Jinyun Shan) is in Zhejiang. It fell under the jurisdiction of Gua County during the Sui. During the Song, this area was known as Chu County (Chuzhou; modern Lishui *xian*, Zhejiang). Fan Chengda served as administrator there in 1168 and 1169.

15   Yandang is Mount Yandang (Yangdang Shan), located in Wen County (Wenzhou), which corresponds to modern Wenzhou *shi*, Zhejiang.

16   Kui County is in eastern Sichuan. Nearby Wu Gorge is one of the famous Three Gorges on the Changjiang.

17   The expression I translate loosely as "senior generation" literally reads "small table and staff" (*jizhang*). This is a term of respect used when referring to older people, based on the idea that members of the senior generation lean on small tables (*ji*) for support when at home and rely on walking sticks or staffs (*zhang*) while away from home.

18   The phrase "stand far above the crowd" has its origin in the *Mencius* (Mengzi), where You Ruo, a disciple of Confucius, remarks about his teacher: "Although he comes from the same stock as everyone else, he stands far above the common crowd" (*Mengzi zhushu*, 2/22/2686).

an azure gauze sash; / The hills resemble jade green hairpins."[19] Liu Zihou's [Liu Zongyuan's] "Account of Zi Family Islet" [Zijia Zhou ji] reads: "Gui county has many numinous hills. From flat ground they thrust upward, steeply and firmly,[20] and like a forest stand erect in the surrounding countryside."[21] Huang Luzhi's [Huang Tingjian's] poem reads: "The heights of Gui encircle the city, just like Yandang; / From level ground their green jade peaks suddenly rise high and steep."[22] When one contemplates the meanings of the three masters' words, then the wondrous nature of the hills of Gui will surely appear right before one's eyes, so there is no need to wait for any additional description from me. I recently sketched a true likeness [of the Gui hills] and sent it to some old friends back in Wu. I did so because convincing them [of Guilin's wondrous scenery] is not something easily accomplished with only a mouth and tongue to work with! The hills here are all hollow and vacuous, so there are many remarkable precipice-grottoes below the peaks. Among them more than thirty are well known and worthy of comment. They are all just seven or eight *li* from the city, with the nearest ones just two or three *li* away. In one day one can visit all of them. Here I will describe the most outstanding ones and provide notes on their essential features.

SINGLE ELEGANCE PEAK [*DUXIU FENG*][23] stands erect behind the

---

19   Cao Yin et al., *Quan Tangshi*, 344.3864. These lines come from the same Han Yu verse mentioned in the Author's Preface, translated in Schafer, *Vermilion Bird*, 26, and in my *On the Road*, 102.

20   Following the alternate reading *qiaoshu* 峭豎 (steeply and firmly). See FCDBJ, 87, n. 1. This reading is supported in *Liu Zongyuan ji*, 27.726 (see n. 21 below).

21   *Liu Zongyuan ji*, 27.726. The complete title of this work, written in 819, is "Account of Gui County Vice Censor Pei's Construction of the Zi Family Islet Pavilion" (Guizhou Pei Zhongcheng zuo Zijia Zhou ting ji). "Vice Censor Pei" refers to Pei Xingli, who served as governor of Gui County during Liu Zongyuan's exile years (815 to 819) in nearby Liu County.

22   These lines are from Huang Tingjian's quatrain "Reaching Gui County" (Dao Guizhou). See *Huang Tingjian quanji*, 10.239. Huang wrote this poem in 1103, when he passed through Gui County on the way to his exile site in Yi County (Guangxi).

23   As noted in *Hu-Tan*, 9, collation note, the text for this entry in all editions of *Treatises* is corrupt, for it conflates descriptive information on two different places: Reading Cave (see below) and Single Elegance Peak. Here I follow *Hu-Tan*, 9, and regard the lines that follow on Single Elegance Peak as a separate

commandery seat [*junzhi*] and serves as the main hill in Guilin. There are no slopes or earthen mounds on its flanks, and it rises abruptly to a height of 1,000 *zhang*.[24]

READING CAVE [*DUSHU YAN*] is located below Single Elegance Peak. The stone chamber [*shishi*][25] at the foot of the peak includes a sitting room [*bianfang*],[26] stone couches [*shita*],[27] and stone windows [*shiyou*], making the chamber seem as if it is encased by a square wall. When Yan Yannian [384–456] served as protector of the commandery, he read therein.[28]

---

entry. The origin of this peak's name is traced to a couplet, cited in numerous sources, attributed to the Six Dynasties writer and official Yan Yanzhi (mentioned in the text below; see also n. 28): "No peak in Guilin is superior to Single Elegance, / Standing lofty and high in the suburbs of the city." See Zheng Shuqi, "Xinkai Shiyan ji," in Dong Hao et al., eds., *Quan Tangwen*, 531.5386; rpt. in *Gudai Guilin shanshui wenxuan*, 110–13. As mentioned below in the text, when Yan Yanzhi served as protector of Guilin, he sometimes repaired to the grotto beneath Single Elegance Peak to read and study. Therefore it became known as the "Reading Cave." In the Yuanyou reign (1086–1094) of the Northern Song, the administrator of the region, Sun Lan, had the name "Master Yan's Reading Cave" (Yangong Dushu Yan) and Yan Yanzhi's famous lampoon "In Praise of the Five Gentlemen" (Wujun yong) engraved on the rocky wall of the precipice-grotto. Xie Qikun, ed., *Guangxi tongzhi*, 94.2b.

24 When describing the heights of Guilin's limestone pinnacles (here and below), Fan Chengda often engages in hyperbole. In fact, the Single Elegance Precipice stands about sixty meters high.

25 "Stone chamber" in this context refers to a smaller, ancillary cave at the foot of the precipice. The "rooms," "couches," and "windows" (or "openings") in the "stone chamber" mentioned in this line were all formed by the natural erosion of limestone.

26 I understand *bianfang*, rendered here as "sitting room," to mean a naturally formed subchamber (that is, a section or part of the larger stone chamber) at the base of the precipice where visitors could stop and rest. Although in some contexts *bianfang* can indicate privies, there is no evidence to suggest that is the case here.

27 "Stone couches," also called "stone beds" (*shichuang*), are in fact stalagmite formations. Read, *Minerals and Stones*, no. 65a.

28 Yan Yanzhi (also known as Yan Yannian) was a major Chinese poet who held several official positions under the first four emperors of the Liu-Song dynasty. Yan's sharp tongue and fondness for wine got him into trouble with many of his contemporaries, resulting in his removal to outlying regions far away from the capital. One of these areas was Shian Commandery, where he served as protector (or governor) around 425.

SUBDUING-THE-WAVES PRECIPICE [*FUBO YAN*][29] rises abruptly and to a height of 1,000 *zhang*. Below it there is a grotto[30] that can accommodate twenty [stone] couches. The grotto bores completely through the precipice, with "windows" [openings] emerging on its flanks. It has stalactites [*xuanshi*] that resemble pillars, which hang down but a thread's distance from the ground, never touching it. The popular name [for these stalactites] is Subduing-the-Waves Ma Tests His Sword Rocks [Ma Fubo Shijian Shi].[31] The front of the grotto sinks down to the riverbank, where waves and billows rush and gush day and night. beating and pounding against the rocks.

FOLDED BROCADE PRECIPICE [*DIECAI YAN*][32] is located behind Eight

---

29   Subduing-the-Waves Precipice stands on the western bank of the Li River in the northeastern corner of modern Guilin. According to popular tradition, the name Subduing-the-Waves derives from a title once given to the Han general Ma Yuan for successively eliminating a southern threat to the Han throne. An alternate name for Subduing-the-Waves Precipice is Whirlpool Waves Precipice (Fubo Yan). Cf. *Hu-Tan*, 10, collation note, which argues the latter is the correct name for the precipice.

30   The unnamed cavern mentioned in this line was originally called the Toying-with-a-Pearl Grotto (Wanzhu Dong), but Fan Chengda's immediate predecessor in Guangxi, Zhang Wei, changed the name to Returned Pearls Grotto (Huanzhu Dong) sometime during the late 1160s, when he served as manager and organizer for pacification and comfort in Guangxi (the same office Fan Chengda held from 1173 to 1175). "Returned pearls" is an allusion to the Han general Ma Yuan. The booty he allegedly accumulated during his military campaign in Yue was supposedly "returned" at this cave, thereby exonerating him from any wrongdoing. See the remarks in Donald S. Sutton, "A Case of Literati Piety: The Ma Yuan Cult from High Tang to High Qing," *Chinese Literature: Essays, Articles, and Reviews* 11 (Dec. 1989): 97. See also Xie Qikun, ed., *Guangxi tongzhi*, 94.11b–12a, which says the name "returned pearl(s)" may also derive from an old folktale in which the cave was inhabited by a dragon and illuminated by a single pearl. A fisherman came by one day and stole the pearl but later returned it because he felt ashamed.

31   According to popular tradition, the Han general Ma Yuan once "tested" (*shi*) his sword on these stalactites. Hence, the name "Subduing-the-Waves Ma Tests His Sword Rocks."

32   The name of this well-known precipice, located in the northeastern precincts of Guilin, derives from the "brocade" patterns of blue-green (*cui*) rock layered throughout its face. See Yuan Hui, "Diecai shan ji," in Dong Hao et al., *Quan Tangwen*, 721.7423; rpt. in *Gudai Guilin shanshui wenxuan*, 82–83.

Cinnamons Hall [Bagui Tang].[33] A side trail ascends the hill. Over halfway up[34] there is a large grotto[35] that, twisting and turning, connects through to the back of the hill.

WHITE DRAGON GROTTO [*BAILONG DONG*][36] is located in a flat area of South Creek [Nanxi], halfway up the hill.[37] The hollow inside it has a large stone chamber. One enters the grotto through the wall on the right side of the chamber. Halfway through the grotto there is a smaller stone chamber.[38]

---

33 Eight Cinnamons Hall was the name of a government office building located just outside the east wall of Guilin. It was so named because it had eight cinnamon trees planted in front of it. Fan Chengda, *Canluan lu*, 60; Hargett, *On the Road*, 203, 246, n. 346. On the history of the hall, see Li Yanbi, "Bagui tang ji," rpt. in Jin Hong et al., eds., *Guangxi tongzhi*, 109.14a–16b. The term "Eight Cinnamons" derives from the expression "cinnamon forest of eight trees" (*guilin bashu*), which appears in the *Mountains and Seas Classic* (Shanhai jing). See *Shanhai jing jiaozhu*, 5.268–69. This expression became a general reference to the Guangxi region after Han Yu used it in the first line of his poem "Seeing Off Great Master Yan to Gui County: Together We Used the Character for 'South' [as Our Lead Rhyme Word]" (Song Guizhou Yan Dafu; tongyong nan zi): "Glossy and green, the luxuriance of Eight Cinnamons; / The land that lies south of the River Xiang." Cao Yin et al., *Quan Tangshi*, 344.3864. Eight Cinnamons Hall was built by Cheng Jie sometime during the Shaosheng reign (1094–1098). Hu and Zhu, eds., *Lingui xian zhi*, 13.34b.

34 *Taiban* 太半 is most likely an error for *daban* 大半 (lit., "over halfway"). See *Hu-Tan*, 11, collation note.

35 Fan Chengda is probably referring to West Precipice (Xiyan), which was also called Phoenix Grotto (Fengdong). Yan Pei notes that this was not a "large grotto" but a rather small one that a person could barely squeeze through. See *Yan Pei*, 14.

36 The undulating ceiling of this cavern, comprised of white limestone, was said to resemble the shape of a dragon's spine. Hence, the name "White Dragon."

37 The hill mentioned here is South Creek Hill (Nanxi Shan), located in the southern section of Guilin. The local waterway (South Creek) from which the hill gets its name joins with the Li River. During the Tang, the area along South Creek was famous for its scenic pavilions and abundant flora, which were built and planted by the official Li Bo when he served as governor (*cishi*) of Guilin in the late 820s. Li's famous "Preface to the South Creek Poems" (Nanxi shi xu), dated 826, carved on the face of South Creek Hill, is extant. The preface is reproduced in *Gudai Guilin shanshui wenxuan*, 145–48.

38 The *Siku quanshu* edition provides additional text in this line. It reads: "Even during the height of summer one enters the grotto wearing a double-layered fur coat." At the end of this entry, there is another line of text: "The scaly snowflakes and flowery luster on the four sides of the chamber formed by all the sta-

LIU-THE-IMMORTAL'S PRECIPICE [*LIUXIAN YAN*] is located on the sunny [or south] side of White Dragon Grotto. This is where the immortal Liu Zhongyuan [eleventh century] once resided.[39] His stone chamber, lofty and cold,[40] is halfway up the hill.

GLORIOUS SCENE GROTTO [*HUAJING DONG*] is lofty and spacious, as big as ten rooms.[41] The grotto entrance is also just as big.

RIVER AND MOON GROTTO [*SHUIYUE DONG*] is located at the foot of Yi Hill [Yishan].[42] Half of it rests against the [Li] River. The forces

---

lactite secretions [*ruye*] resemble a treasury [*baosuo*]." See *GHYHZ* (*SKQS* ed.), 2b; also cited in *FCDBJ*, 87, n. 3.

39   Liu Zhongyuan refers here to Liu Jing. Popular tradition says he was a local butcher who once lived at the foot of South Creek Hill. Later, with help from a formulae gentleman (or Daoist adept, *fangshi*), he became "awakened" and ascended the hill to "cultivate the Way." Liu then traveled for more than forty years to various famous mountains (*mingshan*) throughout the empire, where he gathered herbs, concocted medicines, cured illnesses, and saved numerous people. He later returned to Guilin, where he lived to the age of 118. One day Liu suddenly experienced a "feathery transformation" (*yuhua*) and ascended into the heavens as an immortal. For additional details see Xie Qikun, ed., *Guangxi tongzhi*, 277.6b–7a. Note that this source (6b) gives Liu Jing's courtesy name as Zhongda rather than Zhongyuan.

40   Some editions of *Treatises* instead read "lofty and spacious" (*gaoguang*). See *Hu-Tan*, 13; and *Yan Pei*, 14, n. 31.

41   According to Jin Hong et al., *Guangxi tongzhi*, 30.15b, Glorious Scene Grotto is located below a hill of the same name, north of Treasure Trove Hill (Baoji Shan). The grotto is filled with inscriptions (*timing*), the earliest of which is dated around 845. The Tang official Yuan Hui built a structure near the grotto that he called the Precipice Light Pavilion (Yanguang Ting), but this pavilion was gone by the time Fan Chengda arrived in Guilin in the 1170s.

42   This grotto is located on a hill along the banks of the Li River, near where it merges with the Yang River (Yangjiang). Throughout history this grotto has been known by a host of different names. See Mo Xiufu, *Guilin fengtu ji*, 5b–6a. "River and moon" was one of its earlier names, but in 1166 the well-known writer-official Zhang Xiaoxiang changed the name to "Morning Sun Grotto" (Zhaoyang Dong). Fan Chengda reports, however, that this new name was not well received by the local people because Guilin already had a cavern known by that name, and so in 1173 he changed it back to "River and Moon." See Fan's "Fu Shuiyue dong: bing xu" (Inscription on restoring [the name] "River and Moon Grotto": with preface), in *Fan Chengda yizhu jicun*, 128; also rpt. in *Qi Zhiping*, 82 (see fig. 2 for a photograph of the surviving inscription in Fan Chengda's calligraphy). Because of the similarity in the local Guangxi pronunciation of the characters *yi* 宜 and *li* 漓, the hill that hosted this grotto was known as both Yi Hill and Li Hill (Lishan). Today it is known as Elephant Trunk Hill (Xiangbi

FIGURE 2
"Inscription on Restoring [the Name] 'River and Moon Grotto': With Preface" ("Fu 'Shuiyue Dong ming': bing xu"), written in the calligraphy of Fan Chengda, preserved in the River and Moon Grotto, Guilin. The complete text of the inscription is reprinted in *Fan Chengda yizhu jicun*, 128, and *Qi Zhiping*, 82.

of nature have trimmed and cut away [at the hill], forming a large grotto entrance, which penetrates through to the back of the hill. The summit is several tens of *zhang* high, and its shape is perfectly round. When seen from a distance, the summit is upright and orderly, just like the great disk of the moon. A tributary of the river flows through the grotto. When one squats down on the rocks and sports with the water, it is like sitting in a dome under a huge bridge.[43]

DRAGON-IN-HIDING GROTTO [*LONGYIN DONG*] AND DRAGON-IN-

Shan) because in contour it resembles an elephant dipping its snout into the Li River (see fig. 3).

43　I understand *juanpeng* in this line to function as a noun, referring to a structure or space with a curved or arching (*juan*) top or roof (*peng*), in other words, a dome or archway. The idea here is that if one looks up at the ceiling of the grotto while "squatting down on the rocks and sporting with the water" (*jushi nongshui*), it seems as if you are sitting in a dome (or archway) under a huge bridge.

FIGURE 3
Elephant Trunk Hill, Guilin. Photograph courtesy
of Dongbo of www.mountainsongs.net.

HIDING PRECIPICE [*LONGYIN YAN*] are both located at the foot of Seven Stars Hill [Qixing Shan],[44] inundated in the water of the [Li] River. One takes a boat to a spot below the rocky cliff-wall, where there is an entranceway into a large grotto that is perhaps a hundred *zhang* high. Entering the grotto to the sound of beating oars, when you look up at the grotto ceiling, there are dragon marks that sweep and swirl,

---

44   Seven Stars Hill is on the eastern bank of the Li River. The hill has seven peaks, clustered in the form of a dipper; thus the hill was named "Seven Stars" after the group of stars that form the Northern Dipper (Ursa Major or Beidou). See Fan's comments in the entry below on Perching Aurora Grotto. The seventh peak on Seven Stars Hill is called Gemmy Light Peak (Yaoguang Feng), named after the seventh star in the Northern Dipper. Dragon-in-Hiding Grotto is at the foot of that peak, overlooking the Minor East River (Xiao Dongjiang), a tributary of the Li River that flows into the grotto. Dragon-in-Hiding Precipice stands above the grotto.

just as if they had been made with a seal impression.[45] They extend for the entire length of the grotto.[46] If one's boat proceeds just a short distance farther, there is separate grotto entranceway through which one can exit. The precipice is next to the grotto. Halfway up the hill there is a small Buddhist temple. In fact, the precipice [or cave] serves as a Buddhist worship hall [*fotang*];[47] no [additional] rooms have been added [to the hall].[48]

PHEASANT PRECIPICE [*ZHIYAN*] is also a single hill on the banks of the [Li] River.[49] It has a small grotto. The grotto entrance overlooks the Li River below.

STANDING FISH PEAK [*LIYU FENG*] is located behind West Hill [Xishan].[50] Imposing and magnificent, lofty and pinnacled, it resembles a single fish planted upright. The remaining [nearby] peaks are very numerous. All of them are [covered with] dark green rocks that are sharp and jagged.

45　The term "dragon marks" (*longji*) refers to the rock patterns on the ceiling of the cave, which sweep and swirl "like the spine and vertebrae of a real dragon." *LWDD*, 1.18 (*Netolitzky*, 1.8). *Yinni*, rendered here as "seal impression," usually refers to seal impressions made in red ink. Fan is saying that the markings on the rocks are quite detailed and appear almost as if someone had imprinted them on the cave's ceiling with a seal (or chop).

46　In his "Account of a Trip to Dragon-in-Hiding Grotto and Dragon-in-Hiding Precipice" (You Longyin Dong Longyin Yan ji), the Qing dynasty scholar-official Zha Li quotes these last two lines from *Treatises* and then remarks: "I did not believe his [Fan Chengda's] description until I observed the grotto today." Zha's comments are reprinted in *Gudai Guilin shanshui wenxuan*, 61.

47　This Buddhist worship hall or chamber (*fotang*) was originally called the Śākyamuni Temple (Shijia Si). According to Zhou Kan's "Stele Account of the Śākyamuni Temple" (Shijia si bei ji), the temple was positioned below the first of the seven peaks on Seven Stars Hill. Zhou's "Account" is reproduced in Wang Sen, ed., *Yuexi wenzai*, 41.4a–6a, and in *Gudai Guilin shanshui wenxuan*, 52–53. *Yan Pei*, 15, n. 37, says the temple was built during the Xining reign (1068–1078) of the Northern Song but provides no source for this information.

48　The idea here seems to be that given space restrictions inside the cave, no additional rooms have been added to the worship hall.

49　According to Xie Qikun, ed., *Guangxi tongzhi*, 95.5a, Pheasant Hill was located 3 *li* south of the city wall of Guilin and stood over 500 *chi* in height. The summit of the hill resembled the shape of a bird about to take flight; hence it had the name "Pheasant Hill."

50　This peak, located in the western suburbs of Guilin, is actually one of the three peaks on West Hill. An alternate name for this peak was Stone Fish (Shiyu).

PERCHING AURORA GROTTO [*QIXIA DONG*] is located on Seven Stars Hill.[51] As for Seven Stars Hill, its seven peaks are positioned and arranged like the Northern Dipper. Furthermore, there is a single, small peak located on the side [of the hill], which is called Supporting Star [Fuxing].[52] Stone Grotto [Shidong] is located halfway up, in the belly of the hill. One enters it through a stone entranceway and then descends over one hundred steps to a level spot, which can seat several tens of people.[53] Off to the sides are two paths. The first one leads toward the west. On the two cliff-walls rocky secretions condense and congeal, [resembling] jade snowflakes and [having a] crystal-like luster. The summit is several tens of *zhang* high. The trail is also three or four *zhang* wide, and walking along it is like traveling on a thoroughfare. If you stomp your feet or drag a staff, the sound resonates like the din of drums and bells. There is probably another grotto below this one. A half *li* farther one encounters a large chasm, but one may not go down into it.

The other path leads off to the north, where one proceeds by stooping and bending down. After several double-paces [*bu*], one comes to a broad and open area. Along each side [of the path], measuring ten-some *zhang*, stalactites [*zhongru*] hang down in huddled clusters. As a general rule, stalactite couches [*ruchuang*] must form according to the rock patterns [*shimai*] and do not form in [random] blocks of rock [*wanshi*]. After going on for more than one *li*, what one sees is overwhelming and wondrous. If one proceeds farther, after the time it takes for a meal one reaches many [additional] branch passageways. Sightseers fear they will lose their way and so do not dare to go into them. It is said these passages lead all the way to Nine Doubts Mountain [Jiuyi Shan].[54]

---

51 Located in the southern part of modern Guilin, this grotto was also known as Jade Green Vacuity Precipice (Bixu Yan) and Li-the-Immortal's Precipice (Xian Li Yan). Fan Chengda has left a text "Inscription on Jade-Blue Vacuity" (Bixu ming) on the wall of this cave, the text of which is reprinted in *Qi Zhiping*, 84. See also the remarks on this inscription in *Hu-Tan*, 18–19.

52 Also called Kaiyang, this is the sixth star of the Northern Dipper.

53 There is additional text following this line in the SKQS edition of *Treatises* that reads: "In the sixth lunar month it is not hot [in the grotto], while at the height of winter it is warm" (*GHYHZ* [SKQS ed.], 3b; quoted in *FCDBJ*, 87, n. 4).

54 Also known as Dark Green Paulownia Mountain [Cangwu Shan], this hill is

ARCANE WIND GROTTO [*XUANFENG DONG*][55] is several hundred double-paces off to the side of Perching Aurora Grotto. Wind comes out of the grotto that is as cold as ice and snow.

MASTER ZENG'S GROTTO [*ZENGGONG DONG*] was formerly named Cold Water Precipice [Lengshui Yan]. The stone entranceway at the base of the mountain is worn smooth. The stone bridge where one enters is very ornate. This was built by Grand Councilor Zeng [Zeng Chengxiang], [*zi*] Zixuan.[56] There is a torrential stream [running under the bridge]; no one knows its origin. From the middle of the grotto, the stream turns around to the right, flows eastward under the bridge, and then reenters the grotto from the right. No one knows where it goes. Some say it flows underground and into the [Li] River. Where one crosses the bridge there are several *mou* of transcendent fields [*xiantian*].[57] After passing the fields, the trail becomes narrow and is soaking wet. Looking down, the rock fissures measure more than one *chi* [in width]. One enters by falling prostrate and crawling through. [The passageway] turns and again becomes high and open, and can lead through to Perching Aurora.

STANDING SCREEN PRECIPICE [*PINGFENG YAN*] is located in a flat area below the craggy wall of a sheer mountain.[58] When one goes

---

located south of modern Ningyuan *xian* in Hunan and is said to be the burial place of the mythical sage-king Shun.

55 Although all Qing and modern editions of *Treatises* read "Prime Wind Grotto" (Yuanfeng Dong), this is not the correct name of the cave. As documented in several pre-Qing sources, the correct name is Arcane Wind Grotto. *Yan Pei*, 16, n. 47, notes that Qing editors changed the original *xuan* 玄 (arcane) character to *yuan* 元 (prime). This was a common practice during the Qing because *xuan* formed part of the name of the Qing emperor Shengzu (Kangxi; r. 1661–1722), which was Xuanye, and thus was considered a taboo character.

56 "Grand Councilor Zeng" refers to Zeng Bu. In 1078 he was appointed to serve as administrator and military commissioner of the Guangnan West Circuit. The following year, after the border situation in Guangxi had been stabilized, Zeng visited various scenic sites around Guilin. Zeng supposedly discovered the grotto described in this entry, which bears his name, during one of his sightseeing tours. See Liu Xuan, "Account of Master Zeng's Precipice" (Zenggong Yan ji), rpt. in *Gudai Guilin shanshui wenxuan*, 32–33.

57 Yang Yuxia, in his "Account of a Trip to River and Moon Precipice" (You Shuiyin Yan ji), describes fields of rocks that are "clearly delineated, like the elevated borders between fields. The local people call these 'transcendent fields.'" Yang's account is reprinted in Wang Sen, *Yuexi wenzai*, 21.36b.

58 Standing Screen Precipice is located north of Seven Stars Hill, on Standing

through the entrance of the grotto, above and below and on the left and right, it is high and open for more than one hundred *zhang*. Inside there is a flat area that could host a banquet with one hundred guests. Down below, the stalactites are as thick as trees in a forest. Many of them have toppled over. One [then] treads up rocky steps some fifty in number, where there is a rocky passageway leading to daylight. Once you penetrate through the passageway and then exit [the grotto], the mountains and rivers and inner and outer city walls appear blurry and limitless. It is for this reason that I have built the Gourd Heaven Observatory [Hutian Guan][59] at this place and have commanded that its grotto be called Vacuous and Bright [Kongming].

THE SIX GROTTOES OF HIDDEN HILL [*YINSHAN LIUDONG*] are all located on Hidden Hill in West Lake [Xihu].[60] The first one is called Morning

---

Screen Hill (Pingfeng Shan). This precipice is alternately known as "Master Cheng's Precipice" (Chenggong Yan), named after the Song official Cheng Jie (see n. 33 above), who "opened" the cave in 1102. For additional details see Hou Penglao, "Account of Master Cheng's Precipice" (Chenggong Yan ji), in Zhang Mingfeng, *Gui sheng*, 8.76; rpt. in *Gudai Guilin shanshui wenxuan*, 64.

59   Construction of this observatory (or scenic overlook) was completed in the summer of 1174. Fan has left a wall inscription for the observatory, titled "Inscription for the Gourd Heaven Observatory: with Preface" (Hutian guan ming bingxu), which is reprinted in *Fan Chengda yizhu jicun*, 128 (also rpt. in *Qi Zhiping*, 85–86). Some of the descriptive language in this *Treatises* entry (especially the line beginning: "Once you penetrate through the passageway") is drawn directly from this inscription. As for the name "gourd heaven" (*hutian*), this probably alludes to an account in the *Hou Hanshu* about one Fei Changfang of the Eastern Han, who once saw an old man at a market with a gourd. After the market closed for the day, the old man "jumped into" the gourd. The following day Fei went to visit the old man, who was still in the gourd. Fei peeped in and saw a beautiful "jade hall where a drinking party was going on." See *Hou Hanshu*, 82xia.2743. Later in Chinese literary history the term "gourd heaven" came to symbolize an especially beautiful scene.

60   In Southern Song times Hidden Hill and its famous "Six Grottoes," located in the western suburbs of Guilin, were surrounded by a body of water called West Lake. The person credited with discovering and developing the scenic area around Hidden Hill is the Tang official Li Bo (see n. 37). See *TPHYJ*, 162.4b; Wu Wuling, "Account of the Recent Opening of Hidden Hill" (Xinkai Yinshan ji), in *Gudai Guilin shanshui wenxuan*, 152–54; and Wei Zongqing (Tang), "Account of the Six Grottoes on Hidden Hill" (Yinshan Liudong ji). The accounts of Wu Wuling and Wei Zongqing are preserved in Zhang Mingfeng, *Gui sheng*, 11.92–94, and 11.94–96, respectively. Fan Chengda has left a poem

Sun [Zhaoyang]; the second is called Evening Sun [Xiyang]; the third is called Southern Glory [Nanhua]; the fourth is called Northern Window [Beiyou]; the fifth is called Choice Lotus [Jialian]; and the sixth is called White Sparrow [Baique].[61] One rides across the lake and moors one's boat, then ascends the hill from the southwest[62] and first reaches Southern Glory. [Then] one proceeds west after exiting the grotto and reaches Evening Sun. Next to the grotto[63] there is a stone entranceway through which one can exit and then reach Northern Window. Tensome double-paces after exiting the grotto one reaches Morning Sun. Proceeding farther west, one reaches White Sparrow.[64] The mouth of the passageway is narrow and tight. One leans to one side to enter it. There is a passageway that leads through to Choice Lotus. Since there are four hills surrounding West Lake,[65] with a thousand peaks of jade green that cast their reflections onto the surface of the water, this [view] is certainly already most wondrous and surpassing. And yet the heart of the lake further floods into Hidden Hill.[66] Beyond the various grottoes there are [more] wondrous peaks, [the beauty of] which could never be matched in a painting. Regarding the time when the lotus flowers are in bloom, there is an old tale about someone sailing a boat and how the outstanding scenery is prized as ranking first in the southwest.[67]

---

about a boat outing he once made on West Lake. See *FSHJ*, 14.180 ("Liuyue shiwu ri ye fan Xihu, fengyue wenli").

61　According to Zhang Mingfeng, *Gui sheng*, 11.89, the correct name of this grotto is "Baique" 白雀 (not "Baihuan" 白雈). *Yan Pei*, 17, n. 55, and *Qi Zhiping*, 6, n. 10, both follow this reading.

62　Following *Yan Pei*, 17, n. 56, and reading "southwest" (*xi'nan*) instead of "northwest" (*xibei*).

63　Rather than "next to the grotto" (*dong pang*), some editions of *Treatises* instead read *dong qiong* (in the deepest part of the grotto). See *FCDBJ*, 87, n. 9.

64　Again, reading "Baique" rather than "Baihuan." See note 61 above.

65　"Four Hills" (Sishan) refers to four, connected peaks located about one *li* northwest of Hidden Hill: Thousand Hills (Qianshan), Standing Fish, Guanyin, and West Peak (Xifeng). Natives of Guilin customarily refer to these peaks as the West Hills (Xishan). *Yan Pei*, 18, n. 59.

66　In other words, aside from the beautiful images of the Four Hills, whose reflections are cast downward onto West Lake, the lake is further "flooded by" (*jin*) the reflected image of Hidden Hill.

67　It is unclear which "old tale" Fan Chengda might have in mind here. Some edi-

NORTHERN CONCEALMENT GROTTO [*BEIQIAN DONG*] is located north of Hidden Hill.[68] Inside it are stone chambers, stone terraces [*shitai*], and stone fruits [*shiguo*]. The stone fruits are shaped like lichees [*lizhi*], walnuts [*hutao*], and date-chestnuts [*zaoli*]. People "pick" them so they can play with them. Some arrange them on fruit plates and present them as gifts as they inquire about each other's health.

SOUTHERN CONCEALMENT GROTTO [*NANQIAN DONG*] is located in West Lake, on Luo Family Hill [Luojia Shan].

BODHISATTVA PRECIPICE [*FOZI YAN*][69] is also named Zhongyin Precipice [Zhongyin Yan].[70] It is ten *li* from the city and figures as the most distant. The single hill rises aloft amid a blur of blue. At the belly of the hill there are three grottoes: the upper, middle, and lower. The lower grotto is the most spacious.[71] The middle grotto is bright and roomy, over a hundred *zhang* in height. The upper grotto is a bit narrower. A single small monastery has been erected in the grotto. For

---

tions of *Treatises* instead read "southeast" rather than "southwest." See FCDBJ, 88, n. 12. *Yan Pei*, 18, n. 61, says "southeast" is the correct reading. According to Bao Tong's "Account of the Restoration of West Lake" (Fu Xihu ji), Guilin's West Lake was drained and turned into fields "many years ago" but was restored by one Zhang Huixian during the Qiandao reign (1165–1174) of the Southern Song. Bao's essay is preserved in Zhang Mingfeng, *Gui sheng*, 11.99–100. Zhang Huixian is not further identified. I suspect this refers to Zhang Wei, who served as administrator of Guilin from 1166 to 1170. Li Zhiliang, comp., *Song Liang Guang: Dajun shouchen yiti kao*, 310. In his essay "Account of Opening Concealed Grottoes" (Kai Qiandong ji), Zhang Wei mentions specifically that in early 1168 he dredged West Lake, and in the summer of that same year he "opened up Concealed Grotto." See *Gui sheng*, 11.99.

68   According to the Xie Qikun, ed., *Guangxi tongzhi*, 95.14a, Concealed Grotto Hill (Qiandong Shan) was northeast of Hidden Hill and had two caverns: Northern Concealment (described here) and Southern Concealment (described in the next entry).

69   Fozi usually designates "bodhisattva" in the general sense, although it can also mean a "follower of Buddha" (or practitioner of Buddhism).

70   The scenic area around this precipice, west of Guilin, was developed by Lü Yuanzhong, Zhang Wei, and Zhang Xiaoxiang when they served as administrators of Guilin during the Shaoxing reign (1131–1163). Xie Qikun, ed., *Guangxi tongzhi*, 95.16b–17a.

71   Following the SKQS ed., 5b, and reading *xia dong zui guang* ("the lower grotto is the most spacious"). *Hu-Tan*, 24, cites several sources that note that the lower grotto was the largest of the three.

this reason the stone rooms serve as hall-chambers.[72]

HOLLOW ELEGANCE GROTTO [*XUXIU DONG*][73] is a bit distant from the city. Its large stone chambers face the flat countryside. To the left and right of all the chambers are trails and tunnels, each several thousand double-paces in length. They make passage through to both sides and also overlook the flat countryside below.

The accounts provided above all concern places adjacent to the outer city wall that can be reached in a day. There are still many other precipice-grottoes in outlying areas, but not all of them can be reached [conveniently]. The stone stalactite grottoes in Xing'an Town are the most superior.[74] I visited there after completing my service in the commandery. There are three grottoes: the upper, middle, and lower. These grottoes, along with those at Perching Aurora, rank first and second, respectively. The other grottoes do not approach them [in beauty]. In Yangshuo Town[75] there are also five grottoes: Embroidery Hill [Xiushan], Arhat [Luohan], White Crane [Baihe], Glorious Canopy [Huagai], and Bright Pearl [Mingzhu], all of which are wondrous. I have also heard that Mount Dujiao in Rong 容 County[76] has three

---

72　Presumably, these hall-chambers (*tangshi*) are part of the monastery "complex" in the grotto.

73　The *Shuofu* edition, in *Shuofu sanzhong*, 50.793 (repeated in FCDBJ, 86), reads Luxiu 盧秀, but this is certainly wrong. The correct name of the grotto is Xuxiu (or "Hollow Elegance"). See the discussions on this in *Yan Pei*, 19, n. 68, and *Hu-Tan*, 24, note.

74　Xing'an Town (modern Xing'an *xian*) was located 150 *li* north of Guilin. The three grottoes there described below by Fan Chengda were 12 *li* southwest of the town. TPHYJ, 162.7a. The long passage in Zhu Mu, *Fangyu shenglan*, 38.687–88, describing the grottoes in Xing'an, appears to be have been copied directly from *Treatises*.

75　Yangshuo Town is 140 *li* south of Guilin. TPHYJ, 162.8b.

76　Modern Rong *xian*, Guangxi. Xie Qikun, ed., *Guangxi tongzhi*, 103.10b, places Mount Dujiao 20 *li* south of the town. This peak is important in the history of Daoism, for it functioned as the twentieth of the "Thirty-Six Lesser Grotto Heavens" (Sanshiliu Xiao Dongtian) devised by Du Guangting during the Tang. The official Daoist name for the grotto-heaven under Mount Dujiao was "Grand Supreme and Precious Mystery Grotto-Heaven" (Taishang Baoxuan Dongtian). See Du Guangting, *Dongtian fudi yuedu mingshan ji*, 4a.

grotto-heavens,[77] and in Rong 融 County there is a Perfected Transcendent Grotto [Zhenxian Dong] on Numinous Precipice [Lingyan].[78] The generations have passed down that they are not inferior to those in Guilin, but all of them are located in miasmic regions,[79] and so the scholar-officials who have gone there are especially few in number.

---

77   The term "grotto-heaven" (*dongtian*) is a collective reference to the various caves or grottoes on a given mountain. I have not been able to find any reference to "three grotto-heavens" on Mount Dujiao.

78   Rong County corresponds to what is now the Rongshui Miao People's Autonomous Xian in Guangxi. Zhu Mu, *Fangyu shenglan*, 41.738, marks Perfected Transcendent Grotto five *li* south of the county seat.

79   Government officials posted to south China were always concerned about malaria and other subtropical diseases. The term "miasmic regions" (*zhangdi*), as used by here by Fan Chengda and elsewhere by other Tang and Song officials who spent time in the south, can refer to Guangdong, Guangxi, and Hainan, as well as parts of Fujian, Jiangxi, and Hunan. These areas were thought to be infected by *zhangqi*, or miasmic vapors (that is, noxious fumes rising from marshes or decomposing animal or vegetable matter that were thought to poison and infect the air, causing miasmic diseases [*zhangli*] such as malaria and other dreaded conditions). In his "Miscellaneous Items Treatise" Fan Chengda makes the following statement: "In the Two Guangs [Guangdong and Guangxi], only Guilin is free of miasma. Everywhere south of Guilin is home to miasma." For more information on *zhang* in south China during the Tang and Song dynasties, see Schafer, *Vermilion Bird*, esp. 130–34.

2

METALS AND STONES
(Zhi jinshi)

T HE BASIC PHARMACOPEIA [BENCAO] INCLUDES A "SECTION on Jadelike Stones"[Yushi bu][1] devoted solely to medicinal products [*yaowu*]. These are not cures for illnesses. Although they are important, I do not note them here.[2] This chapter also concentrates on those [minerals] necessary for making prescription medicines [*fangyao*].

RAW GOLD [*SHENGJIN*] comes out of the counties and settlements [*zhoudong*] in the southwest, where it is found in mountain valleys, the open countryside, and sandy soil.[3] It does not come out of mines.

---

1   Several versions of *The Basic Pharmacopeia* (Bencao; sometimes translated into English as *Materia Medica*) were in circulation during the Southern Song. These are described in Hervouet, ed., *A Sung Bibliography*, 245. Most, if not all, of these versions include chapters on medicinal drugs made from inorganic matter, primarily mineral sources. These sections or chapters are usually titled "Section on Jadelike Stones."

2   Tentative translation for *sui zhong bu lu* 雖重不錄. This line of the text is probably corrupt.

3   From the description below it is clear that Fan Chengda is referring to "raw gold" in the sense of "gold in its natural state"; that is, gold found in river and creek beds, as opposed to gold that is refined from ore found in mines. For additional information on raw gold, see the useful comments in *Hu-Tan*, 28–29, n. 1. Panning for gold was a common activity in southwest China dur-

Settlement people make a living mainly by panning for it in sand. When one removes it from the earth with scooped hands,[4] it naturally blends and joins into granules [*ke*]. The larger ones resemble wheat grains [*maili*]; the smaller ones resemble wheat bran flakes [*fupian*]. These can then be tempered to serve medicinal purposes. Only the color is a bit pale, that is all. If one desires to make it pure and first-rate, then it is refined repeatedly. To obtain fullness in color, one expends [loses] two or three parts out of ten [during the refining process]. After refining, it becomes cooked gold [*shujin*].[5] Elixir stove [*danzao*][6] sites require raw gold, and so I have provided a note here on its origins.

Supplementary text: Raw gold comes out of the sandy soil in the Creek Settlements [Xidong][7] and is required by elixir stove masters [*danzao jia*]. [Lumps] of it as large as chicken eggs are used to make mother of gold [*jinmu*].[8]

CINNABAR [*DANSHA*][9] is ranked by *The Basic Pharmacopeia,* with

---

ing the Song dynasty. Zhou Qufei has much to say about this practice in *LWDD*, 7.269–70 (*Netolitzky,* 7.21).

4   Following the *ZBZZCS* ed., 5b, and reading *pou* 抔 (to scoop up with cupped hands). See the comments on this reading in *Yan Pei,* 23, n. 3.

5   "Cooked" in the sense that it has been refined and thus become "mature."

6   Fan Chengda is referring to a special type of heating apparatus (*zao*) used by alchemists when preparing various elixirs (*dan*). Although *zao* usually indicates a stove or furnace, in some cases it denotes an oven or combustion chamber. See *Needham et al.,* 5-4:11–16. For additional description of stoves and other laboratory instruments used by alchemists, see Fabrizio Pregadio, "Elixirs and Alchemy," in Kohn, ed., *Daoism Handbook,* 188.

7   The term "Creek Settlements" appears several times in *Treatises* and usually refers to the various settlements of non-Chinese people who lived along the Left and Right Rivers in Yong County, although on one occasion in *Treatises* Fan Chengda mentions that such settlements also existed in Yi County (see the supplementary entry on Nandan in the "Treatise on the Man"). According to Jin Hong et al., eds., *Guangxi tongzhi,* 6.10a, there were twenty such settlements still in place in Yi County in 1287, occupied by Yao people. Fan Chengda mentions that Lao (or Mountain Lao) people also lived near these settlements (see the entry on the Lao in the "Treatise on the Man").

8   Gold that has been refined in a cauldron and thereby transformed into true cinnabar (*zhendan*) is called "mother of gold." Supplementary text from *HSRC,* 67.50a; *FCDBJ,* 91.

9   Several terms are used interchangeably in Chinese for cinnabar (that is, red

Chen cinnabar [Chensha][10] regarded as the best and Yi cinnabar [Yisha][11] as second. Nowadays natives of Yishan[12] remark that the [main] cinnabar-producing area [in Guangxi] intersects with Hubei.[13] Cinnabar produced north of the mountains [on the border] constitutes Chen cinnabar; that produced south of there constitutes Yi cinnabar. The veins of the earth [*dimai*] in these areas do not vary much, and [so] there are no significant differences [between Chen cinnabar and Yi cinnabar]. As for Yi cinnabar, the mature variety is white in color.[14] It has flat, wall-like sides resembling a mirror, which form on the surface of beds of white rock [*baishi*][15] and can be used in the refining process [of cinnabar]. Its potency rivals that of Chen cinnabar. *The Basic Pharmacopeia Illustrated Gazetteer* [Bencao tujing][16]

---

sulphuret of mercury). Aside from *dansha*, another common name for the mineral is *zhusha*. For other names, see Read, *Minerals and Stones*, no. 43. For more detailed information on mercury in China, see Hanbury, comp., *Notes on Chinese Materia Medica*, 10. Most of Fan Chengda's entry on cinnabar is quoted in BCGM, 9.518 (*Compendium*, 2:9.988).

10   Chen refers to Chen County (Chenzhou), which was located in the area around modern Yuanling *xian*, Hunan. Chen County fell under the jurisdiction of the Jing-Hu North Circuit (Jing-Hu *beilu*).

11   Yi County (Yizhou) corresponds to the area around modern Yishan *xian*, Guangxi. It was part of the Guangnan West Circuit. TPHYJ, 168.13a, mentions a Fu'an industrial complex (Fu'an *jian*) located 130 *li* west of Yi County, which produced cinnabar.

12   Yi County, like the Yi Town established there in 1119, takes its name from the Yi Hills (Yishan), which are clustered within the confines of the Yi County seat. Because of this association between the name of the county and the hills from which it derives its name, Yizhou was sometimes also called Yishan.

13   In this line I follow the punctuation and reading of Yang Wuquan in his "*Guihai yuheng zhi jiaozhu* jiaoji zayi," 53. Cf. the discussions of this line in *Hu-Tan*, 30, and *Yan Pei*, 21, and 23, n. 7, which seem to raise more questions than they answer. The key to understanding the line is reading *quanya* 犬牙 (lit., "dog tooth") as a verb meaning "to intersect with." "Hubei" here indicates the Jing-Hu North Circuit, where Chen County was located. The idea in this line is that the main cinnabar-producing area in Guangxi (Yi County) "connects" or "intersects" with the main cinnabar-producing region across the mountainous border with "Hubei" in the north (Chen County).

14   Quoting this line, HSRC, 67.50a, reads "the color of iron" (*tiese*).

15   I suspect that "white rock" indicates lime or limestone (*shihui*).

16   This work was edited by Su Song, a well-known Northern Song political figure. It is more commonly known as *The Illustrated Gazetteer of the Basic Pharma-*

remarks that Yi cinnabar is found among earth and rocks, and not in beds of white rock. In fact, [cinnabar derived from white rock] is Yi cinnabar that still has not been recognized as such.

There is another variety that is red in color and pliable in consistency, named earthen pit cinnabar [*tukang sha*], which, as it turns out, is reddish black.[17] The variety found among earth and rocks is not very fire-resistant.

Yong County also has cinnabar. The larger lumps are several tens of hundreds of *liang* in weight. They are dark in color and have few flat, wall-like sides. When chewed, this cinnabar assumes a purple and dark black color, which is not desirable for use in medicine. People who burn it do so only to obtain mercury [*shuiyin*].

The Illustrated Gazetteer further remarks that Rong County[18] also has cinnabar. Today we know that Rong County has never had cinnabar. The pronunciation of [the words] Yong and Rong is similar, and so this probably explains the error,[19] or so it is said.

MERCURY [*SHUIYIN*] is obtained by grinding cinnabar from the Creek Settlements in Yong County and heating it on a stove. It is extremely easy to make. One uses one hundred *liang* [of cinnabar powder] to make one *diao*-pot[20] [of mercury]. As for the construction of *diao*-pots, a pig's bladder is used to make the framework. The outside is caulked with several layers of thick paper. When one stores it away, the pot never leaks.

Supplementary text: As for the method used to fire [prepare] mercury, one uses iron to make an upper and lower cauldron. The upper cauldron holds the cinnabar. Between the two cauldrons is placed an iron plate with a tiny eye-hole, which covers the top of the lower

---

copeia (Tujing bencao). See Hervouet, ed., *A Sung Bibliography*, 245.

17   The character 點 in this line, pronounced *dan*, is an alternate written form of *dan* 黕, meaning "reddish." See *Qi Zhiping*, 8, n. 3.

18   Rong 融 County approximately corresponds to today's Rongshui Miao People's Self-Autonomous *Xian* in Guangxi.

19   In other words, cinnabar is found in Yong 邕 County but not in Rong County. Because of the similarity of the pronunciation of "Rong" and "Yong," however, there has been confusion, with some people thinking that cinnabar is produced in Rong County.

20   A *diao* is a small pot with a handle and a spout.

cauldron. The lower cauldron is filled with water and buried in the ground. Facing upward, it is joined with the lip of the upper cauldron, bonded, and tightly sealed all around. [The cauldron is then] scalded with a blazing fire. The cinnabar transforms into a hovering mist, which descends into the water and coagulates to make the mercury.

In Yong County, one obtains cinnabar by chiseling where it is plentiful. The cinnabar then flows out naturally. Cinnabar sold by traveling merchants is always [the variety] produced by firing. One hundred *liang* of cinnabar makes one *diao*-pot. *Diao*-pots are made out of thick paper and pig bladders, and never leak. [21]

STALACTITES [*ZHONGRU*]: [22] Guilin borders with the mountains in Yi and Rong 融 [counties], where grotto-caves [*dongxue*] are extremely numerous and far superior to those in Lian County [Lianzhou]. [23] I have traveled to these grottoes and personally visited them. When you look up at and carefully observe places where the rock patterns [*shimai*] protrude, immediately there are stalactite couches [*ruchuang*] [24] like snow-white jade, made from the blending and joining of mineral secretions. The stalactite beds hang down like inverted peaks and little hills. The tips of the peaks gradually taper to a point and are as long as icicles. The tips of the icicles are light and thin, and hollow in the center, resembling goose quills [*eguan*]. [25] Stalactite water drips and drops and never stops, and as it drips it also congeals. Such is the most outstanding type of stalactite. [To collect the mineral needed for the drug] a bamboo tube is raised aloft, into which the [tip of the] stalactite is fitted and then snapped off and pulled down. Daoist alchemists [*lianye jia*] also regard the tips of "goose quills," which are

---

21   *HSRC*, 67.50a–b; *FCDBJ*, 91.

22   The usual Chinese term for limestone stalactites (that is, carbonate of lime in stalactitic masses), employed here, is *zhongru*, which literally means "milky white [stone] that [hangs down] like bells." See Hanbury, comp., *Notes on Chinese Materia Medica*, 5. Fan Chengda's entry on stalactites, which follows, is quoted in *BCGM*, 9.563 (*Compendium*, 2:9.1059).

23   Lian County corresponds to the area around modern Lian *xian*, Guangdong.

24   "Couches" refer to flat, layered deposits (or "beds") of lime that extend down from the ceiling of the cave.

25   "Goose quills" is another name for stalactites. Read, *Minerals and Stones*, no. 63.

especially light and luminous, resembling mica [*yunmu*][26] and claw-nails [*zhuajia*],[27] as the most outstanding [drug].

Supplementary text: Daoist alchemists regard "goose quills" with patterns resembling cicada wings [*chanyi*] as the most outstanding. In Guangdong they send people gifts of goose-quill rocks [*eguan shi*],[28] which are mostly coarse and yellow. Those that come out of Shu are also dull and heavy. The ones found near the [stone] couches are plugged up [solid] as well as being coarse and rolled. These are commonly referred to as shoots [*nie*].[29]

NATURAL COPPER [*TONG*][30] comes out of the counties and settlements along the Right River in Yong County. When you dig down several *chi* into the soil, you immediately find deposits of it. Thus, the Man people are fond of using copper utensils.

MALACHITE [*LÜ*] is derived from copper.[31] It comes out of those places along the Right River where there is also copper. It is produced in rock. The variety that has a consistency like rock is named rocky malachite [*shilü*]. There is also another variety that is soft and mushy like crushed earth, named muddy malachite [*nilü*]. In grade it is the lowest, and its price is also cheap.

Supplementary text: When washed to bring out its beautiful luster, malachite can be used [as a pigment] for paintings.[32] A secondary use for it is ornamenting homes. . . . .[33]

---

26   *Yunmu* generally refers potash mica or muscovite, a mineral of especially brilliant appearance. The idea here seems to be that the "goose-quill tips" of the stalactites are especially fragile and luminous.

27   The precise reference of "claw-nails" is unclear to me. Fan Chengda seems to be referring to the tapered, sharp tips of the "goose-quill" stalactites.

28   "Goose-quill rocks" is another name for stalactites.

29   HSRC, 67.50b; FCDBJ, 92.

30   "Natural copper" (*tong* or *ziran tong*) is also called pyrite. It is one of the few metallic elements that occur in uncombined form as a natural mineral.

31   That is to say, malachite is the native carbonate of copper. Read, *Minerals and Stones*, no. 84. Other common names for malachite in Chinese are *lüqing* and *tonglü*.

32   Malachite has long been used to produce green pigments for painting. See the remarks by Tao Hongjing, quoted in BCGM, 10.597 (*Compendium*, 2:10.1102–3). Painters sometimes call this pigment *biqing*.

33   HSRC, 67.52a; FCDBJ, 92.

TALCUM [*HUASHI*][34] comes out of all the districts under the jurisdiction of Guilin and the Yao settlements. There are two kinds, white and black, the uses of which are similar.[35] When it first comes out [of the soil] it is like mushy mud, but after exposure to air it hardens. It is also referred to as cold rock [*lengshi*]. Locals use lime [*shihui*] to plaster walls. Before the plaster dries, talcum powder is used to wipe it clean. [The resulting] shiny luster is like jade.

LEAD POWDER [*QIANFEN*][36] that is made in Gui County is the most famous. It is referred to as Gui powder [*Guifen*]. The powder [is made] by taking black lead [*heiqian*] and incubating it in a pickling jar [*zaoweng*], which seals and [thus] transforms it [into powder].[37]

Supplementary text: The government did not start manufacturing [lead] powder until the beginning of the Qiandao reign [1165–1174]. The annual income [it derives] in cash amounts to 20,000 strings.[38]

PYROLUSITE [*WUMING YI*] is small, black pebbles.[39] It is extremely common in the hills of Guilin. One package contains several hundred of them.

Supplementary text: The price [of pyrolusite] is extremely cheap.[40]

FOSSILIZED MEI-TREES [*SHIMEI*] come out of the sea.[41] Each thicket

---

34 The term *huashi* (lit., "slippery stone") is applied to several minerals, including talcum, lardstone, soapstone, and figurestone. Read, *Minerals and Stones*, no. 55. Here the reference seems to be to talcum. During the Song dynasty talcum was often used by painters because of its soft and smooth composition. Hence, an alternate name for the mineral is *huashi*, or "painting stone."

35 The white variety was used mainly for medicinal purposes, while large blocks of the black type were sometimes made into containers and funerary objects. See BCGM, 9.550 (*Compendium*, 2:9.1038–43).

36 "Lead powder" refers to white lead (*fenxi*; that is, carbonate of lead).

37 The process for making carbonate of lead is described in Read, *Minerals and Stones*, no. 12, and in *Hu-Tan*, 36, n. 2.

38 HSRC, 67.53a; FCDBJ, 92.

39 Here I follow the editors of the *Compendium*, 2:9.1056 (BCGM, 9.561), who identify *wuming yi* as pyrolusite. Read, *Minerals and Stones*, 61, follows this same identification. Cf. Wheatley, "Geographical Notes on Some Commodities," 75, which, based on Hanbury, comp., *Notes on Chinese Materia Medica*, 9, speculates that *wuming yi* might be limonite (hydrated iron oxide).

40 HSRC, 67.53b; FCDBJ, 92.

41 Fan Chengda's reports here on "fossilized mei[-trees]" (*shimei*) and below in the entry on "fossilized cypress [trees]" are repeated, with only minor differences, in LWDD, 7.284–85 (Netolitzky, 7.32 and 7.33). BCGM does not include sep-

has several branches, arranged horizontally and slanting downward, which are slim and hard. In shape and color they truly look like a withered mei-tree. Although skilled craftsmen can make them [artificially], the results cannot match [the real thing]. [The substance] that adheres to the trunk resembles the underside of a mushroom. Someone has remarked that[42] fossilized mei-trees were originally a woody substance [that was later] transformed by the sea, like fossilized crabs [*shixie*] and fossilized shrimp [*shixia*].[43]

Supplementary text: Fossilized mei[-trees] and fossilized citrus [*shigan*] come out of the sea. Additional information is unavailable, but they can be used in medicines.[44]

FOSSILIZED CYPRESS TREES [*SHIBO*][45] come out of the sea. Their

---

arate entries on *shimei* and *shibo* but does have an entry on "fossilized crabs" (*shixie*; Fan also has a separate entry on "fossilized crabs"; see the "Treatise on Insects and Fishes"). Li Shizhen suggests these are actually fossilized sea creatures, which can be pulverized and used in the preparation of medicines. Most other explanations in BCGM say the various fossils under discussion here are simply rocks that in shape resemble crabs, shrimp, cypress trees, and so on. See BCGM, 10.622 (*Compendium*, 2:10.1133–34).

42   "Someone has remarked that" refers to Ma Zhi and his team of collaborators, who, in 973, produced *The Basic Pharmacopeia of the Opened Treasure Reign* (Kaibao bencao). Ma's comments on fossilized crabs are quoted in the BCGM, 10.622 (*Compendium*, 2:10.1133). Ma reports that these are just normal crabs that have become fossilized. He says nothing about a "woody substance transformed by the sea" (see below).

43   Cf. LWDD, 7.282–83 (*Netolitzky*, 7.31), which has a joint entry on "fossilized crabs and fossilized shrimp." Zhou Qufei mentions that "fossilized crabs" can cure eye disease but says he is not sure whether "fossilized shrimp" can be used for medicinal purposes. See also Read, *Turtle and Shellfish Drugs*, 37, n. 1, which identifies *shixie* as a fiddler crab or mudskipper (*Macrophthalmus latreillii*).

44   HSRC, 67.54b; FCDBJ, 92.

45   The Song dynasty historian Hong Mai provides a fascinating description of fossilized cypress: "Fan Shihu's [Fan Chengda's] [*Guihai*] *yuheng zhi* has an entry on fossilized cypress. I just got hold of one recently, born from the surface of a rock at the bottom of the sea. The trunk intertwines, while the branches and leaves resemble [those in] a painting. The branches and leaves are purple; the trunk is white. The tree has a fossil-like quality throughout. When skies are overcast and rainy, it will certainly bear watery pearls [dewdrops] on its leaves. Among the branches there will also be cypress-seed [aromatic], all of which is formed from rocky secretions that have congealed. There are also fossilized

single trunk is extremely slender. On top there is a single leaf. They look just like the leaning cypress [*cebo*],[46] luxuriant and well spaced, without the slightest variation. [The substance] that adheres to the roots resembles lindera [*wuyao*].[47] Most of it has already fossilized. Although it is not known for sure whether fossilized cypress trees and fossilized mei-trees can be used in the making of medicines, both are still wondrous products. I have no choice but to provide entries on them.

mei[-trees] and fossilized pine [trees] [*shisong*], but I have never seen these." Hong Mai, *Yijian zhi*, 2:892-93.

46   A "leaning cypress" (also known in Chinese as a *bianbo*, or "flat cypress") is a type of evergreen (*Chamaecyparis*) whose branches are arranged on a horizontal plane.

47   *Wuyao*, literally, "black herb," is *Lindera strychnifolia*. It is so named because the outer portion of the root is black in color. Also known in English as spicebush or Japanese evergreen spicebush, lindera is used for a wide variety of purposes in traditional Chinese medicine.

3

AROMATICS
(Zhi xiang)

THE SOUTHERN QUARTER IS ASSOCIATED WITH THE FIRE phase [*huoxing*].[1] Its air blazes and ascends.[2] The medicinal prod-

---

The word *xiang* 香 can be translated in several different ways, depending on how it is used. In ancient China *xiang* generally fell into two broad categories: spices, that is, dried seeds, fruits, roots, and bark or vegetative substances used as a food additive for the purpose of flavoring; and fragrances or perfumes, which includes aromatic woods. In this chapter of *Treatises* Fan Chengda uses *xiang* in the sense of "aromatic." Most aromatics in China are produced from trees that grow in the tropical and subtropical regions of the south. A substantial amount of the aromatics used in China during the Song dynasty, all ostensibly controlled by a state monopoly, came from foreign lands, including Cambodia, the northern reaches of the Malay Peninsula, and Sumatra. These aromatics were used for a variety of purposes, including medicine preparation, religious rituals (incense), clothing fumigation, and even ornamentation. As noted below, Fan Chengda's main interest is to describe southern aromatics used in the making of medicines.

1   The Five Phases (Wuxing)—water, fire, wood, metal, and earth (this is the customary ordering)—were used in traditional China to describe the basic nature of interactions and relationships between and among phenomena. Each phase (or element) is associated with a particular direction on the compass, with "earth" functioning as the "center." In this system of relationships, "fire" represents "south."

2   The expression "blaze and ascend" (*yanshang*) is drawn from the "Great Design" (Gongfan) chapter of the *History Classic* (Shujing): "[The nature of] fire is said to blaze and ascend." *Shangshu zhengyi*, 2/76/2:188 (Legge, *The Chinese Classics*, 3:325).

ucts it provides as tribute tax[3] all taste bitter but smell fragrant. But the generations have solely referred to products such as *chen* and *jian* as aromatics.[4] In fact, they represent the most outstanding [aromatics].[5]

The generations have all said that the Two Guangs produce aromatics. But aromatics in Guangdong, as it turns out, are shipped there [from elsewhere] by oceangoing junks [*bo*].[6] In Guangyou, aromatics produced in Haibei[7] are also of common grade. Only aromatics from Hainan are superior. Officials [*renshi*] who have never been sent down to the south may not know all there is to know about the subject. Thus, I will write down what information has been in circulation.

SINKING-IN-WATER AROMATIC [*CHENSHUI XIANG*][8] of the high grade

---

3 "Provide as tribute tax" is a wordy translation of *fu* 賦, which refers here to local products sent from the provinces to the capital as a form of tribute.

4 *Chen* and *jian* are names of well-known aromatics (see below). The point in this line is that although *chen* and *jian* are well-known aromatics, there are many other varieties in the south that are generally unknown.

5 The last portion of this line, which reads *you mei zhi suo zhong ye* 又美之所種 也, is corrupt. Rather than 種, FCDBJ, 95, n. 1, provides an alternate reading: 鍾. Kong Fanli suspects this is the correct reading, as do *Yan Pei*, 28, *Hu-Tan*, 39, and *Qi Zhiping*, 9. I follow this reading. The verb *zhong* 鍾 in this line, translated as "to represent," literally means "to concentrate."

6 For a fascinating discussion of the various types of oceangoing vessels used during the Song dynasty for shipping aromatics and other commercial items to Guangdong, see Lin Tianwei, *Songdai xiangyao maoyi shigao*, esp. 15–20.

7 Haibei usually refers to the part of continental China that lies north of Hainan Island. See the comments in *Yan Pei*, 31, n. 4. In the text below, however, Fan Chengda mentions that Haibei includes Jiaozhi, which corresponds to the northern part of modern Vietnam (on Jiaozhi, see below and note 28).

8 *Chenshui xiang* (or *chenxiang*) is an aromatic that derives from gharu-wood (also gahru-wood, garoo-wood; *Aquilaria agallocha* or *Aquilaria sinesis*) and is variously called "aloeswood," "eaglewood," "oud," or "jinko" in English. In its most natural form, *chenshui xiang* is a piece of resinous wood formed by the *Aquilaria* genus of the Thymelaeaceae family of evergreen trees (fig. 4). The formation of gharu-wood aromatic is a natural process in which the *Aquilaria* tree responds to (or rots as a result of) attacks by fungi. The resulting aromatic wood is usually formed inside the tree with no visible indication on the outside. Since the resulting heavily resinous wood sinks when placed in water, it is called *chenshui xiang*, or "sinking-in-water aromatic." It is produced in many different places, both within China and outside, in places such as Sumatra and the Malay Peninsula. The quality of aromatics produced from gharu-wood varies greatly, and its varieties are numerous.

The names of aromatics derived from gharu-wood vary according to the

FIGURE 4

Song dynasty illustration of a
sinking-in-water aromatic tree
from Hainan. Source: *Chongxiu
Zhenghe jingshi zhenglei beiyong bencao*, 12.307.

FIGURE 5

Song dynasty illustration
of monkshood from Zi 梓
county. Source: *Chongxiu
Zhenghe jingshi zhenglei
beiyong bencao*, 10.241.

[variety] is produced in the settlements of the Li people on Hainan.[9]
Another name for it is native sinking aromatic [*tu chenxiang*]. It rarely

---

thickness of the bark of the tree from which they are taken. According to ZFZ,
2.178 (*Chau Ju-Kua*, 208), and Ding Wei's "Account of Heavenly Spices" (Tianxiang zhuan), in Zeng and Liu, eds., *Quan Songwen*, 5:604–7, the aromatic
taken from a living gharu-wood tree is called "fresh aromatic" (*shengxiang*;
this should be distinguished from *shuchen*, or "ripe gharu," which is collected
from rotten logs); that taken from a tree whose bark is three-tenths formed is
called "provisional aromatic" (*zhanxiang*); that taken from a tree whose bark is
half formed is called "quick aromatic" (*suxiang*); that taken from a tree whose
bark is seven- or eight-tenths formed is called "Jian aromatic" (*jianxiang; jian*
in this name probably means something like "writing-paper thin"); and that
taken from a tree whose bark is completely formed is called "sinking aromatic."

For additional information on sinking-in-water aromatic, see Wheatley,
"Geographical Notes on Some Commodities," 69–72; *Fourth Century Flora*,
87–90; LWDD, 7.241–42 (*Netolitzky*, 7.1); and especially ZFZ, 1.174–76, n. 1 (*Chau
Ju-Kua*, 204–6).

9 Lidong, or "settlements of the Li people," is not a specific place-name, but rather
refers to the settlements where the Li people lived in the interior of Hainan.

comes in large lumps.[10] Aromatics secondary to it, like calf horn [*jianli jiao*],[11] monkshood [*fuzi*],[12] polypore mushrooms [*zhijun*],[13] and floss-grass-bamboo leaves [*mao zhuye*][14] are all outstanding. Even varieties [of sinking-in-water aromatic] that are light and thin like paper sink when placed into water.

As for the segments of [sinking-in-water] aromatic, because they hibernate for a long time in the soil,[15] their resin oozes downward, where it comes together to form the aromatic. When harvested, the face of the aromatic is completely below [ground]. Those [segments] with back sides of woody composition consequently emerge from the surface of the soil.[16] The four commanderies encompassing Hainan Island[17] all have sinking-in-water aromatic. The crowning [best] varieties are produced by the various foreign peoples [on Hainan]. The variety that comes out of Wan'an[18] is regarded as the most superior.

---

10   Most sinking-in-water aromatic from Hainan forms in flake-shaped sheets or in long strips of irregular length, so it rarely comes in big lumps (as do some other aromatics).

11   I have not been able to find any information on this aromatic, but the name probably reflects its curved, hornlike shape. See also Wheatley, "Geographical Notes on Some Commodities," 70, who mentions a "rhinoceros-horn gharu" (*xijiao chen*), which was so called because of its shape.

12   The term *fuzi*, usually translated as monkshood or wolfsbane in English, is used to denote different perennial herbs of the genus *Aconitum* (fig. 5). The blue or white flowers of these herbs have large hoodlike upper sepals; hence the name "monkshood." Several different species of aconite were used in traditional Chinese medicine. The aromatic mentioned here, also called *fuzi chen*, resembled aconite roots in shape.

13   *Zhijun*, or polypore mushroom, is probably used here as a synonym for *lingzhi*, which is usually identified as *Ganoderma lucidum*. This mushroom belongs to a large family of fungi called polypores. The medicinal benefits of *lingzhi* are well known and extensively documented.

14   This aromatic is not further identified.

15   Fan Chengda is referring here to decayed gharu-wood trees that are buried in the ground, from which the aromatic could be harvested.

16   I understand this line to mean that the aromatic grows in such a way that its main face/surface is buried in the soil, while the attached woody underside (or back side) emerges from the surface of the ground.

17   The four "commanderies" mentioned here are Qiong County (Qiongzhou), Dan Military District (Danjun), Wan'an Military District, and Yai County (Yaizhou).

18   Wan'an Military District was located in the southeastern part of Hainan, in the general area around modern Wan'an *xian*.

Those who speak about such matters remark that the mountains of Wan'an are due east on the island and thus receive a concentration of morning sun. The aromatics there are especially rich and delicate, abundant and outstanding.

As a general rule, the smell of all Hainan aromatics is pure and gentle, sort of like the smell of lotus flowers [*lianhua*], mei-flowers [*meiying*],[19] goose pears [*eli*],[20] and bee's nests [*mipi*].[21] If you burn one for a little over the time it takes to play a round of dice,[22] a foreboding smell fills the room. But when you turn it over, the four sides all give off a fragrance, so much so that even air with coal cinders in it will not smell foul. This is the distinguishing quality of Hainan aromatics. Most northerners are not very well informed about this. It is likely that even when one [travels] the seas such knowledge is still hard to come by on your own. Government subjects [*shengmin*][23] use oxen [*niu*] to barter for aromatics with the Li people. One oxen is bartered for one *dan* of aromatic. Upon returning home, [government subjects] select and choose [the best of the lot]. Out of ten that are submerged in water, they do not get more than one or two. Government officials from the Central Counties [Zhongzhou][24] only use aromatics that come to Guangdong by oceangoing junks from Champa

---

19   *Meiying* is another name for *Prunus mume*, or mei-flowers.

20   I have not been able to identify precisely "goose (-egg shaped?) pears," though they are mentioned in various sources, including BCGM, 30.1765 (*Compendium*, 4:30.2715) and even in the preface to one of Fan Chengda's poems. See FSHJ, 12.152 ("Neiqiu liyuan").

21   Following Qi Zhiping, 11, n. 3, and reading *mipi* to mean "bee nest." Qi notes that bee nests are constructed in a shape that resembles a human spleen (*pi*); hence the name *mipi* (lit., "bee-spleen").

22   The term *botou* refers to a dice game. Another name for it is *touzi*.

23   "Government subjects" is a general term that refers to people in the border areas living under the control of the central Song government. Here the reference is to traders from outside the confines of the settlements of Li people on Hainan. For additional information on *shengmin* and related terms, see the Introduction.

24   That is, China.

[Zhancheng][25] and Cambodia [Zhenla].[26] In recent years an aromatic from Dengliumei[27] has also been prized. I have tried it. It is not as good as middle- and lower-grade aromatics from Hainan. Oceangoing junk aromatic is often rancid and intense. As for varieties that are not so rancid, their aroma is also short in duration; in nature they are woody. The final fumes will certainly be foul. Those that come out

---

25   During the Tang this state was known to the Chinese as Zhanpo. Hence, it is sometimes called "Champa" or "Campa" in English and some European languages. In the early ninth century this state became known as Zhancheng. During the Song, Zhancheng extended along the central and southern coasts of present-day Vietnam. For additional information, see *Songshi*, 489.14077–86; and especially ZFZ, 1.10, n. 1 (*Chau Ju-Kua*, 47–50).

26   Zhenla (sometimes called Zhanla) roughly corresponds to modern Cambodia, although during the Song it included the southern part of modern Vietnam, a considerable part of lower Thailand, and the Malay Peninsula. In 1296–97 the second emperor of the Yuan dynasty, Temur Khan (Chengzong, r. 1294–1307), dispatched a diplomatic embassy to Zhenla. After his return to China, Zhou Daguan, a member of the embassy, wrote a descriptive account of the people, customs, and material culture of Zhenla, which he titled *Account of the Customs and Geography of Zhenla* (Zhenla fengtu ji). This important work survives in several different editions and has been studied and translated into French by Paul Pelliot. Pelliot first published a translation of Zhou's text in *Bulletin de L'École française d'Extrême-Orient* 2 (1902): 123–77 but continued (until 1924) to revise his translation. His revisions (which were not finished) were published posthumously. See *Mémoires sur les coutumes du Cambodge, récit de Tcheou Ta-Kouan* (Paris: Adrien-Maisonneuve, 1951). This version of Pelliot's French translation has been translated into English by Michael Smithies and published under the title *The Customs of Cambodia* (Bangkok: The Siam Society, 2001).

27   Dengliumei is the name of a state that was located in southern Thailand, in and around what is now the province and city of Nakhon Sri Thammarat (formerly known as Ligor). Chen Jiarong et al., comps., *Gudai Nanhai diming huishi*, 796. This is the first appearance of this place-name in Chinese sources. It is also cited in LWDD, 2.81 (*Netolitzky*, 2.4), and during the Song was written at least two other ways: Dingliumei and Danmeiliu. A passage in HSRC, 67.62b, gives it as Dengloumei. This inconsistency is probably due in part to the similarity in pronunciation during the Song of *deng* 登, *ding* 丁, and *dan* 丹, on the one hand, and *liu* 流 and *lou* 樓, on the other. See the remarks in LWDD, 7.242, n. 2. Scholars differ in their opinions regarding the precise location of Dengliumei, but all agree it was situated somewhere on the Malay Peninsula. For additional information on Dengliumei and various theories regarding its location, see ZFZ, 1.28–30, n. 1 (*Chau Ju-Kua*, 57–58). The ZFZ entry on Dengliumei mentions specifically that sinking-in-water aromatic was a product of that state.

of Haibei are grown in Jiaozhi.[28] When people in Jiaozhi get [such an aromatic] from foreign oceangoing junks, and it is then collected together in Qin County, it is referred to as Qin aromatic [*Qinxiang*].[29] Its quality is heavy and solid, it comes in mostly large chunks, the smell is especially pungent and strong, and [by the time you get some] it no longer has any special quality. It can only be used in medicine. Southerners do not value it.

Supplementary text: Sinking aromatic comes from the settlements of the Li people across the sea. Since aromatic trees grow again after being cut down,[30] sections [of the cut-down tree] hibernate for a long time in the soil. For several hundred years they will not rot but instead become increasingly pure and firm. . . . Most of the [aromatic's] surface is below ground and shaped like mountain peaks, fantastic rocks, fantastic beasts, tortoises, and snakes. . . . If you closely inspect [the aromatics] produced by the various foreign peoples, the variety that comes out of Wan'an in particular is regarded as superior. . . . The smell of all Hainan aromatics is pure and gentle. . . . Their value equals that of silver [*baijin*].[31]

---

28   During the reign of Emperor Wu of the Han, the ancient Nan-Yue region was conquered by Chinese troops and then organized into several commanderies, the administrative center of which was situated in Jiaozhi (sometimes called Cochin in English) Commandery. The name Jiaozhi subsequently became a general reference for the area around modern Hanoi and the northern part of Vietnam. Later in the Han this territory was reorganized into a new administrative entity called Jiaozhou, or Jiao County. Then, in 670, there was yet another administrative reorganization into an even larger unit called Annan, which after the Five Dynasties became an independent kingdom. During the Song dynasty, the name Jiaozhi (or Jiaozhi Guo) seems to have been applied to the entire area of northern Vietnam (Tonkin). On the origin and history of this place-name, see Wang Dayuan, *Daoyi zhilüe jiaoshi*, 52–53, n. 1; ZFZ, 1.1–2 (*Chau Ju-Kua*, 46, n. 1); and Chen Jiarong et al., comps., *Gudai Nanhai diming huishi*, 375–80. Fan Chengda has separate entries on Annan and Jiaozhi in the "Treatise on the Man."

29   The entry on Qin aromatic in LWDD, 7.246 (*Netolitzky*, 7.5), and the entry on the thriving market there in the same work, 5.197–98 (not translated in *Netolitzky*), state very clearly that the aromatic trade in Qin County was substantial during the Southern Song, with commercial traffic between Jiaozhi and Qin County "never stopping."

30   Here I follow the gloss on *nie* 枿 ("trees that grow again after being cut down") in *Yan Pei*, 129, n. 2.

31   HSRC, 67.51b–52a; FCDBJ, 96.

PENGLAI AROMATIC [*PENGLAI XIANG*] also comes out of Hainan. In fact, it is submerged-in-water aromatic that is not yet [completely] formed. It mostly forms into strips, resembling the shape of a cone-shaped bamboo hat or large mushroom.[32] Some are one or two *chi* in diameter and extremely firm and solid. All Penglai aromatics are like submerged-in-water aromatics in color and shape, but they float when placed in water. If you shave off the woody part on their back side, most will also sink in water.

FRANCOLIN-SPOTTED AROMATIC [*ZHEGU BAN XIANG*] is also included among sinking-in-water, Penglai, and the very best Jian aromatics on Hainan. The rough edges are hewn off so it is light and loose, while the color is a brownish black but has white partridge spots and specks like the feathers on the chest of a francolin. Its smell is especially pure and agreeable, similar to that of a lotus flower.

Supplementary text: It is not completely woody in nature, and takes its name from its color.[33]

JIAN AROMATIC [*JIANXIANG*][34] comes out of Hainan. In appearance it resembles hedgehog hide [*weipi*],[35] a bamboo awning, or a fisherman's coir raincoat.[36] Probably when it is refined and processed great labor is required to carve and shape it. The aromatic remains after the wood is removed, and the thorns and pricks are thick and dense. The essence of the aromatic is concentrated in the ends of the pricks. Its fragrant smell is far different from that of Jian aromatic in other places. Jian aromatic that comes out of Haibei is gathered in Qin County, and its grade is extremely common. It is on a par with

---

32   *Jun* used by Fan Chengda here probably refers to some type of mushroom, but his precise reference is not clear.

33   *HSRC*, 67.52a.

34   Jian aromatic is known by several different names: *jianxiang* (writing-paper aromatic), *jianxiang* (simmering aromatic), and *zhanxiang* (timber aromatic). Some sources, such as Tan Cui, *Dianhai yuheng zhi*, 3.22, say that when placed in water Jian aromatic sinks halfway, but is not clear if this quality applies to *jianxiang* from Hainan.

35   The body hair on a hedgehog (*wei*) is stiff and sharp, and presumably similar to the "thorns and pricks" that grow on Jian aromatic (see the description below).

36   The character *xiang* 香 in this line (following *chu Hainan* 出海南) seems superfluous, and so I have not translated it.

the fresh [*sheng*],[37] ripened [*shu*],[38] quick-formed [*sujie*],[39] and other aromatics available from oceangoing junks in Guangdong. Below the Jian aromatic of Hainan there are also the moth secretion [*chonglou*][40] and fresh-formed [*shengjie*][41] varieties of aromatic, both of which are inferior in color.

Supplementary text: The leaves of the [Jian] aromatic tree are like those of the winter pine [*dongqing*] but rounder. The bark resembles paper-mulberry bark [*chupi*] but thicker. The flowers are yellow, sort of like cauliflower [*caihua*]; the seeds are greenish yellow, sort of like sheep dung [*yangshi*]. People on Hainan use an ax to hack a depression [into the tree], which causes its oily resin to congeal and concentrate slowly inside the ax mark, where it is gathered to make an aromatic that is sort of like Jian aromatic. Most such aromatics are man-made.[42]

BRIGHT AROMATIC [*GUANGXIANG*][43] is in the same grade and class as Jian aromatic. It comes out of Haibei and Jiaozhi, and is also gathered in Qin County. It comes mostly in large lumps that resemble bare and lifeless mountain rocks. The smell is coarse and strong, like that when pine [*song*] or juniper [*gui*] [wood] is burned. It can

---

37   The term *shengxiang*, or "fresh aromatic," also known as *shengsu*, or "fresh and fast," refers to aromatic that is procured from a living gharu-woood tree that is cut down for that purpose. ZFZ, 2.177 (*Chau Ju-Kua*, 208).

38   "Ripened" refers to aromatic that is taken from the decayed wood of a gharu-tree that has already fallen down. ZFZ, 2.178 (*Chau Ju-Kua*, 208).

39   I assume that "quick-formed" is another name for "quick aromatic;" that is, aromatic gathered from a tree whose bark is only half formed. See note 8. See also Wheatley, "Geographical Notes on Some Commodities," 71, which does not define *suxiang* but does say that it was a product of Cambodia, Annam, and Java.

40   All surviving editions of *Treatises* read *chonglou* 重漏, but this is probably an error for *chonglou* 蟲漏 (moth secretion), referring to a variety of sinking-in-water aromatic that is made by moths in the crevices of the tree. I have followed this reading in my translation. See BCGM, 34.1938 (*Compendium*, 4:34.2952), and Yang Wuquan's comments in "*Guihai yuheng zhi jiaozhu* jiaoyi zayi," 53.

41   BCGM, 34.1938 (*Compendium*, 4:34.2952) mentions that fresh-formed sinking-in-water aromatic is taken from notches in trees cut by farmers.

42   HSRC, 67.52a–b; FCDBJ, 97.

43   Bright aromatic is a variety of Jian aromatic, but I have not been able to identify it beyond that association. LWDD, 7.245–46 (*Netolitzky*, 7.5), mentions that it was burned at many Buddhist ceremonies and banquets in Guilin.

never compare with Hainan's Jian aromatic. Southerners often use it on a daily basis and in their customary sacrificial ceremonies.

MUDDY AROMATIC [*NIXIANG*][44] comes out of Jiaozhi. It is made of various sweet grasses [*xiangcao*] mixed and matched with honey [*midiao*] and resembles lavender aromatic [*xunyi xiang*].[45] Its smell is warm and pervasive and has a unique aroma, but it is subtle, and reserved and restrained.

AROMATIC BEADS [*XIANGZHU*][46] come out of Jiaozhi. They are made from muddy aromatic kneaded into the shape of little Ba beans [*badou*],[47] with lapis lazuli gems [*liuli zhu*] placed between them. A colored thread runs through them that can be used to make counting beads [*shuzhu*] for Buddhists.[48] They are sold when you enter

FIGURE 6

Ba Beans from Rong 戎 county. Source: *Chongxiu Zhenghe jingshi zhenglei beiyong bencao,* 14.339.

---

44   Since an entry on sinking-in-water aromatic has already appeared earlier in this treatise and because references to "muddy aromatic" appear in two entries that follow this one, it seems likely that the character *chen* 沉 (to sink) in the title of this entry is corrupt. I suspect that it should instead read *ni* 泥 (lit., "mud" or "muddy," referring to the putty-like composition of this aromatic), forming the title *nixiang,* or "muddy aromatic." *Yan Pei,* 34, n. 34, supports this reading. See also the remarks in *Hu-Tan,* 45, note. LWDD, 7.246 (*Netolitzky,* 7.5), repeats this entry almost verbatim and copies the *chenxiang* entry title. Yang Wuquan, 246, n. 3, says he is not sure which of the two readings (*chenxiang* or *nixiang*) is correct.

45   *Xunyi* or *xunyi cao* is lavender (*Lavandula augustifolia*).

46   According to Hong Chu's *Aromatics Manual* (Xiangpu), 2.21, *xiangzhu* (lit., "aromatic gems") are beads made of various aromatics that are worn by Daoists. When the aromatic beads are burned, their fragrance can "permeate to the heavens." This same work also includes a recipe for making "aromatic beads."

47   Native to the Ba and Shu regions (modern Sichuan), this poisonous herb (*Croton tiglium*)—the seeds of which resemble beans—is used extensively in Chinese medicine (see fig. 6). BCGM, 35.2052–58 (*Compendium,* 5:35.3109–17).

48   Although "aromatic beads" are often associated with Daoist religious practices

government territory. In the south married women are fond of wearing them.

SILAO AROMATIC [*SILAO XIANG*][49] comes out of Rinan[50] and resembles frankincense [*ruxiang*].[51] Its resin[52] is yellowish brown in color. Its smell is like maple aromatic [*fengxiang*].[53] The people of Jiaozhi use it to mix and match with various other aromatics.

ALIGNED GRASS [*PAICAO*] aromatic[54] comes out of Rinan. In shape it resembles white thatch-grass [*bai mao*] aromatic.[55] Its aromatic fragrance is strong, resembling that of musk [*shexiang*] and originally

---

(see note 46), here Fan Chengda is clearly referencing *shuzhu*, or the counting beads used by Buddhists (*daoren*) when reciting prayers or scriptures.

49   Silao is probably a place-name, but its precise location is unknown. See also *Fourth Century Flora*, 133–34, which describes a "Silao bamboo" (*silao zhu*) that "grows everywhere in Jiao and Guang."

50   Rinan was one of nine commanderies established by Emperor Wudi of the Han after he pacified the regions of Southern Yue. It was located in the south-central part of modern Vietnam.

51   The term *ruxiang* (lit., "milky aromatic") is a general name for frankincense, of which there are numerous varieties. Frankincense is a gum resin produced by several different species of the *Boswellia* tree (or shrub) when notched with an ax. After the resin hardens, the aromatic is formed. A common pre-Song name for frankincense was *xunlu xiang*. For additional information, see ZFZ, 2.163–64 (*Chau Ju-Kua*, 195–97); *Fourth Century Flora*, 79–80; Schafer, *The Golden Peaches*, 170–71; and Wheatley, "Geographical Notes on Some Commodities," 47–49.

52   Reading *liqing* 歷青 to mean *liqing* 瀝青 (lit., "dripping dark"), which indicates the resin of pine and other sap-yielding trees.

53   Maple aromatic derives from the sap of the maple resin tree (*fengxiang shu*). It is obtained from the trunk of this tree, where it forms in cavities of the bark and is harvested in autumn. CMP, no. 463, and Yang Wuqan, LWDD, 7.247–48, n. 9, both identify the resin as *Liquidamber formosana*. Bernard E. Read in CMP, no. 463, calls it "Formosan storax."

54   *Compendium*, 2:1562 (BCGM, 14.897), identifies *paicao xiang* as "hairy stalk loosestrife" (*Lysimachia capilipes*) and further notes it is produced from the root of an unidentified herb. Alternate names for it include "nine-*li* aromatic" (*jiuli xiang*) and "ten-*li* aromatic" (*shili xiang*), so called because its scent was detectable at a great distance. Schafer, *Shore of Pearls*, 41. BCGM, 14.897 (*Compendium*, 2:14.1562), also mentions that aligned grass aromatic is produced in Jiaozhi, where merchants often mix it with other herbs.

55   "White thatch-grass aromatic" is also a product of Jiaozhi. BCGM, 14.897 (*Compendium*, 2:14.1562), mentions that "it is good for blending with other fragrant herbs to make incense."

was also used to mix with other aromatics. Among the various grass-based aromatics,[56] there is none that matches it.

BETEL PALM MOSS [*BINLANG TAI*][57] comes out of the various islands in the southwestern [sea]. It grows on betel palm trees and resembles the mossy coating [that grows] on the frame of a pine tree. A single burn [of the aromatic] yields an extremely pungent odor. When people in Jiaozhi mix it with muddy aromatic, it can form a warm and pervasive smell. Its function resembles that of shell aromatic [*jiaxiang*].[58]

OLIVE AROMATIC [*GANLAN XIANG*] is the resin of olive trees.[59] In shape it resembles black, sticky rice cakes [*jiaoyi*]. Natives of Jiangdong[60] gather resin from pistache trees [*huanglian mu*][61] and maple trees [*fengmu*][62] to make olive aromatic, so probably [all of these aromatics] fall into the same category. Since they are derived from olives, they alone have a pure and strong, out-of-this-world appeal. In grade and quality olive aromatic is above that of pistache and maple aromatics. The Dongjiang area in Guilin[63] has this fruit [olives]. Residents there gather the aromatic and sell it. They cannot get much of it. The variety that uses pure resin and is not mixed with tree bark is outstanding.

---

56   Reading *caoxiang* to mean aromatics that derive their fragrance from grasses and plants rather than trees.

57   Betel palm moss refers to betel palm aromatic (*binlang xiang*). Since it grows on the trunks and branches of betel palm trees, it is sometimes called "moss."

58   *Jiaxiang*, also known as *jiajian xiang*, is an aromatic drug comprising a mixture of ground sea conch (*hailuo*) shell and other drugs. According to the *Nanzhou yiwu zhi* quoted in BCGM, 46.2546 (*Compendium*, 5:3705), the shell of a sea conch can be as big as a small jar. It is coarse, thorny, and uneven. At the opening of the shell there is a thick, straight edge several *cun* long. Burning the shell with other aromatics increases the intensity of their combined aromas. When burned independently, however, it smells foul.

59   The olive tree (*ganlan shu; Canarium album*) produces a black resin that is burned as an aromatic or incense. BCGM, 31.1822 (*Compendium*, 4:31.2795).

60   The precise geographic reference of "Jiangdong" is not clear. Fan might be referring to the general area east of the Li River in Guilin.

61   *Huanglian mu* here denotes *Pistacia chinensis*, a resin-bearing tree of the family Anacardiaceae. In English it is sometimes called the Chinese pistache tree.

62   On maple trees and maple aromatic, see note 53.

63   Dongjiang, or East River, is an alternate name for the Li River.

LINGLING AROMATIC [*LINGLING XIANG*][64] is common in Yi and Rong 融 Counties. The local people [in those counties] plait it into straw mats [*xijian*] and seat cushions [*zuoru*]. By nature it is warm and pleasing to people. Lingling is today's Yong County. But in fact, it does not have this kind of aromatic.[65]

Supplementary text: The border of ancient Lingling is very distant [from Yong County].[66]

Supplementary entry: **CRAB SHELL AROMATIC [*XIEKE XIANG*]**[67] comes out of Gao and Hua Counties.[68]

---

64   Schafer and Wallacker, "Local Tribute Products of the T'ang Dynasty," 217, identifies *lingling xiang* as a name for both sweet-clover (*Melilotus*) and basil (*Ocimum basilicum*).

65   *LWDD*, 7.248 (Netolitzky, 7.6), echoes Fan's comment that Lingling aromatic in fact did not come from Lingling, which Fan narrowly identifies with Yong County. Li Shizhen, however, correctly points out that Lingling was the name of a Han dynasty commandery, the territory of which included what later became known as Yong County. *BCGM*, 14.901 (*Compendium*, 2:14.1567–68). See also the comments on this in *Hu-Tan*, 49, and in Lin Tianwei, *Songdai xiangyao maoyi shigao*, 52–53.

66   *HSRC*, 67.53a.

67   *LWDD*, 7.245 (Netolitzky, 7.4), mentions that crab shell aromatic is very thin, presumably like a "shell."

68   Gao and Hua Counties correspond to modern Maoming *xian* and Huazhou *xian*, Guangdong. Supplementary entry from *HSRC*, 67.52b; *FCDBJ*, 97.

4

WINES
(Zhi jiu)

BY NATURE I CANNOT DRINK A LOT. AMONG MY OFFICIAL friends who drink little, none drinks less than me. And yet, among those who are informed about wine, none is more informed than me. On a few occasions I formerly served in Court[-appointed positions].[1] When I visited the homes of princes, dukes, and respectable persons, I had not yet begun to be able to recognize famous wines. While serving as an envoy to the caitiffs [*lu*], I reached Yanshan,[2]

---

1   After earning his *jinshi* degree in 1154, Fan Chengda served as a minor official in Hui County (modern She *xian*, Anhui). Thereafter, he served in a succession of posts, both in the capital and in the provinces. After a position in the Pharmacy for Benefiting the People (Humin Yaoju) (1162), he served as inspector of examinations (*dianjian shijuan*) (1163), in various editorial posts (1163–1166), as vice director in the Ministry of Personnel (*Libu yuanwai lang*) (1166), as imperial diarist (*qiju lang*) (late 1169 or early 1170), as Song envoy to the Jin (1170), and as pacification and comfort commissioner for regulation and order (1173–1175).

2   Fan Chengda was sent to the north as Song ambassador to the Jin (or "caitiffs") in 1170. Fan's destination was the Jin capital, which here he calls "Yanshan." Yanshan is a Song administrative name, established in 1122, for the municipality in north China that included modern Beijing, parts of Hebei, and even some sections of modern Tianjin. After the Jin occupation of the north in 1125, Yanshan Municipality was renamed Yanjing Xijin. In 1153 the Jin capital was

where in the [Jin] palace they had some wine known as Gold Orchid [Jinlan].[3] As it turned out, it was truly outstanding! To the west of Yan are the Gold Orchid Mountains [Jinlan Shan],[4] where water is drawn from springs to brew it. But when I got to Guilin and drank some Auspicious Dew [Ruilu],[5] I had then experienced the ultimate in fine wines. The reputation of Auspicious Dew resonates across Hu and Guang.[6] The superiority of Gold Orchid notwithstanding, it certainly still cannot be considered to be in the same class as Auspicious Dew.[7]

AUSPICIOUS DEW [*RUILU*] is the kitchen wine [*chujiu*][8] of the Command Inspectorate Gentleman [Shuaisi Gong].[9] In front of the Management and Comfort Office [Jingfu Ting),[10] there is a well with clear and cool water, which is drawn for brewing the wine. As a result, it has become famous. Now a spring has emerged naturally inside the southern storehouse.[11] In recent years only water from the storehouse well has been used [to brew Auspicious Dew]. The wine is still outstanding.

---

moved to the southwestern section of modern Beijing, and with this move came a new name for the municipality: Zhongdu Daxing. Most sources refer to this city simply as "Zhongdu."

3   Gold Orchid wine was well known to Song ambassadors to the north. See, for instance, the comments in Zhou Hui, *Qingbo zazhi*, 6.269 and 6.270, n. 4.

4   I have not been able to find any references to or information about mountains west of Yanshan bearing this name.

5   Zhou Qufei mentions that the Auspicious Dew produced by the Command Inspectorate in Guilin was the best wine in all Guangxi. He also notes that originally it was produced in He County (southeast of modern He *xian*, Guangxi). See *LWDD*, 6.232 (*Netolitzky*, 6.31).

6   "Hu" refers to the Jing-Hu North and South Circuits, while "Guang" indicates the Guangnan East and West Circuits. Collectively, this area encompasses all of modern Hunan as well as parts of Hubei, Guangdong, and Guangxi.

7   According to Huang Zhen's comments in *HSRC*, 67.53a, Fan Chengda was so fond of Auspicious Dew wine that he later had it brewed in Chengdu when he served as an official there between 1175 and 1177.

8   "Kitchen wine" in fact refers to *guanjiu*, or government-produced wine.

9   The title Command Inspectorate Gentleman refers here to the chief government military officer for the Guangxi region. The more formal designation for this office was managing and organizing commissioner for pacification and comfort in Guangxi (*Guangxi jinglüe anfu shi*). Fan Chengda held this post when he served as an official in Guangxi.

10   That is, the office of the chief military official in the region.

11   The reference here is to a government-operated storehouse or granary (*ku*), which apparently was located in the southern part of Guilin.

GULA SPRING [GULA QUAN] wine derives its name from a market [*xu*][12] between Bin and Heng Counties,[13] whose spring water is used to brew the wine. When mature, the wine is not warmed but buried in the ground. After a full day it is retrieved [for drinking].

Supplementary text: The color is pale red; the taste is sweet but delicate and reserved. Although one may take it out into the burning sun, this does not cause the wine to spoil. People in the Southern Counties value it highly.[14]

VINTAGE WINE [LAOJIU] is brewed with yeast. After it is tightly sealed, the wine can be stored away for several years. Local families[15] especially esteem and value it. Each year in the La month, each and every family makes fish condiment [*zha*],[16] which provides them a means to tide over the year. If esteemed guests come for a visit, then some vintage wine is set out for them. During winter, fish condiment is used to demonstrate frugality. When someone takes a wife, vintage wine is regarded as a lavish gift.

---

12 The Gula market (Gula *xu*; also known as Gula *chang* and Gula *pu*) was famous in Guangxi during the Song and later during the Ming dynasty. A passage in the *Yudi jisheng*, 113.4b, locates the market 110 *li* north of Yongding Town, Heng County (for which see note 13 below). On the possible etymological origins of the term *xu* (market), see Eberhard, *Local Cultures*, 224–26.

13 Bin County corresponds to the area around modern Binyang *xian*, Guangxi. Heng County was located in modern Heng *xian*, Guangxi.

14 Zhu Mu, *Fangyu shenglan*, 39.705.

15 It is likely that *shiren jia* (families of officials) here should instead read *turen jia* (local families), and so I have followed the latter reading. Cf. the comments in *Hu-Tan*, 52, n. 2.

16 Fish condiment is a fermented preparation, usually made with fish (any kind), salt, and rice porridge.

5

IMPLEMENTS
(Zhi qi)

THE CUSTOMS IN THE SOUTHERN COUNTIES ARE JUMBLED and mixed among the Man and Yao. Thus, as a general rule, most of their daily implements [*shiqi*] are strange and odd. As for the designs of the weapons and armor of the Outer Man,[1] these should all be known by those responsible for frontier defense.[2]

BAMBOO BOWS [*ZHUGONG*] are made of bamboo cured [black] with smoke.[3] As for the design of their sinews and adhesives,[4] they are just like a horn bow [*jiaogong*],[5] only when an arrow is drawn it does not require much strength.

LI BOWS [*LIGONG*] are used by the Li people of Hainan. They are

---

TRANSLATOR'S NOTE: As evidenced by the wide range of subject matter in this treatise, the term *qi* covers a broad spectrum of "implements," including weapons, musical instruments, and even clothing and fabrics.

1   Throughout *Treatises* Fan Chengda refers to Man people who lived in areas outside of or beyond Chinese administrative control as "Outer Man."

2   Reading *bianbei* 邊備 (frontier defense) rather than *bianzhen* 邊鎮. See FCDBJ, 102, n. 1.

3   Following the ZBZZCS ed., 11b, and reading *xunzhu* 熏竹 (to cure bamboo until it is black).

4   "Sinews and adhesives" (*jinjiao*) refers to the materials that bind and hold together the various parts of the bow. See *Needham et al.*, 5-6:109–13.

5   That is, a bow made from the curved horn of an animal.

wood bows [*mugong*] with long ears [*changshao*]. The bowstrings are made from vines. Arrows are three *chi* in length, and they have no guide feathers. The arrowheads [*xuan*] are five *cun* in length and resemble arrowhead leaves [*cigu ye*].[6] Since they have no feathers, they are shot no farther than three or four *zhang*. However, anyone hit by one will surely die.

MAN CROSSBOWS [MANNU]. As for the various settlements of Yao and other foreign peoples in the southwest, the crossbows they make all follow about the same [design]. They are made of hardwood, while the posts [*zhuang*] are very short. They resemble the shooting-game crossbows [*shesheng gong*] used by hunters in China but are inferior to a great degree.

YAO PEOPLE'S CROSSBOWS [YAOREN NU] are also called bend-the-frame crossbows [*bianjia nu*].[7] They do not have arrow grooves [*jiancao*]. One bends the frame and then shoots the arrow.

POISON ARROWS [YAOJIAN] are used by the various Man who live beyond civilization [*huawai*].[8] Although their crossbows are small and weak, they dip their arrow tips into poison.[9] Anyone hit by one dies immediately. The poison is made from snake venom and [poisonous] weeds [*shedu cao*].

As for **MAN ARMOR [MANJIA]**, only that of the Dali kingdom [Dali

---

6　*Cigu* (*Sagittaria sagittfolia*) is sometimes called "Chinese arrowhead" or "Old World arrowhead" in English. The leaves of this aqueous plant are shaped like arrowheads. BCGM, 33.1906 (*Compendium*, 4:33.2908–9).

7　In this entry Fan Chengda seems to be using *bianjia* to mean "bend-the-frame [of the bow]," referring to a leaf-spring type of crossbow. Fan's comments in his entry on the Yao people in the "Treatise on the Man," the entry on "Man Crossbows" in LWDD, 6.210 (*Netolitzky*, 6.9) and *Yan Pei*, 44, n. 11, support this reading. See also. *Needham et al.*, 5-6:136, which remarks that the term *bianjia nu* "almost certainly means that the bow stave was made of several pieces of wood or bamboo in leaf-spring form." This type of bow was armed by pushing a stirrup against the ground. According to Shen Gua, the bend-the-frame crossbow was also called a *shenbi gong*, or "magic stock bow," and could propel an arrow 300 *bu* and pierce multilayered armor. See Shen Gua, *Mengxi bitan quanyi*, 19.600–1. Shen Gua's comments are translated in *Needham et al.*, 5-6:156.

8　The expression *huawai*, or "beyond civilization," was sometimes used by Chinese to describe tribespeople who lived in remote areas beyond the influence of Chinese culture.

9　On the use of poison arrows in China, see *Needham et al.*, 5-6:136.

Guo][10] exhibits the finest workmanship. In all cases the armor and helmets [*jiazhou*] are made from elephant hide [*xiangpi*]. The breast and back sides each have a large cuirass [*pian*] that resembles a tortoise shell [*guike*]. As for hardness and thickness, it falls into the same category as iron. Moreover, the type of armor that joins together small strips of hide for the purpose of shielding the shoulders and protecting the neck resembles Chinese iron armor [*tiejia*] in design. The leaves [of the skirting] are all painted vermilion. With helmets [*doumou*] and bodies armored on the inside and out, all lacquered in yellow and black and bearing numerous patterns of flowers, reptiles, and beasts, the armor resembles the lacquered implements [*xipi*][11] used throughout the ages. It is extremely well-crafted and ingenious. Furthermore, the Man use threaded strings of small, white shells to bind the seams of the armor and adorn the helmets as well. I suspect this is the same as the "shells-on-vermilion-strings-adorning-the-helmets"[12] design handed down from antiquity, or so it is said.

LI HELMETS [*LI DOUMOU*] are used by the Li people of Hainan. They are made from woven vines.

YUNNAN KNIVES [*YUNNAN DAO*] are in fact made in Dali. The iron blade is bluish black and resonates with a deep and distant sound that is never muffled.[13] They are most esteemed by southerners. Elephant

---

10   The Kingdom of Dali was located in Yunnan and the southwestern part of modern Sichuan. Founded in 937, this kingdom was ruled by a succession of kings until 1253, when it was destroyed by the Mongols.

11   The term *xipi* is a transcription of a non-Chinese word that originally referred to the animal-ornamented girdle clasps or buckles (*xi* means "buffalo" or "rhinoceros") worn by the Xianbei (or Xianbi), an ancient tribal people who lived in what is now Inner Mongolia. See *Hanshu*, 94*shang*.3758. For additional information on the etymology of the term *xipi*, see especially Peter A. Boodberg, "The Hsien-pei Buckle," in *Sino-Altaica* 3.5, rpt. in *Selected Works of Peter A. Boodberg*, ed. Alvin P. Cohen (Berkeley and Los Angeles: University of California Press, 1979), 136–37. By the Song period *xipi* was used as a general designation for lacquered implements with ornamentation. Cf. below, where Fan uses *xipi* to mean "lacquered designs."

12   This description is quoted directly from the *Poetry Classic* (Shijing; *Maoshi* no. 300). *Maoshi zhengyi*, 20-2/348/616 (Legge, *The Chinese Classics*, 4:626).

13   Strictly speaking, *xian* 銘 (also written 陷) means "to sink" or "fall into." Here, however, Fan Chengda is describing the resonant sound of the iron used to make Yunnan knives, which he says is "never muffled" (*bu xian* 不銘).

hide is used to make scabbards [*qiao*]. These are painted vermilion, and on them are also painted lacquered designs [*xipi*] in ornate patterns. One scabbard has two pockets [*shi*], each holding a knife. The handles [*ba*] are tied and bound with strips of hide. Well-to-do persons [*guiren*] tie them with gold and silver silk threads.

SETTLEMENT KNIVES [*DONGDAO*]. In the counties and settlements along the Two Rivers [Liang Jiang][14] and among the various Outer Man, no one fails to carry a knife. The custom of carrying two knives in one scabbard is the same as that in Yunnan, only in the settlements they use black lacquer and mix leather [strips together] to make scabbards.

LI KNIVES [*LIDAO*] are made by the Li people of Hainan. In length the knives do not exceed one or two *chi*. The handles are thus three or four *cun*. Slender vines are woven together to tie and bind the handles in place. At the end of the handles are inserted strips of segmented horn about one *chi* in length. They resemble the tail feathers of an owl [*chixiao*] and are used for decoration.

MAN SADDLES [*MAN'AN*] are made by the various foreign peoples in the southwest. They do not use saddle blankets [*jian*] but merely two wooden stirrups [*deng*] that hang down in midair. As for the shape of the stirrups, they are carved to resemble little boxes, into which the toes are placed out of fear that thistles and thorns [*zhenji*] will injure the feet. As for the rear hock straps [*qiu*], a lathe-cut [circular piece of] wood is used to make large "coins," several hundred of which are strung together one after the other. In shape they resemble China's mule hock straps [*leilü qiu*].

MAN WHIPS [*MANBIAN*], made of wood carved into section after section, resemble bamboo stalks. They are lacquered in alternating vermilion and black. In length they are merely four or five *cun*. The top is small and has an iron ring with two strips of hide strung through it. This is used to whip the horse.

FLOWERY-SHELL WAIST DRUMS [*HUAQIANG YAOGU*][15] come out of

---

14   "Two Rivers" refers to the Left River and the Right River.

15   Waist drums, usually made of porcelain, iron, or wood and shaped like a dumbbell, were popular percussion instruments in ancient China. According to *LWDD*, 7.253 (*Netolitzky*, 7.10), waist drums made in Guangxi during the

Zhitian Village [Zhitian xiang] in Lingui.[16] The soil there is especially well suited for making drum shells [*guqiang*, "drum cavities"].[17] Villagers make special kilns to fire them. Delicately painted patterns of red flowers are used to decorate the drums.

BRONZE DRUMS [*TONGGU*] were used by the ancient Man people.[18] Tradition has it that the drums excavated from time to time along the southern borders were left by Ma, the Subduer of Waves [Ma Yuan]. Their design resembles a porcelain stool [*zuodun*] but is hollow underneath. The entire drum is covered with delicate flowery patterns of extremely exquisite workmanship. The four corners have little [ornamental] toads [*chanchu*].[19] Two people together carry the drum as they walk along, playing it with their hands. It sounds exactly like a [Chinese] war drum [*pigu*].

BLUNDERBUSS DRUMS [*CHONGGU*] are a musical instrument of the Yao people. In shape they resemble waist drums [*yaogu*]. The shell is twice as long as that of a waist drum. On top it is tapered; below it is

---

Southern Song were especially well known for their deep, sonorous tone.

16 Lingui was the metropolitan town of Jingjiang Municipality. The precise location of Zhitian Village is unknown. Cf. LWDD, 7.253 (*Netolizky*, 7.10), which reads "Zhiyou Village" (Zhiyou xiang 職由鄉).

17 *LWDD*, 7.253 (*Netolitzky*, 7.10), also mentions that the earth in the village was especially well suited for firing drums in kilns. This same source also notes that the head of a waist drum had an iron ring around it, while the drum head was made of goat skin.

18 The use of bronze drums (see fig. 7) by non-Han people in southwest China extends back to the Spring and Autumn period, perhaps even earlier. They were used mostly for religious ceremonies. Later the drums gradually became a symbol of power for tribal chiefs. According to legend, many of the bronze drums excavated in Guangxi, Guangdong, and Yunnan since the Tang dynasty were "left" there by the great Han general Ma Yuan when he carried out a military campaign in the south to eliminate threats to the Han throne. In the next line of the text, Fan Chengda refers to Ma Yuan as "Ma, the Subduer of Waves" (Ma Fubo). For additional information on ancient bronze drums, see Lo Hsiang-lin (Luo Xianglin), "The Yüeh Bronze Drums, Their Manufacture and Use," in *Symposium on Historical, Archaeological and Linguistic Studies on Southern China, South-East Asia and the Hong Kong Region*, 110–14; and Schafer, *Vermilion Bird*, 254.

19 The decorative toads on the top of the drum were believed by many people in south China to have the power to invoke rain. For additional information on this see Lo Hsiang-lin, "The Yüeh Bronze Drums," 112.

FIGURE 7
Bronze Drum, dating from 203-111 B.C.E., discovered in Luobowan 蘿
泊灣, Guigang 貴港 *shi*, Guangxi. Source: http://zh.wikipedia.org/wiki.

broad; and it also uses animal hide for the drum skin. The drum is placed perpendicular to the ground and is played while sitting.

REED PIPES [*LUSHA*][20] are a musical instrument of the Yao people. In shape they fall into the category of panpipes [*xiao*].[21] Lengthwise there are eight pipes [*guan*], with one pipe running crosswise.

GOURD ORGANS [*HULU SHENG*][22] are instruments found in settlements along the Two Rivers.

VINE BASKETS [*TENGHE*] are gnarly vines twined around and coiled into a basketlike shape, which are then lacquered to secure and protect them. They come out of Teng, Wu, and other such commanderies.[23]

---

20   Here I read *lusha* 盧沙 to mean *lusheng* 蘆笙, or "reed pipes." This instru-
     ment, sometimes called a mouth organ, usually has five or six pipes. Below Fan
     Chengda says it has eight pipes, but this is questioned in *Hu-Tan*, 67, n. 1. Hu
     and Tan suspect "eight" might be a mistake for "six." In any case, reed pipes
     are played by various ethnic groups in southwestern China and neighboring
     countries.
21   *Xiao* here refers to panpipes (*paixiao*), a traditional Chinese musical instrument.
22   "Gourd organ" is a reed mouth organ with a gourd wind chest.
23   The two "commanderies" mentioned here are actually counties. Teng County
     corresponds to the area around modern Teng *xian*, Guangxi; Wu (or Cangwu)

CHICKEN-FUR WRITING BRUSHES [*JIMAO BI*]. There are also rabbits in the area Beyond the Ranges [Lingwai],[24] but they are extremely rare. Usually one cannot make rabbit-fur writing brushes; chicken feathers are used most of the time. The ends [of rabbit fur] are unsteady and uneven,[25] and not suitable for use.

LINEN [*SHUZI*][26] comes out of the counties and settlements along the Two Rivers. For the most part it is like ramie cloth [*zhubu*]. There is a flowery patterned variety referred to as flowery linen [*huashu*]. The local people themselves also esteem and value it.

Supplementary text: Natives of Shu are especially fond of linen. When Yao Cha [533–606] of the Chen dynasty [557–589] served as secretary [*shangshu*] in the Ministry of Personnel [Libu], [a disciple from] an influential family [*simen*] sent him one length [*duan*] of southern cloth [*nanbu*] and one bolt [*pi*] of flowery linen. Cha said to the disciple: "I only wear [clothes made of] burlap cattail-linen [*mabu pushu*]. What use would I have for these items?" Fortunately, Cha was not annoyed at this, and so this person then respectfully invited him [to a feast]. Cha then drove him away with an angry look.[27]

WOVEN VELVET [*TIAN*][28] also comes out of the counties and settle-

---

was located near modern Wuzhou *shi* in Guangxi.

24   That is, the area south of the Southern Ranges—Guangxi and Guangdong.

25   In other words, rabbit fur is too soft and pliable to serve as a calligraphy brush.

26   *Shuzi*, rendered here as "linen," is a material made from ramie (*zhuma*; *Boehmeria nivea*). LWDD, 6.225 (Netolitzky, 6.25), mentions that ramie produced in Yong County is "pure and white, thin and light, and that natives there select the thinnest and longest ramie and make it into linen."

27   The incident related in part here comes from Yao Cha's biography in the *History of the Southern Dynasties* (Nanshi). The full text of the story runs as follows: "There was a disciple who didn't dare send his mentor [that is, Yao Cha] a gift of some lavish food. [So instead] he sent a length of southern cloth and a bolt of flowery linen. Cha then addressed him, saying: 'I only wear clothes made of burlap or cattail-linen, so these items are of no use to me.' Afterwards, the disciple wanted to invite his mentor to a feast, thinking it was fortunate that this would not annoy him. When the disciple respectfully extended the invitation, Cha drove him away with an angry look. From this time on, no one dared to invite Yao Cha to a meal." See Li Yanshou, ed., *Nanshi*, 69.1691. Supplementary text from *Yan Pei*, 47, n. 37, quoting from the *Yongle dadian*.

28   Yang Wuquan, LWDD, 6.223 (Netolitzky, 6.21), n. 1, identifies *tian* as a fabric woven from velvet (*sirong*). Later in Chinese history, during the Ming and Qing periods, this material was called *tujin*, or "local damask." Today it is sometimes

ments along the Two Rivers. It resembles China's cotton gauze [*xian-luo*]. On it are patterns of tilted, small overlapping squares.

MAN FELT [*MANZHAN*] comes from the various foreign peoples in the southwest. The variety from Dali is regarded as the best. As for the Man people, during the day they drape a felt fabric over their shoulders; at night they sleep on it. No matter how well-to-do or base, each person has just one felt robe.

Supplementary text: Man felt comes in lengths of perhaps several *zhang*.[29] Two layers are joined together. Thus, it is thin and soft. As for northern felt, it can be slept on for a long time, but it can never guard against the rain. As for southern felt, whether you sleep on it or drape it over the shoulders, you will never be soaked by the rain. [Felt] from Dali is the best.[30]

LI SCREENS [*LIMU*][31] come out of the settlements of the Li people on Hainan. The Li people obtain Chinese multicolored silk [*jincai*], which they cut up to get the colored silk. This is interwoven with cotton [*mumian*]. The screen is completed when the silk and cotton are sewn together. Four widths [*fu*] are joined together to make one screen.

LI SHEETS [*LIDAN*] are also woven by the Li people. They are made of cotton cloth with alternating stripes of bluish black and red. The people of Guilin buy them to serve only as bedding [*woju*].

BETEL PALM BOXES [*BINLANG HE*]. All southerners are fond of eating betel palm nuts. As for the manner in which they are eaten, if

---

called Zhuangjin, or "Zhuang damask."

29   The *LWDD* passage on felt (6.227; *Netolitzky*, 6.27) mentions that Man felt came in lengths of over three *zhang*, with the width extending from one *zhang* six to one *zhang* seven *chi*. It doubles in thickness after the two ends are then sewn together. The felt was wrapped around the body and held in place with a belt. Both men and women followed this practice. The *LWDD* passage on felt is translated in Bertold Laufer, "The Early History of Felt," *American Anthropologist*, new series 32.1 (Jan.–March 1930): 6.

30   Supplementary text from the *Guihai junzhi*. I have not been able to gain access this important work on the history of Guilin compiled by Chen Lian in 1450. The passage cited here is quoted in *Yan Pei*, 48, n. 39.

31   Cf. *LWDD*, 6.228 (*Netolitzky*, 6.28), which uses a different name for Li screens: *Lishi* 黎飾.

one uses lime powder [*shihui*][32] or oyster powder [*xianhui*][33] chewed together with betel vines [*fuliu teng*],[34] then the nuts are not astringent. Prominent families even go so far as to make little boxes out of silver and pewter, which are shaped like silver ingots [*yinding*]. Inside there are three compartments: one for storing powder, one for storing vines, one for storing betel palm nuts.

NOSE-DRINKING CUPS [*BIYIN BEI*]. Southern border peoples are accustomed to drinking through their noses.[35] They have a kind of vessel that resembles a pitcher. On the side of it is a single small tube, resembling the spout of a vase, through which they suck liquor into their noses. During the summer months they use this method to drink water. It is said the water goes from their noses down into their throats with a speed that cannot be described. People in Yong County now follow this custom. I note it here because those who witness such displays have a big laugh.

OX-HORN CUPS [*NIUJIAO BEI*]. People along the coast cut off the horns of oxen and then make them smooth for drinking liquor. This [idea] also comes from the rhinoceros wine goblet [*sigong*] of ancient times.[36]

MAN BOWLS [*MANWAN*] are carved from wood and are lacquered in alternating stripes of vermilion and black. The interior is extravagant; the bowl has legs and resembles the shape of a food vessel [*dui*] or wine vessel [*bu*].[37]

BAMBOO CAULDRONS [*ZHUFU*] are used by the Yao people. They cut

---

32   *Shihui* is a powder (hydrated calcium oxide) obtained by pulverizing seashells. Sometimes in English this is called "slaked lime."

33   *Xianhui* is a powder derived from burning the shell of an oyster. *Hu-Tan*, 75, note.

34   *Fuliu* is the vine of the betel pepper (*Piper betel*). It has large, shiny, oval-shaped leaves and is classified in the pepper genus. *Fourth Century Flora*, 112.

35   For more information on the practice of nose drinking, see Eberhard, *Local Cultures*, 296–97, and *LWDD*, 10.420 (Netolitzky, 10.27).

36   This is a wine goblet made from a rhinoceros horn and is mentioned in the *Poetry Classic* (*Maoshi* no. 154). See *Maoshi zhengyi*, 8-1/124/392 (Legge, *The Chinese Classics*, 4:233).

37   A *dui* (rendered loosely here as "food vessel") is a round or oval vessel with a lid for holding cereals; a *bu* (or "wine vessel") is a dumpy, bowl-shaped vessel with circular foot, used to hold wine or water.

a large bamboo tube to serve as a cooking vessel [*dangding*]. Food is cooked in it, but the bamboo does not snuff out the fire. This is probably due to the innate laws of nature, so there is nothing strange about it.

PERFORMANCE MASKS [*XIMIAN*][38] are human faces the people of Guilin carve out of wood. The workmanship and skill level is extremely high. Just one of them is sometimes worth 10,000 cash.

---

38   These masks were worn during a festival or performance in south China held in the twelfth month, when groups of people would parade through villages and ask for money, food, and wine. Upon receipt of these items, they would then drive and burn all evil spirits from the house. This exorcism rite (*nuo*) is also mentioned in the "Treatise on the Man." For additional information see Eberhard, *Local Cultures*, 328–30.

6

BIRDS
(*Zhi qin*)

THERE ARE MANY RARE BIRDS IN THE SOUTHERN QUARTER that the learned gentlemen [*junzi*] have not heard about.[1] Moreover, since the laws prohibiting the capture and trapping of rare birds are very strict, I have not been able to find out very much about such birds.[2] By chance I was able to see some of these birds in people's homes. Whenever I obtained information about the stranger ones, I would make a note so as to help identify the creatures of the natural world.

PEACOCKS [*KONGQUE*][3] nest in tall trees on lofty mountains. People

---

1 Here I read *wen* 問 to mean *wen* 聞. In this context, "not hear about" means "not know about" or "not have information about."

2 If my understanding of this line is correct, there were laws in place during the Song regarding the "capture and trapping" of rare birds. So far, I have not been able to confirm the existence of any such prohibitions. See also Rudolph, "Literary Innovation and Aesthetic Tradition in Travel Writing of the Southern Sung," 25, whose reading of this line is the same as mine.

3 The Chinese *kongque*, or peacock, is a member of the pheasant family (*Pavo muticus*). Read, *Avian Drugs*, no. 309. This creature is known in English by a host of different names, including "Malayan peacock," "Burmese peacock," and "green peafowl." The bird was especially valued for its glittering coat of bronze and metallic green as well as its multicolored tail feathers dotted with "golden coins." For additional details see Schafer, *Vermilion Bird*, 236–37. Although no peacocks are found in the mountain forests of Guangxi today, during the Song

capture their nestlings and then train them. Peacocks are fond of lying in sand and using it to cleanse themselves. The flapping and fluttering [sound they make when "bathing"] is very fitting. The feathers of males grow to a length of several *chi* but do not reach full length until three years after birth. Each year they shed all their feathers, which grow back in summer and fall. The feathers should not get near the eyes, for they are harmful to humans.[4] [Young] peacocks are fed pig entrails and raw vegetables. The only thing they do not eat is celery cabbage [*song*].[5]

PARROTS [YINGWU][6] are especially numerous in commanderies near the sea. The common people sometimes use parrot flesh to make condiments and moreover use peacock flesh to make dried meat [*xi*]. This is because parrots and peacocks are both easily obtained. These two matters have not yet been chronicled in historical sources. I am the very first to do so. Southerners who raise parrots say this creature is native to the blazing quarter [the south]. If they are taken a short distance to the north, where it is cooler, they shiver and tremble as if being attacked by malaria, similar to when a human contracts chills and fever. If the sick parrot is fed mandarin oranges [*ganzi*],[7] it will recover. Otherwise, it will certainly die.

COCKATOOS [BAI YINGWU][8] are as big as a small goose, and they are

---

they existed in the wild in great numbers. Fan Chengda mentions below that southerners ate both peacock and parrot flesh. He says they ate halcyon king-fishers and francolins as well.

4   Many sources note specifically that the tail feathers are poisonous and hence dangerous to human eyes. See also the comments in Read, *Avian Drugs*, no. 309. An old Chinese tradition says that peacocks copulate with snakes, thus making the peacock's blood and gall poisonous as well. See BCGM, 49.2668 (*Compendium*, 6:49.3841). LWDD, 9.367 (*Netolitzky*, 9.21), warns that one drop of blood from the gall of a peacock can kill a man.

5   Reading *song* 菘 here to mean *baicai*, or "celery cabbage."

6   As noted in Schafer, "Parrots in Medieval China," 271, the Chinese term *yingwu*, usually translated as "parrot," refers to "any and all of the Psittacidae" (that is, true parrots). Many sources record that wild parrots were numerous in south China during the Tang and Song. See, for instance, Duan Gonglu, comp., *Beihu lu*, 1.4. LWDD, 9.368 (*Netolitzky*, 9.24), mentions that "flocks of parrots flew about the Southern Counties like wild birds."

7   The SKQS ed., 17a, instead reads *yugan zi*, or Indian gooseberry fruit, for which see the "Treatise on Fruits."

8   Schafer, "Parrots in Medieval China," 277, remarks that the "white parrots"

also able to speak. Their feathers are [as white as] jadelike snow, and people stroke them with their hands. The feathers carry a powdery substance that adheres to the fingers and palms, resembling that on the wings of a butterfly [*jiadie*].[9]

DARK PHOENIX [*WUFENG*][10] resembles a magpie [*xique*]. In color it is dark purple and jade green, while the neck feathers are sort of like the neck hair on a cock. The head has a crown, and from the tail hang two soft bones, each measuring one *chi*, four or five *cun* in length. It does not grow its first crop of feathers until the end of its first year. The crown and tail are superlative and fantastic; they are about as big as those on a phoenix. Its singing notes are clear and distinct, like a pipe or flute, and it can carry a tune, ingeniously maintaining proper pitch. Moreover, it can also imitate the sounds of the hundred insects [*baichong*]. It is native to the Creeks Settlements along the Left and Right Rivers, and is extremely difficult to catch. However, it has not been chronicled in books that have been passed down, and this is because they are rarely known by man, or so it is said.

HILL MYNAHS [*QIN JILIAO*][11] resemble the true myna bird [*quyu*].

---

mentioned in medieval Chinese literature "are certainly cockatoos." True white cockatoos are members of the *Cacatua* genus, in which there are many species.

9   Fan Chengda probably mentions this "powdery substance" because many people in ancient China believed that stroking the back feathers of a parrot (or cockatoo) could lead to contraction of a fatal disease. Schafer, "Parrots in Medieval China," 279, identifies this as a "virus disease similar to pneumonia now known as psittacosis." Schafer also points out that psittacosis (also known as "parrot fever") is actually transmitted to the lungs in dust contaminated by parrot feces. The entry on "parrots" in Duan Gonglu, comp., *Beihu lu*, 1.4, identifies this disease as "parrot miasma" (*yingwu zhang*).

10   Read, *Avian Drugs*, no. 307B, mistakenly calls this bird *niaofeng* rather than *wufeng* and identifies it as *Psittacula longicauda* (the "long-tailed parakeet"). Read also notes that it comes from the "caves in the hills of Kwangsi (Guangxi) along the Yu Kiang (Youjiang) and Tso Kiang (Zuojiang) rivers, where it is hard to catch them." Yang Wuquan, *LWDD*, 9.369–70, n. 1, identifies the bird as *Paradisea sexsetacea*, or "golden bird of paradise," but does not cite a source for this identification. *Hu-Tan*, 81, note, suspects *wufeng* is the same as the *daijian niao* (*Cuculus paradiseus*, or greater racket-tailed drongo) described in Liu Xun, *Lingbiao luyi*, 2.13. In the final analysis, no one has convincingly identified the *wufeng*.

11   Yang Wuquan, *LWDD*, 9.370, n. 1, identifies the *Qin jiliao* (lit., "the good fortune

They are deep purple and black in color. The beak is vermilion; the legs are yellow. From below the eyes to the nape of the neck, there are dark yellow stripes. The nape feathers are parted, resembling the way humans part their hair. They are capable of human speech and, compared with a parrot, much cleverer. For the most part, the voice of a parrot sounds like that of a child. But the voice of the hill mynah is like that of a full-grown man. It comes out of the Creek Settlements in Yong County. According to the *Tang History* [Tangshu]: "Linyi produces the *jieliao* bird [*jieliao niao*]."[12] Linyi is today's Champa.[13] It is some distance from Yong and Qin Counties but is adjacent to Jiaozhi. I suspect this bird is in fact the hill mynah.

DAMASK PHEASANT [*JINJI*] is also named the golden pheasant [*jinji*].[14] In shape it resembles a small pheasant [*xiaozhi*]. It is also found in Hunan and Hubei.

MOUNTAIN PHOENIX [*SHAN FENGHUANG*][15] in shape resembles a

---

bird of Qin" [Shaanxi]) as the hill mynah or India hill mynah (*Gracula religiosa intermedia*), also known as *liaoge*. Schafer, *Vermilion Bird*, 244, concurs that this bird is the hill mynah and notes that "it is the best of all speaking birds." For additional information on the hill mynah in China see Roderich Ptak's useful article "Notizen Zum Qinjiliao Oder Beo (Gracula Religiosa) In Alten Chinesischen Texten (Tang-Bis Mittlere Ming-Zeit)," *Monumenta Serica* 55 (2007): 447–69.

12   Fan Chengda's reference here is to a comment in the *Jiu Tangshu*, 197.5270: "[The Kingdom of Linyi] has a *jieliao* bird that is capable of understanding human speech."

13   Champa (Zhancheng) and Linyi are names of ancient non-Chinese states that were located in what is now Vietnam. On Linyi and Champa, see the "Treatise on the Man," chapter 13 of this book, notes 198 and 214.

14   The bird described in this entry is *Chrysolophus pictus*, usually called the "golden pheasant" in English. Read, *Avian Drugs*, no. 271. It is also known as *bizhi* or *biezhi*. The multicolored plumage on its breast was said to be as bright as a peacock. See BCGM, 48.2617 (*Compendium*, 6:48.3783–84).

15   As noted by Yang Wuquan, LWDD, 9.366–67, n. 1, Fan Chengda's "mountain phoenix" is probably some variety of hornbill, perhaps the Malabar pied hornbill (*Anthracoceros coronatus*) (fig. 8). During incubation, the female lays her eggs in a tree cavity, which is then sealed with a compound of mud, droppings, and fruit pulp. There is only one small opening, just big enough for the male to transfer food to the mother and chicks. When the chicks and the female are too big to fit in the nest, the mother breaks out and rebuilds the wall, then both parents feed the chicks. My source for this information is http://wikipedia.org/wiki/Malabar_Pied_ Hornbill (accessed 7 September 2008). As for the practice of suf-

goose [*eyan*] and has a beak that resembles that of a phoenix. They nest deep in the woods along the Two Rivers. When it is time to lay eggs, the male uses tree branches mixed with peach-tree sap [*taojiao*] to seal the nest, where the female remains alone at its single opening. The male flies off to search for food to nourish the chicks. When the chicks have matured, they immediately leave the sealed nest. If they do not mature, then the nest opening is plugged up, and the chicks are suffocated to death. This is indeed a strange creature, but I myself have never seen one.

REVERSE FEATHERS FOWL [*FANMAO JI*] have wings and tail feathers that grow in reverse direction and are curved and crooked, facing the outside. They are especially tame and friendly and do not run off and scatter. They are found in both Guangs.

LONG-CROWING FOWL [*CHANGMING JI*][16] are of greater height and size than common fowl. Their crowing lasts for a very long time, wailing and howling all day long without ever stopping. They are native to the Creek Settlements in Yong County.

HALCYON KINGFISHERS [*FEICUI*][17] come out of Hainan and Yong and He Counties. There are also people who dry their flesh and sell it.

GRAY CRANES [*HUIHE*][18] are as big as [normal] cranes [*he*]. The entire body is a gloomy gray color. The feathers begin to turn cinnabar red about two *cun* down from the top of the head, and this

---

focating the chicks if they do not mature properly (see text below), I have not been able to confirm that the Malabar pied hornbill engages in such a practice.

16   The precise identity of the long-crowing fowl is unknown. *LWDD*, 9.380 (*Netolitzky*, 9.35), however, says they come from Nanzhao and are worth one *liang* of silver.

17   The Chinese term *feicui* refers specifically to the white-throated kingfisher (*Halcyon smyrnensis fokiensis*) distributed throughout south and east China, Hainan, and Taiwan (fig. 9). Halcyon kingfishers were especially well known for their brilliant blue plumage, which since the Zhou dynasty was used to embellish clothing. As far as I know, only southerners preserved halcyon kingfisher flesh and ate it (see text below). For more information on the *feicui* in China, see Schafer, *Vermilion Bird*, 238–39.

18   According to *Yan Pei*, 55, n. 19, *huihe* [gray crane] is another name for the redcrested crane (*hongding he*; *Grus japonensis*), also known as the Japanese crane or Manchurian crane. Adults have white primary feathers, while those of juveniles are grayish in color.

FIGURE 8
(*Left*) Malabar
Pied Hornbill
(*Anthracoceros
coronatus*). Photo
by Dave Behrens.

FIGURE 9
Halcyon King-
fisher. Photo by
Jan Sevcik.

extends halfway down the neck. They are also able to sing and dance.[19]

FRANCOLINS [*ZHEGU*][20] are as big as a bamboo partridge [*zhuji*][21] but a bit longer. Their heads resembles a quail [*chun*]; the patterns on their bodies are likewise [similar to a quail]. Only in the front of [or above] the breast there are white spots, perfectly round like a pearl. People [in the south] harvest and eat francolins.

WATER SPARROWS [*SHUIQUE*][22] are dark green in color, resembling a wagtail [*jiling*]. They fly about and congregate in the entrance halls

---

19 All cranes engage in some form of "dancing," which includes movements such as bowing, jumping, running, stick or grass tossing, and wing flapping. They also "sing" in the sense that mated pairs engage in unison calling, which is a complex and extended series of coordinated calls. The paired cranes stand in a specific posture, usually with their heads thrown back and beaks skyward during the display. For additional information on cranes in China, including some discussion of their dancing maneuvers, see Madeline K. Spring, "The Celebrated Cranes of Po Chü-i," *Journal of the American Oriental Society* 111.1 (Jan. 1991): 8–18.

20 The francolin (*Francolinus pitadeanus*) is a white-throat partridge that was common in south China. Read, *Avian Drugs*, no. 274. See also Schafer, *Vermilion Bird*, 240–41.

21 On the bamboo partridge (*Bambusicola thoracica*), see Read, *Avian Drugs*, no. 275.

22 The precise identity of this bird is unknown, so I have translated its name literally as "water sparrow."

of people's homes. As they flit to and fro, they form into ranks along with swallows and sparrows [*yanque*].[23]

Supplementary entry: **MAGIC FALCONS [*LINGHU*]**:[24] If their nesting [tree] cavities are blocked off [by humans], they can use the "Yu step" [Yu bu] method to remove the obstruction.[25]

---

23   Although *yanque* can refer to the brambling or bramble finch, here Fan Chengda seems to be using the term in a general sense to indicate small, common birds like the swallow (*yan*) and sparrow (*que*).

24   HSRC (67.53b) reads *lingque* (lit., "magic magpie"), but this should probably read *linghu* (lit., "magic falcon"). Cf. LWDD, 9.372 (*Netolitzky*, 9.29), which has an entry on the *linghu* bird (translated in note 25 below). I follow this reading. Fan Chengda and Zhou Qufei are referring to some type of woodpecker or falconlike bird, the precise identity of which is unclear. Yang Wuquan, LWDD, 9.373, n. 1, argues that *linghu* refers to the Eurasian kestrel (*Falco tinnunculus interstinctus*), a member of the falcon genus.

25   HSRC, 67.53b; FCDBJ, 105. The remnants of this cryptic and largely unintelligible entry require some explanation. The LWDD entry (9.372; *Netolitzky*, 9.29) on the *linghu* offers more details:

> In Yong county there is a bird called the magic falcon. In shape it resembles a woodpecker [*zhuomu*], but is a bit larger. It nests in tree cavities, where it raises its young. People [sometimes] take a piece of wood and block off entrance to its [nest] cavity. When the falcon arrives back [at the nest] and has no way to get in, it will alight on the ground and pace about with a limp [use the "Yu step"]. After a short while the falcon will dart to where the nest cavity is sealed off, whereupon it will be able to enter it. After this happens, people spread some ashes on the ground and [again] seal off the nest, for they desire to observe the bird's tracks and retrace them [to see how it was able to enter the nest cavity]. When the falcon has finished with its pacing, it immediately uses its talon to erase its tracks and then reenters the [sealed nest] cavity. People desire to retrace the falcon's steps, but there is no way for them to do so.

> So, presumably the *linghu* is "magical" (*ling*) in that it has the skill to dematerialize (*yinshen shu*) and get into its nest cavity even when the entrance is sealed off with a piece of wood. According to popular thinking, the key to unlocking this mystery lies in how the bird paces on the ground before "magically" entering the nest. Aware of this, the *linghu* bird thus "paces about with a limp" to cover its tracks so the "secret" will not be revealed to humans. A variation of this folktale is provided by Shao Bo in his *Shaoshi Wenjian houlu*, 29.228. In this version, however, secret markings (*fu*) scratched out by a woodpecker's beak cause the obstruction across the nest cavity to "open up of its own accord."

7

QUADRUPEDS

(*Zhi shou*)

AMONG QUADRUPEDS, NONE IS MORE MASSIVE THAN THE elephant; none more useful than the horse. Both are well suited to the southlands [*nantu*]. I served as director of the Horse Administration [Mazheng][1] and was very much involved in making up for

1   The main government procurement sites for horses during the Southern Song were in Guangxi and Yunnan. Most of the mounts purchased there came from non-Chinese states along or beyond the border. The Chinese government apparatus charged with buying horses was called the Horse Administration (Mazheng). In Guangxi the government official who supervised these activities initially was the inspector for supervising horse purchases (*tiju maima si*), who from 1133 was based in Yong County. In 1136, however, this responsibility shifted to the command-inspector of Guangxi. *Songshi*, 198.4956. Thus, during his term as command-inspector of Guangxi, Fan Chengda was directly responsible for horse procurement. For a useful overview of the Horse Administration in Guangxi during the Southern Song, see *LWDD*, 5.186–87 (*Netolitzky*, 5.3), and Lin Ruihan, "Songdai bianjun zhi mashi ji ma zhi gangyun," esp. 130. For a more detailed treatment of the entire Horse Administration system under the Southern Song see Jin Baoxiang, "Nan Song mazheng kao," 321–30, and especially Okada, *Zhongguo Hua'nan minzu shehui shi*, 166–245. The most thorough study of the Horse Administration during the Song dynasty in English is Paul J. Smith's *Taxing Heaven's Storehouse: Horses, Bureaucrats, and the Destruction of the Sichuan Tea Industry, 1074–1224* (Cambridge: Council on East Asian Studies, Harvard University Press, 1991).

shortages and deficiencies [*buju louxi*].[2] There is much to be said [about the Horse Administration], but this would be much too involved, and it is not something I can describe [here]. For now, I will just write down some general information [about the Horse Administration] as well as some information about rearing animals that is somewhat different [than in the north]. These are combined into this one chapter.

ELEPHANTS [*XIANG*] come out of the mountain valleys of Jiaozhi.[3] Only the males have two tusks. Buddhist texts mention "four tusk" and "six tusk" varieties,[4] but today such elephants do not exist.

---

2   Fan Chengda was so dissatisfied with the Song horse procurement system in Guangxi that he submitted at least two memorials concerning its various maladies. A portion of one of these memorials survives in HSRC, 67.17a–b. Local officials and horse procurement officers would first use inferior quality horses to establish a fixed market price, then use this fixed price later to buy better quality mounts; these horses would then be resold to the Song at a much higher price. Furthermore, there was no suitable grazing area at the main horse market at the Hengshan Stockade (Hengshan Zhai), and many horses sustained injuries because of the poor roads (many of which had no bridges) they had to traverse on their way to Hengshan. Finally, the horses provided by the Man were of small stature (Fan argued in favor of purchasing mounts no lower than four *chi*, three *cun* in height). For additional information on the problems of procuring horses in Guangxi during the Southern Song, see the comments in *Yan Pei*, 58, n. 1, *Hu-Tan*, 88–90, n. 3, and Okada, *Zhongguo Hua'nan minzu shehui shi*, esp. 236–38. Fan Chengda provides additional information about the horse market at the Hengshan Stockade below.

3   During the Shang dynasty (ca. 2100–ca. 1028 B.C.E.) elephants were common in China's Yellow River valley. Over time, however, deforestation resulting from population increase forced the great beasts to retreat farther and farther south. In the twelfth century wild elephants were still found in Guangdong and Guangxi (Fan mentions this below) and in most, if not all, of the many kingdoms bordering China in the south and southwest. For more information on elephants in China, especially during the pre-Song period, see Bertold Laufer, *Ivory in China* (Chicago: Field Museum of Natural History, 1925), and Schafer, *The Golden Peaches of Samarkand*, 79–83. Laufer mentions that ivory from Annan (or Jiaozhi) is "small and short, and a kind yielding a red powder when cut by a saw was regarded as very excellent" (15). Marks estimates that "by the fifteenth century, elephants had become extinct in Lingnan." See his *Tigers, Rice, Silk, and Silt*, 45. See also Mark Elvin, *The Retreat of the Elephants: An Environmental History* (New Haven: Yale University Press, 2004), especially the chapter "Humans v. Elephants: The Three Thousand Year War," 9–18.

4   Schafer, *The Golden Peaches of Samarkand*, 81, mentions a "four-tusked white elephant" that lived in an unidentified place called Kaga. Six-tusked white

Supplementary text: Elephants come out of Elephant Mountain [Xiangshan][5] in Jiaozhi. The strength of an elephant's entire body is concentrated in its trunk. There are also wild elephants in the Two Guangs. They steal liquor and harm crops, their eyes are tiny, and they fear fire. People in Qin County use a trap[6] to catch them. The hide can be used to make armor [*jia*]. Sometimes the hide is cut into strips to make staffs, which are very sturdy.[7]

Supplementary text: An elephant's head cannot be lowered; its neck cannot turn about. The mouth is hidden in its chin, far from the ground, and it makes use of its trunk [for support] as it moves about. The strength of an elephant's entire body is concentrated in its trunk. When it is about to walk, it first places its trunk on the ground for support and then moves its feet, aware that the strength of its feet is inferior to that of its trunk. The end of the trunk is much tapered and can pick up objects by opening and closing. In the middle of the trunk there is a thin lining of flesh. The trunk can even pick up small or tiny objects. When an elephant picks up food with its trunk, only after its toes knock away the dirt and grime will it curl the trunk so as to place the food into its mouth. When drinking water, it also uses the trunk to suck in the water and curl it into its mouth. The feet resemble columns; they have no toenails. But they do have toes, five in number, which resemble large chestnuts. When climbing lofty mountains, descending steep mountain slopes, or wading through deep rivers, elephants appear to be obese and clumsy, but

---

elephants are common in Buddhist art and textual sources, there representing one of the innumerable previous incarnations of the Buddha. See Lao Kan, "Six-Tusked Elephants on a Han Bas-Relief," *Harvard Journal of Asiatic Studies*, 17.3–4 (Dec. 1954): 366–69. The six tusks in this context also stand for the six pāramitās (*liuzhou* or *liudu*), which can ferry humans beyond the bank of mortality. Sometimes six-tusked elephants are also associated with a particular bodhisattva. For instance, when the Southern Song official Wang Zhiwang visited Mount Emei in Sichuan in the mid-twelfth century, he composed a poem that describes the mountain's resident bodhisattva—Samantabhadra (Puxian)—as riding "a six-tusked white elephant." Wang's poem is translated and discussed in my *Stairway to Heaven*, 120–23.

5   On Elephant Mountain, see below.

6   For more details on the elephant trap mentioned here, see the text below.

7   *HSRC*, 67.53b; *FCDBJ*, 108.

they are very nimble. The place in Jiaozhi that elephants come from is called Elephant Mountain.[8] They are hunted there once a year. The mountain has a stone chamber,[9] through which there is only one passageway, with stone walls all around. First, some hay and beans are placed inside the chamber. A single tame female elephant is then driven inside it. Sugarcane [*ganzhe*] is spread along the passageway so as to attract the wild elephants. When they approach to eat the sugarcane, hunters then release the tame female into the herd of wild elephants, which attracts the wild elephants to return with her into the stone chamber. They then follow her to the entrance of the huge stone chamber.[10] When the elephants start craving more food, the hunters line the stone chamber with fodder [*si*] for the tame female. The wild elephants observe that the female is able to eat it and, feeling at ease, follow along seeking the fodder. When they become more at ease they are whipped [into submission]. In a short time they become tame, and one can ride and control them. After a long time they gradually begin to understand human commands. They are also given names. When you call them by name, they respond. As for their keepers, they are referred to as "mahouts" [*xiangnu*]. They also go by the name "elephant masters" [*xianggong*]. As a general rule, one must use a hook to control an elephant. The mahout sits upright [on the elephant], straddling its neck. He uses an iron hook around its head. If he wants it to turn left, the hook is pulled to the right of the head; if he wants it to turn right, then the hook is pulled to the left. If he wants it to step

---

8   According to Zhu Mu, comp., *Fangyu shenglan*, 40.719, Elephant Mountain was in Xiang County (Xiangzhou; modern Xiangzhou *xian*, Guangxi); specifically, five *li* west of Yangshou Town (Yangshou *xian*). The Xiangzhou to which Fan Chengda is referring, however, was in Jiaozhi (or Annan). Its precise location is unknown. See also LWDD, 1.32 (*Netolitzky*, 1.16), which includes an entry on Elephant Mountain but provides no information on hunting activities there, saying only that cloud formations shaped like a white elephant sometimes appear at the mountain.

9   The term *shishi* (stone chamber) refers to a naturally formed cave with square walls and ceiling.

10 LWDD, 9.345–46 (*Netolitzky*, 9.1), follows Fan's description of elephant hunting in Jiaozhi almost verbatim. This line, however, reads as follows: "After [the wild elephants] enter [the stone chamber], the hunters then seal off the entranceway with a huge boulder."

backward, then he pulls the hook over its forehead. If he wants it to go forward, he does not pull on the hook. If he wants it to kneel and crouch, he uses the hook to press directly down on its brain [or forehead]. If he presses down to the point where it is painful, the elephant will scream and cry out. When people remark that there are elephants that can speak and respond, this is what they are talking about. When elephants are arranged neatly in files, all have a hook to control their movement forward and backward, left and right. Although in size they are huge, elephants cannot bear pain. Thus, humans can tame them with a hook only a few inches in length. As for those who have been tame a long time, when the mahout approaches, the elephant lowers its head and kneels on its front left knee. When a human steps up to mount them, elephants get excited and eager to set out on the journey. In their comings and goings most Man chieftains ride elephants. As for those elephants presented as tribute to China, on their backs are constructed saddles bearing an imperial throne. Such elephants are known as Luowo elephants [*luowo xiang*].[11] On their foreheads are arranged golden bells, several tens in number, so when they walk they make a tinkling-jingling sound. When a native of Jiaozhi commits a heinous crime, he is lain prone on the ground and trampled to death by an elephant. There are also wild elephants in the Two Guangs. When village commoners brew wine, elephants will approach, following the smell of the wine, and even knock down walls to get a drink. People suffer a lot from elephants because wherever they pass by, they trample crops. Their eyes are tiny, and they fear fire. They do not fear humans. If one unexpectedly encounters an elephant, he uses a long bamboo pole lit like a torch to fend it off. Invariably, the elephant will retreat. Although there are many elephant herds, they are not fearsome; only rogue elephants are to be feared. Presumably, their forceful and vicious behavior is not tolerated by the herd. When roaming alone, the rogue elephant has no prohibitions whatsoever. When it encounters someone it thinks will wantonly do it harm, it will roll

---

11   The precise origin and meaning of the term *luowo* is unclear. It could be a local (Guangxi) term of non-Chinese origin. Elsewhere Fan Chengda mentions that a *luowo* "resembles a saddle frame" and was used to ride an elephant. See the supplementary entry on Annan in the "Treatise on the Man," chapter 13.

that person in its trunk, throw him to his death, trample him until his blood flows, and then drink it. Natives of Qin County are able to catch [wild] elephants. As the elephants move along [trails], they set off a trigger; rapiers then shoot down from above and hit them.[12] Elephants that are pierced by the rapiers in vital body parts are sure to die. Just before they die, elephants [intentionally] break their tusks against some rocks, knowing their demise is due only to their tusks.[13] The taking of tusks is regarded as decimation of the elephant's body. If the vital parts are not harmed, they are then carried away on rapiers slung over the hunters' shoulders. If the flesh festers, it is cut away with a rapier. If the elephant's trunk is injured, it will also die. This is because when the trunk is injured, the resulting wound cannot heal. Thus, this also leads to death.[14] The flesh of just one slaughtered elephant can feed an entire village. The flesh of the trunk is the most delicious. Distiller's grains [*zao*] are added when it is cooked. When the distiller's grains permeate the sliced flesh, it is eaten. Elephant hide can be used to make armor. Sometimes it is cut into strips and then hung up until it dries. It is then made[15] into a walking stick, which is very sturdy.[16]

 Supplementary entry: **HORSES [MA]**[17] [come] from the Kingdom of

---

12 The trap described here worked as follows: hunters placed a concealed spring trigger device (*ji*) on the ground and connected it to rapiers (or double-edged swords; *ren*) hung on a tree above. When an elephant walked by, it set off the trigger, sending down the rapiers from above. This hunting technique is also described in *LWDD*, 9.346 (*Netolitzky*, 9.1).

13 Elephants are highly intelligent mammals well known for engaging in various types of social behavior, such as expressing grief, compassion, and even self-awareness. The idea in this line is that the elephants themselves are aware that they are being killed only for their ivory. Thus, before they die, the beasts will destroy their tusks to thwart the hunters' intentions.

14 Cf. *LWDD*, 9.346 (*Netolitzky*, 9.1): "Presumably, in its daily work the elephant uses only its trunk. If the trunk is injured, the wound will not heal. This can lead to death."

15 Reading *zhi* 治 in this line as a variant of *zhi* 製 (to make; to design).

16 Zhu Mu, comp., *Shiwen leiju: houji* [*SKQS* ed.], 36.12b–14b; Wang Sen, ed., *Yuexi congzai*, 22.10a–11a.

17 Since Fan Chengda in his introduction to this chapter first mentions elephants and horses, it seems logical to insert this "lost" entry on horses, preserved in *Mr. Huang's Daily Transcriptions*, at this point in the text.

Ziqi:[18] one bolt of damask [*jin*] will get you three Dali horses; a gold bracelet [*jinzhuo*] weighing one *liang* will get you two horses. The horses are driven thirteen stages [*cheng*] to Sicheng County[19] and then driven an additional six stages to Yong County. There is also the Kingdom of Luodian [Luodian Guo],[20] as well as the villages of the Xiefan and Luokong, whose horses are especially strong. These are driven twenty-two stages to Sicheng County, where they are herded together with horses from Ziqi and other places. They all come in the tenth month. The managing and organizing inspector [*jinglüe si*] annually deals out 1,500 bolts [of damask to purchase horses]. Especially fast horses get several tens of *liang* in gold. Government prices are set at a fixed rate and cannot be increased. Dali is just forty-some stages from the Hengshan Stockade[21] in Yong County. People [horse traders] from

---

18   Ziqi was a small but powerful state that came to prominence in the twelfth century because of its influential position in the horse trade with the Song. As noted here by Fan Chengda, however, the horses that Ziqi sold to the Song were not from Ziqi but rather from nearby Dali. There are various scholarly opinions about the location of Ziqi. *Hu-Tan*, 91, n. 1, says it was south or southeast of modern Kunming, Yunnan. Yang Wuquan marks it along the border of southwestern Guizhou and the southeastern part of Yunnan. *Yan Pei*, 59, n. 5, also favors a Guizhou location. According to Tan Qixiang et al., eds., *Zhongguo lishi ditu ji*, 6:65–66, the geographic center of Ziqi was near what is now Guangyi *xian*, Guizhou. For additional information about Ziqi and its role in the horse trade, see below.

19   Sicheng County (Sicheng *zhou*) corresponds to modern Lingyun *xian*, Guangxi.

20   Chinese contact with Luodian extends back to the Huichang reign (841–847) of the Tang, when the military leader of that state was established (by the Tang) as the "King of Luodian" (Luodian Wang). See *Xin Tangshu*, 222xia.6319. The territory of Luodian was situated in the western part of modern Guizhou.

21   The Song dynasty regarded its relations with the various independent states (such as Dali, Ziqi, and Luodian) and semi-independent tribes in the southwest (such as the Xiefan and Luokong) as important for several reasons. First, Dali provided virtually all the horses the Song purchased in the south. Second, in light of the volatile and threatening military situation along China's northern borders (throughout the entire Song period), it was essential for the southern flank of the empire to be secure. This became very evident in the 1040s when a local rebellion led by a Man chieftain named Nong Zhigao (Vietnamese: Nùng Trí Cao; for additional details on Nong and his uprising, see the "Treatise on the Man") threatened Song control of the south. One tactic used by the Song to ensure military and administrative-political control of Guangxi (and other

Ziqi [are always] scrambling to make a profit but do not dare ford the river from Ziqi [into Dali]. There is an alternate route in the east from Shanchan Municipality[22] through Temodao,[23] which is very fast. Since the people of Temodao[24] are also ravenous and rapacious, travelers cannot get through [Temodao to their destination].[25]

MAN HORSES [*MANMA*] come from the various foreign peoples in the southwest. Most come from the kingdoms of Pina,[26] Ziqi, and the like. Ziqi obtains horses from Dali, which is the ancient Nanzhao. Its territory extends to the Western Rong. The horses are especially wild when they are born. Dali horses constitute the very best among foreign horses in the southwest.[27]

---

areas such as Shaanxi) was the creation of *zhai* or *zhaibao*, which I translate as "stockades." These installations were strategically placed near the bridle and halter areas so as to allow the Song to keep a watchful eye on Man activities nearby. In the event of local unrest, troops were available at the stockade. The most important stockade in Guangxi in the 1170s was the Hengshan Stockade, located on the northern bank of the Right River in what is now Tiandong *xian*, Guangxi. This would put it 520 *li* southeast of Yong County, under whose administrative control it fell. During the Southern Song the Hengshan Stockade served as a key hub for economic and government contact between the Song and various non-Chinese tribes in the southwest. According to Huang Kuanchong's informative essay "Nan Song shidai Yongzhou de Hengshan zhai," 5, the Hengshan Stockade held jurisdiction over eighteen bridle and halter counties along the Right River.

22 Shanchan Municipality (Shanchan *fu* in Dali) corresponds to modern Kunming.

23 Temodao was located in the eastern part of what is now known as the Wenshan Zhuang and Miao's People's Self-Autonomous Prefecture in southeastern Yunnan. During the Ming and Qing periods this administrative area was known as Guangnan Municipality (Guangnan *fu*).

24 The text reads Shimo 時磨, but there was no kingdom or state named "Shimo" in the Guangxi-Yunnan region during the Song or any other period in Chinese history. It seems almost certain that Shimo here is a corruption of Temodao (see n. 23), and I have followed this reading.

25 *HSRC*, 67.53b–54a; *FCDBJ*, 108–9.

26 The location of Pina is unknown.

27 Here I follow *Hu-Tan*, 91, note, and regard this last line as part of the entry on Man horses (rather than as a separate entry). Horses from Dali (or Yunnan) were well known for their strength, stamina, sure-footedness, quickness, and agility and, as mentioned here by Fan Chengda, were regarded as superior to other "foreign" mounts. This explains why the Southern Song government was eager to purchase horses from Dali.

BELOW-THE-FRUIT-TREE HORSES [*GUOXIA MA*] are a local product in the form of a miniature carriage horse.[28] The best ones come out of Longshui Town in Deqing Municipality.[29] In height they do not exceed three *chi*. The fastest ones have two backbones. Thus, they are also known as double-backbone horses [*shuangji ma*].[30] They are vigorous and skilled at galloping.[31]

Supplementary text: In height below-the-fruit-tree horses do not exceed three *chi*, but they are fast and vigorous and have great endurance. Each year on the fifteenth day of the seventh month, they are assembled on the banks of the river[32] for exchange and trade. Shaoyang,[33] Yingdao,[34] and such places in Hunan also produce a variety of diminutive horse [*dima*].[35]

GIBBONS [*YUAN*] come in three varieties: "golden hairs," which are yellow; "jadelike faces," which are black; and "pure blackies," the faces of which are also black.[36] The golden hair and jade-face varieties are

---

28   *Guoxia,* or "under the fruit tree," is a term used to describe horses or oxen that are extremely small in stature, thus allowing riders to pass below the branches of a fruit tree. See Read, *Animal Drugs,* no. 326. On dwarf oxen in China, see Schafer, *The Golden Peaches of Samarkand,* 73. LWDD, 9.351 (Netolitzky, 9.5), provides additional information on these rare "dwarf horses" (*aima*), as they were sometimes called. Schafer says the name *guoxia* must originally have been a word "from some northeastern language, whose meaning was forgotten and then rationalized by the Chinese" (68).

29   Deqing Municipality was located in the area around modern Duanxi *xian,* Guangdong. Longshui Town (Longshui *xian*) was south of there, between modern Luoding *xian* and Yangchun *xian.*

30   Schafer, *The Golden Peaches of Samarkand,* 297, n. 115, speculates that these double-backbone ponies might have a partial Arab origin.

31   Following *Qi Zhiping,* 19, n. 4, and reading *shanxing* 善行 (skilled at galloping) rather than *xixing* 喜行.

32   The river mentioned here is not further identified.

33   Shaoyang was a town under the jurisdiction of Shao County (Shaozhou), which corresponds to modern Shaoyang *shi,* Hunan.

34   During the Song dynasty Yingdao Town (modern Dao *xian,* Hunan) fell under the jurisdiction of Dao County (Daozhou).

35   HSRC, 67.54a–b; FCDBJ, 109.

36   Gibbons are classified under the *Hylobates* genus, which includes many species. Van Gulick is unsure about the identity of the three types of gibbon mentioned in this entry. See *The Gibbon in China,* 90. Yang Wuquan, LWDD, 9.353, n. 1, identifies them respectively as *Hylobates hoolock* (white-cheeked gibbon), *Hylobates concolor* (crested gibbon), and *Hylobates lar* (white-handed gibbon).

both difficult to find. Some say the pure blackies are male, while the golden hairs are female. It is also said that the male can whistle, while the female cannot. Gibbons by nature are not able to endure touching the ground. If they touch the ground, without fail they will develop diarrhea and die. But if one brews a concoction of monkshood juice [*fuzi zhi*][37] and has them drink it, gibbons will immediately recover.[38]

MAN DOGS [*MANQUAN*] resemble hunting dogs. They stand guard and are ferocious.[39]

YULIN DOGS [*YULIN QUAN*][40] come out of Yulin County.[41] They are extremely large in size, their ears droop down, and the tail is curled. They are different from ordinary dogs.

DAPPLED SHEEP [*HUAYANG*]: In the south there are no white sheep. Most are yellowish brown with white spots, resembling oxen [*huang-niu*]. Another variety that is dark brown with a black back and white spots looks exactly like a deer [*lu*].[42]

MILK GOATS [*RUYANG*] originally came out of Ying County.[43] That area produces fairy floss-grass [*xianmao*].[44] After the goats eat the

---

For additional information on gibbons, see *LWDD*, 9.352 (Netolitzky, 9.7).

37   Presumably, "monkshood juice" was produced from an extract of the root of the *fuzi* plant, for which see the "Treatise on Aromatics" and figure 5.

38   Fan Chengda's entry on the gibbon is also translated and discussed in van Gulick, *The Gibbon in China*, 90.

39   According to the *Guilin junzhi*, cited in *Yan Pei*, 61, n. 12, when Man peoples brought horses to sell at the Hengshan Stockade, they used Man dogs as guards, with the result that "no thief would ever dare to approach."

40   Although Yulin dogs are native to Yulin County, they are common throughout Guangxi and Yunnan.

41   Yulin County corresponds to the area around modern Yulin and Bobai *xian*, Guangxi.

42   In this entry Fan Chengda is not referring to any particular species of sheep but is speaking in general terms about wild sheep in Guangxi. Zhou Qufei also includes an entry on "dappled sheep" and mentions that they could be "seen off in the distance in mountain valleys." Zhou also says *huayang* were "true deer" (*zhenlu*). *LWDD*, 9.358 (Netolitzky, 9.12).

43   Ying County was part of the Guangnan East Circuit, located in the general area around modern Yingde *xian*, Guangdong.

44   "Fairy floss-grass" is actually an herb (common *Curculigo*) native to the western regions of China, whose thick stem and root are used in Chinese medicine. Read, *Animal Drugs*, no. 324, says milk goats live on *Curculigo ensifolia* and are very fat, and that the flesh of these animals is "very tender and tasty." For addi-

grass, their bodies change completely into fat, and no longer do they have any flesh and blood.⁴⁵ Eating them is beneficial to humans.

COTTON SHEEP [*MIANYANG*]⁴⁶ come out of the Creek Settlements in Yong County and the various Man kingdoms [of the southwest]. They are no different from the Hu sheep [*huyang*] in Shuofang.⁴⁷

MUSK DEER [*SHEXIANG*]⁴⁸ that come from the Creek Settlements in Yong County go by the name local musk deer [*tushe*]. The odor [of their musk] is foul and intense, and inferior to that [from musk deer] of the Western Fan [Xifan].⁴⁹

CIVETS [*DALI*]⁵⁰ differ from other species of leopardlike cats [*li*].

---

tional information on fairy floss-grass, see BCGM, 12.752–53 (*Compendium*, 2:12.1336–39).

45   Cf. *Yan Pei*, 61, n. 16, which says that "fat" (*fang* 肪) in this line refers to the white-colored flesh of the milk goat. Zhou Hui, *Qingbo zazhi*, 3.125, has an entry about goats in Ying County that says their white color comes not from eating fairy floss-grass but rather from drinking the secretions produced by stalactites in caves. See also BCGM, 12.754 (*Compendium*, 2:12.1338), which quotes this line from *Treatises*. The translators of the *Compendium* render *fang* as "tendon" ("Sheep ["sheep" here should probably read "goats"] eat the herb, and develop plenty of *tendons* [italics mine] instead of flesh and muscle").

46   LWDD, 9.359 (*Netolitzky*, 9.13), provides the following additional information on *mianyang*, or cotton sheep: "They are black and white in color. Their hair resembles silk floss from a cocoon, is cut to make rugs, and is even superior to that produced in Shuofang [on Shuofang, see note 47 below]." Based on this description Yang Wuquan identifies *mianyang* here as the Angora sheep (*roumao yang*; *Capra angorensis*). See LWDD, 9.359, n. 1.

47   Shuofang is a Han dynasty name for a commandery established in 127 B.C.E., located in what is now Inner Mongolia. The government seat, Shuofang, was situated north of modern Hangjinqi.

48   Read, *Animal Drugs*, no. 369, identifies *shexiang* as *Moschus moschiferus*, which is commonly known as the Siberian musk deer. A more likely candidate is *Moschus berezovskii*, or Chinese forest musk deer. See BCGM, 51.2867 (*Compendium*, 6:51.4066–71). There is an entry on *shexiang* in LWDD, 9.363 (*Netolitzky*, 9.19).

49   The term "Western Fan" probably refers to the various non-Chinese tribes of Yunnan that gathered deer musk and traded it to the Chinese. See also Yang Wuquan's comments in LWDD, 9.364, n. 2, arguing that "west" here refers to the Qinghai-Tibetan Plateau region and Yunnan, the two areas that produced China's best musk aromatic. This reading is possible, but Fan Chengda's point here seems to be that deer musk from Yong County was inferior to that produced in other non-Chinese areas along the border.

50   There are differing opinions among the commentators regarding the precise

Yong County has its own separate variety. The color of its fur is like a gold-coin spotted leopard [*jinqian bao*],[51] only its gold-coin spots are greatly inferior. Someone said that after a civet reaches maturity it turns into a leopard [*bao*]. Its patterns indeed at first sight resemble those on a leopard.

WIND CATS [*FENGLI*][52] resemble the yellow gibbon [*huangyuan*][53] in shape and eat spiders [*zhizhu*]. During the day they curl up like a hedgehog. When it becomes windy, they then fly about in midair.

---

identity of this creature, which in all editions of *Treatises* is identified as *huoli* 火狸, or "fire fox." *Yan Pei*, 62, n. 22, says these creatures feed on insects, mice, and fruit, and are also known as *baoli*. Yang Wuquan, *LWDD*, 359, n. 1, argues that the character *huo* 火 in *huoli* is a scribal or printing error for *da* 大, leaving us with a creature named *dali* 大狸. Since Zhou Qufei's description of *dali* in *LWDD*, 9.359 (*Netolitzky*, 9.14), is based directly on Fan's entry, it seems almost certain that *huoli* in our text should instead read *dali*. This argument seems credible also because the characters *da* and *huo* are similar in appearance and thus could easily be confused. Moreover, with reference to animals and birds, *huo* usually indicates the color red, which is not mentioned at all by Fan Chengda. For these reasons I follow the *dali* reading. I strongly suspect that the mammal in question here is some kind of civet cat (*lingmao*). According to the *BCGM*, 51.2871 (*Compendium*, 6:51.4071–72), civet cats live in the mountain valleys of the south and "resemble the leopard." This same source (2871) also cites the following remark from Yang Shen's *Danqian zonglu*: "I once saw a kind of *xiangmao* like a leopard, covered with designs like a gold-coin leopard."

51   This creature is also known as the "guinea leopard" (*Lespardus japonicus*). Read, *Animal Drugs*, no. 352.

52   Yang Wuquan tentatively identifies this animal as a flying squirrel (*da wushu*; *Petanrista petanrista*). *LWDD*, 9.360–61, n. 1. Read, *Turtle and Shellfish Drugs*, no. 289, describes the flying squirrel of China, but nothing in his description resembles Fan Chengda's "wind cat." But then in his *Animal Drugs*, no. 373, Read specifically identifies the *fengli* or "wind cat" as the sloth monkey. Li Shizhen includes an entry on "wind cats" in the *BCGM* but does not identity the creature. His description in part reads: "It is as big as a leopard cat or otter. It looks like a monkey but is smaller. Its eyes are red and its tail is so short it looks like it has no tail. It is blue-green, yellow, and black. It has leopardlike designs. . . . Its urine looks like milk. It likes to eat spiders and frankincense. During the day, it curls up and stays as quiet as a hedgehog. At night, it jumps over cliffs and trees like a bird flying in the sky" (*BCGM*, 51.2877 [*Compendium*, 6:51.4080]).

53   Fan here is probably referring to the "golden hair" variety of gibbon mentioned above.

Their urine [*ni*] and milk [*ruzhi*] are used to treat leprosy [*dafeng*][54] and are amazingly effective.

LAZY WIVES [*LANFU*][55] resemble the wild porcupine [*shanzhu*][56] but are smaller. They are fond of eating grain. When farmers take the shuttle of a loom and hang it in the fields, the lazy wives will no longer approach.[57] They are found in Anping, Qiyuan, and such counties.[58]

WILD BOARS [*SHANZHU*] are in fact porcupines [*haozhu*].[59] Their bodies have prickly quills, which they can rouse to stick humans. Two or three hundred of them form into a pack[60] and thereby bring harm to grain crops. In the counties and settlements they cause much suffering.

VOLES [*SHISHU*][61] eat only wild bean roots [*shandou gen*].[62] People in Bin County take the stomach and dry it into powder, which is used to treat throat disorders. Its effect is like magic. This medicine is referred to as vole belly [*shishu du*].

MUSK MICE [*XIANGSHU*][63] are extremely small, only about as big as a

---

54   *Dafeng* here refers to *da mafeng* (also known as *mafeng bing*, or leprosy).

55   The name "lazy wife" stems from an old folktale with many variations. Essentially, the story goes that once there was a wife who worked as a weaver. Oftentimes she would doze off at her loom, whereupon her mother-in-law would beat her with the loom's shuttle. Eventually, the wife suffered a bitter death because of the beatings. *LWDD*, 9.364–65 (*Netolitzky*, 9.20), has additional information on the origin of this tale. The "lazy wife" described in this entry might refer to some small variety of wild boar. See also the comments on *lanfu* (lazy wife) in *BCGM*, 51.2892 (*Compendium*, 6:51.4027).

56   On the wild porcupine, see the entry on wild boars below.

57   Presumably, the "lazy wives" do not approach the fields out of fear of being "beaten" with the shuttle of the loom.

58   Anping County and Qiyuan County fell under the administrative jurisdiction of the Left River Circuit in Yong County. Both were located in the general area west of modern Daxin *xian*, Guangxi.

59   That is, the common porcupine (*Hystrix cristata*). Read, *Animal Drugs*, no. 360.

60   Following the *ZBZZCS* ed., 18b, and reading "two or three hundred."

61   My translation of *shishu* as "vole" is based on the comments in *BCGM*, 51.2908 (*Compendium*, 6:51.4115–16). Voles are rodents that resemble mice, but their bodies are stouter. They have a short, hairy tail, a slightly rounder head, and smaller ears and eyes.

62   Wild bean roots (*shandou gen*; *Sophora subprostrata*) are a common additive used in traditional Chinese medicinal preparations.

63   *Xiangshu* (lit., "musk mouse") is probably some type of musk-producing mole

thumb. They dig their holes into pillars and scurry along the ground in hurried fashion, as swiftly as arrows.

WILD OTTERS [*SHANTA*][64] come out of the Creek Settlements in Yi County. According to popular tradition, they serve as supplements for essential medicines. Residents of the settlements say that by nature the wild otter is lewd and malicious. Such creatures are found in the mountains. As a general rule, [other] female animals avoid them by running off. Otters do not take mates. They will embrace a tree [trunk] and die there.[65]

Lao people in the settlements especially honor and value the wild otter, saying it can provide an antidote for arrow poison.[66] As for persons hit by [poisonous] arrows, a small quantity of otter bone is ground up and applied to the wound, which immediately dispels the poison. One dose is worth a *liang* of gold. People sometimes try to find some to buy, but by the time it gets to the victim, the effect of the antidote is very minimal.

---

shrew (*yanqu*). See Yang Wuquan's comments in *LWDD*, 9.362, n. 1. The entry on *xiangshu* in *LWDD*, 9.362 (*Netolitzky*, 9.17), repeats Fan's entry almost verbatim and then adds: "Musk mice are especially numerous in government administration buildings."

64   Read, *Animal Drugs*, no. 383, identifies the *shanta* as the common Chinese river otter (*Lutra lutra chinensis*). Yang Wuquan, *LWDD*, 9.365, n. 1, says *shanta* is another name for the *hanta*, or marmot (*Marmota bobak*). BCGM, 51.2892 (*Compendium*, 6:51.4098), does not identify the *shanta* but only says the name literally means "mountain otter."

65   In other words, the *shanta* will embrace a tree trunk in a sexual way and remain there until it dies (*ku*; lit., "withers away").

66   BCGM, 51.2892 (*Compendium*, 6:51.4098), mentions that a powdery drug made from the penis of a *shanta* is useful in treating human impotence, while its pulverized bones can be used to detoxify arrow poison. See also the comments on *shanta* in Zhou Mi, *Qidong yeyu*, 20.372.

8

INSECTS AND FISHES
(Zhi chongyu)

A S FOR THE MINUTE CREATURES AMONG THE INSECTS AND fishes that extend all the way to the sea—how could one possibly calculate their extensive numbers? I will list only a minuscule number of those that, by chance, I have seen or heard about.

PEARLS [ZHU][1] come out of the sea in Hepu Town.[2] There is a place there, the Pearl Pool [Zhuchi],[3] where the coastal boat people [danhu][4]

TRANSLATOR's NOTE: The title of this treatise, which translates literally as "Insects and Fishes," does not do justice to the wide range of its contents. Here *chong* indicates insects, spiders, and reptiles, while *yu* refers to various aquatic creatures such as fish, amphibians, and crustaceans.

1   *Zhu* refers to *zhenzhu*, or true pearls, that is, pearls formed by bivalves (organisms comprised of two shells, such as oysters and mussels). Read, *Turtle and Shellfish Drugs*, no. 211. See also LWDD, 7.258–59 (*Netolitzky*, 7.14), much of which is repeated in ZFZ, 2.203–4 (*Chau Ju-kua*, 229–30).

2   The pearl fisheries of Hepu, located off the coast of Guangxi in modern Hepu *xian*, have existed since the Han dynasty. During the Tang, local government officials gathered the gems and shipped them to the capital. In Southern Song times Hepu Town (Hepu *xian*) fell under the jurisdiction of Lian County (Lianzhou). For a useful overview of the history of pearl harvesting in Hepu, see Schafer, "The Pearl Fisheries of Ho-p'u," 155–68.

3   Zhou Qufei's entry on the Pearl Pool in LWDD, 7.258 (*Netolitzky*, 7.14), includes additional information about pearl diving around Hepu.

4   Without citing his source, Wheatley says the pearl fisheries in the shallow

dive in the water to get them from oysters [*bang*]. Each year yields either a good or a bad harvest. When divers get a lot of them, this is referred to as a "pearl-ripening [harvest]" [*zhushu*].[5] Tradition has it that there is a place at the bottom of the sea that is as big [around] as a city wall. The oysters dwell therein. A scary creature guards it, and no one can get to them. Only when the oysters are broken into pieces and spread and sprawl outside [the city wall] can they be found and harvested.

Supplementary text: As for pearls, there is a pool in front of a solitary island in the sea at Hepu that is named Obstructed View Pool [Duanwang Chi]. When you gaze at the island, located several tens of *li* from shore, it resembles a single fist. The depth of the pool is possibly ten *zhang*. Around it on all four sides, there seems to be a city wall. When the oysters are abundant outside the city wall, they can then be harvested.[6] . . . Each time [the coastal boat people dive in the water] to search for clams, they take a long rope and heavy bamboo basket. Sometimes, when they encounter a ferocious fish or sea monster, they die.[7]

GIANT CLAMS [*CHEQU*][8] resemble large oysters. Mariners grind and shape their shells, making them into various kinds of playthings.

---

seas off Hepu were banned to Chinese divers throughout much of the Song, though the Dan people were allowed to continue their harvesting of pearls ("Geographical Notes on Some Commodities," 89). On the Dan, or coastal boat people, see the "Treatise on the Man."

5   LWDD, 7.259 (*Netolitzky*, 7.14), mentions that bumper crop years for pearls were rare, "less than one or two out of a hundred."

6   The characters *xiling* 細零 seem to be irrelevant in this line, so I have not attempted to translate them. See also LWDD, 7.259, which copies this line verbatim less the two characters *xiling*.

7   LWDD, 7.259 (*Netolitzky*, 7.14), mentions specifically that "among the dangerous fish in the sea none posed a greater threat to pearl divers than the *lasha*. Yang Wuquan, LWDD, 260, n. 2, identifies *lasha* as the great white shark (*Carcharodon carcharias*). Supplementary text from HSRC, 67.54b; FCDBJ, 111–12.

8   *Chequ* is *Tridaena gigas*, or giant sea clam. Read, *Turtle and Shellfish Drugs*, n. 230. According to Zhao Rukuo (cited in Wheatley, "Geographical Notes on Some Commodities," 91), the shells of this creature were imported into China from Jiaozhi and perhaps also from Persia. See ZFZ, 2.206–7 (*Chau Ju-kua*, 231–32). The entry on *chequ* in LWDD, 7.265 (*Netolitzky*, 7.18), offers additional information on the various uses of giant clam shells. On the possible non-Chinese origins of the term *chequ*, see Hirth and Rockhill, *Chau Ju-kua*, 231, note.

Supplementary text: Giant clams fall into the category of large oysters. Their shells can be made into lotus leaf cups [*heye bei*].[9]

PYTHONS [*RANSHE*][10] can be as big as pillars and match [a pillar] in length. Their gall bladders [*dan*] are used as an ingredient in medicine.[11] Southerners cure their skin and peel off the scales, and use it to make drum skins. Pythons usually go out and hunt deer for food.[12] Stockade soldiers [*zhaibing*] are skilled at catching them. Several soldiers, with their heads completely adorned with flowers,[13] hasten forward toward the python. Since pythons are fond of flowers, they will certainly halt to have a look. As the troops gradually come forward, eventually they will pat [the flowers on] their heads and call out "the young lady in red" [*hongniangzi*] [has arrived].[14] The python's head increasingly lowers, [then] remains still. Then a stout lad with a large knife lops off its head.[15] Everyone then scatters hastily and, from a distance, they watch the python. After a short time, the snake loses consciousness [but still] turns and thrashes about. From the flank small wooden spears are all drawn [by the troops]. With great thrusts

9   *HSRC*, 67.54b; *FCDBJ*, 112.

10 *BCGM*, 43.2397 (*Compendium*, 5:43.3535), identifies the *ranshe* as *Python molurus bivittatus*, known in English as the "Burmese python" or "boa." Yang Wuquan, *LWDD*, 385–86, n. 1, agrees with this identification. Liu Xun, *Lingbiao luyi*, 3.22, mentions that the larger varieties of *ranshe* can grow to a length of five or six *zhang*, with a girth of three to four *zhang*.

11 The bile (*danzhi*) of the python was used to concoct medicines to treat a wide variety of ailments, including eye swelling, abdominal pain, and ulcers of the external genitals. *BCGM*, 43.2398 (*Compendium*, 5:43.3536–37). See also Schafer, *Vermilion Bird*, 216–17.

12 Several sources note that pythons fed mainly on deer, which they reportedly swallowed whole. See, for instance, the remarks in Liu Xun, *Lingbiao luyi*, 3.22.

13 The idea here is that the soldiers have adorned their heads with flowers, pretending to be young women.

14 I understand this line to mean that the soldier-hunters, with the heads adorned with flowers like a woman, are pretending to be a potential "bride" (lit., "young lady in red") for the snake. Shao Bo, comp., *Shaoshi Wenjian houlu*, 29.228, also mentions that hunters in Guangxi would chant "young lady in red" to entice a python into a trap.

15 Several different methods were used to catch and kill pythons. See *LWDD*, 10.385 (*Netolitzky*, 10.1). See also Yang Wuquan's comments on 386, n. 2. The usual method was to stab them with bamboo or wooden skewers, or to stake them down alive. Schafer, *Vermilion Bird*, 217.

FIGURE 10
Hawksbill Turtle.
Photo courtesy of
www.commons.
wikimedia.org.

of force, the python is thereupon killed. Several tens of men carry it off on a pole. The snake's meat provides enough food to feed an entire village.

Supplementary text: Pythons are as big as pillars. They hunt musk deer [*zhanglu*][16] in the fields. Southerners adorn themselves with flowers and call out "sister-in-law"[17] or "young lady in red" to lure the python. Flowers are placed on the python's head.[18] When the python bows its head and becomes still, they kill it.[19]

HAWKSBILL TURTLES [*DUMAO*][20] in shape resemble the great sea turtle [*guiyuan*]. The plates on the carapace [back] number thirteen.

---

16 *Zhanglu* is a variety of musk deer, specifically, *Moschus chinloo.*

17 The character 姼 is pronounced *da* and means "the wife of one's younger brother" (*di*). Kong Fanli, *FCDBJ*, 112, n. 2, says he suspects that 姼 should instead be read *yao* 妖 (seductive; bewitching; alluring). Cf. *LWDD*, 10.385 (*Netolitzky*, 10.1), which gives a different character: *ta* 姼, which is defined as "elder sister" (*zi*).

18 Although in Fan Chengda's entry on the python it is the soldier-hunters who adorn themselves with flowers to attract the snake's attention, in the *LWDD* entry on pythons, the hunters place the flowers on the *snake's* head. See *LWDD*, 10.385 (*Netolitzky*, 10.1). This source also mentions that the hunters sing songs to the python which, when heard by the snake, cause it to become docile and lower its head.

19 *HSRC*, 67.54b; *FCDBJ*, 112.

20 The Chinese characters for the hawksbill turtle (*Eretmochelys imbricata*) (see fig. 10), given here as *dumao* 蝳蝐, are also written 玳瑁 and 瑇瑁 (both pronounced *daimao*). Read, *Turtle and Shellfish Drugs*, no. 202; see also *ZFZ*, 2.214 (*Chau Ju-kua*, 238).

Patterns of regularly alternating black and white stripes and irregular lines form the entire carapace. The side skirts,[21] serrated and jagged, are clenched like the teeth of a saw. They have no feet but do have four fins. The two fins in front are longer and shaped like a paddle. The two fins in back are considerably shorter. On the back sides [of the rear fins] are scales and shells. They use the four fins to move through the water. Mariners raise them in saltwater, nourishing them on small fish. Popular tradition says one must absolutely not eat them on *jiazi* and *gengshen* days. These are referred to as the "hawksbill turtle fasting days" [*dumao zhairi*]. Such nonsense is very ridiculous.

FIGURE 11

Centipede. Source: *Chongxiu Zhenghe jingshi zhenglei beiyong bencao*, 22.449.

Supplementary text: [The carapace] . . . is covered entirely with flowery patterns.[22]

CENTIPEDES [*WUGONG*][23] may be extremely large.

AZURE SNAILS [*QINGLUO*][24] in shape resemble paddy snails [*tianluo*].[25] They are as big as two fists. When you scrub and rub them clean, the coarse skin resembles a halcyon kingfisher color. They are carved and polished into wine cups.

PARROT SNAILS [*YINGWU LUO*][26] in shape resemble common snails

---

21   "Side skirts" (*bianqun*) here refers to the edges of the carapace.

22   HSRC, 67.55a; FCDBJ, 112.

23   BCGM, 42.2345 (*Compendium*, 5:42.3468), identifies *wugong* as the red-headed centipede (*Scolopendra subspinipes mutilans*) (fig. 11). It averages about eight inches in length and lives in an aquatic environment. For additional details see *Hu-Tan*, 107, note.

24   Read, *Turtle and Shellfish Drugs*, no. 236, identifies the *qingluo* as the azure snail and notes that "it is like the kingfisher in color."

25   *Tianluo* refers to river snails (*Cipangopaludina chinensis*), which thrive in rice paddies, lakes, and ponds. BCGM, 46.2547 (*Compendium*, 5:46.3706).

26   Both Read, *Turtle and Shellfish Drugs*, no. 236, note, and Schafer, *Vermilion Bird*, 208, identify the *yingwu luo* as "the pearly nautilus"—a cephalopod of the Indian and Pacific oceans having a spiral shell with pale pearly partitions. See also Zhou Qufei's remarks in LWDD, 6.204 (*Netolitzky*, 6.5).

[*woniu*].²⁷ Their shells are polished to reveal a brilliant color. They are also carved and polished into cups.

COWRY SHELLS [*BEIZI*]²⁸ are found everywhere along the seashore. The larger ones resemble a fist and have purple markings;²⁹ the smaller ones are about as big as the surface of a finger and are as white as jade.

Supplementary text: Not only have the generations not esteemed the common cowry, but people rarely gather them.³⁰

FOSSILIZED CRABS [*SHIXIE*]³¹ are native to Hainan. In shape they truly resemble a crab. It is said they are fossilized by froth from the sea. The reason this happens cannot be discerned. There are also fossilized shrimp,³² which fall into the same category [as fossil crabs].

DEMON BUTTERFLIES [*GUI JIADIE*]³³ are as big as a hand fan, with

---

27 *Woniu* are common helicoid land snails. Read, *Turtle and Shellfish Drugs*, no. 239.

28 Cowry (also spelled cowrie) shells are marine snails of the genus *Cypraea*. The shell itself is almost always smooth and more or less egg-shaped, with a long, narrow, slitlike opening. Almost all varieties have a porcelainlike shine, and many have colorful patterns. Although cowry was highly valued in remote antiquity and sometimes used as a form of currency, in twelfth-century China they were regarded as "the equivalent of clams and oysters." LWDD, 7.268 (*Netolitzky*, 7.20).

29 Fan Chengda's reference here may be the purple cowry (*zibei*; shell of *Erosaria caputerpentis*), described in BCGM, 46.2542 (*Compendium*, 5:46.3686), and Read, *Turtle and Shellfish Drugs*, no. 232. See also the comments in Schafer, *Vermilion Bird*, 208. LWDD, 7.268 (*Netolitzky*, 7.20), has an entry on "Large Cowries." Yang Wuquan identifies the "larger ones" as *Mauritia arabica* and the "smaller ones" as *Erosaria caputerpentis*.

30 HSRC, 67.55a; FCDBJ, 112.

31 *Compendium*, 2:10.1133 (BCGM, 10.622), identifies *shixie* as the fossil crab (*Fossilia brachyurae*). Read, *Turtle and Shellfish Drugs*, no. 214C, says the fossil crabs mentioned in the BCGM are fossilized *Macrophthalmus latreillii*. Cf. LWDD, 7.283, n. 1, which identifies them as Lithodes, or the king crab. See also Fan Chengda's entries on fossilized mei-trees and fossilized cypress trees in the "Treatise on Metals and Stones."

32 *Shixia* are also mentioned in LWDD, 7.282 (*Netolitzky*, 7.31), but few details are provided except that "in shape they resemble a shrimp."

33 The precise identity of *gui jiadie*, translated literally here as "demon butterflies," is unknown. See also the comments by Yang Wuquan in LWDD, 10.395, n. 1. The LWDD entry on *gui jiadie* (10.395; *Netolitzky*, 10.9) does mention, however, that the butterfly's wingspan reaches a diameter of six or seven *cun*, that it has a basic color of brown but with various other colors mixed in, and that it is dazzling in appearance.

four wings. They are fond of alighting on the branches of lichee trees.

BLACK BUTTERFLIES [*HEI JIADIE*][34] are as big as bats [*bianfu*], and metamorphose from tangerine grubs [*judu*]. Northerners sometimes call them arcane warrior cicadas [*xuanwu chan*].

BARBEL FISH [*JIAYU*][35] in shape resemble a small shad [*shiyu*].[36] They are very fatty, and their taste is extremely full and wonderful. They come out of Mount Huo [Huoshan] in Wu County.[37] People there use them to make fish condiment, which is sent as native produce to friends in far-off places.

Supplementary text: Barbel fish come out of the Bing Cave [Bingxue] below Mount Huo in Wu County.[38] . . . When frying them, one does not use oil. Some also come out of Bing Cave in Shu, which are similar [to these] in their plumpness.[39]

---

34 *LWDD*, 10.395 (*Netolitzky*, 10.9), includes an entry on black butterflies but essentially repeats what Fan Chengda says here. The black butterfly is otherwise unidentified.

35 The term *jiayu* is sometimes used in the general sense to mean "fine fish" or "beautiful fish." Here, however, the reference is to a small, carplike freshwater fish with fine scales similar to those on a trout, known to live in streams inside stalactite caves. *BCGM*, 44.2437 (*Compendium*, 5:44.3576-77). Western scholars often identify the *jiayu* as the barbel, a large, carplike fish of the *Barbus* genus. The barbel is well known in China. There is even a verse in the *Poetry Classic* (*Maoshi* no. 171) titled "In the South there are barbel" (Nan you jiayu). See *Maoshi zhengyi*, 9-4/150/418 (Legge, *The Chinese Classics*, 1:270). It is said to "have the body of a carp and the scales of a rudd." See also Read, *Fish Drugs*, no. 144, which renders *jiayu* as "char" and notes that char are said to reside in lakes situated in large, stalagmite caves; Knechtges, *Wen xuan*, 1:347, n. 70, which follows Read's "char" identification; and *LWDD*, 10.392, n. 1, which identifies *jiayu* as a variety of carp known as *Ptychidio jordani*.

36 *BCGM*, 44.2436 (*Compendium*, 5:44.3577), and Read, *Fish Drugs*, no. 143, identify *shiyu* as a Hilsa herring. This same fish is also known as the Reeves shad (*Macrura reevesii*).

37 Wu County corresponds to the area around modern Cangwu *xian*, Guangxi. Mount Huo stood just south of the county wall. *TPHYJ*, 164.10b–11a.

38 There were several caverns in China, many of them in Sichuan, known as Bing Caves. They were so called because the barbel in these caves supposedly would emerge in the streams flowing out of the cave in the third, or *bing*, month on the lunar calendar. See also Knechtges' note on a *bing* cave in Shaanxi in *Wen xuan*, 1:346, n. 70.

39 *HSRC*, 67.55a; *FCDBJ*, 112.

SHRIMP FISH [*XIAYU*][40] come out of the Li River. Their flesh is white and plentiful. The taste is like shrimp but lighter and more wonderful.

GOBY FISH [*ZHUYU*][41] come out of the Li River. In shape they resemble black carp [*qingyu*];[42] they taste like the mandarin fish [*guiyu*].[43] In the south, varieties of fish such as the common carp [*li*][44] and golden carp [*ji*][45] are both available, but the shrimp fish and goby fish are regarded as precious.

CELESTIAL SHRIMP [*TIANXIA*][46] in shape resemble large flying ants [*feiyi*]. After the autumn altar sacrifice [*qiushe*],[47] if there is wind and rain, then they swarm and descend into the rivers. They have small wings. People wait until they descend into the rivers and then gather them to make fish condiment.

---

40   "Shrimp fish" is not further identified. Cf. LWDD, 10.394 (*Netolitzky*, 10.8), which adds that the taste of shrimp fish is similar to that of freshwater shrimp (*xia*). See also Fan's comment about shrimp fish below.

41   Read, *Fish Drugs*, no. 134, citing T. Saiki et al., identifies the *zhuyu* as the goby, a fish similar to the black carp (see below) but "larger with fewer bones and spines." It is the color of bamboo, hence the literal name *zhuyu*, or "bamboo fish."

42   Read, *Fish Drugs*, no. 133. This is a common freshwater fish, especially plentiful in south China. It is often used to make fish condiment.

43   Read, *Fish Drugs*, no.150, identifies the *guiyu* as *Siniperca chuatsi*, a common fish in China that closely resembles a rock bass. It is generally known as the "Mandarin fish" but is also sometimes called the "Chinese perch."

44   Read, *Fish Drugs*, no.128. The common carp is *Cyprinus carpio*.

45   Read, *Fish Drugs*, no.146, identifies *jiyu* as the golden carp (*Cyprinus auratus*).

46   BCGM, 44.2478 (*Compendium*, 5:44.3624), identifies *tianxia* as a "kind of worm the size of a shrimp," which, after the day of the fall sacrifice, "descend into the rivers and change into shrimp." The entry on *tianxia* in LWDD, 10.398 (*Netolitzky*, 10.11), provides some additional description; Yang Wuquan cites explanations from various sources on the possible identity of *tianxia* (396–97, n. 1). Hu and Tan, suspect it is some variety of water beetle (*longshi*) (*Hu-Tan*, 112, note).

47   This fall sacrifice to the earth gods is usually carried out on the fifth day after the start of autumn on the lunar calendar.

9

FLOWERS
(Zhi hua)

UILIN POSSESSES VARIOUS KINDS OF PLANTS, FLOWERS, and trees, including the tree peony [*mudan*],[1] herbaceous peony [*shaoyao*],[2] peach [*tao*],[3] and apricot [*xing*].[4] But if great effort is not taken to nurture and water them, they will [all] merely maintain a similar likeness [to their northern counterparts] and nothing more. Here I will describe only those [flowers] uniquely suited to local con-

---

1   On the origins, history, and characteristics of the tree peony (*mudan*; *Paeonia suffruticosa*), see H. L. Li, *The Garden Flowers*, 22–31. The native habitat of the tree peony was in the mountainous regions of Shaanxi, Gansu, and Sichuan.

2   The habitat of the herbaceous peony (*shaoyao*; *Paeonia albiflora*) extends to several parts of China but not the south. According to H. L. Li, *The Garden Flowers*, 34, "the plant does not adapt well to the hot climate" there. Fan's comments in the next line confirm that *shaoyao* did not grow well in Guangxi.

3   The peach tree (*Prunus persica*) is native to China. The scientific name *persica* derives from an early European belief that peaches were native to Persia (or Iran). The modern botanical consensus is that they originate in China and were introduced to Persia and the Mediterranean region via the Silk Road in early historical times, probably around the beginning of the Common Era. Laufer, *Sino-Iranica*, 539–40.

4   Despite the literal meaning of its scientific name (*Prunus armeniaca*, or "Armenian plum"), the apricot tree is native to China. Laufer, *Sino-Iranica*, 539.

ditions.[5] As a general rule, none of those found in the northern counties[6] will be noted.

LANTERN FESTIVAL REDS [*SHANGYUAN HONG*][7] are deep red in color. They look exactly like the flowers of the red papaya [*hong mugua*][8] but do not bear fruit. Because they bloom around the time of the Lantern Festival Eve,[9] they are so named.

WHITE CRANE FLOWERS [*BAIHE HUA*][10] resemble white cranes and bloom at the Beginning of Spring [Lichun].[11]

SOUTHERN CAMELLIA [*NAN SHANCHA*][12] flowers in the south have a corolla [*pa*] and calyx [*e*] twice the size of those in the Central Counties, but the color is slightly paler. The leaves are more pliant and thinner and have hairs. Aside from the southern camellia there is another, separate variety, which resembles those native to the Central Counties.

---

5   That is to say, Fan will only describe those flowers that are uniquely suited to conditions in the south.

6   Fan Chengda uses the term "Northern Counties" (Beizhou) to refer to China in general.

7   The precise identity of this flower is unknown. *Hu-Tan*, 114, note, suggests Fan Chengda might be referring to the crane plant (*hecao*), which H. L. Li identifies as a type of orchid, probably *Pecteilus susannae*, found in south China (*Fourth Century Flora*, 40–41). But this identification is tentative at best. Fan's entry on the *shangyuan hong* is simply too brief to make a positive identification.

8   The gourd-shaped fruit of this tree, sometimes called the Chinese flowering quince, is the papaya (*mugua; Carica papaya*).

9   Lantern Festival Eve falls on the fifteenth day after New Year's on the lunar calendar, when colorful lanterns are put on display.

10   Hu and Tan provide some additional information on the white-crane flower (*Hu-Tan*, 114). They suspect it is the same as the "crane plant" mentioned in the *Nanfang caomu zhuang* (Descriptions of the herbaceous plants and trees of the Southern Quarter), for which see *Fourth Century Flora*, 40–41.

11   Lichun marked the official start of spring on the lunar calendar. At the same time, it marked the first day of the New Year. This explains why China's New Year's festival is sometimes called the "Spring Festival."

12   *Shancha* is one of two Song dynasty names for the camellia, the other being *chahua*. Before the Song, camellias were popularly known as *hai shiliu*, literally, "sea pomegranate." See Harper, "Flowers in T'ang Poetry," 140. As noted by Yang Wuquan in LWDD, 328, n. 1, *nan shancha* is *Camellia reticulata*, a cultivated species of the camellia that is especially common in Yunnan. Hence, it is also known as *Yunnan chahua*. The entry on this flower in the LWDD, 8.328 (*Netolitzky*, 8.25), provides some additional information. Fan Chengda's entry here on *nan chahua* is also translated in *Needham et al.*, 6:1.461.

RED CARDAMOM FLOWERS [*HONG DOUKOU HUA*][13] grow in clusters. The leaves are slender, resembling those of a jade green reed [*bilu*]. They come out in late spring. Before their flowers blossom, they first grow forth a single stem, enclosed by a large bract [*tuo*]. When the bract is shed, the blossom appears. Each spike [*sui*] has several tens of stamens [*rui*], which are pink and vivid like the color of peach and apricot blossoms. When the stamens double up [and become heavier], they droop down like grapes, which in shape resemble fire-regulating pearls [*huoqi*][14] and pearl-jade necklace [*yingluo*][15] as well as the cut ribbon [*jiancai*] and simurgh branch [*luanzhi*].[16] This flower produces no fruit and is not the same variety as the herbaceous cardamom [*cao doukou*].[17] Each style [*ruixin*] has two tips [*ban*] side by side, so poets employ metaphors comparing [the double tips] to the paired-eye fish [*bimu*][18] and trees with interlocking branches, or so it is said.

---

13 H. L. Li, in comments about the cardamom (*doukou hua*; *Amomum cardamo-mum*), an herb of the ginger family, mentions that an alternate name for the wild ginger (*shanjiao hua*; *Alpinia chinensis*) is *hong doukou* and that it grows in Guangxi and northern Vietnam. This might be the flower to which Fan is referring, but it is uncertain because the name *doukou* is used to indicate a number of different plants. See *Fourth Century Flora*, 38–40. See also *Needham et al*, 6:1.462, which says Fan's plant has been identified as *Languas galangal* but could also be *Languas officinarum* (*gaoliang jiang*) or even *Languas japonica* (*shanjiang*), and *Compendium*, 2:14.1516, which identifies *hong doukou* as *Fructus alpiniae officinarum*. Fan Chengda wrote a poem on red cardamom flowers. See FSHJ, 14.173 ("Hong doukou hua").

14 *Huoqi* (lit., "fire-regulating") is the name of a crystal-like substance probably made from mica, sometimes also called fire pearl (*huozhu*) or rose pearl (*mei-gui zhu*). According to the BCGM, 8.506 (*Compendium*, 2:8.972), it forms into a transparent egglike shape and can emit light for several feet. *Huoqi* is also an alternate name for *liuli*, or colored glass.

15 *Yingluo* is probably the name of a flower, but I have not been able to identify it.

16 "Cut ribbon" and "simurgh branch" also appear to be names of flowers but are otherwise unidentified.

17 Yang Wuquan, LWDD, 8.333, n. 3, identifies *cao doukou* as *Alpinia katsumadai*, also sometimes called "Katsumada's galangel." Cf. Wheatley, "Geographical Notes on Some Commodities," 87, which says *cao doukou* is *Amomum globulo-sum*.

18 Read, *Fish Drugs*, no. 177, says *bimu yu* is a flounder. See also Knechtges' comments in *Wen xuan*, 1:142, line 434 note, where he identifies the paired-eyed fish as the *die*, a sole-shaped flatfish that can move one of its eyes to the other side of its head to join with the other eye.

STEEPING FLOWERS [*PAOHUA*][19] among southerners sometimes go by the name pomelo flowers [*youhua*].[20] They blossom in late spring. The stamens are round and white, resembling a big pearl. When you snap one off [a branch], it resembles a camellia. Its smell is clear and fragrant, on par with that of Arabian jasmine [*moli*] and royal jasmine [*suxin*].[21] Foreign people[22] collect them in order to steam them into a fragrance [or air freshener]. The aroma is surpassing and superior.

Supplementary text: Steeping flowers are gathered in order to steam them into a fragrance [or air freshener]. This method uses thin slices of outstanding sinking aromatic,[23] which are placed in a clean vessel. When the steeping flowers are halfway to bloom, they are layered together with sinking aromatic inside it. The vessel is then sealed tightly. After one day the contents are changed [the flowers and aromatic are replaced with fresh ones]. One does not wait until the flowers have withered. Once the [fresh] flowers are in place, the fragrance reaches full strength. Among the natives of Fanyu, Wu Xing[24] makes heart-character aromatic [*xinzi xiang*] and rose-gem aromatic [*qiongxiang*]. The [steeping] method that employs royal jasmine and Arabian jasmine [flowers] is also like this. As a general rule, once the steeping [method] obtains the aroma, it never cooks out. In Jiang and Zhe they make sweet osmanthus [*muxi*][25] and lakawood [*jiangzhen*][26]

---

19   Yang Wuquan, in LWDD, 334, n. 1, identifies *paohua* as *Citrus aurantium*, sometimes called the bergamot orange in English, whose sweet fragrant flowers were steeped in tea for flavoring. This explains the name "steeping flowers." *Paohua* were also used in the south as an air freshener. See the comments in *Hu-Tan*, 115–16.

20   On the pomelo, see the "Treatise on Fruits."

21   See below for Arabian jasmine and royal jasmine.

22   LWDD, 8.333 (Netolitzky, 8.32), quotes Fan's entry on *paohua* almost verbatim. However, instead of "foreign people" (*fanren*) the LWDD text reads *Fanyu ren*, or "natives of Fanyu." Fanyu corresponds to modern Guangzhou.

23   For sinking-in-water aromatic, see the "Treatise on Aromatics."

24   During the Song dynasty the Wu family of Fanyu (or Guangzhou) was famous for making aromatics. See the comments in Ye Zhi, *Tanzhai biheng*, 18.4b. Wu Xing is probably the name of the patriarch of the Wu family.

25   The fragrance referenced here is made from the sweet osmanthus (*Osmanthus fragrans*) shrub (or small tree), the fragrant flowers of which are usually called *guihua*, or "cinnamon flowers."

26   *Jiangzhen xiang* (lit., "truth-descending aromatic"), also known as *jiangxiang*

aromatics [or air fresheners] on the surface of a steaming soup. That is not the same as this method.[27]

RED CANNA FLOWERS [*HONG JIAOHUA*][28] have slender leaves, similar to those on reeds [*lu*] and Indocalamus bamboo [*ruo*].[29] In the center[30] [of the style] they sprout branches. The branch tips sprout blossoms, while the leaves are in several layers. Each day they lose one or two leaves. The color of the leaves is pure red, resembling those of the pomegranate [*liuhua*][31] and lichee. On the end of each leaf there is a single dot of bright green, which is especially attractive. The red canna blooms in summer and autumn but even during very cold winters still maintains its sweet fragrance. There is also another variety of canna with roots that come out of the ground, which is especially full and plump, like a vase with a slender neck and bulging body. It is known by the name slender-neck bulging-body canna [*danping jiao*].[32]

(descending aromatic) and *ziteng xiang* (purple-vine aromatic), is an aromatic made from the lakawood or rosewood tree (*Dalbergia odorifera, Dalbergia sissoo,* or *Dalbergia parviflora*). For additional information see the entry on *jiangzhen xiang* in ZFZ, 2.183 (Chau Ju-kua, 211), BCGM, 34.1945–46 (*Compendium,* 4:34.2963–64), and especially Derek Heng Thiam Soon, "The Trade in Lakawood Products between South China and the Malay World from the Twelfth to the Fifteenth Centuries AD," *Journal of Southeast Asian Studies* 32 (2001): 133–49.

27   HSRC, 67.55b–56a; FCDBJ, 115.

28   There is an entry on *hongjiao hua* in LWDD, 8.327 (Netolitzky, 8.24). Yang Wuquan, 327, n. 1, identifies this as a variety of *meiren jiao* (*Canna indica*). Cf. CMP, no. 652, which says *hongjiao* is a variety of the *bajiao,* or the *Musaceae* genus. This genus includes plantain and bananas.

29   Yang Wuquan, LWDD, 8.327, n. 2, identifies *lu* in this line as *zongye lu* (*Thysanolaena maxima*) and *ruo* as *Indocalamus tessellates. Ruo* here probably indicates some slender-leaf species of Indocalamus bamboo.

30   Following *Hu-Tan,* 116, note, and reading *zhongxin* 中心 (in the center).

31   The pomegranate (*liuhua; Punica granatum*) is more commonly known in Chinese as *shiliu* or *anshi liu.* For a general description, see H. L. Li, *The Garden Flowers,* 192–93. On the role of the pomegranate in Tang poetry and its earlier transmission from Persia to China via western Asia, see Harper, "Flowers in T'ang Poetry," 139–53.

32   The precise identity of this variety of canna is unclear. In his entry on *danping jiao,* Zhou Qufei says that this flower is also called the *xiangti hua,* or elephant foot flower. LWDD, 8.326 (Netolitzky, 8.22). Fan Chengda, however, includes a separate entry on the *xiangti hua,* for which see below. This suggests that Fan regarded the *danping jiao* and *xiangti hua* as different flowers.

OLEANDER FLOWERS [*JUNA HUA*][33] have long, slender leaves, somewhat resembling those of the willow [*yangliu*]. In summer they make pink flowers, each cluster comprising ten calyces. Even in late autumn they still have their flowers.

RANGOON CREEPER FLOWERS [*SHI JUNZI HUA*][34] grow on tendriled vines [*wan*]. Trellises are made to cultivate the vines. They bloom in summer. Each cluster of flowers has ten or twenty corollas, which are light and full, sort of like those of the flowering crabapple [*haitang*].

WEST-OF-THE-WATER FLOWERS [*SHUIXI HUA*][35] have leaves resembling those of the day lily [*xuancao*].[36] Their flowers are yellow, and they bloom in summer.

WRAPPED MEI-FLOWERS [*GUO MEIHUA*] are in fact shrubby althea [*mujin*].[37] There are two varieties: red and white. The leaves resemble those of the hollyhock [*Shukui*].[38] Those who select the red variety [take] the joined leaves[39] and wrap them together with ripened mei

---

33   *Juna* (sometimes called *juna yi*) denotes the white-flower oleander (*Nerium indicum*). The LWDD, 8.335–36 (*Netolitzky*, 8.34), entry on *juna hua* has additional descriptive information. See also H. L. Li, *The Garden Flowers*, 194.

34   CMP, no. 245, and Yang Wuquan, LWDD, 8.330, n. 1, both identify the *shi junzi hua* as *Quisqualis indica*, or the Rangoon creeper (fig. 12). This shrub, which was used to treat childhood diseases, was also known before the Tang as *liuqiu zi*. During the Tang, however, it became associated with the famous pediatrician Guo Shijun; hence the name *shi junzi*. *Fourth Century Flora*, 55.

35   Zhou Qufei copied this entry verbatim into the LWDD, 8.337 (*Netolitzky*, 8.35). The precise identity of *shuixi hua*, however, is uncertain. See Yang Wuqian's comments in LWDD, 8.337, n. 1, and *Hu-Tan*, 117, note.

36   The yellow-flowered day lily is a common plant, indigenous to China, of the genus *Hemerocallis* (in the lily family). It includes some fifteen species and is known mainly for the medicinal properties of its tubers and leaves. See H. L. Li, *The Garden Flowers*, 109–11. Among these fifteen species, several have yellow flowers and bloom in summer. Fan Chengda's *shuixi zi* is probably one of these.

37   CMP, no. 279, identifies *mujin* as *Hibiscus syriacus*—an ornamental, deciduous shrub. See also n. 54 below. This identification is confirmed in BCGM, 36.2128 (*Compendium*, 5:36.3207). In English it is known as "shrubby althea," "morning flower," and "rose of Sharon."

38   The hollyhock is *Althaea rosea*. CMP, no. 275; see also H. L. Li, *The Garden Flowers*, 143.

39   "Joined leaves" (*lianye*) are connected or joined clusters of leaves that grow from different branches.

FIGURE 12
Rangoon Creeper Flowers (*Quisqualis indica*) from Mei 眉 county, Sichuan.
Source: *Chongxiu Zhenghe jingshi zhenglei beiyong bencao*, 9.239.

[-fruit], a salty solution, and sun-dried meat [*baogan*], which is then served with wine; hence the name.

YUXIU FLOWERS [*YUXIU HUA*][40] are pink in color and blossom throughout the four seasons.

ELEPHANT HOOF FLOWERS [*XIANGTI HUA*][41] resemble the cape jasmine [*zhizi*],[42] but the leaves are smaller. They blossom in summer and last until late autumn.

ROYAL JASMINE FLOWERS [*SUXIN HUA*][43] are rarer than those that come out of Fanyu. This is because of the differences and advantages of local conditions [in Guangxi].

---

40   This same entry is repeated verbatim in *LWDD*, 8.338 (*Netolitzky*, 8.37). No other information on this flower seems to be available.

41   Yang Wuquan, *LWDD*, 326, n. 1, identifies the *xianti hua* as the elephant banana (*Ensete glaucum*).

42   This is *Gardenia jasminoides*, an evergreen shrub widely cultivated for its large fragrant, waxlike white flowers and glossy leaves.

43   Also known as *yeximing hua*, royal jasmine is a common species of wild jasmine (*Jasminum grandiflorum*) of Persian origin that flourished in Guangdong and Fujian. For additional information, see *Fourth Century Flora*, 35–38. On the foreign origins of the name *yeximing* and its relation to the word "jasmine," see Laufer, *Sino-Iranica*, 331. See also Edward H. Schafer, "Notes on the Chinese Word for Jasmine," *Journal of the American Oriental Society* 68 (1948): 61, which observes that from beginning of the eleventh century the term *yeximing* was replaced with *suxin*.

ARABIAN JASMINE FLOWERS [*MOLI HUA*][44] are also rare [in Guangxi], as in Fanyu.[45] If they are irrigated daily with washed rice and broth, flowers are then produced constantly. This can last an entire summer. The flowers are also large and have numerous leaves, and the flowers are quite extraordinary. If on the sixth day of the sixth month[46] they are watered once with specially prepared fishy-smell solution [*yuxing shui*],[47] the flowers are even more remarkable.

POMEGRANATE FLOWERS [*SHILIU HUA*][48] are a distinct variety in the south and bloom steadily throughout the four seasons. After they bear fruit in summer, in late fall they suddenly flower fully once again and bear fruit a second time. The very large fruits on the tips of the branches crack and split open, but the red beauties [flowers] beside them shine brilliantly. Together the flowers and fruits are picked and set out for a feast, which is absolutely wonderful.

ENHANCED-COLOR HIBISCUS FLOWERS [*TIANSE FURONG HUA*][49] when they open in the morning, are pure white; following the *wu* double-hour,[50] they turn slightly red; at night they become deep red. Master

---

44   *Moli* is probably a name of Indian origin and usually refers to the Arabian jasmine (*Jasminium sambac*). Its white flowers have an especially rich fragrance. H. L. Li, *The Garden Flowers*, 127.

45   Jasmine was cultivated extensively in the area around modern Guangzhou. See the entry on *moli hua* in LWDD, 8.329 (Netolitzky, 8.27), which says "they are also quite numerous in Fanyu"; see also the comments in *Fourth Century Flora*, 36. Fan's comment about *moli hua* being "rare" in Fanyu cannot be correct.

46   Arabian jasmine is especially sensitive to cold temperatures and hence was planted at the height of summer (around the time of the sixth day of the sixth lunar month), when temperatures were the hottest. See the remarks in LWDD, 8.329, n. 2.

47   *Yuxing shui* (lit., fishy-smell water) is probably a liquefied version of *Houttuynia cordata*, or the chameleon herb (*yuxing cao*). Yan Pei, 79, n. 22, says this fertilization method is still in use today.

48   For more information on the pomegranate (*Punica granatum*), see H. L. Li, *The Garden Flowers*, 192–93; Laufer, *Sino-Iranica*, 276–87; and CMP, no. 250. Fan's entry on the pomegranate is quoted almost verbatim in LWDD, 8.329–30 (Netolitzky, 8.28).

49   Based on Fan Chengda's description, Yang Wuquan, LWDD, 8.331, n. 1, correctly identifies this flower as *Hibiscus mutabilis*, which is the most celebrated hibiscus in Chinese horticulture. This flower is also known as *mu furong*, or woody hibiscus.

50   The *wu* double-hour falls between 11:00 a.m. and 1:00 p.m.

Ouyang's *Tree Peonies Manual* [Mudan pu][51] includes an "enhanced red" type, which is the same idea as described here. Branches of these flowers go thorough the entire winter without withering, and some of them [on trees] are higher than a house. In Jiang and Zhe these flowers must have a perennial root that is doubly thick and sturdy. The Shu variety is also like this.

TILTING GOLD POT FLOWERS [*CE JINZHAN HUA*][52] resemble those of the small yellow mallow [*huangkui*],[53] while the leaves are sort of like those on the common hibiscus.[54] They bloom at the end of the year, at the same time as the mei-flower.

Supplementary entry: **MĀNDĀRA FLOWERS [*MANTUOLUO HUA*]** Māndāra [*mantuoluo hua*][55] grow everywhere in the open country. They have large leaves and white flowers, with fruit that resembles the eggplant [*qie*]. Tiny prickles grow all over them. Thugs gather the flowers to make them into a powder. When placed into human food and drink, it immediately makes one faint and drunk. Locals also use

---

51   "Master Ouyang" (Ouyang Gong) is Ouyang Xiu, a leading statesman and writer of the Northern Song. The full title of Ouyang Xiu's study of the peony is *Account of the Tree Peonies of Luoyang* (Luoyang mudan ji).

52   According to CMP, no. 18, *jinzhan hua* is the marigold or pot marigold (*Calendula officinalis*). Both *Yan Pei*, 80, n. 27, and *Hu-Tan*, 122, however, identify the *ce jinzhan hua* as a different flower altogether, specifically a member of the Ranunculaceae, or buttercup family. They provide little information beyond this.

53   This is a type of Chinese mallow (*kui*), specifically *Hibiscus manihot*. CMP, no. 280.

54   I suspect Fan Chengda here is referring to *mujin hua*, or shrubby althea. See n. 37 above.

55   The name *manduoluo* comes from the Sanskrit *māndāra* (alternately, *māndārava*) and refers to a fragrant red flower mentioned in various Buddhist scriptures. This red flower should be distinguished from the white flower described here by Fan Chengda, which Yang Wuquan, LWDD, 335, n. 1, identifies as *Datura stramonium* (see also CMP, no. 112). This is a common poisonous weed in the nightshade family, which contains tropane alkaloids that can be used as a hallucinogen. Common English names for *Datura stramonium* include loco weed, mad hatter, crazy tea, gypsum weed, and devil's trumpet (from their large trumpet-shaped flowers). The entry on *mantuoluo hua* in LWDD, 8.334–35 (Netolitzky, 8.33), is based almost entirely on Fan Chengda's description.

it to make a laxative⁵⁶ for children. When someone took a branch of *māndāra* and hung it in a government warehouse in Zhao County,⁵⁷ those who drank [wine infused with *māndāra* powder there] easily became drunk.⁵⁸

---

56   Tentative translation for *qu ji yao* 去積藥 (lit., "a medicine for removing build-ups [of food]").

57   Zhao County was located in the area around modern Zhaoping *xian*, along the middle reaches of the Gui River (Guijiang) in what is now eastern Guangxi.

58   *HSRC*, 67.56a; *FCDBJ*, 115. A portion of this entry is quoted in Chu Renhuo's *Jianhu ji*, 2:7b. At the end of this quotation, we find the following comment, which presumably is from Fan Chengda: "I suspect these are in fact *utpala* flowers [*youboluo hua*]." This comment does not appear in any extant editions of *Treatises*. *Utpala* is a Sanskrit term that designates lily- and lotuslike flow-ers. As far as I know, *utpala* flowers are not generally associated with *Datura stramonium*.

10

FRUITS
(Zhi guo)

THE GENERATIONS HAVE PASSED DOWN THAT FRUITS IN THE south with names carrying the suffix *zi* number 120.[1] Half of these are herbaceous and woody [tree] fruits in the mountainous wilds, which are the delight of apes and monkeys [*yuanju*]. People have stubbornly regarded them as fruits and have named them as such, so I cannot know about all of them. Here I will list those I know about that are edible, which number fifty-seven varieties.[2]

---

1   The noun suffix *zi* 子 used as an indicator of fruit and nut names should be distinguished from *zi* (the same Chinese character) meaning "seed," indicating immature fruit in "seed" or "bud" form. In the short preface to his entry on the "Hundred Fruits" (Baizi), Zhou Qufei repeats the number 120 but adds that sometimes the number is alternately given as 100 (as he does) or 72. See *LWDD*, 8.308 (*Netolitzky*, 8.19). On the classification scheme that identifies seventy-two southern fruits and nuts, see Zhou Hui, *Qingbo biezhi*, 2.1b.

2   Fifty-five fruits are listed under separate entries in my translation of this treatise. This number falls two short of Fan's "fifty-seven varieties." For various textual reasons, explained in the notes, I have combined the entries on *luowang zi* 羅望子 and *luohuang zi* 羅晃子 (see n. 23), as well as the entries on *buna zi* 不納子 and *buna zi* 布衲子 (see n. 93). Only fifty-five fruits remain. As for the two "missing" fruits, I have no explanation. Perhaps they were lost in the textual transmission process, but there is no way to verify this.

LICHEES [*LIZHI*][3] are found along a stretch of land extending just 100 or so *li* from the border of Hunan into Guilin. They have never been very plentiful there. Zhaoping Town produces shrunken-pit [*youhe*] lichees,[4] while the green variety that comes out of Linhe[5] is especially superior. Lichees are found in all the various commanderies south of here.[6] None are suitable for drying. The flesh of the fruit is meager, while the taste is superficial, and they are inferior to the lichees produced in Min.[7]

LONGAN [*LONGYAN*][8] are found in all of the Southern Counties. The extremely large ones come out of Yong County. In circumference they are about the size of two cash coins, but the flesh of the fruit is scanty, and they are no better than common longan from elsewhere, which is regrettable.

STEAMED-BUN MANDARIN ORANGES [*MANTOU GAN*][9] that rise up

---

3   Lichee (also spelled "litchi" or "lychee") is *Litchi chinensis*, a tropical fruit tree native to south China. The fruit consists of a layer of sweet, translucent white flesh, with a texture somewhat similar to that of a grape. On the long history of lichee in China, see *Fourth Century Flora*, 113–15, and especially Simoons, *Food in China*, 206–10. See also Groff, *The Lychee and Longan*.

4   Fan's reference here is to a fleshy variety of lichee with tiny, "shrunken" pits. Zhaoping Town, also known as Longping Town, was 162 *li* southeast of Zhao County. *TPHYJ*, 163.10b. For additional information on Zhaoping lichees, see Cai Xiang, *Lizhi pu*, 4.

5   Linhe is a town under the jurisdiction of He County (southeast of modern He *xian*, Guangxi).

6   That is, south of Guilin.

7   According to the *BCGM*, 31.1817 (*Compendium*, 4:31.2788), and many other sources, the best quality lichee fruit comes out of Min (or Fujian). Those produced in Sichuan are of secondary quality, while those grown in Lingnan rank third.

8   *CMP*, no. 302, and Yang Wuquan, *LWDD*, 8.300, n. 4, both identify *longyan* (lit., "dragon eyes") as *Euphoria longan*. This botanical relative of the lichee is also a well-known fruit in south China and was generally used in preserved form. *Fourth Century Flora*, 122–23; Simoons, *Food in China*, 210–12. See also Groff, *The Lychee and Longan*.

9   *Gan* refers to the sweet-peel tangerine (sometimes also called the mandarin orange; *Citris nobilis*). This sweet and delicious fruit differs from the *ju*, or sour-peel tangerine (*Citris deliciosa*), mainly in that it is more spherical in shape and has a thicker and coarser rind. Modern classification often combines these two fruits under one species (*Citris reticulate*). See, for instance, *Fourth Century Flora*, 119–20. See also *CMP*, no. 348. The precise identity of *mantou*

near their footstalk [*di*], resembling the end of a steamed bun [*mantou*], are superior in taste and fragrance, and can be likened to the sweet-peel tangerine [*rugan*][10] of Yongjia.

KUMQUATS [*JINJU*][11] that come out of Yingdao[12] are premier in the world. Those that come out of Jiang and Zhe have sweet rinds and sour flesh, and are inferior.

SOFT PLUMS [*MIANLI*][13] are sweet and wonderful in taste and superior to the common grade. If you split one in two with your hands, it resembles a peach with the kernel separated from the flesh.

STONE CHESTNUTS [*SHILI*][14] are round like pellets. Each one has a

---

gan is uncertain. Meng Yuanyao, "Guoming kao," 6, speculates that *mantou gan* might be another name for *penggan* (*Citris poonensis*), or the Chinese honey orange.

10   Following *Yan Pei*, 87–88, n. 10, and *Hu-Tan*, 126, note, and reading *rugan* 乳柑. The *rugan* of Yongjia (modern Wenzhou, Zhejiang) were well known in the Song. See, for instance, the remarks in Zhang Shinan, *Youhuan jiwen*, 5.45, which identifies the *gan* of Yongjia as "premier in the world." This praise is repeated in Han Yanzhi's *Julu* 橘錄 (SKQS ed.), 1.1b, which also remarks that *rugan* fruit carries the name *ru* (literally, "milk") because it has a creamy taste. For an English translation of Han Yanzhi's entry on *rugan*, see Hagerty, "Han Yen-chih's *Chü lu*," 74–76.

11   *CMP*, no. 345.

12   Yingdao is a Song town name. This town, on the border between Guangxi and Hunan, fell under the jurisdiction of Dao County (modern Dao *xian* in southern Hunan).

13   The *li* (*Prunus salicina*) is a common flowering fruit tree in China, usually translated as "plum" in English, of which there are many varieties. *Mianli* is certainly one of these, but its precise identity is unknown. Meng Yuanyao, "Guoming kao," 2, notes that the name *mianli* seems to be drawn from the Zhuang language and means "cotton" (*mianhua*) and by extension "soft" (*ruan*). He further notes that *mianli* fruit is "quite large, with a diameter of four to five centimeters. The outer rind is greenish yellow. . . . The flesh of the fruit is red and has a sweet-and-sour taste. After ripening, when *mianli* is split apart with the hands, the pit and flesh completely separate."

14   *Shili* is certainly some variety of wild chestnut or acorn, but its precise identity is uncertain. Yang Wuquan, *LWDD*, 8.304, n. 1, identifies *shili* as the candlenut or kukui nut (*Aleurites moluccana*). This is a large brown fruit with little pulp and a thick rind that encloses one or two very large seeds (or nuts). See also the comments in *Fourth Century Flora*, 131, which identifies a fruit tree with the same name (*shili*) listed in the *Nanfang caomu zhuang* as chinkapin (*Castanopsis indica*). The description of this tree in the *Nanfang caomu zhuang* is different from the fruit tree described here by Fan Chengda. Yang Wuquan contends

stalk wrapped around it that looks like a ladle handle [*shaobing*]. The flesh is yellowish white.[15]

SWEET-SWORD ALMONDS [*GANJIAN ZI*] resemble the sweet almond [*balan zi*].[16] The almond is attached to the pulp and has white dimples [or dots]. It is not edible. If eaten, it will trigger illness. Northerners sometimes refer to sweet-sword almonds as "walnuts from across the ocean" [*hai hutao*].[17]

DRAGON LICHEES [*LONGLI*][18] have shells resembling those of a small lichee; the pulp tastes like longan. The tree and leaf of this fruit resemble those of the two fruits [lichee and longan]. Thus, they are so named. [The fruit] can be steamed and eaten, but one must not eat

---

the *shaoli* described in the *LWDD*, 8.305 (*Netolitzky*, 8.15), is the same as Fan Chengda's *shili*: "The *shaoli* is gray and brown, and perfectly round with a shell that is hard. It has a stem [*bing*] that resembles a ladle [*shao*]." Cf. the following comments in Liu Xun, *Lingbiao luyi*: "There are no *li* in Guang, except for the *shili* that grow in the mountains of Qi County. They mature once a year and are round like pellets. The peel is thick, and the taste is like the kernel of a walnut [for which see n. 17]" (2.11). Also note Laufer, *Sino-Iranica*, 263, 408, where *shili* is identified as *Aleurites triloba*, which also goes by the name "candlenut" in English.

15   As correctly pointed out in *Hu-Tan*, 128, note, in all surviving editions of *Treatises* the entries for *shili* and *ganjian zi* (just below) are wrongly joined into one entry. From quotations in the *BCGM*, 33.107 (*Compendium*, 4:33.2910), and other sources, however, it is clear that these are two separate entries, and here I have treated them as such.

16   *Hu-Tan*, 129, note, identifies the *balan zi* as the *badan xing* (*Prunus amygdalus*), or sweet almond. See also *CMP*, no. 443. Cf. the following remarks from H. L. Li, *Garden Flowers of China*: "The almond, *Prunus amygdalus*, is rather rare in China. It was brought from Persia in medieval times and is now grown only in the northwestern part of China" (157). Laufer, *Sino-Iranica*, 406, notes that *badan* comes from the Persian word *bādām*, meaning "almond."

17   The earliest Chinese term for the cultivated walnut (*Juglans regia*) is *hutao*; lit., "foreign peach." Later it was also known as *hetao*, or "peach with a kernel." Laufer, *Sino-Iranica*, 256. "Walnuts from across the ocean" (*hai hutao*) is probably an extended form of the word *hutao*.

18   Both Meng Yuanyao, "Guoming kao," 2, and Yang Wuquan, *LWDD*, 301, n. 6, identify *longli* as *Dimocarpus confinis*. Meng also mentions that *longli* are also known as "wild lichees" (*ye lizhi*) because they grow wild in mountainous areas. Several sources, including *LWDD*, 8.300, mention that the skin of this fruit resembles the lichee, while the flesh tastes like the longan (for which, see above).

it raw, for this will trigger the onset of epilepsy [*xian*] or apparitions of monsters [*guaiwu*]. The small white flowers bloom in the third month, at the same time as the lichee.

WOODY BAMBOO FRUIT [MU ZHUZI][19] has the exact skin color and shape of a large loquat [*pipa*].[20] The flesh is sweet and wonderful. It bears fruit during autumn and winter.

WINTER PEACHES [DONGTAO][21] are shaped like the jujube [*zao*].[22] Deep jade green and shiny, soft and mushy, sweet and sour, they ripen in spring and summer.

LUOWANG FRUIT [LUOWANG ZI][23] shells are several inches in length.

---

19   The precise identity of the *mu zhuzi* is unknown. According to the *Leizhou fu zhi* (Gazetteer for Lei County) quoted in LWDD, 8.313, n. 7, the common name for this fruit is "mountain bamboo" (*shan zhuzi*). The LWDD entry on *mu zhuzi* (8.308; *Netolitzky*, 8.19) provides some additional information on the fruit: "The flesh is sweet and wonderful, and slightly mushy. Its nuts [*zi*] also resemble the kernels [*he*] of the loquat. . . . When it is half green and half yellow, it is picked for eating. It can be stored up to three or four months without spoiling." I suspect Fan might be referring to a variety of *Garcinia*, perhaps *Garcinia multiflora*, which is sometimes referred to as *mu zhuzi*. The leaves of this fruit tree are shiny green but reddish when young. The fruit is yellow, thin-skinned, and smooth, while its yellow flesh has a butterlike consistency and pleasant acidic flavor.

20   The loquat (*Eriobotrya japonica*) is also known as the Japanese medlar. CMP, no. 427; Simoons, *Food in China*, 212–13. The English word "loquat" derives from *lougwat*, the Cantonese transliteration of *luju* (lit., "reed tangerine"), an ancient name for the loquat. This fruit is more commonly known as *pipa* because of its physical resemblance to the Chinese musical instrument *pipa* ("lute" or "balloon guitar").

21   CMP, 137, no. 448, identifies *dongtao* as a late-ripening variety of the peach (*Prunus persica*). Meng Yuanyao, "Guoming kao," 2, however, says *dongtao* here refers to *dong mangguo* (*Mangifera sylvatica*), a variety of mango that ripens during the winter months. If this identification is accurate, then Fan Chengda's comment that *dongtao* "ripen in spring and summer" would seem out of place. Cf. BCGM, 29.1741 (*Compendium*, 4:29.2684), which does mention a variety of winter peach but says it is red on both the inside and the outside, so this is probably not the *dongtao* Fan Chengda is describing in this entry. See also Li Zailong and Zhang Caixi, "Woguo de dongtao ziyuan,", which notes that there are numerous varieties of late maturing peach in China that vary according to fruit size and other attributes.

22   The jujube (or Chinese date) is *Zizyphus vulgaris*. Schafer and Wallacker, "Local Tribute Products of the T'ang," 219. See also Simoons, *Food in China*, 223–25.

23   *Luowang zi* 羅望子 (*Sterculia nobilis*) is a fruit-bearing variety of the *wutong* (*Firmiana simplex*) tree. See Yang Wuquan's comments in LWDD, 8.312, n. 6.

They resemble soap [*feizao*] beans[24] and also resemble knife beans

---

It is sometimes called the "noble bottle tree" in English. In modern botanical nomenclature, *luowang zi* is usually distinguished from *luohuang zi* 羅晃子, or sweet tamarind, a bean-shaped fruit that grows in pods on a species of evergreen tree (*Tamarindus indica*) and is sometimes called Indian date. In all of the received editions of *Treatises*, we find separate entries for *luowang zi* and *luohuang zi* (see FCDBJ, 117 and 119, respectively). Some modern commentators, such as Hu and Tan (*Hu-Tan*, 131, note), and Meng Yuanyao ("Guoming kao," 3), say these are two names of the same fruit (that is, *Sterculia nobilis*) and that the separate entries on *luowang zi* and *luohuang zi* in *Treatises* are both part of one original entry in Fan Chengda's text that somehow became separated in the textual transmission process. Others commentators, such as Yang Wuquan, in LWDD, 312–13, n. 6, argue that we are dealing here with two separate and distinct types of fruit. Yang further argues that Zhou Qufei's entry on *luohuang zi* (8.308; *Netolitzky*, 8.19), in which Zhou says that *luohuang zi* and *luowang zi* are two names for the same fruit, is wrong. While in modern botanical classification, *luohuang zi* and *luowang zi* are distinct varieties of fruit, we should not assume this was the case during the Song. Judging from the description of *luowang zi* in this entry, it seems that Fan Chengda is describing *Sterculia nobilis*: First, the length of the pods, seeds wrapped in red legumes, and the fact that the seeds need to be steamed before eating all indicate the fruit of the *Sterculia nobilis*. In addition, the fruit names *luohuang zi* and *luowang zi* sound the same in the Zhuang language of Guangxi, which suggests they might refer to the same fruit. Zhou Qufei's single entry on *luohuang zi* in LWDD, 8.308, is undoubtedly drawn from Fan's separate entries on *luohuang zi* and *luowang zi*. This strongly suggests that Fan's original entry on *luowang zi* was somehow split into two entries, with the second of these entries at some time in the textual transmission process picking up the name *luohuang zi*. *Hu-Tan*, 131, has taken Fan Chengda's separate entries on *luowang zi* and *luohuang zi* and convincingly reconstructed them into a single entry. My translation follows this reconstruction.

24   Use of the English word "soap" here requires some explanation. In traditional times the Chinese did not use true soap in the modern sense; that is, soap made from animal fat. Instead, they used detergents usually made from the seeds (or beans) of the soap bean tree (*zaojia*; *Gleditschia sinensis*) or from bodhi seeds (*feizhu zi*; *Sapindus mukorossi*). The detergents functioned as films that were placed either inside one's clothing or directly on the body, which would be employed to lift off dirt or soil. To make the detergent, pharmacists would mix the pulverized beans with flower, minerals, and aromatics, which were mixed into "soap balls" for washing. See the remarks in Charles Benn, *China's Golden Age: Everyday Life in the Tang Dynasty* (Oxford: Oxford University Press, 2001), 116; see also Edward H. Schafer, "The Development of Bathing Customs in Ancient and Medieval China and the History of the Floriate Clear Palace," *Journal of the American Oriental Society* 76.2 (Apr.–June 1956): 57–82 (see esp.

[*daodou*].[25] They moreover resemble olives.[26] The peel has seven layers.[27] True cinnabar red in color, inside [the shell] are two or three seeds [or fruits; *shi*]. Stew the fruit for eating. It is sweet and delicious.

HUMAN FACE FRUIT [*RENMIAN ZI*][28] resembles a large mei-fruit or plum [*li*]. The kernel resembles a human face, complete with two eyes, a nose, and a mouth. The flesh is sweet and sour, and well suited for stewing in honey.[29]

BLACK OLIVES [*WULAN*][30] resemble the common olive. Bluish black in color, the flesh is mushy but sweet.

SQUARE OLIVES [*FANGLAN*][31] also resemble the common olive. They have three or four corners and come out of the counties and settlements along the Two Rivers.

COCONUT-PALM FRUIT [*YEZI*].[32] Its tree and leaves are both similar to the windmill palm [*zonglü*][33] and the sugar palm [*guanglang*].[34] The fruit [the coconuts] grows among the leaves. Each spike holds several stems, the stems being as large as a five-*sheng* vessel. As for the largest

---

the remarks on 64).

25   Knife beans (*Canavalia ensiformis*) are also sometimes called broad beans or jack beans. *CMP*, no. 376.

26   This is the common or "Chinese" olive (*ganlan*; *Canarium album*).

27   Yang Wuquan, *LWDD*, 8.312, n. 5, citing several sources, argues this should instead read "nine layers" (*jiuchong*).

28   Yang Wuquan, *LWDD*, 313, n. 8, and Simoons, *Food in China*, 229, both identify *renmian zi* as *Dracontomelon duperreanum* (or *Dracontomelon dao*), which is sometimes called "yanmin" (from the Cantonese) in English. See also *Fourth Century Flora*, 132.

29   In other words, the fruit can be stewed in honey and thereby made into a preserve. For additional information on *renmian zi* fruit, see *LWDD*, 8.308 (Netolitzky, 8.19).

30   *Wulan* is identified as *Canarium pimela*, or the black olive, in Meng Yuanyao, "Guoming kao," 3; Yang Wuquan, *LWDD*, 8.306, n. 1; and *CMP*, no. 338. For additional information, see *LWDD*, 8.306 (Netolitzky, 8.17).

31   Both Yang Wuquan, *LWDD*, 8.307, n. 3, and Meng Yuanyao, "Guoming kao," 3, identify *fanglan* as *Canarium bengalense*. It is also known as the "East Asian copal."

32   Coconut-palm fruit (or simply "coconut") is *Cocos nucifera*.

33   The windmill palm, also known as the Chusan palm, is *Trachycarpus excelsa* or *Trachycarpus fortunei*.

34   *Guanglang* is the sugar palm (*Arenga pinnata*). See the "Treatise on Herbaceous Plants and Trees."

fruits, the coconut and the jackfruit [*boluomi*] are simply in a class all by themselves.[35] The fruit-shell inside the outer skin can be made into a vessel. The pulp inside the fruit is as white as jade; the flavor is as wonderful as cow's milk. As for the liquor inside the pulp, when fresh, the liquor is extremely clear and fragrant. But if it gets old, it becomes turbid and murky and is unbearable to drink.[36]

BANANA FRUIT [*JIAOZI*][37] of the extremely large variety does not wither even in winter. A single stem grows from the center of the plant[38] several *chi* in length, with flowers on each and every joint. When the flowers shed their leaves, fruit grows on the stems. When the outer skin is peeled, the pulp of the banana is obtained. It is as soft and mushy as green persimmon [*lüshi*][39] and is extremely sweet and refreshing. The banana bears fruit throughout the four seasons. Locals feed the fruit to their babies, saying its cooling quality eliminates guest heat.[40] [To preserve it] soak the fruit in mei-juice [*meizhi*],[41] and dry it in the sun. Then press it flat.[42] Its flavor is sweet

---

35   For jackfruit, see below.

36   Cf. the entry on *yezi* in LWDD, 8.295 (*Netolitzky*, 8.8), which is quoted almost in its entirety in the ZFZ, 2.188 (*Chau Ju-Kua*, 214).

37   As noted in Schafer, *Vermilion Bird*, 186, the taxonomy of the banana (*Musa*) in China is difficult to sort out. *Hu-Tan*, 135, note, describes three varieties of banana and how they relate to the entries on banana fruit, fowl banana fruit, and bud bananas. The first, called *dajiao* (*Musa sapientum*), is referred to by three different names in this entry: *jiaozi*, *bajiao*, and *niu jiaozi*. The fruit of these trees is large and flat, lacks sweetness, and in fact is quite sour. This fruit is good for making *bajiao gan*, or dried banana. The second variety is *ganjiao* (*Musa paradisiaca*), or plantain banana. Fan Chengda's fowl banana fruit (*ji jiaozi*) falls into this category. The final variety is the *longya jiao*, which corresponds to Fan's bud banana (*ya jiaozi*). Also known as *xigong jiao*, its fruit is small and twisted around; it is soft and smooth and has a very sweet smell.

38   Following *Hu-Tan*, 134, and reading *zhong chou yi gan* 中抽一幹 (a single stem grows from the center [of the plant]).

39   CMP, no. 187, identifies *lüshi* is an alternate name for *beishi* (*Diospyros embryopteris*), or varnish persimmon.

40   In other words, the fruit has a "cooling quality" (*xingliang*) that helps dispel illnesses resulting from unwanted "guest heat" (*kere*) in the body.

41   Mei-juice is a concentrate made from *Prunus mume*. Cf. BCGM, 15.1004 (*Compendium*, 3:15.1711), which identifies *meizhi* as a decoction made from *wumei*, or black mume (*Fructus mume*).

42   Following *Hu-Tan*, 134, and reading *pian* 楄 to mean *bian* 扁, or "flat."

and sour, and [its color] is a bit frosty white. This is what the generations have referred to as dried banana. It also goes by the name ox
banana fruit [*niu jiaozi*],[43] and it too bears fruit throughout the four
seasons.

FOWL BANANA FRUIT [*JI JIAOZI*] is smaller than the ox banana. It
also bears fruit throughout the four seasons.

BUD BANANAS [*YA JIAOZI*][44] are smaller than fowl banana fruit and
are especially fragrant and soft, sweet and wonderful. They bear fruit
in early autumn.[45]

RED-AND-SALTY CARDAMOM [*HONGYAN CAOGUO*][46] is derived from
freshly cut herbaceous cardamom [*cao doukou*],[47] which is processed
with mei-juice and soaked in salty water until it turns red. It is then
dried in the sun and served as a tidbit with wine. Parrot tongue [*yingge
she*] is in fact the most prized type of red-and-salty cardamom. When
herbaceous cardamom first begins to bear fruit, it is immediately

---

43 Some editions of *Treatises* instead read *niuzi jiao*. See FCDBJ, 121, n. 5.

44 Reading *ya jiaozi* 芽蕉子 rather than *mao jiaozi* 茅蕉子. See FCDBJ, 131, n. 6.
This reading is the same as that in LWDD, 8.305 (Netolitzky, 8.22). See also *Yan
Pei*, 91, n. 30, and Yang Wuquan, LWDD, 306, n. 1.

45 Fan Chengda's descriptions of these three varieties of *jiao* plants are also translated by Philip K. Reynolds (in collaboration with Mrs. C. Y. Fang) in "The
Banana in Chinese Literature," *Harvard Journal of Asiatic Studies* 5.2 (June
1940): 175.

46 Schafer, *Vermilion Bird*, 194–96, identifies two general types of red cardamoms
in south China and north Vietnam. The first is described as "Chinese equivalents of our familiar nutmeg" (194). Schafer further distinguishes three species:
(1) black or bitter cardamom (*caoguo; Amomum amarum* or *Amomum tsao-
ko*), which was used as a food additive and for medicinal purposes; (2) "true
cardamom" (*Elettaria cardamomum*), the usual referent of the word *doukou*;
and (3) "Chinese" or "herbaceous" cardamom (*cao doukou; Amomum globosum*). The second general type of red cardamom, which Schafer describes as
"botanically close to cardamoms," is a gingerlike galangal or galangal cardamom (*Alpinia officinarum*). This entry of *Treatises* describes a process whereby
some non-red flowered variety of herbaceous cardamom is placed into a solution that turns its flowers (or fruits) red so as to resemble the true, red-flowered
variety of cardamom.

47 Cf. *Compendium*, 2:14.1516–17 (BCGM, 14.865-66), which identifies *cao doukou*
(also known as *doukou*) as Katsumade galangal (*Alpinia katsumadai*). Apparently, the term *cao doukou* was used to refer to both Katsumade galangal
(*Alpinia katsumadai*) and herbaceous cardamom (*Amomum globosum*). Fan
Chengda's reference seems to be to the latter.

picked and then dried through the red-and-salty process, and only then does it resemble a tiny [parrot] tongue.[48]

STAR ANISE [*BAJIAO HUIXIANG*][49] is acquired by northerners to use as a tidbit with wine. After [it is chewed] a short while, it becomes very fragrant and sweet. It comes out of the counties and settlements along the Left and Right Rivers.

INDIAN GOOSEBERRY FRUIT [*YUGAN ZI*][50] is mostly trafficked in the Northern Counties, where everyone knows about it. Its wood can be used to make implements.

Supplementary text: As for Indian gooseberry fruit, its aroma is superior to the common olive. Even when the fruit rots and spoils, it remains firm and crisp.[51]

CARAMBOLA FRUIT [*WULENG ZI*][52] in shape is very strange and unusual. Its five segments protrude, resembling the shape of stone rollers [*liuzhou*] used by farmers. The taste is sour, but if chewed for a long time it becomes slightly sweet. In Min it is referred to as the goat peach [*yangtao*].[53]

---

48   All surviving editions of *Treatises* list red-and-salty cardamom and parrot tongue as separate entries. I agree with *Hu-Tan*, 136, however, that they probably form one single entry, as they do in LWDD, 8.301 (*Netolitzky*, 8.11).

49   CMP, no. 506. Star anise is used to make a spice that closely resembles anise in flavor. It is made from the fruit of a small evergreen tree of the Magnolia family (*Illicium verum*) native to southwest China. The star-shaped fruits are harvested just before ripening. For additional information, see Simoons, *Food in China*, 386–89.

50   The Indian gooseberry (*Phyllanthus emblica;* also known as the emblic tree and the Malacca tree) produces a small, yellow round or oblate fruit with an acidic flavor. The wood of the Indian gooseberry tree is hard but flexible and can be used to make various types of implements and furniture. CMP, no. 330. See also LWDD, 8.303 (*Netolitzky*, 8.13); Laufer, *Sino-Iranica*, 378.

51   HSRC, 67.57a; FCDBJ, 122.

52   *Wuleng zi* (lit., "the fruit with five ridges"), also known as *wuhan zi*, is *Averrhoa carambola*. *Fourth Century Flora*, no. 68. Other English names for this fruit include star fruit, five-angled fruit, and star apple. Carambola has a unique taste—something like a mix of apple, pineapple, and kiwi fruit. See LWDD, 8.308 (*Netolitzky*, 8.19), for additional information. Schafer, "Kiwi Fruit," 1, notes that the carambola plant of south China is sometimes known in English as the "Coromandel gooseberry."

53   Schafer, "Kiwi Fruit," 1, and 3, n. 1, notes that the name "goat peach," sometimes altered to *yangtao*, or "sun peach," was also applied to kiwi fruit in north China

WILD LEMON FRUIT [*LIMENG ZI*][54] resemble large mei-fruits and also are like a small sour-peel tangerine. The taste is extremely sour.

JACKFRUIT [*BOLUOMI*][55] is as big as a winter melon.[56] The outer skin is covered with kinky nodules like Buddha's topknot [*foji*].[57] One removes the peel and eats the fruit. The taste is extremely sweet. The fruit segments[58] resemble those of the winter melon. Jackfruit grows on huge trees and ripens in autumn.

POMELOS [*YOUZI*][59] in the Southern Counties go by the name stinky pomelo [*chouyou*] and are as big as melons. They are also edible. The rind is very thick. Those who make rubbings from stone tablets roll up pomelo peels and dip them into ink rather than use a brush. It is

---

because goats were fond of eating it. Judging from Fan Chengda's comments here, this same name was also used for carambola in the south.

54 Yang Wuquan, *LWDD*, 8.313, n. 11, identifies *limeng zi* as Rangpur fruit (*Citrus limonia*), also called lemanderins. This is a hybrid between an orange and a lemon. Because this fruit has a sour, lemony taste, many confuse it with the common lemon (*Citrus limon*), known to modern Chinese speakers as *ningmeng*. Meng Yuanyao, "Guoming kao," 6, points out that these are two different fruits. He further notes that the *limeng zi* is found in the wild in China and that it grows from the earth (rather than from a tree).

55 The *boluomi*, sometimes translated into English as "jackfruit" (*CMP*, no. 596), is *Artocarpus integrifolia* (*CMP*) or *Artocarpus heterophyllus*. See Yang, *LWDD*, 8.296, n. 2, following *BCGM*, 31.1839 (*Compendium*, 4:31.2817). On the Central Javan origins of the name *boluo*, see *ZFZ*, 2.185, n. 1, and especially the notes in *Chau Ju-Kua*, 212–13.

56 *Donggua*, or "winter melon," indicates the gourd melon (*Benincasa cerifera*; also called wax gourd or white gourd). *CMP*, no. 56.

57 Buddhas and bodhisattvas are often depicted with specific hairstyles, sometimes with their long hair tied up in an elegant chignon or bun. Images of the Buddha also depict a protrusion on the top of his head (a sign of great wisdom and an enlightened state) surrounded by tightly curled knots of hair. The "kinky nodules" mentioned here likely refer to this type of hairstyle. For additional information, see Meher McArthur, *Reading Buddhist Art: An Illustrated Guide to Buddhist Signs and Symbols* (London: Thames and Hudson, 2002), 97.

58 Most editions of *Treatises* read *zilian* 子練, which makes no sense to me. Here I follow the *SKQS* ed., 29a, and read *ziban* 子瓣, which I take to mean "fruit segments."

59 Pomelo (or Chinese grapefruit) is *Citris grandis* (also *Citris maxima*). See *BCGM*, 30.1794 (*Compendium*, 4:30.2756–57); *CMP*, no. 344. The reference here could be to the large pomelo produced in Guangxi known by the local name *shatian you*.

good for the ink and does not damage the paper, and it is extremely convenient to use.[60] This technique could be passed on to others, but in the Northern Counties such large pomelo simply do not exist.[61]

LUGU FRUIT [*LUGU ZI*][62] is as big as a half-*sheng* bowl. If you examine it closely, several tens of spathes [*fang*] accumulate and form into a sphere. Each spathe is separated from the others by a crevice. In winter they are blue-green, but by summer they are red. Break off a section of the fruit and eat it. It is slightly sweet.

RUBBING-AND-SCRATCHING NUTS [*CUOCA ZI*][63] resemble *zhuili*.[64] The flesh is sweet but slightly astringent.

EARTHWORM FRUIT [*DICAN ZI*] grows in the ground, and [its roots] resemble little worms. They also look like artichokes [*ganlu zi*].[65]

---

60   Sometime during the seventh century, or perhaps earlier, the Chinese invented a technique of using paper and ink that allowed one to make copies of the texts inscribed on stone tablets (or stele; *shibei*). These ink rubbings (*taben*) made a print of the inscription. To make a rubbing, a sheet of moistened paper is laid on the inscribed surface and tamped into every depression with a writing brush, usually made of rabbit fur. When the paper is almost dry, its surface is tapped (or rolled) with an inked pad. The paper is then peeled from the stone. Since the black ink does not touch the parts of the paper that are pressed into the inscription, the process produces white characters on a black background. Fan Chengda's point here is that in the south pomelo rinds are used in this process rather than a standard writing brush.

61   Reading *xu* 許 here to mean "like this." Long Qian'an, comp., *Song Yuan yuyan cidian*, 355.

62   Yang Wuquan, *LWDD*, 8.314, n. 13, and *Netolitzky*, 272, n.12, both identify *lugu zi* as *Pandanus tectorius*. This is a species of the screwpine tree (*Pandanus*), which is cultivated widely across the Pacific. In Hawaii it is called the Hala tree. Cf. *Hu-Tan*, 141, note, who say this is a variety of jackfruit. The *LWDD* entry on *lugu zi* (8.309; *Netolitzky*, 8.19) has additional information.

63   The *LWDD* entry (8.309; *Netolitzky*, 8.19) on this fruit gives the characters as *cuoca* 搓擦, literally, "rub and scratch," which I follow here. It also mentions that the shell of the fruit has many white hairs, which must be "rubbed and scratched away" before the fruit can be eaten. Yang Wuquan, *LWDD*, 8.314, n. 14, speculates *cuoca zi* might be *heiye zhui* (*Castanopsis nigrescens*) but does not provide any further information. No doubt Fan Chengda is referring to some edible variety of nut, but its precise identity is unknown.

64   Yang Wuquan, *LWDD*, 8.314, n. 15, says that *zhuili* refers to *zhenzhu li* (*Castanea henryi*, or Henry's chestnut). *Hu-Tan*, 141, note, identifies *zhuili* as another name for hazelnut (*zhenli*) or oak chestnut (*xiangli*).

65   The precise identity of *dican zi* is unclear. While Fan Chengda and Zhou Qufei

Supplementary text: They resemble artichokes but are not pointy. They are served as a tidbit with wine.[66]

FIERY-RED POMELOS [*CHI YOUZI***]**[67] resemble the common olive. The skin is green, and the flesh is fiery red.

[The varieties of fruit grouped together below bear fruit in the spring.][68]

FIERY CHARCOAL NUTS [*HUOTAN ZI***]**[69] resemble black plums [*wuli*].[70]

WILD RAMBUTAN [*SHAN SHAOZI***]**[71] is red in color. The flesh resembles that of a lichee.

[The eight varieties of fruit grouped together below bear fruit in summer.]

WILD LONGAN [*SHAN LONGYAN***]**[72] is green in color. The flesh resembles that of the longan.

(*LWDD*, 8. 309; *Netolitzky*, 8.19) both mention that *dican zi* and *ganlu zi* are similar (but different), the BCGM, 27.1683 (*Compendium*, 4:27.2605), says both names refer to the Chinese artichoke (*Stachys sieboldii*). Li Shizhen also mentions that the root of this herb looks like a hairpin covered with hair. See also the comments in *Hu-Tan*, 141, note.

66   HSRC, 67.57a; FCDBJ, 122.

67   Meng Yuanyao, "Guoming kao," 6, says Fan is probably talking about some variety of pomelo here, the flesh of which is pink or purplish red in color.

68   Although this line appears in all surviving editions of *Treatises*, it is probably an interpolation added by some later editor. Hence, I have enclosed it (and similar comments that follow below) in brackets. See the remarks in *Yan Pei*, 96, n. 50.

69   Yang Wuquan, *LWDD*, 8.315, n. 18, identifies *huotan zi* as a synonym for *xiao putao* (*Acmena acuminatissima*). Cf. *Hu-Tan*, 142, note, which suggests Fan's *huotan zi* is either the cashew (*Anacardiaceae occidentale*; *duxian shu*) or some similar nut. Meng Yuanyao, "Guoming kao," 7, speculates that *huotan zi* might be another name for a common fruit in Guangxi called *huoguo* (fiery-red fruit), which he identifies as *Baccaurea ramiflora*, known in English as the Burmese grape.

70   *Wuli*, rendered literally here as "black plum," is unidentified.

71   Yang Wuquan, *LWDD*, 8.315, n. 20, identifies "wild *shaozi*" as *Nephelium topengii*, while CMP, no. 301, says it is *Nephelium lappaceum*. Both are types of rambutan tree. Trees of the *Nephelium* genus produce a lichee-like fruit covered with a reddish leathery skin with fleshy pliable spines. The fruit flesh is translucent, whitish, or very pale pink, with a sweet, mildly acidic flavor. Fruit names bearing the prefix "mountain" (*shan*) are wild, uncultivated fruits.

72   Meng Yuanyao, "Guoming kao," 2, points out that there are no less than nine varieties of wild longan in Guangxi.

SOAPBERRY FRUIT [*KU TIZI*][73] is yellow in color and resembles the pomegranate.

MULAI FRUIT [*MULAI ZI*][74] resembles a pale yellow large plum.

NIAN FRUIT [*NIANZI*][75] is about as big as the print of a finger and is brown in color.

THOUSAND-YEAR FRUIT [*QIANSUI ZI*][76] resemble green and yellow plums. The taste is sweet.

FIERY-RED JUJUBES [*CHI ZAOZI*][77] resemble the sour jujube [*suanzao*].[78] The taste is sour.

---

73 This fruit appears under different names in different editions of *Treatises*. In *FCDBJ*, 119, it is given as *kuti* 苦提, while in the 1646 *Shuofu* (*Shuofu sanzhong*, 6:2869) and *ZBZZCS* (26b) eds. it is written *budi* 部諦. The *SKQS* ed. and *LWDD* (8.309), however, read *buti* 部蹄. See *FCDBJ*, 121, n. 8. These all seem to refer to the same fruit. The written form may be confused because of the similar pronunciations. *CMP*, no. 304, and Meng Yuanyao, "Guoming kao," both identify the fruit in question as *Sapindus mukorossi*, or Chinese soapberry (Read in *CMP* calls it "Bodhi seeds"; this name derives from the Buddhist practice of using dried soapberry fruit to make beads). *Compendium*, 5:35.3072–73 (*BCGM*, 35.2024) also confirms the *Sapindus mukorossi* identification.

74 This fruit is not further identified.

75 Yang Wuquan, *LWDD*, 8.316–17, n. 24, argues that *nianzi* is another name for *luofu shi* (*Diospyros morrisiana*), or the "Morris persimmon." Meng Yuanyao, "Guoming kao," 7, says *nianzi* fruit comes from a variety of clove tree (*taojin niang*; *Eugenia caryophyllata*). Based on a entry in Liu Xun, *Lingbiao luyi*, Hu-Tan, 143, note, identifies *nianzi* as *daonian zi*, a persimmon-like fruit that is purple on the outside and red on the inside. See also *BCGM*, 31.1843 (*Compendium*, 4:31.2822).

76 *BCGM*, 33.1908 (*Compendium*, 4:33.2912), identifies Fan Chengda's *qiansui zi* as a "creeping herb" produced in Jiaozhi. Li Shizhen further mentions that the pulp of *qiansui zi* is similar to a chestnut and tastes just like it. As noted by Ma Tai-loi, some scholars have identified the *qiansui zi* as the peanut (*Arachis hypogaea*), but there is insufficient description in *Treatises* to draw such a conclusion. See Ma's "The Authenticity of the *Nan-fang ts'ao-mu chuang*," 251.

77 "Fiery-red jujubes" is another name for hawthorn fruit (*Crataegus pinnatifida* or *Crataegus cuneata*), which in fact are bright red berries. A more common name for this wild fruit is *shanzha*. *BCGM*, 30.1773–74 (*Compendium*, 4:30.2727–26).

78 The "sour jujube" (or "sour date") is the wild jujube (*shanzao*; *Zizyphus vulgaris*). *CMP*, no. 294. See also Simoons, *Food in China*, 224.

CREEPING RAMBUTAN FRUIT [*TENG SHAOZI*][79] is as big as a wild duck egg [*fuluan*]. The footstalk is red.[80]

[The thirteen varieties of fruit grouped together below bear fruit in autumn.]

GUMI FRUIT [*GUMI ZI*][81] shells are yellow. Inside there is flesh that resembles grains of rice.

QIAO FRUIT [*QIAOZI*][82] resembles a green mei-fruit [*qingmei*].[83] The taste is sweet.

CREEPING HE FRUIT [*TENG HEZI*] grows on white vines[84] and resembles small grapes [*putao*].[85]

WOODY LOTUS FRUIT [*MU LIANZI*][86] resembles walnuts. It is purple in color.

---

79 As noted in BCGM, 31.1844 (*Compendium*, 4:31.2824), "creeping rambutan fruit" refers to some unidentified species of *shaozi* (or rambutan), for which see above. Cf. Yang Wuquan, LWDD, 8.316, n. 27, which identifies *teng shaozi* as *Nephelium chryseum*. Trees of the *Nephelium* genus produce edible oval red fruit with soft spines.

80 Following LWDD, 8.309, and *Hu-Tan*, 145, and reading *Teng shaozi da ru fuluan, di hong se* 藤韶子大如鳧卵, 蒂紅色.

81 *Gumi zi* (lit., "ancient rice fruit") is unidentified. Yang Wuquan speculates that it might be some variety of pomegranate. See LWDD, 8.316, n. 28. The LWDD entry on *gumi zi* adds that "each single pellet [*ke*] [of fruit] has several tens of beads [*li*]." LWDD, 8.309 (Netolitzky, 8.19).

82 *Hu-Tan*, 145, note, tentatively identifies *qiaozi* (sometimes pronounced *kezi*; lit., "shelled fruit" or "fruit in pods") as another name for *dujiao[jue] zi*, which CMP, no. 84, identifies as *Genipa americana*, a variety of gardenia sometimes known in English as "genipap" or "marmalade box." The fruit produced by this tree is as large as an orange and is green or reddish brown in color. Cf. Yang Wuquan, LWDD, 8.316, n. 29, which suspects that *qiaozi* is a variety of olive.

83 Fan Chengda's precise reference here is unclear. He may be referring to the *lü'e mei*, or green calyx mei-flower, which has a greenish calyx and white single or double petals.

84 There are many varieties of vines or climbing plants bearing the name *baiteng* (lit., "white rattans"). Yang Wuquan, LWDD, 8.316–17, n. 30, speculates that Fan Chengda's reference here might be a fruit-bearing plant called *Calamus faberi*, a very slender, climbing rattan with sparsely armed canes about as thick as a finger and bearing small, pinnate leaves.

85 The written form for "grape" given here (*putao* 蒲桃) is a precursor to the familiar modern form *putao* 葡萄. Laufer, *Sino-Iranica*, 225.

86 The "woody lotus" is *Manglietia fordiana*.

LUOMENG FRUIT [*LUOMENG ZI*][87] is yellow and as big as a sour orange [*cheng*][88] or pomelo.

MAO CHESTNUTS [*MAOLI*][89] resemble oak chestnuts [*xiangli*].[90]

TENAI NUTS [*TENAI ZI*][91] in shape resemble torreya nuts [*fei*][92] but are rounder and longer, and stand upright.

BUNA FRUIT [*BUNA ZI*][93] resembles a yellow and ripe small mei-fruit. They spoil extremely easily. Once they spoil, the peel and flesh immediately start to ferment. The kernel can be made into Buddhist prayer beads [*nianzhu*] that resemble bodhi seeds [*puti zi*].[94]

GOAT-DROPPINGS FRUIT [*YANGSHI ZI*][95] in color and shape com-

---

87   Yang Wuquan, *LWDD*, 8.317, n. 33, thinks *luomeng zi* might in fact refer to the citron (*gouchuan*; *Citris medica*). For additional information on the citron in China, see Simoons, *Food in China*, 201–3; and *Fourth Century Flora*, 66–67.

88   The sour orange (*cheng* or *suancheng*; *Citris aurantium*) is quite common in south China, where several varieties are cultivated.

89   *Maoli* probably refers to some variety of the well-known "Chinese chestnut" (*Castanea mollissima*), a member of the family Fagaceae and the most common variety of chestnut grown in China. The nuts are sweet and considered by some to have the best taste of any chestnut.

90   The "oak nut" or "saw tooth oak nut" (*xiangli*) tree (*Quercus acutissima*) is especially well known for its prolific production of acorns.

91   The precise identity of "tenai nuts" is unclear. Yang Wuquan, *LWDD*, 8.317, n. 35, speculates that *tenai zi* refers to nuts produced by a variety of evergreen called *bashan feizi* (*Torreya fargesii*).

92   *Fei* (or *feizi*) is *Torreya grandis*, sometimes called the "Chinese nutmeg tree."

93   Both *Treatises* (*FCDBJ*, 120) and *LWDD* (8.310), contain separate entries on *buna zi* 不納子 and *buna zi* 布衲子. As confirmed by *Hu-Tan*, 147, note, however, these are two different names for the same fruit. Here I follow *Hu-Tan*, which combines both *buna zi* entries into one. Cf. Yang Wuquan, *LWDD*, 8.320, n.52, who argues against combining these entries. The precise identity of *buna zi* is unclear. *LWDD*, 8.310 (*Netolitzky*, 3.19), provides the following additional information on this fruit: "Someone mentioned that recently *buna zi* was sent to the national capital as tribute, but was rejected" [*buna* 不納 literally means "not accepted"]. Hence, it is so named." Yang Wuquan, *LWDD*, 8.318, n. 38, suggests it might be a type of fruit similar to the apricot or mei. Li Tiaoyuan thinks that *buna zi* is a variety of "small apple." See *Yuedong biji*, 56:13.6a.

94   Fan Chengda's reference here is not to seeds from the famous Bodhi tree under which the historical Buddha sat before his enlightenment. Rather, he is probably referring to seeds or kernels produced by the Chinese soapberry tree (*Sapindus mukorossi*). See notes. 24 and 73 above.

95   Here I follow Yang Wuquan, *LWDD*, 8.318, n. 40, who contends that *yangshi* 羊

pletely resembles[96] goat droppings [*yangshi*]. The taste is also not outstanding.

RITOU FRUIT [*RITOU ZI*][97] in shape resembles a cherry [*yingtao*]. The color resembles that of a grape. It grows in spikes.

BISHOP TREE FRUIT [*QIUFENG ZI*][98] in color and shape completely resembles the chinaberry [*lianzi*].[99]

WAMPEE FRUIT [*HUANG PIZI*][100] resembles small jujubes.

矢 in fact should be read *yangshi* 羊屎 (lit., "goat droppings"), referring to a type of fruit tree of the same name, which is a wild variety of longan sometimes called "Cochin-China helicia." The LWDD entry on *yangshi zi* (8.310; *Netolitzky*, 8.19) states that "in the center [of the flesh] is a small kernel."

96 *FCDBJ*, 120, has a misprint here. Rather than *jinsi* 金似 the text should instead read *quansi* 全似 (completely resemble). This reading is confirmed in the ZBZZCS edition of *Treatises*, 27a.

97 This fruit is not further identified. Cf. Yang Wuquan, LWDD, 8.318, n. 41, who says this fruit might also be known as *tianxian guo* (*Ficus formosana*). This identification seems tentative at best. Cf. also LWDD, 8.310 (*Netolitzky*, 8.19), which adds the following information on *ritou zi*: "The taste is extremely sweet, and they are especially plentiful in Bin County (modern Binyang *xian*, Guangxi).

98 Meng Yuanyao, "Guoming kao," 7, identifies *qiufeng zi* as *Bischofia javanica*, or the bishop tree. The LWDD entry on *qiufeng zi* (8.310; *Netolitzky*, 8.19) provides the following additional information: "The taste is sour and astringent. They grow in Yong County. Sometimes they are called *suifeng zi*. Zengcheng has its own variety of *suifeng zi*, which is used in medicine. This is not the same type of *suifeng zi* described here." Zengcheng was located east of modern Guangzhou. For additional information on the *suifeng zi* of Zengcheng, also known as *hezi*, see LWDD, 8.319, n. 45.

99 CMP, no. 335, identifies *lianzi* as *Melia azedarach* (also known as *kulian* or *ku lianzi*). In English this tree is usually called the chinaberry or bead tree. The hard, spherical seeds were widely used for making rosaries and other products requiring beads. Chinaberry fruit is harmful to humans. Presumably, the fruit of the Bishop's tree was not.

100 Also known as *huangpi guo* or *huangdan*, this is *Clausena lansium*, or wampee fruit—a grapelike fruit with brownish-yellow skin and white pulp and an acidic-sweet flavor. Meng Yuanyao, "Guoming kao," 7, mentions that the wampee tree bears fruit in summer, not in autumn (as classified here). The LWDD entry on *huangpi zi* (8.310; *Netolitzky*, 8.19) provides the following additional information: "It is sweet and sour and its outstanding taste can last quite a long time. It can be sent to far-off places."

ZHUYUAN FRUIT [*ZHUYUAN ZI*][101] is perfectly round and deep red. In shape it resembles the chinaberry [*ku lianzi*].

[The six varieties of fruit grouped together below bear fruit in winter.]

OBLATE PEACHES [*BIANTAO*][102] are as big as a peach but oblate. The color is pure green.

FEN'GU FRUIT [*FEN'GU ZI*][103] has yellow skin. The flesh seems to be powdery.[104]

TAGU FRUIT [*TAGU ZI*][105] is oblate in shape, like a large sweet orange. The interior of the skin is empty and hollow.[106]

YELLOW BELLY FRUIT [*HUANGDU ZI*][107] resembles small pomegranates.

---

101   The *LWDD* entry on *zhuyuan zi* (8.310; *Netolitzky*, 8.19), literally, "vermilion ball fruit," mentions this perfectly round fruit "can be played with . . . and it also resembles the *tang qiuzi* [*Crataegus cuneata*; sometimes translated as the "red haw" or "hawthorn"; see *CMP*, no. 422] and is slightly sweet. It bears fruit in winter."

102   Meng Yuanyao, "Guoming kao," 2, identifies the "oblate peach" (sometimes called the "peento" in English) as *Mangifera persiciformis*, which in fact is a variety of mango. Here I read *bian* 匾 to mean *bian* 扁, "oblate" (flat on the top and bottom, round on the sides).

103   *Fen'gu* fruit is not further identified.

104   Here I follow the *SKQS* ed., 30b, of *Treatises* and *LWDD*, 8.310, and read *rou ru fen* 肉如粉, or "the flesh seems to be powdery." "Powdery" in this context probably means something like "flaked with white spots." The entry on *fen'gu zi* in *LWDD*, 8.310 (*Netolitzky*, 8.19) mentions that the taste of the fruit is sour.

105   This same entry appears in *LWDD*, 8.310, but the first character in the fruit's name is written *da* 搭 rather than *ta* 塔. Yang Wuquan speculates that it might refer to a variety of bitter orange called *xiangyuan* (*Citris wilsonii*) (320, n. 51).

106   Tentative translation. I do not understand how the "interior (or lining) of the skin" (*pili*) could be "empty and hollow" (*kongxu*). The *ZBZZCS* ed., 27b, reads *piguo* 皮裹, but this variant reading does not help to make the meaning of the line any clearer.

107   Yang Wuquan, *LWDD*, 320, n. 54, citing Wu Qijun's *Zhiwu mingshi tukao*, identifies *huang duzi* as another name for *fan shiliu* (*Psidium guajava*), or the "foreign pomegranate." The *LWDD* entry on *huang duzi* (8.310; *Netolitzky*, 8.19) adds the following information: "The skin is dry and hard, like that of oak galls [*mo shizi*]. The dry stalk resembles a thorny bramble, on the surface of which grow ornamental patterns. It is not edible." Oak galls, also known as Aleppo galls, are the globelike excrescences of gall wasps or gall flies, which accumulate when wasps (or flies) deposit eggs in the tissues of the buds of certain oak trees. For additional information, see *ZFZ*, 2.190, note (*Chau Ju-Kua*, 215–16); and Wheatley, "Geographical Notes on Some Commodities," 72.

11

HERBACEOUS PLANTS AND TREES
(Zhi caomu)

U NUSUAL PLANTS AND RARE TREES GROW MOSTLY ON remote mountains and in desolate wilderness. As for those specimens not suitable for Physician He [Yi He] and Carpenter Shi [Jiang Shi],[1] people do not gather them either. Thus, I know very little about them. But those in the category of bamboo are so much more outstanding and unusual that I have appended them to my notes.

CINNAMON [*GUI*][2] in the southern quarter is a wondrous tree and is

---

1   Physician He was a famous doctor from the ancient state of Qin who was once dispatched to serve as medical advisor to King Jing of the Zhou (Zhou Jingwang; r. 571–545 B.C.E.). See *Chunqiu Zuozhuan zhengyi*, 1906/26/204 (Legge, *The Chinese Classics*, 5:580–81). Sometimes Yi He's name is given as Yi Huan. Carpenter Shi was a talented and discerning craftsman whose skills are described in the *Zhuangzi*. See, for instance, *Zhuangzi*, 8.16a. The idea here is that plants and trees unsuitable for medicine or for the building of furniture, vessels, and so forth, would generally be unknown because they would not be harvested.

2   Fan Chengda's reference here is *Cinnamomum cassia*, or true cinnamon, the most prized species of the genus *Cinnamomum*. Common in Guangxi, Guangdong, and Annan (Jiaozhi), the bark and branches of the cinnamon tree have long been valued and used in China as a condiment and in medicinal prescriptions. Although the names used for cinnamon in premodern texts vary and at times are confusing, essentially there are two varieties: meaty cinnamon (*rou-*

used to produce superior-grade medicine. Guilin takes its name from the cinnamon. Cinnamon fruit is not produced locally.[3] It comes out of Bin and Yi Counties.[4] As a general rule, all tree leaves have a single, vertical pattern in the center. Only the cinnamon has two veins [*wen*],[5] which in shape resemble a jade scepter-tablet [*gui*].[6] Those concerned with the composition of Chinese characters think that the character cinnamon is probably derived from scepter-tablet.[7] The taste of the leaves is bittersweet, no different from the bark, but they are more fragrant and enjoyable. People like to chew on them.

Supplementary text: The flowers [of the cinnamon tree] resemble the flowering crabapple. They are pale, and the petals are small. The fruit resembles little acorns [*xiangzi*]. Flowers that have been collected before they blossom are dried and can be peeled for five years [and still maintain their fragrance].[8] Three types [of cinnamon products] are

---

gui) and cinnamon twigs (*guizhi*). These are described in the text below. For additional information, see *Fourth Century Flora*, no. 35; Schafer, *Vermilion Bird*, 195; and Laufer, *Sino-Iranica*, 542–43.

3   Judging by the statement here, which is repeated in LWDD, 8.287 (Netolitzky, 8.1), by Southern Song times virtually all of the cinnamon trees in and around Guilin had already been cut down. As mentioned in the next line, to find forests of the richly aromatic tree, one needed to travel southwest to either Bin or Yi County.

4   Song dynasty illustrations of cinnamon trees from Bin and Yi Counties are preserved in Tang Shenwei, ed., *Chongxiu Zhenghe jingshi zhenglei beiyong bencao* (fig. 13). The Bin County cinnamon tree illustrations (top left) and the accompanying cinnamon branch illustration (lower right) provide pictorial examples of the three-vein-style leaves described in note 5.

5   This line should read "three veins" (*sanwen*) rather than "two veins" (*liangwen*). One of the distinguishing features of cinnamon leaves is that they have three veins. See Song Liren, "Gui de kaozheng," 74. Quoting *Treatises*, Song Liren states specifically that Fan Chengda's text should read "three veins."

6   A jade scepter-tablet is an elongated, pointed tablet held by ancient rulers (and sometimes envoys) on ceremonial occasions.

7   In other words, the pictographic and phonetic aspects of the graph *gui* 圭 (scepter-tablet) were borrowed to form part of the new character *gui* 桂 (cinnamon).

8   That is to say, individual layers of the dried, immature fruit (not the flowers) can be removed one by one for a very long time and still maintain their fragrance.

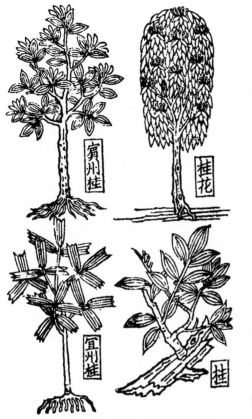

FIGURE 13
Cinnamon tree leaves
from Bin and Yi
counties in *Chongxiu
Zhenghe jingshi zhen-
glei beiyong bencao,*
12.289.

cinnamon twig,[9] meaty cinnamon,[10] and cinnamon heart [*guixin*].[11]
As for cinnamon twig, its texture is thin, and the smell is light. As

---

9   The term "cinnamon twig" refers to thin strips of cinnamon that remain after
    the coarse branch bark is removed. Li Shizhen says it is also called *mugui*, or
    "woody cinnamon." BCGM, 34.1925 (*Compendium*, 4:34.2938).

10 *Rougui*, or "meaty cinnamon," also refers to bark taken from the trunk or a
    branch of a cinnamon tree—ideally, one that is about five or six years old. It is
    much valued as a medicine and as a condiment. After harvesting, it is dried in
    the sun for a day or two, after which time it is rolled up into a "stick."

11 "Cinnamon heart" is a term used for the very best cinnamon, derived from
    the internal layers (or "heart") of young branches. Cf. Schafer and Wallacker,
    "Local Tribute Products of the T'ang Dynasty," 218, which identifies *guixin* as
    the "scraped bark of young branches."

for cinnamon bark, its texture is thick, and the smell is heavy. As for cinnamon heart . . . [12] To shave thicker cinnamon [bark], one uses a sharp [strip of] bamboo, which is bent and curved, to shave down very close to the wood, where there is lots of tree sap. [The cinnamon strips obtained] resemble a coarse linen mourning sash [*diedai*].[13] The flavor is especially intense. The herbaceous plants and trees of Guilin do not flourish.[14]

BANYAN [*RONG*][15] is a tree that grows easily and moreover can easily become lofty and huge. Those that can cover several *mou* of land are very numerous. The roots emerge halfway up the frame. Auxiliary [or aerial] trunks [*fugan*] hang down and penetrate the soil, hence the expression "the banyan tree has reverse-growing roots." Birds bearing banyan seeds in their mouths spread them so they grow on other trees, which results in [increased] luxuriance and growth. Since the roots extend down to the ground and derive emanations from the soil, after a long time proliferation exceeds that which has been spread [by birds].

Supplementary text: The leaves resemble those of a sophora tree [*huai*].[16] Its shade can extend for several *mou*.[17]

---

12   This line (beginning with *gui xin ze* 桂心則) is incomplete. See the comments in *Yan Pei*, 137, n. 2.

13   In most editions of *Treatises,* the last two characters of this line read *jingdai* 經帶, which does not make sense to me. Zhou Qufei's entry on the cinnamon tree, which is based directly on Fan's entry, instead reads *diedai* 绖帶. LWDD, 8.287 (*Netolitzky*, 8.1). I follow this reading. *Diedai* refers to a sash or belt, made of simple coarse linen, worn during periods of mourning. See Yang Wuquan's commentary in LWDD, 8.289, n. 6.

14   HSRC, 67.57a–b; FCDBJ, 126. The last line seems out of place here. Cf. the opening remarks to the "Treatise on Flowers," where Fan Chengda mentions that many of the plants, flowers, and trees imported from north China do not grow well in Guilin unless great care is taken to nurture them.

15   The *banyan* is a species of fig tree. Fan Chengda's reference is probably the Chinese banyan (*Ficus microcarpa* or *Ficus retusa*), which is still common in Guilin. This giant tree often spreads over a large area because of the many aerial roots that descend from the branches and develop into additional trunks, forming a canopy of shade. For additional information on the banyan tree, see the comments in Edward H. Schafer's "Li Kang: A Rhapsody on the Banyan Tree," *Oriens* 6.2 (Dec. 1953): 344–53, and *Fourth Century Flora*, no. 33.

16   The *huai* tree is *Sophora japonica*, sometimes called the "Chinese bayberry" or "pagoda tree."

17   HSRC, 67.57b; FCDBJ, 126.

SHA TREES [*SHAMU*] fall into the same species as the grand conifer [*shan*].[18] They are especially lofty and big. The leaves are pointy and form into clustered spikes. Their small size distinguishes them from those of the grand conifer.

Supplementary text: People in the Yao settlements split the wood into boards, which are sent down to Guangdong by boat for trading.[19]

SUGAR PALM TREES [*GUANGLANG MU*][20] have a frame as straight as a grand conifer. Moreover, they resemble the windmill palm.[21] They have segments like those on big bamboo. The one, single trunk extends straight up, standing several *zhang* in height. Their flowers blossom in several tens of spikes, which are green in color.

Supplementary text: The sugar palm has a hollow core, which is scraped out and used as a water bucket.[22] The outside is firm and can be made into crossbow arrows.[23]

XILEI TREES [*XILEI MU*][24] grow in the counties and settlements along the Two Rivers. [The wood] is solid and firm. If soaked in salty water, it [hardens and] will not rot for a hundred years.

ROUGE TREES [*YANZHI MU*][25] are solid and exquisite, while the color

---

18   Many traditional sources, including BCGM, 34.1923 (*Compendium*, 4:34.2931–32), and modern reference works, such as CMP, no. 786b, identify the *sha* tree as an alternate name for the *shan* tree, or grand conifer (*Cunninghamia sinensis* or *Cunninghamia lanceolata*). Clearly, however, Fan Chengda's description (repeated in LWDD, 8.290; *Netolitzky*, 8.3) concerns a variety of conifer that is similar to but not the same as the grand conifer.

19   HSRC, 67.57b; FCDBJ, 126.

20   This is *Arenga saccharifera* or *Arenga pinnata*—the sugar palm. The juice from its fleshy spadix can be converted into sugar. *Fourth Century Flora*, 90–92; Schafer, *Vermilion Bird*, 175–76.

21   On the windmill palm, see note 33 in the "Treatise on Fruits."

22   Reading *chenglou* 承漏 as a noun meaning "a bucket used to hold [*cheng* 承] leaking or excess water [*lou* 漏]."

23   HSRC, 67.58a; FCDBJ, 127.

24   *Xilei mu* 息欇木 is probably an alternate written form of *silei mu* 思儡[欇]木, for which there is an entry in LWDD, 8.292 (*Netolitzky*, 8.5). As far as I know, this tree is not precisely identified in any source, though Zhou Qufei mentions that its hard wood was used to make bows.

25   The expression *yanzhi* has a long and obscure history in China, which is outlined in part in Laufer, *Sino-Iranica*, 325–28. Although the origins and precise meaning of *yanzhi* are unclear, it is often associated with a wild flower in Guangdong that produced seeds used in the preparation of a cosmetic known

resembles that of rouge [*yanzhi*].[26] [Wood from these trees] can be lathed into vessels.[27] They come out of Rong 融 County as well as other counties and settlements, and are also found in the towns under the jurisdiction of Guilin.

JITONG [*JITONG*][28] leaves resemble those of the chinaberry. The leaves are cooked in a stew and used to treat foot and knee ailments.

LONGGU TREES [*LONGGU MU*][29] are bluish green in color. In shape they resemble a skeleton [*kugu*].

FENGGAO HERB [*FENGGAO YAO*][30] has leaves like those of the winter pine. It can be used to treat sun stroke [*taiyang ji*], when the head and eyes become dizzy and confused.

SOUTHERN LACQUER [*NANQI*][31] resembles liquid malt sugar [*xiyi*]. The smell resembles pine resin [*songzhi*]. It is soggy and sodden and lacks strength.

DANG BAMBOO [*DANGZHU*][32] leaves are big and moreover dense,

---

as *yanzhi fen*, which was used as a dye for textiles and as a facial cosmetic for women. Because of its red color, it is sometimes translated as "rouge" in English. The precise identity of Fan Chengda's "rouge tree," however, is uncertain. See also the speculative comments in *Sino-Iranica*, 328, and Yang Wuquan, *LWDD*, 8.291–92, n. 1.

26   That is, red.

27   Here I follow the emendation suggested by Lu Xiang, cited in *FCDBJ*, 125, n. 3, and read *ke xuan zuo qi* 可鏇作器 (can be lathed into vessels). The *LWDD* entry on the rouge tree (8.291; *Netolitzky*, 8.4), which quotes from Fan's entry almost verbatim, has the same reading.

28   The precise identity of the *jitong* (lit., "fowl-*tong* [tree]") is unknown, but its use in treating arthritis in the knee and feet (see below) is documented in *BCGM*, 35.2002 (*Compendium*, 5:35.3041).

29   I have not been able to identify this tree. "Longgu" literally means "dragon bones."

30   *Yan Pei*, 106, n. 15, without citing any source, says *fenggao yao* is a type of medicated compress made from *fengcao*, a wild plant found only in caverns near Gaoyao Town (modern Gaoyao *shi*) in Guangdong.

31   During the Song dynasty, Guangxi served as a major source of lac [*qi*], which is the gray, syrupy sap from the lac tree (*qishu; Rhus vernicifera*). *CMP*, no. 318. It is not clear if Fan Chengda is referring to the true lacquer tree or a different southern variety of that tree.

32   Many sources define *dang* or *dangzhu* simply as "big bamboo." See, for instance, Carr, "A Linguistic Study of the Flora and Fauna Sections of the *Erh-*

slightly resembling those of a reed [*luwei*].[33]

ABRASIVE BAMBOO [*SEZHU*][34] has coarse and abrasive skin and resembles the sandpaper [*shazhi*] used by woodworkers. It can be used to trim and smooth fingernails and toenails.

Supplementary text: Abrasive bamboo can be smoothed down and used to make armor.[35]

HUMAN FACE BAMBOO [*RENMIAN ZHU*][36] has segments that are dense and bulge outward, and look just like human faces. People gather it in order to make walking sticks.

FISHING LINE BAMBOO [*DIAOSI ZHU*][37] is similar to Dang bamboo. Its branches are extremely fragile and flimsy.

---

ya," 146, and the various citations quoted in Li Kan, *Zhupu xianglu*, 5.20b. Yang Wuquan, *LWDD*, 8.298, n. 5, identifies *dangzhu* as a variety of common bamboo known as *mazhu* (*Sinocalamus latifeorus*), or wideleaf bamboo. This giant plant can sometimes grow to a height of 50 meters. See also Hui-lin Li's comments on the Yunqiu bamboo (*yunqiu zhu*) in *Fourth Century Flora*, no. 75.

33　*Luwei* (reed) here probably refers to *luye*, also known as *zongye lu* (*Thysanolaena maxima*), a bamboolike tropical grass (sometimes called "tiger grass") known for its elongated leaves.

34　Li Kan, *Zhupu xianglu*, 5.27b, notes that an alternate name for *sezhu* is *silao zhu*, which is *Schizostachyum pseudolima*, or "Silao bamboo." *Silao zhu* was often used to make flutes. It was also split for weaving and sometimes used for walling homes. While this attribution is possible, Fan Chengda's reference here is probably to a species of *Equietum*, or "horsetail," a bamboolike plant but not a true bamboo. Its rough, coarse surface is the result of accumulated deposits of siliceous materials. See the description and commentary in *Fourth Century Flora*, no. 78; see also the remarks in Yang Wuquan, *LWDD*, 8.297, n. 3, and *Hu-Tan*, 158, note.

35　*HSRC*, 67.58b; *FCDBJ*, 127.

36　Yang Wuquan identifies *renmian zhu* as *Phyllostachys aurea*, or "golden bamboo." I have not been able to confirm this identification. The *LWDD* entry (8.297; *Netolitzky*, 8.9) on *renmian zhu* explains that each segment bulges outward in a shape that is long and round, "just like a human face." Cf. the *renmian zi* tree described in *Fourth Century Flora*, no. 74.

37　*Diaosi zhu* is *Sinocalamus affinis* (also known as *Bambusa emeiensis*, or "Mount Emei bamboo"). Yang Wuquan, *LWDD*, 8.299, n. 12. The *LWDD* entry on *diaosi zhu* (8.297; *Netolitzky*, 8.9) mentions that its branches "hang down and gently sway in the wind . . . like fishing line."

MOTTLED BAMBOO [*BANZHU*][38] contains layered halos [*dieyun*].[39] The mottled bamboo in Jiang and Zhe has continuous tear stains[40] throughout and lacks halos.

Supplementary text: [Mottled bamboo . . .] originally came out of Qingxiang Town in Quan County.[41] Guilin also has it.[42]

MAOTOU BAMBOO [*MAOTOU ZHU*][43] is similar to tendon bamboo [*jinzhu*][44] in consistency and quality.

PEACH BRANCH BAMBOO [*TAOZHI ZHU*][45] grows mostly on the surface of rocks. The leaves resemble those of a windmill palm. People use the larger ones to make walking sticks.

LE BAMBOO [*LEZHU*][46] is thorny bamboo [*cizhu*]. Its barbs and

---

38 The mottled (or "spotted") bamboo is *Phyllostachys bambusoides*, a variety of bamboo distinguished by its circular, purplish maculation.

39 "Halo" here refers to the circular spots on the inside of the bamboo.

40 Here I follow the SKQS ed., 32a, and read *leihen* 淚痕, or "tear stains." See the collation note in FCDBJ, 125, n. 6. The "tear stains" on mottled bamboo are often linked to a tale about two consorts of the legendary ruler Shun, both of whom were also goddesses of the Xiang River. Tradition says they cried as they searched for their king's body. The spots on the bamboo were said to be vestiges of their tears. See the comments in Schafer, *Vermilion Bird*, 179.

41 Modern Quanzhou *xian*, Guangxi.

42 HSRC, 67.58b; FCDBJ, 127.

43 According to a gloss in Chen Yuanlong's *Gezhi jingyuan*, 67.15b, quoting the *Qunfang pu*, *maozhu* 猫竹 was also known as *maozhu* 茅竹 (lit., "floss-grass[like] bamboo") and *maozhu* 毛竹 (lit., "hairy bamboo"). This same source mentions that the trunk "is huge and thick, and different from common bamboo," and that it was used to construct boats. *Hu-Tan*, 159, note, argues that *maotou zhu* (lit., "cat's head bamboo") in the title of this entry should probably instead read *maozhu* 猫竹, or "*mao* [cat] bamboo." The various *mao* characters were probably used to designate a local dialect word that had a similar sound. The physical appearance of the bamboo itself, as far as I can tell, had nothing to do with cats or cat heads.

44 The precise identity of *jinzhu*, or "tendon bamboo," is unknown. An entry in the *Youyang zazu*, 18.172, however, mentions that it was used by southerners to make crossbow strings. Cf. the comments in *Hu-Tan*, 160, note.

45 Peach branch bamboo has a red cortex that is smooth and strong; it can be used to make matting and, as mentioned below, staffs. Cf. the comments in Hagerty, "Tai K'ai-chih's *Chu-p'u*," 395–96. See also *Yan Pei*, 107, n. 23, and *Hu-Tan*, 160, note.

46 Although there are many species of thorny or spiny bamboo in China, I suspect the reference here is to *Bambusa bambos*, a giant-size thorny bamboo of the *Bambusa* genus. Because of its size, this variety of bamboo would have been

thorns [*mangji*] are dense and thick.

ARROW BAMBOO [*JIANZHU*][47] is found everywhere in the mountains.

PERENNIAL EGGPLANT [*SUGEN QIE*][48] never withers and dies [in winter]. It bears fruit year after year.

BRONZE DRUM PLANTS [*TONGGU CAO*][49] bear a fruit that resembles a melon and can be used to treat skin disease [*chuangyang*] toxins.

BIG ARTEMISIA [*DAHAO*].[50] Nowhere on the road to Rong 容 and Wu Counties has it frosted or snowed for a long time. Thus the year is extended and the growing season is long. The larger trees can be used to make support columns for houses. The smaller ones can also be used as shoulder poles [*kang*] on a sedan chair [*jianyu*].

---

ideal for constructing walls and barriers (see below). For additional information see the LWDD subentry on *lezhu* (8.296–97; *Netolitzky*, 8.9), which mentions that *le* 竻 (alternately written 勒) is a word southerners use for *ci* 刺 ("thorn" or "bramble"). This same source also mentions that in Xin County (Xinzhou; modern Xinxing *xian*, Guangdong) thorny bamboo was planted all around the county seat in lieu of a protective wall. This follows a general custom in south China of using thorny bamboo to make barriers or fences. See also the comments in Hagerty, "Tai K'ai-chih's *Chu-p'u*," 390–91.

47   Arrow bamboo is so called because it is slender but strong and has a solid center and no nodes, which made it ideal for arrow construction. See LWDD, 8.297 (*Netolitzky*, 8.9), which mentions that military weaponry in the various commandery seats includes arrows made with this variety of bamboo. The precise botanical referent of Fan Chengda's "arrow bamboo" is uncertain. See also Carr, "A Linguistic Study of the Flora and Fauna Sections of the *Erh-ya*," 270, and Yang Wuquan, LWDD, 8.299, n. 13, which identifies *jianzhu* as *Sinarundinaria nitida*, sometimes called "fountain bamboo" in English. Yang's attribution seems tentative at best.

48   Here Fan Chengda is referring to eggplant that is grown as a tree (*Solanum melongena* or *Solanum esculentum*) that could produce fruit year after year; hence Fan describes it as a perennial (*sugen*). Liu Xun mentions that "eggplant trees in Jiaozhi and Lingnan do not lose their leaves in winter and after two or three years become large trees with fruits as big as melons" (*Lingbiao luyu*, 2.8).

49   This herbaceous plant is not further identified. The LWDD entry on the bronze bell drum (8.342; *Netolitzky*, 8.42) mentions that, when treating skin disease (see below), it is ground down with vinegar and then applied to the skin.

50   Hundreds of varieties of *hao*, or artemisia, grow in China, so it is difficult, if not impossible, to identify Fan Chengda's "big artemisia." See *Hu-Tan*, 162, note; LWDD, 8.339–40 (*Netolitzky*, 8.39).

ROCK HAIR [*SHIFA*][51] is indigenous to the sea coast. They are tiny and long, resembling silk threads.

OBLATE VEGETABLES [*BIANCAI*][52] are slender like fringed waterlilies [*xingdai*][53] and oblate like shallots [*xiecai*]. They grow to a length of one or two *chi*.

DUGUAN PLANTS [*DUGUAN CAO*][54] have stems with six leaves. They ward off centipedes and snakes.[55]

PATTERNED VINES [*HUATENG*][56] are lathed in order to make them into implements. The core has a decorative pattern.

HU HANGING VINES [*HU MANTENG*][57] are poisonous plants. When they are kneaded and soaked in water, death is immediate if [the poi-

---

51   Judging from the description that follows, "rock hair" probably refers to some type of algae that grows on the surface of rocks in tangled clumps that look like human hair. CMP, no. 857, identifies *shifa* as one of several names for a variety of algae known by the scientific name *Ceramium rubrum*. Yang Wuquan, LWDD, 8.342, n. 1, thinks *shifa* here might refer to a soft, silky aquatic plant known as *Ulothria flacca*. The LWDD entry on *shifa* (8.342; *Netolitzky*, 8.43) mentions that it is light green in color and when used to garnish meat dishes is "extremely adorable." See also the comments on edible algae in China in Simoons, *Food in China*, 182.

52   According to Yang Wuquan, LWDD, 8.343, n. 1, *biancai* refers to *haima lan* (*Zostera marina*), or wild eelgrass, a flowering plant that grows in shallow water.

53   *Xingdai* here likely refers to the fringed water lily (also called "floating heart"; *Limnanthemum nymphoides* or *Limnanthemum peltatum*).

54   *Duguan cao* (lit., "military coordinator plant") is listed in BCGM, 13.795 (*Compendium*, 2:13.1410) but is not identified by scientific name. CMP, no. 204, identifies *duguan cao* as *Angelica kiusiana* (also known as *Angelica japonica*), but I have not found any source that corroborates this identification.

55   LWDD, 8.341 (*Netolitzky*, 8.40), mentions that when *duguan cao* is placed in a room, centipedes and snakes dare not enter.

56   LWDD, 8.325 (*Netolitzky*, 8.21), mentions that *huateng* is common in Rong 融 County and that its vines have multicolored bands, the flowery patterns of which resemble those on gingko (*yinxing*) leaves. Otherwise, it is unidentified.

57   This alkaloid-based poisonous vine is also known as *hu mancao* (lit., "foreign creeper"), *gouwen* (lit., "to hook the throat"), and *duanchang cao* (lit., "the plant that splits your intestines"). *Compendium*, 3:17.2018 (BCGM, 17.1227); CMP, no. 174; Yang Wuquan, LWDD, 8.344, n. 1; and Laufer, *Sino-Iranica*, 106, all identify it as *Gelsemium elegans*. In English this creeping plant is sometimes called the "jassamine." *Sino-Iranica*, 107, notes that there is no apparent reason for the word *hu* (which usually indicates plants, fruits, and so on, of non-Chinese origin) to be prefixed to this plant name.

son] enters the mouth.

Supplementary entry: **XIUREN TEA [*XIUREN CHA*]:**[58] Xiuren is the name of a town[59] under Jingjiang Municipality. [The tea leaves] are cut into strips about two *cun* in length. Strips that have the words "presented to the immortals" [*gong shenxian*] on them are superior.[60] As for the larger strips, they are coarse and pallid.[61]

Supplementary entry: **BETEL NUTS [*BINLANG*]**[62] grow in the settlements of the Li people [on Hainan]. Those gathered at the time of Ascendant Spring [Shangchun][63] are made into soft betel nuts [*ruan binlang*]. Those gathered in summer and fall and dried are made into rice betel nuts [*mi binlang*]. The smaller and pointy ones are made into chicken-heart betel nuts [*jixin binlang*]. Oblate ones are made into big bellies [*da fuzi*].[64] All of these can give off an [identifi-

---

58   In a note appended to one of his poems, Fan Chengda mentions that Xiuren tea was also called "Man tea" (*Mancha*) and that it was a "great remedy for head-aches." See *FSHJ*, 14.179 ("Shi ba shuzi").

59   Xiuren Town (made a market town between 1071 and 1078) was located 340 *li* northwest of Guilin. *TPHYJ*, 162.8b. This roughly corresponds to the general area west of modern Lipu *xian*, Guangxi.

60   The strips of tea described here, after being cut into lengths about two *cun* in length, were presumably then pressed (or "branded") with the words "presented to the immortals."

61   *HSRC*, 67.58a. This entry and those that follow do not appear in any of the surviving versions of *Treatises*. They are all retrieved from Huang Zhen's *Mr. Huang's Daily Transcriptions* and are listed here in the order in which they appear in Huang's text.

62   Betel nuts, also known as areca nuts, are the acrid and mildly intoxicating seeds of the betel nut palm tree. The people of south China were (and many still are) fond of peeling these nuts and then rolling them in the leaves of the betel vine (or betel pepper), after which the leaves were powdered with lime derived from pulverized oyster or clam shells and then chewed. See the comments on this below. For additional information on betel nuts, see Wheatley, "Geographical Notes on Some Commodities," 67–68; Schafer, *Vermilion Bird*, 175; and *ZFZ*, 2.186–87 (*Chau Ju-Kua*, 213–14).

63   That is, the first lunar month.

64   Wheatley, "Geographical Notes on Some Commodities," 69, says that during the Song the "chicken hearts" and "big bellies" "were mostly exports from the Philippines" (rather than coming from Hainan). Wheatley's brief discussion of trade terms for betel nuts under the Song, which he traces to Zhou Qufei's *LWDD*, 8.292–3 (*Netolitzky*, 8.6), is in fact based on information in this passage, which Zhou Qufei copied.

able] odor.[65] Those preserved in a salty solution are made into salty betel nuts [*yan binlang*]. The Qiong County[66] Administration collects taxes on betel nuts, which accounts for half its annual budget. Guang County also collects several tens of thousands strings of cash in taxes. From Min to Guang betel nuts are chewed with lime powder and betel vine leaves [*louye*]. Only after one spits out the fiery red liquid, which resembles blood, can one swallow the remaining juice. In Guang County they add cloves [*dingxiang*], cinnamon flowers [*guihua*], and ginger [*sanlan zi*][67] to make "aromatic-medicinal betel nuts" [*xiangyao binlang*].[68]

Supplementary entry: **EBONY [*WULAN MU*]**[69] is well suited for making boat rudders [*duo*],[70] ranking first [among all woods]. The rudders come out of Qin County.[71]

Supplementary entry: **KAPOK [*JIBEI*]** trees[72] resemble a small mul-

---

65   Although *xiaqi* is a term used in traditional Chinese medicine meaning "to fart," here I read it to mean "give off an odor."

66   That is, Qiong County on Hainan.

67   *Sanlan zi* probably refers to *shannai* (also known as *sannai*), a plant in the ginger family (*Zingiberaceae*; specifically, *Alpinia galanga*) sometimes called the "galanga resurrection lily" in English. BCGM, 14.859 (*Compendium*, 2:14.1508).

68   HSRC, 67.58a.

69   *Wulan mu* (*Diospyros ebenum*) is usually identified in English as Ceylon ebony or Ceylon persimmon, or simply as "ebony." BCGM, 35.2046 (*Compendium*, 5:35.3101–2). See also ZFZ, 2.190 (*Chau Ju-Kua*, 216); and Wheatley, "Geographical Notes on Some Commodities," 75.

70   The entry on boat rudders in LWDD, 6.21–20, notes that ebony was used to construct the rudders of large, oceangoing vessels. The LWDD entry on ebony is translated and discussed in Shiba Yoshinobu, *Commerce and Society in Sung China*, trans. Mark Elvin (Ann Arbor: The University of Michigan, Center for Chinese Studies, 1970), 8; a portion of the same passage is also translated in Marks, *Tigers, Rice, Silk, and Silt*, 41–42.

71   HSRC, 67.58a.

72   The term *jibei* (from the Malay word *kapas*, meaning "cotton"; Sanskrit: *karpàsa*; sometimes alternately written in Chinese as *gubei*) refers to the kapok tree (*Ceiba pentandra*). The pods (or "fruits") of this tropical tree contain seeds surrounded by a fluffy, yellowish fiber that is a mix of lignin and cellulose. The fiber is harvested and woven into fabrics for such things as mattresses, pillows, and (as mentioned below by Fan Chengda) sitting mats. For additional information, see LWDD, 6.228 (*Netolizky*, 6.28); Hirth and Rockhill's extended comments in *Chau Ju-Kua*, 218–20, note; and the comments by Wheatley in "Geographical Notes on Some Commodities," 59.

berry tree, while their leaves are like those of the hibiscus. The [fibers of the tree] are woven into mats.[73]

Supplementary entry: **JU PLANTS** **[*JUCAO*]**[74] ward off mosquitoes and flies [*ying*].[75]

---

73   *HSRC*, 67.58a.

74   According to Isaac Henry Burkhill, *A Dictionary of Economic Products of the Malay Peninsula* (London: London Crown Agents for the Colonies, 1935), 792–96, quoted in *Netolitzky*, 276, n. 41, *jucao* is *Desmodium laburnifolium*, a flowering plant of the family Fabaceae, sometimes called beggar lice, tick clover, or tick trefoil. See also *LWDD*, 8.341 (*Netolitzky*, 8.41), which says it "grows to a height of 1 of 2 *chi*, and in shape resembles floss-grass or cogon-grass (*mao*, or *maocao*). If, during summer, a sprig of *ju* plant is placed on a sitting mat, mosquitoes and flies will not approach."

75   *HSRC*, 67.58b.

12

MISCELLANEOUS ITEMS

(Zazhi)

AS FOR THE UNUSUAL NATURE OF THE CUSTOMS AND GEOG-raphy in Lingnan,[1] these are worth noting in order to provide such information to learned persons.[2] But since I cannot classify this

---

1   Rather than Lingnan (South of the Mountain Ranges), some editions of *Treatises* instead read Jiaonan (South of the Pointy Peaks). *Yan Pei*, 110, and *Hu-Tan*, 166, both follow this reading. Lingnan and Jiaonan refer to the same general geographic region. The "mountain ranges" (*ling*) and "pointy peaks" (*jiao*) in these toponyms are references to the so-called Five Mountain Ranges (Wuling), which stretch across Jiangxi, Hunan, Guangdong, and Guangxi (there is disagreement among scholars about the precise locations and individual names of the ranges). "Lingnan" thus indicates the area south of the Five Ranges (this region is also sometimes called Lingbiao or Lingwai). During the Tang this part of China was called the Lingnan Circuit (Lingnan *dao*) and encompassed most of Guangdong and Guangxi, Hainan, and the northernmost part of modern Vietnam. In 862 the Lingnan *dao* was split in two, making separate "eastern" (Guangdong) and "western" (Guangxi) circuits, each headed by a order and rule commissioner (*jiedu shi*). During the Song these administrative areas became the Guangnan East and West Circuits (see Introduction, note 2). I suspect Fan Chengda's use of the term Lingnan (or Jiaonan) here, however, refers only to the Guangnan West Circuit, or modern Guangxi.

2   I read *bowen* 博聞 (lit., "extensive learning") to mean *bowenzhe* 博聞者, or "persons with extensive learning."

information separately [into individual treatises], I call this chapter the "Miscellaneous Items Treatise."

SNOW [XUE]. Snow and frost are rare in the Southern Counties,[3] and none of the herbaceous plants and trees there alter their branches or change their leaves.[4] Only in Guilin does it snow year after year.[5] Sometimes in the La month there are three snowfalls,[6] but in the end it never snows as much as in the Northern Counties. In the mountains that sit between Lingchuan and Xing'an,[7] where it is only wide enough for one horse—this is referred to as Yan Pass [Yanguan].[8] In the first lunar month, the snowfalls invariably stop when they reach the pass. When there is a heavy snowstorm, it crosses the pass and reaches the city wall of Guilin, going no farther south. In the northern section of the city, formerly there was a tower called the "Snow Observatory" [Xueguan], [the name of] which was used as a means to boost the reputation of the Southern Counties.[9]

---

3   "Southern Counties" (Nanzhou) refers generally to Song administrative areas in Guangdong and Guangxi. The "Northern Counties" (Beizhou; mentioned below) are Chinese administrative regions north of Guangxi.

4   In other words, the plants and trees in the Southern Counties are perennials that keep their leaves year round. The phrase "alter branches, change leaves" (*gaike yiye*) is drawn from the *Record of Rites* (Liji). See *Liji zhengyi*, 1430/23/202.

5   As mentioned here by Fan Chengda, Guilin is the only place in Guangxi that has snowfall during the brief, two-month winter there. Fan Chengda has left three poems that describe snowfalls in Guilin. See *FSHJ*, 14.176–77. In the long title to the first of these verses (176), Fan mentions that "over a foot" of snow fell in Guilin on the second day of the La month in the ninth year of the Qiandao reign period (6 January 1174 on the Western calendar). For more information on snowfall in Guilin, see *Hu-Tan*, 167, n. 2.

6   In other words, it snows quite often during the La or final month of the lunar year (roughly January on the Western calendar). In traditional China it was considered auspicious to see "three snowfalls" (*sanbai*), especially during the last month of the year, for this was believed to signal the coming of a prosperous New Year.

7   Lingchuan Town (near modern Lingchuan *xian*, Guangxi) was 60 *li* east of Guilin, while Xing'an Town was 150 *li* to the north. *TPHYJ*, 162.6b–7a. Yan Pass stood between the two towns, closer to Xing'an. See note 8 below for additional details.

8   According to *Dushi fangyu jiyao*, 106.4361, Yan Pass is 17 *li* southwest of Xing'an Town. In a note appended to his poem "Yan Pass," Fan Chengda mentions that it was also called "Flaming Heat Pass" (Yanguan) and regarded as the "demarcation point between north and south." See *FSHJ*, 15.189.

9   The last line of this entry does not appear in any of the surviving editions of

Supplementary text: Only in Guilin is there snow. From Guilin south to Haibei, people know nothing about snow. Someone might remark that it once snowed several decades ago, and that year was a great disaster. Presumably, the temperature of the soil is usually warmed by the sun, and plants are soft and fragile. So, when it suddenly snows, everything becomes stiff [freezes] and dies.[10]

WIND [FENG]. There are typhoons [*jufeng*] along the Southern Sea [Nanhai] in Guangdong. None of the counties and towns slightly to the north on the [Guangnan] West Circuit has them. Only in Guilin is it windy. In autumn and winter the winds are severe. Trees are uprooted and roof tiles fly about, never stopping day or night. Popular tradition relates that if the wind starts blowing in the morning, it will stop after one day; if it starts at dusk, then it will last for seven days; if it starts at midnight, then it will blow for a full ten days. [Guilin] is more than 1,000 *li* from the ocean, so these are not typhoons. The local people here do not know what they are talking about. I will try to explain: The elevation[11] of Guilin is taken to be 1,000 *zhang* higher than that of Changsha and Fanyu.[12] It is high and [thus] very windy. This no doubt explains things.

Supplementary text: The two rivers, the Xiang and the Li, both come out of Mount Haiyang [Haiyang Shan][13] in Lingchuan Town.

Treatises but has been recovered by Kong Fanli from a Qing dynasty commentary to Du Fu's poetry by Qiu Zhaoao. See *Du Shaoling ji xiangzhu*, 9.132; cited in *FCDBJ*, 131, n. 1. The same line is also recovered and reproduced in *Qi Zhiping*, 30 (see 32, n. 3).

10   *HSRC*, 67.58b–59a; *FCDBJ*, 131.

11   "Elevation" is a loose translation of *dishi*, literally, "land configuration."

12   Changsha refers to Changsha Town (Changsha *xian*) in Tan County (Tanzhou; modern Changsha, Hunan); Fanyu is an old name for the area around modern Guangzhou. Fan Chengda's figures here regarding the elevation of Guilin vis-à-vis Changsha and Fanyu are off the mark. Changsha stands just over 200 feet above sea level, while the elevation of Fanyu (or Guangzhou) is only about 50 feet. Guilin stands higher than both of these cities, but not "1,000 *zhang*" higher. Its elevation today is about 545 feet.

13   Mount Haiyang (also known as Yanghai Shan, or Mount Yanghai) is located 170 *li* north of Xing'an Town. *TPHYJ*, 162.7a. The idea that the source of the Xiang and Li Rivers is Mount Haiyang goes back at least to the Tang period. See Mo Xiufu, *Guilin fengtu ji*, 6. While the source of the Xiang is still regarded as Mount Haiyang, modern experts say the origin of the Li River is the Mao'er

They course [together] for a hundred *li*, then split off to the north and south, and proceed onward. The river to the north is called the Xiang. It proceeds onward for 2,000 *li* to Changsha. Only then does the river begin to slow down. The river to the south is called the Li. It passes through 360 shoals [*tan*] and then continues on for 1,200 *li* to Fanyu, where it enters the sea. Guilin alone serves as the backbone of the Xiang and Li, and stands 1,000 *zhang* above Changsha and Fanyu. Beyond the cloudy forms [*yunwu*],[14] it is high and [thus] very windy. This no doubt explains things.[15]

GUI RIVER [*GUISHUI*]. There is an ancient account about Guilin that local elders have transmitted orally. Briefly, it goes: "Since the Gui River courses around the eastern city wall, it will forever be free of weapons and war."[16] "Gui River" is the Li River.[17]

MIASMA [*ZHANG*].[18] In the Two Guangs only Guilin is free of miasma.

Mountains (Mao'er Shan) in Xing'an. For additional information on Mount Haiyang as it relates to the Xiang and Li Rivers, see especially Tang Zhaomin, comp., *Lingqu wenxian cuibian*, 1–14.

14   I understand this phrase to mean that Guilin is located in a remote place, even "beyond the clouds."

15   *HSRC*, 67.59a; *FCDBJ*, 131.

16   As mentioned here by Fan Chengda, "Gui River" is another name for the Li River. The character *gui* 癸, here an abbreviation for *rengui* 壬癸, represents "north," indicating that the Li River flows down to Guilin from the north. *LWDD*, 1.29 (*Netolitzky*, 1.14), notes that the course of the Gui (or Li) River flowed south along the eastern wall of Guilin, thus forming a natural moat. This same source also mentions that "long ago" a moat had been dug at the northeastern corner of the Guilin city wall, allowing water from the Gui River to flow completely around the Guilin city wall and then come together on the eastern side (see map 2), and that Fan Chengda had the moat dredged when he served as administrator of Guangxi.

17   While serving as an official in Guilin, Fan Chengda built (in 1174) a pavilion he called the "Gui River Pavilion" (Guishui Ting). See Kong Fanli, comp., *Fan Chengda nianpu*, 259. His poem celebrating its construction is found in *FSHJ*, 14.178 ("Guishui ting . . . "). The pavilion was situated on the riverbank, below Subduing-the-Waves Precipice and in front of the Eight Cinnamons Hall. See *LWDD*, 1.30 (*Netolitzky*, 1.14).

18   "Miasma" refers to noxious fumes rising from marshes or decomposing animal or vegetable matter that was thought to poison and infect the air, causing miasmic diseases (*zhangli*) and other dreaded ailments. For additional information on miasma in south China during the Song, see *LWDD*, 4.152–53 (*Netolitzky*, 4.4). See also Schafer, *Vermilion Bird*, esp. 130–34. Cf. the comments on

Everywhere south of Guilin is home to miasma! As for miasma, it is caused by mountain mists and watery poisons, together with foul exhalations from wild grasses and steamy swelter from lush vegetation. People who have come down with miasma look like they have malaria [*nüe*]. Although there are many treatment methods, usually monkshood[19] is used in extreme cases, while pinellia, atractylodes, and agastache formula [*buhuan jin zhengqi san*] are used in common cases.[20] [Along] the Two Rivers in Yong County, the water and soil are especially foul. Over the course of an entire year, there is never a time when there is no miasma. In the spring it is called green grass miasma [*qingcao zhang*]; in summer it is called yellow-mei miasma [*huang-mei zhang*]; in the sixth and seventh months it is called new grains miasma [*xinhe zhang*]; in the eighth and ninth months it is called yellow floss-grass miasma [*huangmao zhang*]. Local people regard yellow floss-grass miasma as being especially toxic.

Supplementary text: Miasma, as it turns out, relates to the blazing quarter [*yanfang*; the south], where the pulse of the land is dispersed and the air is drained.[21] People are baked by its constant heat. As for the veins and arteries in the skin [of southerners], they are flat and smooth, and never thick. Moreover, for several tens of *li* there is no tree shade, wells, hostel accommodations [*nilü*], or medicinal herbs [*yiyao*]. Illnesses caused by the heat are not necessarily all the result of miasma. Rocky Lake's[22] "Account of the True Summer Hall"

---

malaria in Lingnan in Marks, *Tigers, Rice, Silk, and Silt*, 71–76. Marks seems to think that *zhang* always indicates malaria, but this is not the case. Below Fan Chengda draws a clear distinction between miasma and malaria.

19   This root (see fig. 5 in the "Treatise on Aromatics") is native to Sichuan and is used for a variety of medicinal purposes. *CMP*, 522a.

20   *Buhuan jin zhengqi san* (lit., "priceless *qi*-correcting powder") is the name of a medicinal formula composed of pinellia, atractylodes, and agastache. For additional information, see Guo Jinlong, "Buhuan jin zhengqi san fangxiang hua shixing pi de shiyan yanjiu," 25–28.

21   I understand this line to mean that the extreme heat in the south causes the geographical features, or "veins of the earth" (*dimai*), to be dispersed (or "unsteady"; *shu*), while the air is drained (*xie*) and thus lacking in its usual nourishing qualities.

22   The last line of supplementary text here was probably added by Huang Zhen, for Fan Chengda rarely uses his nickname "Rocky Lake" when referring to himself.

[Zhengxia Tang ji] discusses this in great detail.[23]

CINNAMON MOUNTAIN RANGE [*GUILING*]: In the past I did not know its true location. Five *li* north of the Guilin city wall, there is little slope one *xunzhang* in height. A stone [stele] stands on it inscribed with the words "Cinnamon Mountain Range."[24] He County has its own Guiling Town [Guiling *xian*],[25] and tradition has passed down that the Initial Security Mountain Range [Shian Ling] was located there.[26] The little slope here today does not mark that place.

VULGAR CHARACTERS [*SUZI*].[27] Since the distant border regions are

---

23   Unfortunately, Fan Chengda's commemorative essay on this hall is not extant. In a colophon to one of his Guilin poems, Fan mentions that he planted cinnamon trees in front of the True Summer Hall in 1174. See *FSHJ*, 14.183 ("Chunxi jiawu Guilin . . . "). Supplementary text from *HSRC*, 67.60a; *FCDBJ*, 132.

24   Fan mentions in the *Canluan lu* that this stone stele was erected by an official named Lü Yuan, who served as military governor of Guilin between 1125 and 1126. See Fan Chengda, *Canluan lu*, 60; Hargett, *On the Road*, 204.

25   He County (southeast of modern He *xian*, Guangxi) was originally on the Guangnan East Circuit but after 1126 was transferred to the Guangnan West Circuit. *Songshi*, 90.2237. Guiling, located 82 *li* northeast of He County, was one of three towns under its jurisdiction. *TPHYJ*, 161.5a.

26   Here I follow the *SKQS* (34b) and *ZBZZCS* (30b) editions and read *xiangchuan Shian ling zai qi di* 相傳始安嶺在其地. See *FCDBJ*, 131, n. 2. Just about all of Fan's comments in this entry about the Cinnamon Mountain Range are drawn from the *Canluan lu*. There Fan states outright that the words "Cinnamon Mountain Range"—inscribed on the stone stele north of Guilin—are a mistake. He further remarks that Cinnamon Mountain Range is actually in He County and that it is also known by the name Shian Ling, or Initial Security Mountain Range. See Fan Chengda, *Canluan lu*, 60; Hargett, *On the Road*, 203. Cf. *Yan Pei*, 114, n. 9, which says Fan's identification of Initial Security Mountain Range as an alternate name for the Cinnamon Mountain Range in He County is mistaken. I agree with this assessment. See my comments in *On the Road*, 246, n. 347. *Yan Pei* correctly points out that "Initial Security Mountain Range" was an alternate name for the Yuecheng Range (Yuecheng Ling), the westernmost of the Five Ranges located in Xing'an Town (the ancient name for this area was Shian, lit., "Initial Security"). Yan further notes that Guiling was an alternate name for the Mengzhu Mountain Range (Mengzhu Ling), one of the Five Mountain Ranges (see note 1 above) located on the border between Hunan and Guangxi.

27   After the reforms during the Qin and Han dynasties that sought to standardize the written forms of Chinese characters, a distinction was made between *zhengzi*, or standard-form characters (used in official documents), and *suzi*, or vulgar characters. The latter were often, but not always, simplified versions (that is, with fewer total strokes) of the former and varied from region to

unrefined and vulgar, legal petitions [*diesu*] and contracts [*quanyue*] use local and vulgar writing forms exclusively. This is the case in all the districts of Guilin. For now I will just list several characters from Lingui.[28] Although they are very crude and rustic, I nevertheless also append a list of them below:

> 𡚻, pronounced *ai* 矮, means "not lengthy."
>
> 閞, pronounced *wen* 穩, means "sit within the confines of a door/ gate; to be secure."
>
> 𡋯, also pronounced *wen* 穩, means "a large seat"; it also means "to be secure."
>
> 仈, pronounced *niao* 嫋, means "a young boy."
>
> 奀, pronounced *dong* 動, means "persons who are skinny and weak."
>
> 歪, pronounced *zhong* 終, means "persons who die and disappear."
>
> 𠀚, pronounced *la* 臘, means "unable to raise one's foot."[29]
>
> 妑, pronounced *da* 大, means "a daughter who has grown as big as her older sister."
>
> 𡼥, pronounced *kan* 勘, means "precipice cavities in mountain stone."
>
> 閂, pronounced *shuan* 橏,[30] means "a door that is locked with a crossbar."

As for the others, I am not able to list them all here.[31] I read legal petitions for two years [in Guilin] and got used to seeing them.

---

region. The vulgar characters used in Guilin listed below all fall into the category of "associative" (*huiyi*) characters, whereby two separate and independent characters are combined to form a new character with a related meaning. For instance, the first vulgar character listed below takes the elements *bu* 不 (not) and *chang* 長 (long) and combines them to form a new, single character (𡚻) meaning "not lengthy" or "short."

28   Lingui is the name of the principal administrative town of Jingjiang Municipality.

29   This probably refers to someone who is disabled and unable to walk.

30   Following *LWDD*, 4.161, and reading *shuan* 橏.

31   In *LWDD*, 4.161 (*Netolitzky*, 4.11), Zhou Qufei lists several vulgar character forms, many of which are still used by Zhuang people in Guangxi today, that are not mentioned in this entry by Fan Chengda. See also *LWDD*, 4.162–63, n. 5, where Yang Wuquan provides useful references to other sources that list and describe vulgar characters. See also the remarks in *Yan Pei*, 114, n.10, and *Hu-Tan*, 172–73, n. 1.

WRITTEN DOCUMENTS [*WENSHU*] from the Kingdom of Dali [Dali Guo] sometimes reach the southern border of China, and merchants from Dali carry Buddhist sūtras from their kingdom with heading titles [*tishi*] that still use the character *guo* 圀. As for *guo* 圀, this was the written form devised by Empress Wu [Wuhou][32] and used for *guo* 國 [state or kingdom]. The *Tang History* [Tangshu] refers to the Kingdom of Dali using the characters 大禮國.[33] The kingdom has stopped using the character *li* 理.

ABDUCTING A PARTNER [*JUANBAN*].[34] The legal system in the South-

---

32　Zhang Zhuo notes that during the Tianshou reign (690–692) of the Tang someone submitted a memorial to Empress Wu (Wu Zetian) pointing out that the *huo* 或 element "inside" the character *guo* 國 "deludes and causes disorder among celestial phenomena" (*huoluan tianxiang* 或亂天象; *huo* 或 here is used as a synonym for *huo* 惑, meaning "to delude"). This memorial further proposed that the *huo* component of the character *guo* be replaced with *wu* 武 (martial; valiant) in order to "provide security" to the area within the boundaries of the empire (*wei* 囗). See *Chaoye qianzai*, 1.12. Apparently, though, this character was never officially adopted. *Hu-Tan*, 173, n. 2, based on information culled mainly from Zheng Qiao's *Tongzhi*, identifies eighteen substitution characters promulgated by Empress Wu. The graph 圀 appears on this list, but the one described above (with the *huo* 或 element "inside") does not.

33　Fan's reference to the *Tang History* is probably to a passage in the *Xin Tangshu*, 222*zhong*.6282. Dali 大禮 here refers to the name of a new state declared by the ruler of Nanzhao in the ninth century, just after Nanzhao's formal dependency on China ended. After the overthrow of the Nanzhao kingdom in 902, a new state was formed in 937 in what is now Yunnan called Dali 大理. Fan Chengda's comment in the next line that "the kingdom has stopped using the character *li* 理" is wrong. See the comments in Fang Guoyu, *Zhongguo xi'nan lishi dili kaoshi*, 1:431. The state of Dali 大理 (which, incidentally, took its name from its capital city located near what is now Kunming in Yunnan) lasted until 1253, when it was destroyed by invading Mongols.

34　The term *juanban*, a local expression in twelfth-century Guangxi, literally means "sweep away a partner." As will soon become evident, however, Fan Chengda is describing a custom here whereby women were abducted and then removed to another location. For additional information on the history of this practice in south China, see Anne B. McLaren, "Marriage by Abduction in Twentieth Century China," *Modern Asian Studies* 35.4 (2001): 953–85. See also Eberhard, *Local Cultures*, 277, which describes "ceremonial bride captures" in Yunnan and Guizhou. These staged captures should be distinguished from the abductions described in this entry by Fan Chengda, which seem to be very real. See also *LWDD*, 10.430 (*Netolitzky*, 10.35), where *juanban* is used to refer to merchants who "secretly entice away" local women in Guangxi and take them north.

ern Counties is sketchy and imprecise [regarding this practice]. Most marriages are improper.[35] People in the villages are violent and brutal. Men kidnap the wives and daughters of others and run off with them. They then move to a different place and live there peacefully and contentedly. This is referred to as "abducting a partner." Although they use the word "abduct" [*juan*], they take it to mean "[select a] mate" [*banlü*]. Later the woman could again be abducted by some other person. There are even women who have had this experience several times with the abductions still not having ended. As for the [abducted] woman's parents-in-law or former husband, if they make inquiries and discover her whereabouts, they will go to [a local] government official and personally state their case. The official will then look into the situation on the former husband's behalf. Oftentimes the so-called former husband got the woman through abduction as well and afterward said she was abducted by someone else. Only in [court] cases brought by [a woman's] own father and mother, brothers, or the man who first married her are women in fact returned to the family from which they were abducted earlier.

Supplementary text: Regarding the practice of abducting a partner, this form of marriage does not follow any ritualistic practice. It is [just] a name for secretly luring someone away.[36]

FEVER [*CAOZI*] is in fact [a term describing] the "cold and hot epidemic" [*hanre shiyi*].[37] In the south, minor officials [*lizu*] and com-

---

35   A "proper" (*zheng*) marriage in traditional China involved negotiations between families concerning the bride's dowry, the price paid for her by the groom's family, and related matters. The marriage custom described below included no such negotiations. Hence Fan calls it "improper" (*buzheng*).

36   *HSRC*, 67.60b.

37   The local Man term *caozi* (original meaning unknown), rendered loosely here as "fever," is defined by Fan Chengda as the "cold and hot epidemic." This condition also falls under the more general category of miasma or miasmic diseases, which were believed to be contagious. The treatment method described below, which is called *tiao caozi* (translated as "break the fever"; *tiao* literally means "stab" or "prick"), is described in greater detail in *LWDD*, 4.153 (*Netolitzky*, 4.4). Zhou Qufei mentions that the *tiao caozi* method was only used in cases involving *rezhang*, or "hot miasma." According to Zhou, persons suffering from more serious cases of hot miasma "feel like they are sleeping on a bed of ashes and fire."

moners [*xiaomin*] never inquire about the source of an illness but only report they have a headache or are not feeling right. They refer to this as "the fever." They do not take medicine but instead have someone use a small awl [or needle] and pierce their lip and the tip of their tongue to draw blood. This they refer to as "breaking the fever" [*tiao caozi*].[38] Actually, this does not make their illness any worse, but they must definitely take medicine before they can get better.

Supplementary entry: **DIVINATION WITH CHICKENS [*JIBU*]:** As for the divination methods [*zhanfa*] of southerners, they take a young rooster, hold it by its two legs, burn incense and divine through prayers, and beat the chicken to death. They then extract the two thigh bones, clean and wash them, and bind them together with a cord. Next they insert a small bamboo branch where the bones are bound, causing the two bones to align symmetrically at the end of the branch. Holding the bamboo branch, they offer blessings a second time. The left bone functions as the *nong. Nong* means "I." The right bone functions as "the other person" [*ren*]; this means the matter that the other person is divining. They then inspect the minute holes on the sides of the two bones by taking a slender bamboo branch a little over an inch long and inserting it into all the holes—obliquely, straight in, from the side, and through the very center, always following the natural contour of the holes, so as to determine the auspicious and inauspicious. There are eighteen variations of this method. As a general rule, the straight and centered ones and some of those that are close to the bone are mostly auspicious, while the crooked and oblique ones and some of those far away from the bone are mostly inauspicious.[39]

There are also persons who divine with chicken eggs. They divine by grasping the eggs and writing in ink on the shell, indicating the four directions. They boil the eggs until they are cooked and then cut

---

38   According to Zhao Fengyan and Li Xiaocen, the acupuncture-bloodletting treatment described here, common in Guangxi, can be traced through archaeological evidence back to remote antiquity. Later, they say, it was transmitted to Chinese civilization in the Central Plains. See their "Cong *Lingwai daida* kan Guangxi Songdai de kexue jishu chengjiu," 42–43.

39   The practice of divining with chicken bones was quite common in south China. See the remarks in Eberhard, *Local Cultures*, 422–23. See also LWDD, 10.442 (*Netolitzky*, 10.44). On the practice of divining with chicken eggs, see below.

them crosswise, inspecting the place that has the ink and distinguishing the thickness or thinness of the white part in the shell so as determine the "I" person's auspiciousness or inauspiciousness.[40]

Supplementary entry: **QIN CITY [QINCHENG]**[41] is the place where the First Emperor [of Qin] earlier dispatched troops to guard the area of the Five Ranges.[42]

Supplementary entry: **NUMINOUS CANAL [LINGQU]**[43] is located in Xing'an Town, Gui County, where the Xiang River flows down from Hunan in the north. Moreover, as for the Rong River [Rongjiang], this is [another name for] the lower reaches of the Zanghe [River].[44] It flows south and down into Guangxi. The two rivers [the Xiang and Rong Rivers] are far apart and have no interaction. Censor Lu [Shi Lu][45]

---

40 Sima Guang, *Zizhi tongjian*, 21.683. This entry does not appear in surviving editions of *Treatises*. It has been recovered by Kong Fanli from Hu Sanxing's commentary in the *Zizhi tongjian*. See FCDBJ, 131, n. 3. Egg divination is also discussed in Eberhard, *Local Cultures*, 420–21.

41 My placement of this supplementary entry is arbitrary. Gu Zuyu, comp., *Dushi fangyu jiyao*, 106.4806, quoting the line that follows, provides additional description of Qin City that presumably is quoted from the original, more complete version of this passage on Qincheng in *Treatises:* "Qin City is located south of the Xiang River, between the Rong and Li Rivers. Its ruins still exist; its brick-lined wells are in good shape. The northern part of the city is near Yan Pass, which is surrounded by clusters of mountains. The bird-track trail there will not allow two carriages to travel abreast."

42 HSRC, 67.59a; FCDBJ, 131.

43 The Numinous Canal (sometimes called in English the "Magic Canal" or "Magic Transport Canal") is located in modern Xing'an *xian*, near Guilin. For additional information, see LWDD, 1.27–28 (*Netolitzky*, 1.13). Fan Chengda's entry on the Numinous Canal is also translated and discussed in *Needham et al.*, 4.3:303–5.

44 Fan Chengda is mistaken here. The Rong and Zanghe are two different rivers with separate origins and courses. See the comments in Tang Zhaomin, comp., *Lingqu wenxian cuibian*, 94. Zhou Qufei also mistakenly thought that the Rong and the Zanghe were two different names for the same river. See LWDD, 1.24 (*Netolitzky*, 1.11). On the place-name and administrative designation Zangge, see the "Treatise on the Man," note 167.

45 During the Qin dynasty it was customary to append the given name (*ming*) of government officials to their office titles. In this case, the given name is Lu, and the office title is Shi, the latter being an abbreviation for *jianyu shi*, or supervising censor. Censor Lu's family name is unknown. Virtually no details are available on his life except that he served as an official under the Qin and was sent to

piled rocks on the sandy bank[46] to make a ploughshare beak [*huazui*],[47] diverting the flow of the Xiang into the Rong. It [then] surged onward for 60 *li*, where thirty-six sluice gates [*doumen*] were put in place.[48] When a boat enters a sluice gate, a second one is then flooded, causing the water level to rise and gradually pass into the first one. Thus, boats are able to rise by "following the cliff" [*xunyai*][49] and descend by "turning over the jar" [*jianling*].[50] Of the ingenious and skillful ways of controlling water, none is better than [that of] the Numinous Canal.[51]

Supplementary entry: **CHAOZONG CANAL [CHAOZONG QU]:**[52] After it

---

the south to open up a canal (that is, the Numinous Canal) that would facilitate shipment of food and supplies to Qin troops engaged in military campaigns in the south. See Sima Qian, *Shiji*, 112.2958.

46 Reading *shake* 沙磕 to mean *shaqi* 沙磧, or "sandy bank." Cf. *LWDD*, 1.27, which reads *shaqi*.

47 That is, a dam or dike shaped like a ploughshare (*hua*). *Needham et al.*, 4.3:303–5, translates *huazui* as "division-head." The preface to Fan Chengda's poem "Ploughshare Beak" notes that the "beak" was located about five *li* outside of Xing'an Town. See *FSHJ*, 15.190 ("Huazui"). Fan Chengda suggests that the ploughshare beak and sluice gates described here were built by Censor Lu during the Qin, but this is not the case. According to Yu Mengwei's "Account of the Repairs Made on the Numinous Canal in Gui County" (Guizhou chongxiu Lingqu ji), dated 868, the person responsible for this construction (in 825) was the Tang official Li Bo and not Censor Lu. Dong Hao et al., eds., *Quan Tangwen*, 804.10b–12b. Yu's account is also cited in Tang Zhaomin, comp., *Lingqu wenxian cuibian*, 148–50 (see also Tang Zhaomin's comments on 132).

48 "Sixty *li*" refers to the entire length of the canal. It is uncertain how many sluice gates may have existed on the canal when Li Bo made his repairs in 825. In 868, however, when Yu Mengwei made further repairs, the number of sluice gates apparently was "increased to eighteen." See the remarks in Tang Zhaomin, comp., *Lingqu wenxian cuibian*, 158. It is not clear exactly when thirty-six sluice gates were in place on the canal. Tang Zhaoming discusses this issue on 164.

49 In other words, as the water level rises, the boat "follows" or "hugs" the sides of the sluice gate (here called "cliffs") as it ascends.

50 *Jianling* is an abbreviation of *jian lingshui*, literally, "turn a water jar upside down." This expression is drawn from Sima Qian, *Shiji*, 8.382. Here the idea is that as water is drained from the sluice gate, the boat inside it descends.

51 *HSRC*, 67.59a–b; *FCDBJ*, 131–32.

52 This canal was located right before Single Elegance Peak. It served several purposes but was used mainly for local water transportation. See the comments on this and other uses of the canal in Lin Zhe, "Guilin Duxiu fengshan qian chengshi xingtai kongjian lishi yanbian," 161. Fan Chengda supervised repairs on the canal in 1174. Kong Fanli, comp., *Fan Chengda nianpu*, 259–60. The

was dug, there were then people who passed the civil service examination.[53]

Supplementary entry: **BRONZE PILLARS [TONGZHU]**[54] were erected in the state of Jiaozhi by Subduing-the-Waves Ma.[55] When people pass below the pillars, they invariably bank them with rocks. A craggy mound has formed as a result.[56] When Ma Zong served as protec-

---

Chaozong Canal connected the Li River with Guilin's West Lake, which in turn connected with the Yang River. Gu Zuyu, comp., *Dushi fangyu jiyao*, 107.4819. Initial construction of this waterway is usually attributed to Wang Zudao. Wang's biography in *Songshi*, 438.11040–42, mentions many of his activities in Guilin but says nothing about construction of a canal.

53 HSRC, 67.59a–b; FCDBJ, 131–32. The following report appears in a Song text titled *Guilin shengshi ji*, written by Zhang Zhongyu: "The [Li River] channel's flow from the north was diverted to the west, causing water to pour into the [Guilin] city moat. [This layout] resembled blood vessels encompassing an entire human body. This event subsequently became known to the court, and so in the second year of the Daguan reign [1108] authorization was given to issue an imperial edict ordering that anyone blocking up the new channel would be treated legally the same way as brigands who destroy the dikes of the Yellow and Bian Rivers, and be thrown in prison. That year a great many scholars from Gui passed the civil service examination." Quoted in Wang Sen, ed., *Yuexi jinshi lüe*, 8/9b–10a. Zhang Zhongyu hailed from Lingui Town, and it seems likely that Fan Chengda met him in Guilin. See Kong Fanli, comp., *Fan Chengda nianpu*, 241. It also seems likely that either Zhang or his account was the source of the comment about "many scholars from Gui passing the civil service examinations" (in 1108).

54 The LWDD entry on bronze pillars (10.404; *Netolitzky*, 10.17) offers additional details.

55 There are numerous theories concerning the location of the Han general Ma Yuan's famous bronze pillars, presumably erected to celebrate his military victories in the south. Many scholars believe the pillars were cast and erected to mark the demarcation point between the Han empire and Jiaozhi. The precise location of the pillars, however, is uncertain. On the many theories regarding the location of the pillars, see Yang Wuquan's critical summary in LWDD, 10.404–5, and Liam C. Kelley, *Beyond the Bronze Pillars: Envoy Poetry and the Sino-Vietnamese Relationship* (Honolulu: Association for Asian Studies and University of Hawai`i Press, 2005), 5–9. One modern scholar, Donald S. Sutton, thinks the story about Ma Yuan's bronze pillars was "probably invented" as a "symbol" that "stood as a barrier between what was known and controlled and what was beyond the [Chinese] empire." See Sutton, "A Case of Literati Piety: The Ma Yuan Cult from High-Tang to High-Qing," 105.

56 Fan Chengda is repeating a well-known legend here, which runs as follows: Ma Yuan's famous bronze pillars supposedly bore an inscription that reads "If these pillars are ever removed, Jiaozhi will be annihilated." Whenever local

tor-general [*du(du) hu*] of Annan, the Yi and Liao people erected two bronze pillars [in his honor].⁵⁷ Also, when He Lüguang of the Tang pacified Nanzhao,⁵⁸ he erected a second bronze pillar for Subduing-the-Waves [Ma Yuan].⁵⁹ This was in Dali.⁶⁰

Supplementary entry: **BUDDHISTS AND DAOISTS [SENGDAO]**⁶¹ are all those who lack ordination certificates [*dudie*]⁶² and have wives and children.⁶³

---

residents would pass by the pillars, they would thus shore them up with stones, out of fear that the pillars might fall down and Ma Yuan's pledge would come true. It seems possible that the report on this legend in Wang Xiangzhi's *Yudi jisheng*, completed in 1227, is based, at least in part, on this entry in *Treatises*.

57   Ma Zong (fl. late eighth to early ninth centuries) believed that he was a descendant of Ma Yuan, and so he (or the local Yi and Liao people) erected bronze pillars to celebrate the accomplishments of his illustrious ancestor. This event took place during the Yuanhe reign (806–821) and is mentioned in Ma Zong's biography in *Xin Tangshu*, 163.5033.

58   He Lüguang (eighth century) was a native of Hainan who distinguished himself as a military official and officer under the reigns of the Tang emperors Xuanzong (r. 712–756) and Suzong (r. 756–762). According to Sima Guang, *Zizhi tongjian*, 216.6918, the pacification of Nanzhao mentioned here took place in the summer of 753.

59   *Xin Tangshu*, 222shang.6270, mentions that He Lüguang erected "bronze pillars for Ma Yuan" in Anning City (Anning *cheng*; southwest of modern Kunming) after his military campaign in Nanzhao.

60   HSRC, 67.59b; FCDBJ, 132.

61   I strongly suspect the text of this entry is corrupt. Cf. LWDD, 147 (Netolitzky, 3.26), which provides a much more detailed description of *sengdao*, or Buddhist and Daoists. Zhou Qufei's entry says nothing about "wives and children."

62   During the Song dynasty Buddhist monks and Daoist priests were considered legal only if they possessed official certificates issued by the state. Throughout most of the Song one could purchase an ordination certificate from the government, but they were expensive and beyond the means of most people. LWDD, 3.147 (Netolitzky, 3.26), mentions that there were very few legal Buddhists and Daoists (*sengdao*) in the Southern Counties because they could not afford to purchase ordination certificates. As a result, most only had novice (*tongxing*) status. One attraction of possessing an ordination certificate is that once one had it in hand, one did not have to become a monk or a priest. One could go back to one's usual secular life but still be exempt from taxes, military service, and so on. A useful overview of the ordination certificate system under the Tang and Song appears in Kenneth Ch'en, "The Sale of Monk Certificates during the Sung Dynasty: A Factor in the Decline of Buddhism in China," *Harvard Theological Review* 49.4 (1956): 307–27.

63   HSRC, 67.60a; FCDBJ, 132.

Supplementary entry: **MOON CROPS** [*YUEHE*] are not planted when there is no moon.[64]

Supplementary entry: **LOCAL MILITIA** [*TUDING*][65] wear uniforms[66] resembling those of the imperial troops [*jinjun*].[67]

Supplementary entry: **SECURITY GUARDS** [*BAODING*][68] serve under the security head [*baozheng*]. They were formed after pacifying the

---

64   *HSRC*, 67.60a; *FCDBJ*, 132. This six-character entry is incomprehensible because the text is corrupt. Based on the entry on *yuehe* in *LWDD*, 8.338–39 (*Netolitzky*, 8.38), the word *he* (lit., "grain," "cereal," "seedling") was used in Qin County to indicate the different crops of paddy rice (*shuidao*) harvested there year round. Fan Chengda's incomplete line is probably a corruption of the following, which appears in *LWDD* (8.338): "The land is warm [in Qin County], so there is no month when they do not plant and no month when they do not harvest." Zhou Qufei mentions that paddy rice planted in the eleventh and twelfth lunar months is called "the moon crop" (*yuehe*).

65   A much longer and detailed description of local militia in Guangxi appears in *LWDD*, 3.132–33 and 140 (*Netolitzky*, 3.16 and 3.21), and in Okada, *Zhong-guo Hua'nan minzu shehui shi yanjiu*, 117–30. These units were composed of local Chinese men (from tax-paying households) requisitioned by the Song for defense. According to the *Songshi*, 191.4744, one male member of five in each household had to serve as a *tuding*. This same source also mentions that in 1062 there were 39,800 officially registered local militia on the Guangnan West Circuit. The local militia, security guards, and stockade troops described in this and the next two entries were recruited from tax-paying Chinese households. The settlement militia (*dongding*), described below, and able-bodied men subject to military service (*zhuangding*) were drawn from the local, non-Chinese population.

66   Reading *zhi* 制 to mean *zhi* 製 (dress; uniforms).

67   *HSRC*, 67.60a; *FCDBJ*, 132. "Imperial troops" here refers to regular government troops, in this case Song forces stationed in Guangxi.

68   "Security guards" were a type of local militia that developed from the *baojia* system established in the Northern Song as a result of the reforms of Wang Anshi. More specifically, the formation of the *baoding*, or "security guard" system, in Guangxi was a direct result of a local rebellion there during the Northern Song. See the "Treatise on the Man," note 34, for information on the "Nong bandits." Essentially, *baoding* were part of a community-based system of law enforcement and civil control. One *bao* consisted of ten *jia*, which in turn comprised one hundred households. According to the *Songshi*, 192.4790, each Chinese family in the Two Guangs was required to supply one male to serve as a *baoding*, but this policy was abolished during the Qiandao reign (1165–1174) because of the hardship it brought on families. The leaders of the *bao*, called security heads (see text below), were given authority to maintain local order.

Nong bandits.[69] Now they are compelled to serve through private corvée [*siyi*].[70]

Supplementary entry: **STOCKADE TROOPS [*ZHAIDING*]**[71] are those
organized along the Creek Settlements.[72]

Supplementary entry: **SETTLEMENT MILITIA [*DONGDING*]**[73] are composed of people from the Creek Settlements.[74]

Supplementary entry: **BRINGING BACK TO LIFE [*TIAOSHENG*]**[75] is a

---

69 On the Nong bandits, see the "Treatise on the Man."

70 *HSRC*, 67.60a; *FCDBJ*, 132.

71 In twelfth-century Guangxi stockades or forts (*zhai*) were put in place near
    the various bridle and halter counties so activities could be watched and moni-
    tored. In addition to regular Song government troops and local militia, these
    stockades also quartered *zhaiding*, or "stockade troops" recruited from the
    local Chinese population. See *LWDD*, 3.137–38 (*Netolitzky*, 3.20), and Okada,
    Zhongguo Hua'nan minzu shehui shi yanjiu, 130–32.

72 *HSRC*, 67.60a; *FCDBJ*, 132.

73 According to the *Songshi*, 191.4746, in the sixth year of the Xining reign (1073)
    there were 45,200 registered "settlement militia" in Yong County. This num-
    ber is repeated in *LWDD*, 3.136 (*Netolitzky*, 3.20). For additional information
    on *dongding* on the Guangnan West Circuit during the Song, see An Guolou,
    Songchao zhoubian minzu zhengce yanjiu, 79–85.

74 *HSRC*, 67.60a; *FCDBJ*, 132.

75 I read *tiao* 挑 in *tiaosheng* 挑生 to mean "arouse" or "provoke." Cf. *Netolitzky*,
    10.48, which translates *tiaosheng* as "Mord durch Wiederbeleben" (murder by
    means of resuscitation). In order to understand the meaning of this expression,
    it must be considered together with the subject of the entry that follows on *gu*
    poison. A number of different ideas and practices have been associated with
    gu poison during its long history, all of which involve a type of black magic or
    witchcraft intended to harm or kill people. A primitive form of the character
    gu 蠱 has even been identified in some of the recovered oracle bone descrip-
    tions dating from the Yin-Shang period (fourteenth century–1045 B.C.E.). H. Y.
    Feng and J. K. Shryock, in their informative article "The Black Magic in China
    Known as *Ku*," 2–9, identify five meanings (or uses) of the term *gu* in pre-Han
    literature. Among these, the one most relevant to Fan Chengda's entries on
    tiaosheng and *gudu* concerns the illegal practice of using *gu* poison to kill peo-
    ple. Most often, *gu* poison was made by placing insects, worms, snakes, or other
    poisonous creatures into a large cauldron (the character *gu* 蠱 itself comprises
    an "insect" [*chong* 蟲] positioned above a vessel [*min* 皿]). These creatures
    were allowed to eat each other until only one was left. The survivor was the *gu*.
    The *gu* (which supposedly could change its shape and appearance at will) was
    administered as a poison in food and drink. Beginning in the Tang period, the
    practice of using *gu* as a form of witchcraft or black magic was largely confined
    to south China and, more specifically, the aboriginal tribes of the south (Feng

variety of witchcraft [*yaoshu*] that uses fish or meat to harm people. If the spell is situated in the diaphragm [*xiongge*], ingesting bugbane [*shengma*][76] will induce one to vomit it up. If it is situated in the lower back or stomach, aromatic turmeric [*yujin*][77] will pass it down

---

and Shryock, 10). The earliest reference I have found concerning the practice of "collecting all different kinds of insects to make *gu* and poison people" appears in Liu Xun, *Lingbiao luyi*, 1.1, written around 900. During the Tang and Song, those who practiced this form of sorcery suffered severe punishment, usually exile. See Brian E. McKnight, *Law and Order in Sung China* (Cambridge: Cambridge University Press, 1992), 76.

Fan Chengda's entry on *gu* poison (below) is corrupt and incomplete. The entry on *gudu* in the LWDD (10.448; *Netolitzky*, 10.49), however, provides some fascinating information on the use of *gu* poison in Guangxi in the twelfth century. Among other things, Zhou Qufei mentions: "If you want to know if a family keeps *gu* poison or not, just go inside their house. If there is not the slightest trace of dust anywhere, then they do." This same comment is repeated, in abbreviated form, in Fan's entry on *gu* poison. Eberhard observes that *gu* raised in pots or cauldrons would "magically keep the house clean" (*Local Cultures*, 150).

Tiaosheng is a type of *gu* poison. While Fan Chengda mentions only that *tiaosheng* is a variety of sorcery (*wushu*), Zhou Qufei says that "in Guangxi *tiaosheng* is used to kill people." See LWDD, 10.448 (*Netolitzky*, 10.48). This is accomplished by serving the intended victim some fish or meat tainted with *gu* poison and then reciting a spell. The fish (or animal from which the meat originated) "comes back to life in the victim's stomach, and the person dies as a result" (LWDD, 10.448). This explains the meaning of the term *tiaosheng*, or "bringing back to life." In other words, the fish, foul, or animal meat in the victim's stomach is aroused back to life. See Feng and Shryock, 15–16, for a complete and accurate translation of the LWDD entry on *tiaosheng*. Later reports on *gu* poisoning in Guangxi and the lore associated with this practice—in particular, those recorded by Kuang Lu in the *Chiya*—are discussed by Steven B. Miles in "Strange Encounters on the Cantonese Frontier," 140–47. One of the *Chiya* passages translated and discussed by Miles (140) describes *tiaosheng* as a type of light produced by flying *gu*, the shadow of which is shaped like a living man. The shadow can, in turn, produce a form capable of having sexual intercourse with a woman. Clearly, this meaning of *tiaosheng* is very different from that described by Fan Chengda and Zhou Qufei in the twelfth century.

76   *Shengma* is used to designate various species of *Cimicifuga*. Here it probably denotes *Cimicifuga foetida* (large, trifolious bugbane). Read, CMP, no. 529. BCGM, 13.796 (*Compendium*, 2:13.1412), says bugbane "neutralizes toxins of a hundred kinds" and is useful in treating "diseases due to noxious agents produced by various parasites."

77   Read, CMP, 646a, identifies *yujin* as *Curcuma aromatica*, or aromatic turmeric, also known as wild turmeric.

[through the digestive system]. When the attendant esquire [*shilang*] Li Shouweng served as a judge [*tuiguan*] in Lei County, he discovered these prescriptions during some judicial hearings.[78]

Supplementary entry: **GU POISON [*GUDU*]:**[79] If you enter[80] [the homes of those who make it], there is not the slightest trace of dust.[81]

---

78   HSRC, 67.60b; FCDBJ, 132. These prescriptions were discovered in a case in Lei County involving someone who practiced *tiaosheng* poisoning. The judge, Li Shouweng (or Li Chun), later had the prescriptions mentioned here (which were obtained directly from the defendant) printed and distributed throughout the county. See LWDD, 10.448 (*Netolitzky*, 10.48). According to the BCGM, 14.882 (*Compendium*, 2:14.1541), the judge in Lei County was not Li Chun but rather the famous historian Li Tao (*zi* Xunyan). This same source also reports that the prescriptions "saved numerous people."

79   The LWDD entry on *gudu* (10.449; *Netolitzky*, 10.49) describes two varieties of *gu* poison, one that immediately kills the victim and another "slow" type that takes six months before finishing the job.

80   The character *ren* 人 here is certainly a misprint for *ru* 入 (to enter).

81   HSRC, 67.60b; FCDBJ, 132.

13

THE MAN
(Zhi Man)

THE COMMANDERIES UNDER THE JURISDICTION OF THE managing and organizing commissioner [*jinglue shi*][1] of Guangxi number twenty-five.[2] In addition to these, there are the various Man administrative units of the southwest. As for the tribal settlements [*quluo*] of the Man, I cannot note them all. So for now I will just record what I have heard about them and the contacts that have taken place between us. The Command Inspectorate [Shuaisi][3] often has dealings with several tribes [*zhong*] in their territory, which are known as the

---

1   *Jinglue shi* is an abbreviation for the office title *jinglue anfu shi*, or managing and organizing commissioner for pacification and comfort. During the Song dynasty this was functionally the chief military official of a circuit.

2   Fan Chengda uses "commanderies" (*jun*) here in the general sense of administrative districts. After the Jin invasion and occupation of north China in the mid-1120s, the Guangnan West Circuit comprised two municipalities, twenty counties, and three military districts, which altogether numbered twenty-five. These are listed in *Songshi*, 90.2239. The Chinese administrative units on this list should be distinguished from the Man "bridle and halter" districts described below.

3   This government agency served as the dominant regional authority on the Guangnan West Circuit and was charged with coordinating all civil and military affairs. *Hucker*, no. 5483.

bridle and halter counties and settlements [*jimi zhoudong*].[4] These tribes are known as the Yao, Lao, Man, Li, and Dan. They are collectively referred to as the Man.

BRIDLE AND HALTER COUNTIES AND SETTLEMENTS [*JIMI ZHOUDONG*] subordinate to Yong County along the Left and Right Rivers are the most numerous. Formerly, there were four circuits [*dao*] of the Nong clan [Nongshi],[5] called Anping,[6] Wule,[7] Silang,[8] and Qiyuan.[9] Everyone in those four counties[10] had the Nong surname. There were also four circuits of the Huang clan [Huangshi],[11] called Ande,[12] Guile,[13] Lucheng,[14] and Tian counties [Tianzhou].[15] Everyone in those four counties had the Huang surname. There were also the people of the four market towns [*zhen*] of Wuhou, Yanzhong, Shimen, and Gande,[16]

---

4   On the *jimi zhoudong*, or "bridle and halter counties and settlements," and the translation of *dong* as "settlements," see the Introduction.

5   The Nong was one of two major tribal clans in Guangxi (the other being the Huang; see the text below). According to Fan Chengda, during the Southern Song the Nong clan was concentrated in the four counties or circuits mentioned here, located along the modern border between China and Vietnam. For additional information on the home region of the Nong, see Anderson, *The Rebel Den*, 74.

6   Anping County corresponds to modern Daxin *xian*, Guangxi.

7   Wule was located in the area around modern Fusui *xian*, Guangxi.

8   Following the sĸǫs ed., 36a, and reading Silang 思浪 rather than Zhonglang 忠浪. Silang, which was near modern Daxin *xian*, Guangxi, is undoubtedly the correct name of this county. See *Songshi*, 90.2240.

9   Qiyuan County was in the general vicinity of modern Pingxiang *shi*, Guangxi.

10   The "four counties" refer to the four circuits just mentioned. All fell under the jurisdiction of the Yong County Commanding General's Headquarters (Yongzhou Dudu Fu).

11   The Huang clan was concentrated in the four bridle and halter counties mentioned here.

12   Ande County was near modern Jingxi *xian*, Guangxi.

13   Guile County corresponds to Baise *xian*, Guangxi.

14   Lucheng was in modern Tianlin *xian*, Guangxi.

15   During the Song, two of the four counties mentioned here, namely Guile and Tianzhou, were on the Right River Circuit in Yong County. Tianzhou corresponds to modern Tianyang *xian*. Ande and Lucheng were not official county names during the Song. Fan Chengda is using the former Tang dynasty "bridle and halter" county names here. See also *Qi Zhiping*, 38, n. 6.

16   The modern locations of these Song dynasty market towns are unknown.

who have had affiliation[17] since the Tang.[18]

When the government demarcated their tribal areas, the larger ones were made into counties, the smaller ones into towns, and the still smaller ones into settlements. As a result of the present dynasty's expansion efforts and increased presence [in the south], there are more than fifty such counties, towns, and settlements.[19] Those individuals who are imposing and senior [*xiongzhang*] are selected to be leaders [*shouling*]; their people are registered as able-bodied men [*zhuangding*].[20] Their manner[21] is fierce and ferocious; their customs and habits are preposterous and strange. It is not possible to completely rein in and rule them by means of the teachings and laws

---

17   The term *neifu* 內附 (lit., "interior dependency" or "attached to the center"), translated here (and below) as "affiliation," requires explanation. Chinese government administrators like Fan Chengda used this expression to describe Man tribes or administrative districts, especially bridle and halter counties, that had willingly submitted to Chinese authority. This status placed a Man region under the direct protection of the Chinese government. Submission to the "center" (China) was expressed formally by sending missions to the Song capital bearing tribute for the Chinese emperor, thereby acknowledging China's ritual supremacy. In return for their submission, Man leaders would often be conferred prestige-bearing Chinese office titles such as "governor" (*cishi;* lit., "prodding scribe," referring to the chief administrative officer in a county). An example is given in the text below. On the history of the Chinese tribute system in the south, see Anderson, *The Rebel Den*, esp. 15–29.

18   Fan Chengda's description in this paragraph of the administrative organization and distribution of the Nong and Huang clans in Yong County refers to the period before the rebellion there led by Nong Zhigao (Vietnamese: Nùng Trí Cao) in the late 1040s and early 1050s (see text and note 34 below). The next paragraph in the text describes the key changes that took place after the rebellion was suppressed. Note that during the Southern Song the bridle and halter administrative districts in Yong County were organized into two circuits along the Left and Right Rivers. These are listed in *Songshi*, 90.2240. Some of the counties associated with the Nong clan are classified under the Left River Circuit, while some of those associated with the Huang clan are classified under the Right River Circuit.

19   The figure "more than fifty" here refers to bridle and halter administrative units that fell under the jurisdiction of Yong County. Fifty-six such units are listed in the *Songshi*, 90.2240–41; these are also listed in *Hu-Tan*, 182, n. 5.

20   *Zhuangding* denotes adult men subject to military and other types of government service.

21   Reading *renwu* 人物 to mean "outward appearance" or "manner."

[*jiaofa*] of the Middle Kingdom, so for now all we can do is to bridle and halter them.

[Within the bridle and halter administrative districts] there are county administrators [*zhizhou*], provisional[22] county administrators [*quanzhou*], county supervisors [*jianzhou*], town administrators [*zhixian*], and settlement administrators [*zhidong*]. On the next level below are the joint emissaries [*tong faqian*] and provisional emissaries [*quan faqian*],[23] who are referred to as officials-in-charge [*guandian*], each of whom receives commissions from their respective county. Each village group also selects one person to serve as a head [*zhang*], who is referred to as the village chief [*zhuhu*].[24] All the remaining people are called *tituo*,[25] which is the same as saying the hundred surnames [*baixing*].

Fields are supplied to the people [by village chiefs] based on the

---

22 When *quan* appears as a prefix to Song dynasty official titles, it can mean either "probationary" or "provisional." *Hucker*, no. 1704. Since context must be relied on to determine which meaning is appropriate, and since context is lacking here, I translate *quan* here and below arbitrarily as "provisional."

23 The title "provisional emissary" was often used during the Song to refer to officials who rose rapidly through the local bureaucracy but were light on qualifications and experience. "Emissary" (*faqian*) is probably used here in the figurative sense. Note the various Song office titles that include *quan faqian* cited in Gong Yanming, comp., *Songdai guanzhi cidian*, 120–22. See also *Songshi*, 158.3716 (quoting Cheng Dachang), which mentions that the rank of *quan faqian* is two grades lower than that of *quanzhi*, or provisional administrator.

24 The expression *zhuhu* (lit., "head of the household"), rendered here as "village chief," has many meanings. In Chinese historical sources it most often refers to a landowner subject to taxation by the government. Here, however, *zhuhu* is a title conferred by the Chinese government to the leader of a bridle and halter village. See *Hucker*, no. 1387. This line of the text is woefully incomplete in all surviving editions of *Treatises*, so I have followed *WXTK*, 330.2589 (*FCDBJ*, 136).

25 The origin of the Man expression *tituo*, for which the Chinese used the characters 提陀, is unknown. Tan Xiaohang speculates that it might relate to a Mulam (Mulao) expression originally meaning "livestock" (*xusheng*). See *Lingnan gu Yueren mingcheng wenhua tanyuan*, 106–7. While *tituo* appears to be used here in a general or neutral sense, referring to the "hundred surnames" (the common people), it can also function as a derogatory form of address. Kuang Lu defines *tituo* as "people who can be sniveled at [*ti* 涕] and spat upon [*tuo* 唾]." See *Chiya kaoshi*, 5. Note that the characters in Fan Chengda's *tituo* share the same sounds as the *ti* and *tuo* in Kuang Lu's gloss.

number of persons [in a family]. The fields cannot be mortgaged or sold, and can only be used by the people themselves to open up new land for cultivation. These are referred to as inherited-and-apportioned fields [*zuye koufen tian*]. County administrators separately receive support-the-seal-of-office fields [*yangyin tian*], which are the same as sacrifice fields [*guitian*].[26] Those below the rank of provisional county administrator who lack an official seal of office [*yinji*] receive hereditary-privilege exemption fields [*yinmian tian*].[27]

Not only does each of them [the tribal chiefs] subordinate his own people; others serve as slaves [*shengkou*] as a result of [being captured in] attacks and raids on the Mountain Lao [Shanlao] and through purchase and marriage. Men and women are matched and supplied with fields to till and trained in the martial arts [*wuji*].[28] They remain subordinate for generation after generation and are referred to as domestic slaves [*jianu*].[29] They are also called domestic

---

26   The character *gui* 圭 in the term *guitian* 圭田 (sacrifice fields) literally means "clean." The expression *guitian* dates from the Han period, if not earlier. As used in the *Mencius*, "clean fields" were originally intended to yield produce for sacrifices. *Mengzi zhushu*, 5/42/2702 (Legge, *The Chinese Classics*, 2:244). Here the idea is that harvests received from the premium "support-the-seal-of-office fields" would be used to generate income for county administrators.

27   "Hereditary-privilege exemption fields" were tax-exempt fields used to generate salaries for lower-ranking local officials who were awarded office through the *yin* privilege system, whereby established officials could place their sons directly into office. The land system described here was organized and managed by the local tribal chief. Farmland was organized into two broad categories: the best land was called "support-the-seal-of-office fields" and "hereditary-privilege exemption fields"; the other was known as "inherited-and-apportioned fields." The latter were supplied to people by the tribal chief, for whom they worked. These same people were also called upon to work the support-the-seal-of-office fields and hereditary-privilege exemption fields for the tribal chief and his subordinates, and could be summoned for local corvée or military service as well.

28   Presumably, martial arts training was provided so the common people could protect the fields of their chief and his subordinates as well as their own. See the comments in note 31 below.

29   *Hu-Tan*, 243, n. 12, notes that a portion of the contents of this paragraph (up to this point) appears to be drawn from an essay by Wang Anshi titled "On Matters of Concern in the Yong Administration" (Lun Yongguan shiyi). This essay is preserved in the Ming collectanea *Baibian* (SKQS ed.), 117.15b–18b (the passage in question appears on 17b). There is little doubt that Fan drew upon Wang

laborers [*jiading*]. Strong and sturdy males from civilian households [*minhu*][30] who can be persuaded to [Chinese ways] through teaching are referred to as field sentinels and field militia.[31] They are also called cavalry escorts [*maqian pai*][32] and are referred to generally as settlement militia [*dongding*].[33]

At present there are still many people [in the bridle and halter districts] with the Huang surname, but those with the Nong surname are extremely few. Presumably, after the Zhigao rebellion[34] the Nong

---

Anshi's essay, for other portions of the *Wenxian tongkao* excerpt translated here also reveal the same influence. Moreover, Fan's descriptions of Man winter and summer clothing and the inventory of Man weapons in his "Treatise on Implements" also seem to be drawn from Wang Anshi's essay.

30   "Civilian households" were those expected to pay taxes and provide occasional state labor service.

31   Following *Yan Pei*, 119, n. 10, and reading *tianzi jia* 田子甲, or "field sentinels." *LWDD*, 3.135 (*Netolitzky*, 3.18), also has an entry on field sentinels. Zhou Qufei explains that these skilled fighters tilled the fields while they were also responsible for guarding them. Zhou mentions that the very best mounts owned by the Song Horse Administration were kept in these same fields. This, presumably, explains why field sentinels were trained in the martial arts.

32   *LWDD*, 3.135 (*Netolitzky*, 3.18), explains that, when local settlement officials (*dongguan*) would travel through their jurisdictions, there would be "one thousand mounted riders in front and several tens behind." *Maqian pai* 馬前牌, rendered here as "cavalry escorts," literally means "shields before [the local official's] horse." Cf. *LWDD*, 3.135, which reads *maqian pai* 馬前排, or "ranks before [the local official's] horse."

33   On settlement militia, see also the "Miscellaneous Items Treatise" supplementary entry. According to *LWDD*, 3.136 (*Netolitzky*, 3.18), there was a supervisor (*tiju*) of settlement militia in Yong County, and during the Xining period (1068–1078) the number of registered settlement militia numbered over 40,000. *Songshi*, 191.4746–47, gives higher and more precise figures of 44,500 for the year 1065 and 45,200 for 1073. This same source (4746) also notes that thirty men composed one *jia*, or platoon, of sentinels.

34   Nong Zhigao was an ambitious and powerful Man chieftain. During the Huangyou reign (1049–1054) he received a mandate from the state of Jiaozhi to serve as administrator of his home county of Guangyuan (modern Quảng Nguyên in Cao Bằng Province, northern Vietnam). Guangyuan was a bridle and halter county that fell officially under Chinese jurisdiction but in fact had been under the control of Jiaozhi since the late Tang. Ignoring Song and Jiaozhi authority in the region, Nong Zhigao in 1045 established his own state, which he called "Kingdom of the Southern Heaven" (Nantian Guo). He also styled himself the "Humane and Benevolent August Emperor" (Renhui Huangdi). Later, after Nong and his followers stormed and captured several surround-

clan became genial and well behaved, and was permitted to use the surname of the imperial family [*guoxing*], so today there are many families surnamed Zhao.[35] In those selected settlements where there is only one surname, marriage [between people with the same family name] is not regarded as inappropriate.[36] Tribal leaders sometimes take several wives, all of whom are called "enchanting ladies" [*mei-niang*].

There are also more than ten bridle and halter counties and towns under the administrative control of Yi County. Its legal system is especially loose, and the people there seem to be beyond change.[37] This is especially the case in Nandan County [Nandan *zhou*],[38] which is treated differently than other [bridle and halter] counties and settlements. By special decree its leader from the Mo clan [Moshi] is known as "governor."[39] Each month he receives support [payment] in the form of salt and food provisions[40] as well as money to support

---

ing counties, the Song emperor Renzong (r. 1022–1063) dispatched the capable general Di Qing to crush the rebellion. *Songshi*, 290.9719; see also Anderson, *The Rebel Den*, esp. 107–112. Nong Zhigao supposedly escaped to Nanzhao (or Yunnan), where he later died, but this is not confirmed in the sources. The standard Chinese account of Nong Zhigao's life and rebellion appears in *Songshi*, 495.14215–18. The best modern scholarship on Nong has been done by Japanese historians. See the extensive list of these works cited in Araki, "Nung Chih-kao and the *K'o-chü* Examinations, 73, n. 1. The most complete and scholarly study on Nong Zhigao in modern Chinese is Huang Xianfan's *Nong Zhigao*. A useful outline in English of Nong Zhigao's exploits is provided in Barlow, "The Zhuang Minority Peoples of the Sino-Vietnamese Frontier in the Song Period," 256–61, but a much fuller treatment appears in Anderson, *The Rebel Den*.

35   Zhao was the surname of the family that ruled China during the Song dynasty.
36   *WXTK*, 330.2588, here reads: "In those selected settlements where there is only one surname, marriages are handled naturally and smoothly."
37   That is to say, the people there are beyond changing to Chinese ways.
38   Nandan County was located in what is today Nandan *xian*, in the very northwest part of modern Guangxi, along the border with Guizhou.
39   In 974 the leader of the Nandan bridle and halter county, Mo Hongyan, sent a tribute emissary to Kaifeng seeking affiliation with the Song. *Songshi*, 3.41. Another tribute embassy followed two years later, seeking bestowal of a tally and seal (*paiyin*), which would formally legitimize Nandan's status as a county under the Song. This request was granted, and thereafter leaders of the Mo clan there were known by the title "governor." *Songshi*, 494.14199.
40   As pointed out in Took, "A Twelfth Century Monograph," 80, n. 23, the salt and food provisions (*yanliao*) mentioned here were intended to serve as a supple-

[local] security officials [*shouchen*].⁴¹ The explanation for this runs as follows: beyond the border of Yi County is in fact the territory of the Huang Tribe bandits [*Huangjia zei*] of the Tang,⁴² and so Nandan was reestablished⁴³ to control it. Members of the Mo clan have also attacked each other from time to time. Recently, Governor Mo Yanshen expelled his younger brother [Mo] Yanlin and set himself up as an independent ruler.⁴⁴ Yanlin fled to the [Song] imperial court,⁴⁵ which is referred to as "selling out to the Song" [*chu Song*]. Note: In general, people in the counties and settlements who have "returned to the court" [*guichao*] are known as having "sold out to the Song."

Supplementary entry: **NANDAN** (county) is on the western border of Yi County. Its local products include wondrous materials and unusual medicines, fierce beasts and venomous snakes. Its people, brave and fierce, use stiff timber to make crossbows and collect poison to apply to arrows.⁴⁶ People hit by them die immediately.

The Gaofeng Stockade [Gaofeng Zhai] of Yi County is on the site

---

ment to official salaries. They came from the government storehouses in nearby Yi County. See *LWDD*, 1.48–49 (Netolitzky, 1.26).

41 The term "security officials" probably refers to local senior military men hired by the governor to manage security matters in the county. Cf. *Yan Pei*, 120, n. 13, which cites an alternate reading of this line from the *Tushu jicheng*: *shou cheng gong ji qian* 守城供給錢 (money to support the security of the county seat).

42 The powerful Huang Tribe bandits (also known as the Huang Settlement Man) held control over more than ten bridle and halter counties along the Left and Right Rivers in the 740s and maintained close relationships with the nearby Wei and Nong clans. In 756 the leader of the clan, Huang Qianyao, rebelled against Tang authority. Two years later, at the beginning of the Qianyuan reign (758–760), an agreement was reached between the Tang and other Man leaders in the region. These leaders requested that the Tang dispatch troops to suppress Huang Qianyao and his followers. The Tang complied with this request and later captured and executed Huang. These events are described in the *Xin Tangshu*, 222xia.6329.

43 This happened in 1161. See *Songshi*, 494.14201.

44 Independent, that is, from Song influence and control.

45 In other words, Mo Yanling pledged allegiance to the Song court. This happened in 1164. *Songshi*, 494.14202.

46 The deadly, poisonous arrows produced in Nandan were well known. Zhou Qufei mentions them in his entry on "Poison Arrows" in *LWDD*, 6.215 (Netolitzky, 6.13).

of ancient Guan County [Guanzhou].⁴⁷ It borders Nandan, where the land elevation is extremely high. The opposite border in Nandan is also high. The two fortifications⁴⁸ [in Gaofeng and Nandan] are within arrow shot of each other.

Nandan engages in commerce at the Gaofeng Stockade on a daily basis. If there is the slightest dissatisfaction, hatred and trouble follow. Nandan's chieftain is from the Mo clan. The present dynasty has decreed that he be designated as "governor." Each month he receives support [payment] in the form of salt and food provisions, and is supplied 150 full strings⁴⁹ of cash for security officials as well, as is the case with the inner tribes.⁵⁰ He styles himself "Great King of the Mo" [Mo Dawang]. From time to time, when he would visit Yi County, he would be received ceremoniously as [head of] one of the aligned commanderies [*liejun*].⁵¹ He has been coming [to Yi County] for several decades now. The explanation for this is that the territory of the Petty Man [Xiao Man] in Xiyuan,⁵² Huang Settlement [Huangdong],⁵³ and

---

47   Guan County was established on the Guangnan West Circuit in 1107 but was lost to local tribal control in 1110. The county was then reestablished but under a new name and administrative category—Gaofeng Stockade—in 1134. *Song-shi*, 90.2248. The stockade was located between what is now Nandan *xian* and Hechi *xian*.

48   I understand *erlei* 二壘, rendered here as "the two fortifications," to refer to the Gaofeng Stockade and a nearby Nandan fort just across the border. Judging from the remarks in the next paragraph, a good deal of commerce took place between these fortifications.

49   In theory, strings of cash in traditional China carried one thousand coins, but for various reasons this was not always the case. Here, however, Fan Chengda notes that the governor was to be paid in full strings (*qian*).

50   Tentative translation. The idea here seems to be that the monthly stipend received by the head of the Mo clan for serving as governor of Nandan is the about the same as that received by other local governors serving in bridle and halter counties (or "inner tribes").

51   "Aligned commanderies" in this context means "major counties."

52   Xiyuan was the name of a Tang bridle and halter county. During the Tang it fell under the jurisdiction of Yong County. *Xin Tangshu*, 43*xia*.1145. During the Song, however, it came under control of the Protector General's Headquarters (Duhu Fu) in Annan. This county was located in the area west of the Right River, on the modern border between China and Vietnam.

53   The precise location of the Huang Settlement is unknown. Yang Wuquan argues convincingly that it was situated along the upper reaches of the Left

Wuyang[54] commandery, [all] beyond the border of Yi County, are in
fact the land of Huang family bandits of the Tang dynasty. Nandan
was reestablished to control them. But from time to time members of
the Mo family also attack and plunder each other. Recently, Governor Mo Yanshen expelled his younger brother, Yanlin, and set himself up as an independent ruler. Yanlin fled to the [Song] imperial
court, which is referred to as "selling out to the Song." Note: In general, counties and settlements that have "returned to the court" are all
known as those who have "sold out to the Song." Yanshen is licentious
and cruel, and incapable of serving his kind. He is an enemy with the
Wang clan [Wangshi][55] of Yongle County [Yongle *zhou*],[56] and they
attack each other every year.

In the *dinghai* year of the Qiandao reign [1167] Mo Yanshen suffered defeat in a battle with the Wang clan and asked for emergency
assistance from the Command Inspectorate. The Command Inspectorate dispatched officials to reconcile the situation. Yongle became
increasingly encouraged to take further action and, with ten thousand crack troops [*shengbing*], was determined to wipe out the Mo
clan. Yanshen thereupon became increasingly arrogant, disrespected
the law, and went so far as to secretly carve [copies of] the seals of the
managing and organizing inspector for pacification and comfort and
the Creek Settlements inspector [*Xidong si*] in Yi County, and forged
the commandant's signature on government communiqués in order
to intimidate the various foreign tribes.

In the *jichou* year [1169], he himself [Mo Yanshen] remarked that
it was not a great distance from [Yi] County to the horse-rearing
Man and that he was willing to purchase horses for the [Song] state.
He begged that a [horse] market be set up in Yi County. The plan
[behind this proposal] was that he desired to use court-appointed
envoys to intimidate and control Yongle. The frontier general Chang

---

River and Ming River (Mingjiang) basin. See *LWDD*, 10.415, n. 6.

54   Wuyang was probably located south of Huang Settlement. See *Xin Tangshu*,
222*xia*.6329; and Yang Wuquan, *LWDD*, 10.415, n. 6.

55   Here and below *WXTK*, 331.2597, reads Yushi 玉氏, but this should read Wangshi 王氏, or Wang clan. See the remarks by Yang Wuquan in *LWDD*, 10.415, n. 9.

56   The precise location of Yongle County is unknown.

Gong [twelfth century] had dealings with Mo Yanshen, to the extent that Chang Gong sent memorials to the throne on Mo's behalf without going through the [local] Command Inspectorate. The Bureau of Military Affairs [Shumi Yuan] affirmed Mo Yanshen's plan and sent officials to establish an inspectorate in Yi County. I sent a memorial to the throne: "Yi County is adjacent to the interior areas. There is no reason to establish relations[57] with the various Man [therein]." Moreover, some hostilities have taken place along the border, and so I have not dared to accept the imperial rescript [concerning the creation of an inspectorate in Yi County]. Moreover, on my own initiative I have placed Chang Gong under arrest at my headquarters. He is in jail, and I have sought his impeachment through a memorial to the throne. The imperial court was greatly startled to hear about all this. After he was removed from office, Chang scurried off to Jiujiang[58] and was never allowed to return.[59]

Beyond [Yi County] there are government people who violate the law [*changfa*]. The traders who go into Nandan and receive registration certificates [*tiedie*] that allow them to proceed to the interior areas are mostly from Xing'an in Gui. I am hunting for them as well and have captured their boss [*qu*]. He has been sent to prison and his crimes elaborated according to the law. Nandan has been somewhat cowed into submission.[60]

Supplementary entry: **ANHUA COUNTY [ANHUA ZHOU]**[61] is the most

---

57   The expression *tongdao* 通道 literally means "open up a road," but here Fan Chengda probably means "establish relations with."

58   Jiujiang is a Han dynasty commandery name referring to the immediate area around Mount Lu in northern Jiangxi.

59   Little is known about Chang Gong except that he served as a military inspector (*xunjian*) in several counties in Guangxi. This explains why Fan Chengda refers to him as a "border general" (*bianjiang*). Judging from remarks here and comments by Zhou Bida in "Shendao bei," 117, Fan Chengda saw Chang Gong and his efforts to open a road for horse trading between Yi County and the "inner areas," along with his dealings with Mo Yanshen, as "illegal" (*feifa*) and serious threats to border security. Fan threw him in jail for his collusion with Mo Yanshen and his attempt to bypass local authority (that is, the Command Inspectorate) in setting up a horse-trading route in Yi County.

60   *WXTK*, 331.2597–98; *FCDBJ*, 139–40.

61   Anhua County, formerly (before 1017) known as Fushui County (Fushui *zhou*), was located in the general area around modern Huanjiang and Luocheng *xian* in Guangxi.

fierce and cruel. It is situated on the western border of Yi County.[62] [Chinese] officials provide [the Man leaders of Anhua County] monthly allowances of food provisions and salt in order to pacify them. Yet still they trespass on government land on a daily basis in order to farm.[63] Local people[64] dare not oppose them; nor does anyone in the county dare to stop them.

Recently, there were two generals, Ling and Luo, who during the Jianyan reign [1127–1131] led [local] settlement militia on a campaign to support the imperial throne.[65] The bandit Cao Cheng entered Guangxi and erected a large banner, offering a reward for the two men.[66] The two men dispatched several tens of crack troops who were short in stature,[67] and who cut their hair to make themselves look like young cowherds. They waited until Cheng's troops passed by and then from the backs of oxen drew their crossbows and shot at them with poison arrows. Those hit died immediately. Cheng was shocked and made a complete retreat. At that time brigands were everywhere in the four directions. The only comfort found in Guangxi resulted from the efforts of the two generals. To this day they are still praised by the southern people. Some of their descendants hold office in the counties and towns.[68]

---

62   Cf. *Songshi*, 495.14205, and *Song huiyao jigao*, "Fan Yi" 5.5a, which say that Anhua County (or Fushui County) is south of Yi County.

63   According to the account in *Songshi*, 495.14205–210, despite the Song policy of appeasing the Man leaders in Anhua County with salt and food provisions, the "fierce and cruel" nature of the people there often led to unrest and hostilities. This, in turn, drove many of its residents to farm in the safer Chinese-controlled areas (or "government land").

64   "Min" 民 here is an abbreviation of *shengmin* 省民, referring to local subjects who lived on government land.

65   The standard histories on the Song say nothing about these two generals.

66   No further information seems to be available on the incident mentioned here and described below. As for Cao Cheng, the biography of Yue Fei in the *Songshi*, 365.11380–81, mentions that in the second year of the Shaoxing reign (1132), Cao had more than 100,000 supporters. Yue Fei was then sent to Hunan to suppress Cao Cheng's rebellious activities. Cao's followers were later routed in Guangxi, but the ultimate fate of Cao Cheng is unknown.

67   The term *zhuru* usually indicates dwarfs, but here I suspect Fan Chengda means men especially short in stature.

68   *WXTK*, 331.2598; *FCDBJ*, 140–41.

Supplementary entry: **BORDER HISTORY AND ADMINISTRATION:**[69]
After Nong Zhigao rebelled, the imperial court put down the revolt. Because Nong's territory was a border area, the Song followed the precedent of the Tang system and demarcated his tribal areas. The larger ones were made into counties, the smaller ones were made into towns, and the still smaller ones were made into settlements. In all there are fifty-some [such administrative] units. . . . In order to fence off these inner areas and provide defense against the Outer Man, an emergency response team [*jizhui ji*] for defense has been assembled, which in design resembles those comprising regular [Song] government troops. Their chieftains [the chieftains of the bridle and halter counties, towns, and settlements] all hold hereditary positions and are now subordinate to [officials at] the various stockades and in general are subordinate to the supervisors.[70] As for the four military stockades in the Left River region, there are two supervisors. As for the four military stockades in the Right River region, there is one supervisor.[71] The

---

69   This entry has no title in the original text. The general heading "Border History and Administration" has been supplied by the translator.

70   "Supervisors" (*tiju*) here refer to Chinese officials in Yong County posted at the various stockades along the Left and Right Rivers mentioned in the next line, who were nominally in charge of local settlement militia. Fan Chengda is probably exaggerating when he uses the expression "subordinate to" (*li*) in this line. Cf. the following remarks by Zhou Qufei in *LWDD*, 3.136 (*Netolitzky*, 3.18): "As for the office title supervisor (*tiju*), in fact they did not have control over one single local soldier [*ding*]. Whether they are allowed to live or are killed, whether they are rewarded or punished, rests entirely with their chieftain."

71   Stockades (*zhai*) were common in Guangxi during the Southern Song. The ostensible purpose of these military-administrative organizations was to control local, non-Chinese officials and the residents of the bridle and halter settlements. The number of troops posted at these stockades varied. According to the *Song huiyao jigao*, "Fang Yu" 19.24b, troop strength could sometimes reach five hundred men. *Songshi*, 90.2240, lists four original stockades in Yong County—Yongping, Taiping, Guwan, and Hengshan—but says later only one of these (Taiping) was maintained. *LWDD*, 3.137 (*Netolitzky*, 3.19), mentions the following stockades for Yongzhou: Hengshan, Wenrun, Taiping, Yongping, and Guwan. According to *LWDD*, 5.186 (*Netolitzky*, 5.3), only one supervisor was assigned to manage the various stockades in Yong County. This differs from what Fan says in this line about there being two supervisors for the Left River region in Yong County.

stockade officer [*zhaiguan*] is a civil official [*minguan*].[72] Each stockade
has one administrator [*zhizhai*] and one assistant magistrate [*zhubu*],
who manage the finances and taxes in the various settlements. In the
Left River region, troops are garrisoned in Yongping[73] and Taiping;[74]
in the Right River region troops are garrisoned at Hengshan.[75] These
[garrisons] manage firewood [collection] [*yanhuo*][76] and the citizen
militia [*minding*],[77] and employ government troops [*guanbing*] to protect the border to the fullest. For the most part, the appearance and
manner of these people is fierce and ferocious, while their customs
are preposterous and strange. They are not capable of being fully dis-
ciplined and ruled by the teachings and laws of the Middle Kingdom.
So, for now we can only bridle and halter them.

There are county administrators, provisional county administrators, county supervisors, town administrators, and settlement
administrators, all of whom are under the orders of the pacification
and comfort commissioner for the Guangnan West Circuit.[78] The
commissioner's duties are similar to those of a supervising inspec-

---

72 *Minguan* designates a civil official as opposed to a military official (*junguan*).

73 The precise location of the Yongping Stockade is uncertain. Yang Wuquan
    thinks it was near the famous Friendship Pass (Youyi Guan), the main land
    route between Vietnam and China near modern Pingxiang *shi* in southwest
    Guangxi. *LWDD*, 2.61–62, n. 7.

74 The Taiping Stockade was probably located in the general area northwest of
    modern Longzhou *xian* in Guangxi. See Yang Wuquan's comments in *LWDD*,
    2.62–63, n. 11.

75 The garrison at Hengshan, located in modern Tiandong *xian*, Guangxi, also
    served as a horse trading center. See the "Treatise on Quadrupeds," note 21.

76 The precise meaning of *yanhuo* 煙火, rendered here as "firewood," is unclear. It
    could also mean "fire control" or "supplies" in a general sense (firewood, grain,
    and so on).

77 "Citizen militia" (*minding*) are the same as *zhuangding*, or "able-bodied men."
    See note 20. These were adult men subject to military and other types of gov-
    ernment service.

78 The various offices mentioned in this line were held by local leaders or Man
    chieftains, all of whom had been ennobled (*feng*) by the Song government.
    These positions were hereditary. In other words, upon the death of a local
    leader or Man chief, his son would inherit the office. To enhance the prestige
    and legitimacy of these "bridle and halter officials," the Song government sup-
    plied them with official government document stationery imprinted with Chi-
    nese seals of office. See text below.

tor [*jiansi*],[79] who supplies them with official government stationery [*wentie*] bearing vermilion seals [*zhuji*]. On the next level below them are the joint emissaries and provisional emissaries, who are referred to as officials-in-charge, each of whom receives commissions from the county. Each village also selects one person to serve as head, who is referred to as the village chief. All the remaining people are designated *tituo*, which is the same as saying the hundred surnames. When settlement militias have a dispute, each will present a legal petition [*song*] to the various chieftains. If the chieftains are unable to resolve it or the chieftains themselves are in dispute [about a matter], then they present a legal petition to the various stockade [officials] or a supervisor. If they are also unable to resolve it, then they present a legal petition to the Yong Administration [Yongguan][80] and continue from there all the way up to the command inspector [of the Guangnan West Circuit].

Before the Huangyou reign [1049–1054], appointment to the office of county administrator would not be a higher rank than chief troops and horses commissioner [*duzhi bingma shi*][81] and was merely equal to that of a lieutenant [*huixiao*].[82] At the time of the [Nong] Zhigao rebellion, settlement residents [*dongren*] established merit, and only then were appointments made to the companies and columns.[83] The

---

79   "Supervising inspector" is a general reference to the various coordinating inspectors on a circuit, who oversaw military, judicial, fiscal, and various other matters.

80   In the early Tang period various "administrations" (*guan*; this is an abbreviation for *zongguan fu*, or "general administration headquarters") were established on the Lingnan Circuit to oversee matters (especially military matters) along the border. One of these was the Yong Administration. Although by Southern Song times this designation was no longer an official government administrative name, Fan Chengda still uses it here.

81   As noted in *Hucker*, no. 4784, *bingma shi*, or troops and horses commissioner, was a "common designation for military officers on duty assignments in frontier areas or in armies on campaign, with varying prefixes and other forms." The prefix *duzhi* (translated here as "chief") designates a military rank in the Palace Infantry Army (Dianqian Mabu Jun).

82   The term *huixiao* 徽校 designates a low-ranking military officer. The component *hui* 徽 in this title refers to the flag or standard of a commandant, while *xiao* 校 indicates the low-level field officers under his command.

83   "Establish merit" (*ligong*) in this context means "submit to Song authority."

various settlement and county administrators would never dare sit above them [assume a superior position], for they view official ranks decreed by the court with respect and esteem. After the Yuanfeng reign [1078–1086], they progressively assumed offices in the Central Counties.[84]

In recent years, many settlement chieftains have transferred their [domicile] registration to internal [or Chinese controlled] areas. They receive corn [*su*] allowances and office appointments but only at the rank of senior and junior envoy [*daxiao shichen*]. If some [of these envoys] ventured to visit the palace [*que*] and presented a report concerning advantages and disadvantages, they would gain temporary office at the gallery grade, which is equivalent to a commandant-protector [*shuaishou*].[85]

Those who function as horse procurement officers [*zhaoma guan*] are especially familiar with [activities] in the counties and towns.

Once this submission process began, the court began awarding selected "settlement residents" in the bridle and halter areas with appointments in the Song civil service system. The various grades within that system are sometimes called "companies and columns" (*banhang*). Based on the comments that follow in the next line, "settlement residents" (or leaders) who held such appointments commanded more prestige in the bridle and halter counties than local administrators.

84   That is to say, regular Chinese civil service positions. During the Song it was possible for non-Chinese living on the two Guangnan circuits to take the Chinese civil service examinations. See the remarks on this in note 85 below. Judging from Fan's comment here, some passed and won appointments in the Chinese bureaucracy.

85   I understand this line to mean that if the envoys (or local officials) in the service of Man chieftains were to travel to the capital (here designated by the term *que*, or "palace") in Hangzhou and present a plan to the court outlining the (many) advantages and (few) disadvantages of expanding the Song presence in Guangxi, these leaders might become eligible for Chinese office appointments at the gallery grade (*gezhi*). This refers to appointments in Song government organs called "galleries" (*ge*), each of which was staffed by academicians (*xueshi*) and other officials. These offices were high in the bureaucracy. For instance, appointment as an academician in the Longtu Gallery (Longtu Ge Xueshi) would be grade 3 (there were altogether nine grades in the bureaucracy, with each subdivided into an "upper" and "lower" category). "Commandant" is an alternate name for the managing and organizing commissioner, who also served as the chief administrative officer on a circuit. These were precisely the government posts Fan Chengda held in Guangxi.

There are young men[86] [from among the Man] who, when they come into Yong County in response to the civil service examinations,[87] recruit "itinerant scholars" [*youshi*].[88] Many [of these "scholars"] have set up spy networks, so before an official document is made public in the counties and towns, they already know about it. [As for the horse procurement officers,] their carriages and horses, houses and dwellings, and clothing and daily accoutrements all compare to those of someone of noble rank [*gonghou*]. Examples would include Li Yu of Anping County and Huang Xie of Tian County [Tianzhou], both of whom command some formidable soldiers. . . . [89]

In the past, one [bridle and halter] county would at most have no more than five or six hundred residents. Now there are some that have a thousand. During the Yuanfeng reign [1078–1086] over 100,000 persons were registered [in each county], not including the old and weak.

---

86   Reading *zidi* 子弟 (lit., "sons and younger brothers") to mean "young men."

87   As pointed out by Araki Toshikazu in his informative article "Nung Chih-kao and the *K'o-chü* Examinations," 80–86, during the Southern Song (or perhaps earlier) Chinese civil service examinations (*keju*) at the county (Araki's "prefecture") level could be taken by non-Chinese people in the border regions of the south. In fact, citing this line from *Treatises,* Araki argues convincingly that Nong Zhigao sat for the Chinese civil service examination in Yong County sometime in the 1040s (83) and probably passed it (86).

88   The expression *youshi* (lit. "itinerant scholars") usually means either an "advocate-persuader" (a professional intermediary hired by one person to persuade someone else) or simply a learned person who offers his services as a scholar while traveling from one place to another. Here, however, the context suggests that *youshi* are unemployed persons in the bridle and halter counties and towns who in fact were recruited to work as spies.

89   *Songshi,* 24.450 and 198.4956, identifies Li Yu as a supervisor of settlement militia in Guangxi (*tiju Guangxi dongding*) who was active in promoting the development of the horse market there during the Jianyan reign (1127–1131). *Songshi,* 25.469, mentions that in 1133 Li Yu was ordered to set up a horse breeding enterprise (*muyang wu*) in Yong County. These horses were needed by Song armies in the north, who at this time were engaged in war with the Jin. Li Xinchuan, *Jianyan yilai xinian yaolu,* 10.12a, says Li Yu was a native of Yong County; the *Xin'an wenxian zhi,* a Ming work compiled by Cheng Minzheng, identifies him as a "tribal chief from Anping County" (69.6a). See also the remarks on Li Yu in Okada, *Zhongguo Hua'nan minzu shehui shi yanjiu,* 176. Anping County fell under the jurisdiction of Yong County. I have not been able to find any biographical information on Huang Xie. Tian County was a bridle and halter county located southeast of modern Tianyang *xian,* Guangxi.

And this [census] register has not been updated for a long time now!

Settlement militias are often strong and agile, and able to endure severe hardship. They wear leather shoes [*pilü*] and can ascend and descend mountains without getting tired. Their weapons and implements include barrel armor [*tongzi jia*],[90] long spears [*changqiang*], *shoubiao*,[91] *pian* knives [*piandao*],[92] arrow shields [*tipu pai*],[93] mountain crossbows [*shannu*], bamboo arrows [*zhujian*], and sugar-palm arrows [*guanglang jian*]. When a fight to the death breaks out between them, they align in battle formation, each side making two flanks so as to surround the other. The side that has more men and a more extended flank is the victor. There is nothing else remarkable about it.

The people live in thatch-covered [structures] that are two-storied sheds [*peng*] referred to as pile houses [*malan*].[94] The upper level is used as living quarters; the lower is used for housing cows and pigs. On top of the shed, bamboo is woven into a platform [*zhan*]; only one ox hide is used to make a padded mat [*yinxi*].[95] Stench from the cows and pigs rises and can be smelled through the cracks in the floor, but the people are used to it. Also, there are many tigers and wolves where they live, so if they do not live in this way, neither the people nor

---

90   The term *tongzi jia* probably refers to a type of body armor that resembles a barrel (*tong*) or tub, which is held over the torso by attached shoulder straps.

91   I have not been able to identify *shoubiao*, though *shou* 手 (lit., "hand") might indicate some sort of guidon used for signaling or indicating one's battle position.

92   *Piandao* (lit., "flat blade") probably indicates some type of sidearm designed for close combat.

93   A *tipu pai* is a shield designed to protect one from arrows shot from far away. *Qi Zhiping*, 39, n. 20.

94   "Pile houses" (*malan*; lit., "hemp sheds") is Eberhard's translation for these Thai-style homes. See *Local Cultures*, 318. See also LWDD, 10.155–56, n. 1. These structures, supported by bamboo poles and high above ground, were so designed in order to ward off moisture and provide protection from snakes, insects, and other pests. Pile-house architecture still exists in Guangxi. Tan Xiaohang, *Lingnan gu Yueren mingcheng wenhua tanyuan*, 66–70, argues that the term *malan* comes from the Zhuang (or Man) language and discusses its possible origins in some detail. For details on the long history of pile-house architecture in south China, see especially *Hu-Tan*, 244–45, n. 16.

95   In pile houses people slept on an upper platform constructed of bamboo. The platform (or floor) was covered in mats. See Eberhard, *Local Cultures*, 320.

the livestock would be safe. Most of the people in the deepest part of Guang also live in this way.

As for the settlement people, their way of making a living is especially basic and simple. For winter they weave goose feathers [*emao*] and woody cotton [*mumian*] [into clothing];[96] for summer they stitch banana and bamboo [*jiaozhu*],[97] and jute and grass cloth [*mazhu*][98] into clothing. They roll rice into balls and scoop up water with their hands when taking meals. Household utensils are hidden away in ground pits as a precaution against bandits and looters. The local land yields gold, silver, copper, lead, malachite, cinnabar, halcyon kingfisher feathers [*cuiyu*],[99] settlement woven velvet [*dongdian*],[100] sackcloth [*shubu*], fennel [*huixiang*], herbs and fruits, and various medicines. Each person pursues whatever brings him profit, never tiring or growing weary. . . .

The chieftain leaders [*qiuhao*] sometimes take several wives, all of whom are called "enchanting ladies." In the families of settlement officials, marriages that are uninhibited and unrestrained in their extravagance and lavish manner are highly esteemed by both sides. The engagement is made by sending presents and carrying out ceremonies, with the presents weighing as much one thousand *dan*.[101]

---

96   Reading *mumian* 木綿 to mean *caomian* 草棉 (lit., "grassy cotton"), which in this context probably refers to *Gossypium herbaceum* (Levant cotton) or some similar species of cotton that grows wild as a perennial shrub.

97   According to Yang Wuquan, *jiaozhu* (lit., "banana and bamboo") refers to (1) *ganzhu*, a name that can indicate numerous kinds of Musaceae, or banana and plantain; and (2) *danzhu* (*Lingnania cerosissima*), sometimes called waxy lingnania in English. The fibers of these plants were used to make cloth known as banana cloth (*jiaobu*) and bamboo cloth (*zhubu*). *LWDD*, 10.414, n. 3.

98   *Ma* and *zhu* probably refer to jute (*huangma*; *Corchorus capsularis*) and the grass cloth plant (*zhuma*; *Boehmeria nivea*), respectively. See Smith and Stuart, *Chinese Materia Medica: Vegetable Kingdom*, 70–71.

99   The bright and colorful feathers of the halcyon kingfisher (*feicui*; see the "Treatise on Birds" and figure 9 in that chapter) were highly sought after, not only as a tribute or commercial item to send to the north, but also locally (in the south) for making feathered clothes and women's ornaments. See Schafer, *Vermilion Bird*, esp. 238; Eberhard, *Local Cultures*, 287.

100   On the woven velvet produced in Man settlements, see the "Treatise on Implements."

101   One *dan* equaled almost 158 pounds, so wedding presents weighing 1,000 *dan*

Anything less would at least be half that amount. When the new son-in-law arrives to begin the marriage, the woman's family builds a straw dwelling with a hundred-some rooms five *li* distant [from the woman's home], where they will live together. This is referred to as "entering the hut" [*ruliao*]. Each of the two families provides music accompanied by drumbeats to welcome the bride and groom to the hut. The woman's slaves and maids [*biqie*] number over one hundred; the man's houseboys and servants [*tongpu*] can number as many as several hundred.

On the evening of the marriage, each of the two families provides an abundant array of soldiers standing ready. At the slightest verbal provocation, the soldiers will draw their swords in opposition. After the wedding, the son-in-law will often draw his sword. If the wife's slaves and maids express opposition, he will then kill them with his bare hands. The more slaves he can kill from the time when they [the bride and groom] enter the hut, the more the wife's faction will fear him. Otherwise, they will refer to him as a coward [*nuo*]. After half a year they return to the husband's home.

People who have returned after traveling afar halt at a place 30 *li* from home. The family dispatches a shaman [*wu*] carrying a bamboo basket to welcome them. The shaman removes the undergarments of the person returning home, stores them in the basket, and then leads the person home. This is said to "bring home the spiritual soul" [*shouhun*] of the traveler.[102]

Just after a relative dies, family members let down their hair[103] and, holding an earthen jar, wail sorrowfully at a riverbank and throw cop-

---

would indeed have been a formidable array of gifts. Cf. LWDD, 10.418 (Netolitzky, 10.24), where Zhou Qufei remarks: "Presents are sent to fix the ceremonies [for the wedding], with as many as a thousand people attending."

102   *Hu-Tan*, 247, n. 22, says that this custom is still practiced today among some of the Zhuang people living in Guangxi.

103   The expression "let down one's hair" (*beifa*) is well known from a passage in the *Analects* (Lunyu), 14.18, where it is mentioned as a "characteristic of the eastern barbarians." See *Lunyu zhushu*, 14/56/2512 (Legge, *The Chinese Classics*, 1–2:282). Here, however, the expression seems to imply "go into mourning." Cf. LWDD, 6.239 (Netolitzky, 6.37), where *beifa* is described as an action performed by filial sons when a family member passes away.

per coins and paper money into the water. [River] water is then drawn, and the relatives return home to bathe the corpse. This is referred to as "buying water" [*maishui*]. [If the family was to do] otherwise, the neighborhood would consider them unfilial.

As for these counties and towns, although they are called bridle and halter, yet everyone there tills and works government land[104] and annually pays taxes in rice to the government. Earlier, when the scale and scope of the nation was broad and far reaching, they were governed and administered by civil officials. [Song] military officials [*bingguan*] suppressed and quelled them, and used the financial resources of the various settlements to maintain government troops and kept [local] able-bodied males on call for standby military service.[105] The upper and lower ranks are well coordinated, while the latter group is responsive and agile.[106]

Although village chieftains are known as administrators of counties and towns, most wear black and white cloth robes similar to those of village heads [*lizheng*] and household heads [*huzhang*]. All the adjutant stockade officers [*canzhai guan*][107] hold clubs in the horizontal position[108] and style themselves "guardians and suppressors against bandits and thieves in such and such county" [*mouzhou fang'e daozei*]. As a general rule, a stockade administrator is regarded in a way similar to the manner in which a village head is seen as a senior

---

104   As mentioned in the Introduction, land on the Guangnan West Circuit under the administrative control of the Song government was called "government land." One reason Man people farmed these lands was security and safety threats in the bridle and halter areas. See above.

105   The phrase translated as "standby military service" literally reads "summon together and quickly dispatch" (*zhao ji qu shi*).

106   "Responsive and agile" is a loose translation of the phrase *you bizhi zhi shi*, which in this context means something like "the upper ranks command the lower ranks just like arms control the movement of fingers."

107   "Adjutant stockade officer" was not an official title in the Song civil service system. Judging from the description that follows, the main responsibility of these local officials was to punish bandits and thieves.

108   The text of *WXTK*, 330.2589, reads *hengting* 橫挺, but this is sometimes also written as 橫梃 (lit., "[to hold] a club in a horizontal position"). In this context the idea is that the stockade officers stand ceremoniously in the ready position to fend off bandits and thieves.

official; a supervisor is respected in a way similar to the manner in which ranks of soldiers [*zuwu*] look up to a commanding general [*zhujiang*]. The Yong Administration is viewed [by the local people] as if it were an imperial court. When they gaze off at the Managing and Organizing Commandant's Headquarters [Jinglüe Shuaifu], [Chinese officials there] are seen as gods and deities [*shenming*]. Their orders and commands are followed and obeyed, which protects and safeguards their majestic and weighty image.[109]

But in recent years this has not been the case. The various settlements have not submitted their land taxes, so there was no grain with which to support the troops of the supervisor. Since the power of the supervisor's troops has become frail and weak, his mighty commands have not been obeyed. Not only were stockade officers derelict in carrying out their duties, but daily they would go to the gates [homes] of settlement officials and work out [private business] deals.[110] The supervisors did not [take action to] restore the stockade officers' dignity and reputation, and instead became involved in shady deals with them. Among the supervisors are some self-respecting men who would like to take action to rectify the situation. The various settlements must unite to defile and dishonor them [the corrupt officers and supervisors] and cause them to be sent away for punishment, and in extreme cases kill them with poison wine [*zhen*]. The source of this state of affairs is the illegal methods used by all border officials [*bianli*] to seek profit. It is still not easy to calculate the complete extent of their corruption and obstinacy.

Here is the background: when the pacification and comfort commissioner for management and organization [*anfu jinglue shi*][111] first opened up his field headquarters [*mufu*] [in the region], he issued salt and multicolored silk as a reward to all the [local] leaders, and official documents were issued making this public. This was referred to as "making concessions" [*weiqu*]. For the most part, the commissioner

---

109 Here I follow *Qi Zhiping*, 39, n. 22, who glosses *yinran* 隱然 as *weizhong zhi mao* 威重之貌 (lit., "descriptive of looking majestic and weighty").

110 Literally, "agree on a business deal with a hand shake" (*woshou wei shi*).

111 This office title is usually given as *jinglue anfu si,* or managing and organizing inspector for pacification and comfort.

secured and defended the borders and gave comfort and relief to able-bodied men, or so it is said. In the past security officials in Yong County never rashly paid out funds [to subordinates]. The garrisoned troops there number about five thousand. The National Capital sends people to serve as supervisors of major military fortifications,[112] where border defense is very well organized. Recently, Yong County has been short on funds and lax and negligent in carrying out its responsibilities. All that remains is several hundred first-rate troops [*yingzu*].[113] Its protective walls and military weapons are dilapidated and have not been repaired. The administrations of the pacification and comfort commissioner and director-in-chief [*dujian*][114] have crumbled and weakened. In the counties and settlements [the people have become] sneaky and cruel, fearing nothing. It has reached a point where government subjects and travelers are robbed, tied up, and then sold [as slaves] to the various Man in Jiaozhi. [The two administrations just mentioned] also recruit government subjects who are dissatisfied [with local conditions] as well as those who seek refuge as subordinates in order to increase their profits. [Moreover,] the field sentinels rebelled and in their haughty manner viewed the pacification and comfort commissioner and director-in-chief as their equals.[115] This situation cannot be maintained for a long time. If we view the rebellion in Guangyuan during the Qingli reign [1041–1049] as a mirror [for what is happening

---

112   The term Jingshi, or National Capital, also refers by extension to the imperial court. In other words, the court sends Chinese officials from Lin'an (or Hangzhou) to Guangxi to serve as supervisors of military fortifications along the border. "Military fortifications" (*bingcheng*) refers to the various stockades along the Left and Right Rivers in Yong County, described earlier.

113   At one time during the Northern Song there were five thousand Song regular army troops stationed in Guangxi. See *LWDD*, 3.129 (*Netolitzky*, 3.15).

114   *Dujian* here is probably an abbreviation for *bingma dujian*, or director-in-chief for troops and horses. Officials holding this office had authority over the military forces in their jurisdiction and were concerned mainly with bandit suppression and other types of public security. *Hucker*, no. 4687.

115   I suspect that this line of the text is corrupt. In classical Chinese, the verb *fan* 反 (to rebel) almost always comes directly after a person's name. Also, it seems extremely unlikely that field sentinels would, under any conditions, view the pacification and comfort commissioner and director-in-chief as their "equals."

now],[116] the situation indeed is no different at all![117]

THE YAO originally were descendants of Pan Hu in the Five Creeks [Wuxi].[118] Areas in Guangyou bordered by their land include Jingjiang Municipality's Xing'an, Yining, and Gu Towns.[119] [The area along] Rong 融 County's Rong River[120] and the borders of Huaiyuan Town[121] both have Yao people. They live deep in the mountains among the streams, wear their hair bundled like a mallet,[122] go barefoot, and

---

116   This is a reference to the Nong Zhigao rebellion. The rebellion originated in Guangyuan, the home county of Nong Zhigao, where in 1048 he proclaimed the founding of his Kingdom of the Southern Heaven. The official start of the rebellion, however, is usually dated 1052, when Nong and his troops attacked and took control of Yong County.

117   *WXTK*, 330.1588–89; *FCDBJ*, 135–39.

118   The so-called Wuxi, or Five Creeks, were located in western Hunan and eastern Guizhou, and supposedly served as the ancient home of tribes descended from Pan Hu, a five-colored, doglike creature associated with the legendary emperor Gaoxin (r. ca. 2436–2366 B.C.E.). According to tradition, Pan Hu (lit., "platter gourd") once subdued a troublesome barbarian general. After delivering the general's head to Gaoxin, the emperor rewarded Pan Hu with the hand of one of his daughters. The dog then carried off his bride to the "southern mountains," where their six sons and six daughters later became the progenitors of the Man people. Some early texts cite this legend to explain the origin of all Man peoples in the south. See, for instance, *Hou Hanshu*, 116.2829. This account is translated and discussed by Bertold Laufer in his "Totemic Traces among the Indo-Chinese," *Journal of American Folk-Lore* 30.118 (1917): 419–21; and in David Gordon White, *Myths of the Dog-Man* (Chicago: University of Chicago Press, 1991), 140–60 (White's discussion of the Pan Hu tradition is especially insightful and informative). Later accounts, however, associate this legend exclusively with the Yao people and their relatives. See Eberhard, *Local Cultures*, 45.; White, *Chinese Dog-Man Traditions*, 145; and especially Okada, *Zhongguo Hua'nan minzu shehui shi yanjiu*, 77–99. According to *Hu-Tan*, 188, n. 2, this entry in *Treatises* marks the first time in Chinese historical records that the Pan Hu legend is directly associated with the origins of the Yao people in the Five Creeks area.

119   Yining Town (Yining *xian*) was located in the area around Wutong *zhen*, northwest of modern Lingui *xian*. Gu *xian*, also a Song dynasty town, was situated in what is now Lipu *xian*.

120   On the Rong River, see the supplementary entry on the Numinous Canal in the "Miscellaneous Items Treatise."

121   Gu Zuyu, comp., *Dushi fangyu jiyao*, 109.4904, places Huaiyuan Town 30 *li* north of Liu County.

122   Eberhard, *Local Cultures*, 50, mentions this hairstyle "was achieved by rolling the hair up around a small board," which Eberhard says represented a "dog

do not provide corvée service [*zhengyi*].[123] In each of their respective locations, they form military units [*wu*].

Supplementary text: The Yao originally were descendents of Pan Hu. The mountains and streams in their territory are high and deep, and border Ba, Shu, Hu, and Guang,[124] stretching on without interruption for several thousand *li*. They wear their hair bundled like a mallet, go barefoot, and dress in brightly colored coarse clothing.[125] They go by the name Yao but in fact do not provide any corvée service. . . .

They use tree leaves to cover their huts and grow grain, millet [*shu*], corn, beans [*dou*], and taro [*shanyu*], which are mixed together into a cereal [*liang*]. They break off sections of bamboo tubes and use them for cooking.[126] In their spare time they hunt for animals in the mountains to supplement their diet. The mountain trails are danger-

---

hairstyle." He relates this hairstyle to the Pan Hu dog myth origins of Yao culture. On Pan Hu, see note 118.

123   Fan Chengda is making a pun here, for an alternate term for compulsory labor for the state, or corvée, given here as *zhengyi* 征役, is *yaoyi* 徭[繇]役. The character *yao* in *yaoyi* and the name of the Yao people sound exactly the same and are often (but not always) written the same. The main reason most Yao people in Guangxi "did not provide corvée service" is that most of them lived "deep in the mountains among the streams" and thus far away from Chinese government influence and control. On the possible connections between corvée *yao* and the ethnic designation *yao,* see Cushman, "Rebel Haunts and Lotus Huts," 55–59.

124   Ba and Shu together refer roughly to what is now Sichuan. Hu and Guang correspond to Hunan and Guangxi, respectively.

125   Judging by the description in *LWDD*, 6.224 (*Netolitzky*, 6.23), and commentary in Eberhard, *Local Cultures,* 273, both Zhou Qufei and Fan Chengda are referring to a variety of patterned (*ban* or *banlan;* Eberhard uses the word "spotted") cloth produced by a particular carving and dyeing technique. Here is Zhou Qufei's description: "This method employs two flat wooden boards, onto which are carved intricate, flowery patterns. The boards are used to press the cloth, while [hot] wax is poured [ahead of time] into the carved patterns. After this is done, the boards are removed and the cloth is retrieved, whereupon the cloth is immersed in various types of indigo dye. Following the dyeing process, the cloth is boiled to remove the wax. Thus, the extremely fine patterned flowers are revealed." The process, known as *laxie* or *laran,* is sometimes called "batik" in English. See Yang Wuquan, *LWDD*, 6.224, n. 2.

126   These bamboo tubes (also called "bamboo cauldrons"; see the "Treatise on Implements") were filled with food and then placed in a fire or in hot ashes until the food inside was cooked. See Eberhard, *Local Cultures,* 100–101.

ous and difficult to climb. Those with burdens all carry them on their backs and, with support ropes tied around their foreheads, hunch over and forge ahead.[127]

They customarily enjoy killing,[128] are suspicious and ruthless, and treat death lightly. They can also endure hunger [for a long time] when they are away in battle. Long swords are carried on the left side of their waists, large crossbows on the right side, while in their hands is carried a long spear. They ascend and descend the precipitous mountain trails as if they were flying.

As soon as a boy can walk, they heat up a piece of iron and sear the heels and soles of his feet, making them insensitive and numb. This way, the child will be able to tread on thorns, vines, roots and stumps without getting hurt. When a son is born, they weigh him, and the same weight in iron is soaked in a poisonous solution. After the son has grown up, they temper the edges [of the iron] so it can be made into a sword, which the son uses for the rest of his life. The sword must be tested by slaying an ox. The blade is angled below the nape of the ox's neck, while the [young man's] shoulders are used to support the sword. Swords that sever [kill] the ox after one thrust are considered fine swords.

Their crossbows go by the name bend-the-frame crossbows.[129] As they bound about in their travels, they use one foot to cock the crossbow, while arrows are drawn from [quivers on] their backs. Most often they hit their target. Their spears go by the name "hanging spears" [*diaoqiang*]. Over two *zhang* in length, they are only used to

---

127   Zhou Qufei, LWDD, 3.119 (*Netolitzky*, 3.11), mentions that most of the local products produced by the Yao people were heavy and could not be carried on the shoulders. Instead, large back baskets (*nang*) were used to transport these goods, which included conifer boards (*shanban*) and talcum (this mineral was an important local product gathered and sold by Yao; see the "Treatise on Metals and Stones"). Zhou also mentions that a leather strap (Fan's "support ropes"), attached to the bamboo basket, was looped around the bearer's forehead for balance and support. These baskets are still used today by Yao people living in the remote mountainous regions of Guangxi.

128   *Chousha* usually means "killing for revenge," but here it seems to be used in the more general sense of "killing people."

129   For additional information on this type of crossbow, see the entry on Yao people's crossbows in the "Treatise on Implements."

protect the [person shooting the] crossbow and are not relied upon to win victory [in battle]. In battle one person mans a crossbow while another mans a [hanging] spear, and together they advance forward. It is not unusual, however, for those manning the spears to be in front so as to protect the crossbows. Those manning the crossbows hold a knife in their mouths and shoot at people using their hands. The enemy might launch a flurry of rapiers in order to hold back the Yao warriors, in which case there is no way to use the spears. The crossbow archer then puts down his bow and takes the knife from his mouth, and then makes a spirited attack to save the spear man. When crossing a dangerous place, they join into orderly ranks; if they retreat, they will certain have concealed crossbow archers [protecting the rear]. Archers [*gongshou*] from local military units are skillful and adept in battle, and vie for a strategic advantage. Often, however, it is not possible for them to win a decisive victory.

At the start of each year, they offer sacrifices to Pan Hu. They mix and blend fish, meat, wine, and rice in a wooden trough, then perform a ritual by beating the trough and then calling out in unison.

On the first day of the tenth month, each village offers sacrifices to the Great King Dubei [Dubei Dawang].[130] Young men and young women each form into separate lines. Then, side by side, and hand in hand, they dance. This is referred to as "the stomping Yao" [*tayao*].[131] If both partners agree, then the young man will cry out "yippee" [*yi*] and leap over to the group of young women, taking over his shoulder the one he likes. They then become husband and wife. [Matters concerning marriage] are not decided by the parents. Those who do not find a

---

130   The New Year for the Yao people began in the tenth lunar month. The divinity mentioned here, Dubei Dawang, was an important god in Yao culture during the Song. The origins of this god are unclear. See the remarks on this in LWDD, 10.423, n. 2, and Eberhard, *Local Cultures*, 48–49.

131   As noted by Charles Hartman, "Stomping Songs: Word and Image," 4, *tayao* 踏傜 might be a mistake or an alternate written form of *tayao* 踏謠, or "stomping song," a combined song and dance routine that included rhythmic stomping of the feet. The remarks in *Hu-Tan*, 193, n. 14, confirm that Hartman is correct. Cf. also LWDD, 10.423 (Netolitzky, 10.29), which reads *tayao* 踏搖 (lit., "stomping and shaking"). Yang Wuquan says that during the Song dynasty "stomping and shaking" often referred to a musical routine that "included dance but no song" (see LWDD, 10.423. n. 1).

match wait until the following year's gathering. If, after two [additional] years, a woman has no future [no hope of getting married], her parents might want to kill her for being rejected, or so it is said.[132]

For music they have instruments such as reed pipes, blunderbuss drums, gourd panpipes,[133] and bamboo flutes [*zhudi*]. When they join together to make music, there is a massive wall of sound that is complete noise. They beat on a bamboo tube in order to provide rhythm, then gather in a circle, jump and leap up and down, and shout and chant in order to maintain unison.

At the close of the year, groups of them, playing music, go into the counties and towns on government lands, where they knock on doors and beg for money, rice, wine, and cooked meat, as if they are carrying out an exorcism.[134]

As for Yao who fall under the jurisdiction of Guilin, the various districts of Xing'an, Lingchuan, Lingui, Yining, and Gu[135] are all close to the Mountain Yao [Shanyao]. The most aggressive are the Luoman Yao and the Mayuan Yao. The remaining Yao, such as the Huangsha, Jiashi, Lingtun, Baojiang, Zengjiao, Huangcun, Chishui, Lansi, Jinjiang, Songjiang, Dinghua, Lengshi,[136] Baimian, Huangyi, Dali, Xiaoping, Tantou, Danjiang, and Shanjiang,[137] are beyond number.

---

132   Zhou Qufei's entry on Yao New Year and marriage customs, LWDD, 3.118–19 (*Netolitzky*, 3.11), is more detailed than Fan's report here. Zhou's entry is translated and discussed in Hartman, "Stomping Songs: Word and Image," 4–5.

133   On reed pipes, blunderbuss drums, and gourd panpipes, see the "Treatise on Implements."

134   "Exorcism" is my translation of the Chinese word *nuo*. Fan Chengda's description here is based on an ancient festival in south China held in the twelfth month where people would parade through villages and ask for money, food, and wine. The masks worn during these processions are described in the "Treatise on Implements." Upon receipt of these items, they would then expel all resident demons and drive away pestilence from the house. Fan Chengda describes this as an exclusively Yao custom, but Eberhard, *Local Cultures*, 329, demonstrates this is not necessarily the case.

135   The five "districts" mentioned here are actually towns. On Yining and Gu, see note 119 above.

136   Cf. LWDD, 3.118, which reads *lengshi keng* 冷石坑. *Lengshi* (cold stone) is another name for talcum. See the "Treatise on Metals and Stones."

137   The eighteen Yao areas listed here all fell officially under the administrative jurisdiction of Yining Town.

In the mountain valleys, rice fields are few and rainfall is scarce. If there is no harvest of rice crops, they have nothing to eat and thus will go out and attack government lands in the four directions, where they seek out a peck or a pint [of rice] in order to avoid starvation. For a long time they have become [increasingly] irreverent and insulting, and even in abundant years they still continue to plunder and loot.

As for government subjects along the border who live in mixed company with the Yao, their language and customs as well as their strength and skills are roughly the same [as those of the Yao]. Some intermarry [with the Yao], producing hatred and resentment. Often government subjects are guided along [mountain] trails by the Yao but then are taken to an alternate location where they are plundered and robbed by them. Since the Yao have personal knowledge about the back trails [along the border], time after time they have launched surprise attacks. Border subjects are unable to prevent[138] [these incursions]. The Yao attack and destroy their farmhouses, plunder their grain and cattle, and this goes on every year without a break. They slither and slip off into the bamboo groves, from where they swiftly and fleetingly come and go [as they please]. By the time the counties and towns become aware [of their actions], they have already taken refuge in their cubbyholes and crannies. Government troops cannot go in there but only garrison road intersections at certain intervals. The mountains have many footpaths, so they cannot all be secured. Doing so over time would become a waste of labor.

Moreover, Yao people often deal in mountain commodities [*shanhuo*], such as conifer boards and talcum[139] and secretly exchange them with government subjects for salt and rice. Mountain fields dry up easily. If the Yao become completely cut off [from the outside] and have nothing to eat, then they will risk death by suddenly breaking out [from the mountains] and bringing harm, which is becoming increasingly violent. Some government subjects along the border, because they have dealings with the Yao, profit at the Yao's expense, which creates enmity between them. This leads to personal

---

138   Reading *sheihe* 誰何 to mean *jinzhi* 禁止, or "prevent." See *Qi Zhiping*, 43, n. 6.
139   On conifer boards and talcum, see n. 127 above.

vendettas for revenge killing on both sides.

After I found out about this situation, in the summer of the ninth year of the Qiandao reign [1173], I dispatched some officials to deal with it. All of the government troops were relieved of duty, and border citizens were used specially [for the task]. Those who were registered and thus could be used [for military service] numbered over seven thousand and were divided into fifty regiments [*tuan*]. As for the commissioned commanders [*zhang*] and deputy commanders [*fu*], and the men within the clearly defined upper and lower ranks, none were allowed to communicate with the Yao. I provided them with weapons and training,[140] and allowed them to take strong measures against petty bandits without waiting to first notify officials. If the Yao attacked one of the regiments, the other regiments would beat their drums to sound the alarm.

Next I ordered that we have closer relations with the Yao. When I also saw that government subjects were united [in their support of me] and incapable of doing anything illegal, I then opened up their trade routes.[141] Otherwise, the routes would have been cut off. They [the Yao] then realized that the border citizens were now united, and the land and terrain [along the border] were difficult and forbidding,[142] and thus they could not easily launch an attack. Fortunately, because we were able to open up trade communication, the Yao now enjoy the benefits of salt and rice, and all happily submit to [Chinese] orders.

In the end, I selected a brave and courageous local official who got fifty-two Yao headmen [*toushou*] to Sangjiang [Stockade],[143] where they changed sides and pledged allegiance [to the Song]. He traveled

---

140   The organizational and training efforts described here were implemented by Fan Chengda himself. He speaks about this in his memorial on the deficiencies in the Horse Administration in Guangxi. See HSRC, 67.17a–b.

141   This line might also be paraphrased "I gave official Chinese government approval for trade activities between Chinese residents and Yao people along the border."

142   The expression *xingge shijin* (the land and terrain was difficult and forbidding) is drawn from the biography of Sun Wu (better known by his honorific title, Sunzi) in the *Records of the Historian* (Sima Qian, *Shiji*, 65.2163).

143   Sangjiang was the name of a stockade, located in what is now the western part of Longsheng Gezu Zizhiqu, Guangxi.

deep into the Shengjing, Luoman, and other settlements, where the Yao are especially ruthless and vicious and ordinarily do not welcome change. There he also explained the advantages and disadvantages of [the Chinese government] having closer contacts with the Yao, which they all went along with.

Thereupon two trade and exchange markets [*boyi chang*] were established: one in Yining[144] and another in Rongxi,[145] Rong 融 County. [Every year] on the Son of Heaven's birthday, chieftains are able to go to the towns under their jurisdiction, [where Chinese officials] host a banquet for services rendered by the chieftains. The various Yao are greatly pleased about this. Registration of their military units was then stabilized, which upheld the majestic and weighty image [of the chieftains]. In the unlikely event that the distant Yao do not follow our leadership, they will first need to destroy the closer Yao. If the closer Yao desire to make a move [against us], then they will also first need to defeat our border regiments [*biantuan*]. Only then will they be in a position to scale our city walls, but that would indeed be difficult for them.

After several months, various Yao regiment commanders [*tuanzhang*], such as Yuan Tai and several tens of others, paid an official courtesy call on the managing and organizing inspector [Fan Chengda himself] to offer their respects and give thanks. All of them wore purple robes and held horizontal clubs wrapped in cloth. They rewarded [the inspector] with gifts consisting of silver bowls [*yinwan*], colorful silk fabrics [*caishi*], salt, and wine, which were presented in recognition for service provided [to them by the inspector]. Moreover, each of them came with a written pledge of allegiance [*shizhuang*],[146] which essentially read as follows:

> I so-and-so, have already assumed official appointment in the
> mountains, and now should make sure there are restraints on the

---

144   On Yining Town, see n. 119 above.
145   The precise location of Rongxi (lit., "Rong Creek") in Rong County is unknown.
146   *LWDD*, 10.424–25, has a complete entry devoted to written pledges of allegiance (*shizhuang*), which Zhou Qufei calls *kuansai* and *nakuan*.

young men and women [of the tribes].[147] Males in their daily routine [may] carry clubs [for hunting]; women in their daily routine [may] hold hemp [for weaving]. They may come and go [across the border with Chinese territory] as they please, but cannot make trouble. [Those who make trouble should know that] above there is the sun; below is the earthly abode. As for those who turn their backs on this pledge, they will bear sons who become donkeys, bear daughters who become swine, and their entire family will be extinguished and wiped out! They are not allowed to say nice things in front of one's face but then bad things behind one's back. Nor are they allowed to flatter and toady. When they go to the mountains, they will follow the same route; when they go down the rivers, they will take the same boat. Males [will still] carry their knives on the same side of their body. In every respect everything is the same. Together they will kill brigands and bandits. Those who do not follow these stipulations will equally be subject to mountain law [*shanli*].

Those subject to mountain law are put to death. Man speech is vulgar and base,[148] but I do not desire to hide the truth about them, and so I have briefly provided a treatise on them here.

Despite my unworthy nature, for two years I managed military affairs [in Guangxi]. [During that time] not a single trace of the various Yao reached government land. Thereupon, I submitted a report to the court concerning all aspects of the accord [with the Yao], after which an imperial edict was issued granting permission to follow and implement it.[149]

THE LAO are located beyond the Creek Settlements along the Right River and are customarily referred to as the Mountain Lao.[150] They live close to the mountains and forests, and have neither tribal chiefs nor

---

147 Following *LWDD*, 10.424, and reading *jin dang qianshu nannü* 今當鈐束男女 (now should make sure there are restraints on the young men and women [of the tribes.]).

148 The reference here is to the coarse Man language in the pledge.

149 *WXTK*, 328.2575; *FCDBJ*, 141–44.

150 Although in modern Chinese the character 僚 is usually read as *liao*, when denoting the specific tribespeople of Sichuan, Shaanxi, Guizhou, Hunan, Guangdong, and Guangxi known by that name, it is pronounced *lao*.

household registers [*banji*]. Among the Man people they are the ones who are [the most] erratic and unstable. They live by bow hunting and eating game. Any insect that can wriggle is taken [by them] for food. They neither calculate years of age nor have names. In any one village, only the person who commands [the greatest] ability and strength is called the *langhuo*.[151] The others are simply known as *huo*. In former accounts[152] their varieties include some twenty-one tribes, including Flying Heads [Feitou],[153] Knocked-Out Teeth [Zaochi],[154] Nose Drinkers [Biyin],[155] White Smocks [Baishan], Flowery Faces [Huamian], and the Fiery-Red Pants [Chiku].[156] Today they are prevalent in the area southwest of the Right River,[157] numbering close to over one hundred tribes.

---

151 The Chinese term *langhuo*, used here to describe a type of native headman, is derived from one of the Man languages of the south. Tan Xiaohang makes a strong case that *langhuo* in fact is borrowed from a Mulam expression meaning "headman" (*touren*). See *Lingnan gu Yueren mingcheng wenhua tanyuan*, 101–5, and also Shin, *The Making of the Chinese State*, 147–48.

152 These former accounts (*jiuzhuan*) are not identified, but Fan must be referring to earlier geographic or ethnographic works on Guangxi.

153 There are numerous accounts in traditional sources about people in the south who can supposedly let their heads fly away, and this practice is often associated with the Lao people. Fan Chengda offers additional description of the Flying Head Lao below. For additional information see the comments by Lang Hong'en in Kuang Lu, *Chiya kaoshi*, 43–44, and Eberhard, *Local Cultures*, 447. Eberhard also mentions (450) that these flying heads bite people.

154 The practice of knocking out teeth as an initiation rite is a long-standing custom among the Lao people. Usually, one upper molar and one incisor are knocked out. Eberhard, *Local Cultures*, 450.

155 According to Kuang Lu, this subgroup of the Lao was also called the Bi Yi. They were known to drink wine through their noses. See *Chiya kaoshi*, 44–45. Fan Chengda has an entry on nose-drinking cups. See the "Treatise on Implements."

156 The names for the various "types" of Lao people enumerated here were coined by the Chinese. As for the White Smocks, Flowery (Tattooed?) Faces, and Fiery-Red Pants, more specific information does not seem to be available. See the comments in *Hu-Tan*, 203, n.6.

157 In many sources, such as the *Xin Tangshu*, 222xia.6329, the tribes in the area of southwestern Guangxi were sometimes collectively called the Southwest Man (Xi'nan Man) or Settlement Lao (Donglao). On several occasions in *Treatises*, Fan Chengda also calls these people the Mountain Lao. Although during the Southern Song these Lao people did live in the bridle and halter areas, because of their remote location Chinese authorities in Guangxi had no control over or influence on them.

Supplementary text: At the beginning of the year the Lao take twelve clay cups to hold water and arrange and align them according to the positions of the chronograms [*chenwei*].[158] The *langhuo* offer prayers to them and then gather together the multitudes to come and observe. If the *yin* cup has water but the *mao* cup has dried up, then they know there will be rain in the first month [of the new year] and drought in the second month. They themselves regard this [prediction] method to be accurate.

The various foreign tribes annually sell horses to the [Song] government. [When government officials] travel the road into their territory, the Lao will demand goods as well as salt and oxen. Otherwise, they will block the horse road.[159] Government officials also use salt and multicolored silk to placate them. Over time some Lao gradually came to acquire titles [from the Chinese government] indicating superior and inferior ranks, which then entered the Man groups. . . .

In his *Treatise on Unusual Things* [Yiwu zhi] Fang Qianli [fl. ca. 840] of the Tang says: "After a Lao woman gives birth to a child, she will then immediately leave [the room]. The husband then lies down, [pretending to be] fatigued [after having given birth], and acts as if he was a nursing mother. If he is not attentive [to these duties], the wife will become ill. If he is attentive, the wife will not encounter hardship [in the future]."[160] The [*Tangzhi*] says: "As for the Flying Head Lao, when their heads wish to fly, scars resembling threads appear all around the napes of their necks. The wives and children together stand watch. By nighttime, when the man seems to be taken

---

158   The "chronograms" mentioned here are actually the twelve terrestrial branches (*dizhi*), arranged to represent the twelve months of the year. In this scheme, *yin* represents the first month, *mao* the second month, and so on.

159   On the horse trade between the Song government and foreign peoples in the southwest, especially Dali, see the "Treatise on Quadrupeds."

160   A text attributed to Fang Qianli with a very similar title—*Treatise on Unusual Things in the Southern Quarter* (Nanfang yiwu zhi)—is listed in *Xin Tangshu*, 58.1507. This is probably the work to which Fan Chengda is referring. This text is not extant. The custom described here, sometimes called *chanweng* (birth father) or *changong* (birth husband), is mentioned in many sources. The earliest reference I have found appears in the *Taiping guangji*, 483.3981, quoting a work titled *Reports from Southern Chu* (Nan Chu xinwen), a late Tang text attributed to Wei Chishu.

ill, his head suddenly disappears. It returns at dawn the next day.

There are also the Black Warrior Lao [Wuwu Lao], whose territory is filled with miasmic poisons. Those who come down with such illness cannot drink any medicine. So they knock out their own teeth."[161]

THE MAN. In the southern quarter they are called the Man.[162] Today, although [residents of] the bridle and halter counties and settlements beyond the commanderies and towns are all Man, their territory remains close to the Chinese government areas, and the people pay taxes and supply corvée labor, and so they are not designated as Man. But once you pass beyond the bridle and halter areas, there you find people who are referred to as "beyond civilization." These indeed are the true Man [*zhen Man*]!

The tribal settlements [of the true Man] stretch on continuously and [eventually] join with the [territory of the] Western Barbarians [Xi Rong].[163] Their ethnic group [*zhonglei*] is odd and strange, and their numbers are beyond calculation,[164] so for now I will only

---

161 The lines quoted here are drawn (with minor variation) from *Xin Tangshu* (referred to in the previous paragraph as *Tangzhi*), 222*xia*.6326. Supplementary text from *WXTK*, 328.2579; *FCDBJ*, 145–46.

162 Several texts, such as the *Jinshu*, 97.2531–32, drawing on terms from Zhou dynasty works used to indicate foreign, "barbarian" peoples along and beyond the borders of China, designate the "Four Yi" (Si Yi), or "Four Barbarians": Yi, Rong, Di, and Man. Each of these names is associated with a particular direction and hence a particular region, namely, east, west, north, and south, respectively. The last of these terms, Man, was used as an all-purpose, generic reference to the various non-Chinese peoples who lived in south China and beyond its borders. Other generics employed by Fan Chengda for these same people include Southwest Man and Southwest Fan. All of these terms carry a pejorative connotation of "barbarian." Cf. *LWDD*, 3.120–21 (*Netolitzky*, 3.12), which calls these same tribes the Southwest Yi (Xi'nan Yi). During the Southern Song the term Southwest Fan was often used specifically to indicate tribes in and around the ancient Zangge region of modern Guizhou (see below) that periodically sent tribute to the Song Court. *LWDD*, 3.120–21 (*Netolitzky*, 3.12) provides some useful details on these tribute missions.

163 Non-Chinese peoples along the western border and beyond were sometimes collectively referred to by Chinese as the Xi Rong, or "Western Barbarians." Xi Rong is among the earliest collective ethnonyms used for "barbarian" in China. See Wilkinson, *Chinese History*, 710, n. 4.

164 Here I follow the text of *WXTK*, 328.2578, and read *bu ke sheng ji* 不可勝計 (their numbers are beyond calculation).

report on the Man near Guilin.

In Yi County are the Southwest Fan, [which includes] the Major and Minor Zhang [Daxiao Zhang], the Major and Minor Wang [Daxiao Wang], the Long, the Shi, the Teng,[165] and the Xie,[166] whose territory borders with Zangge.[167] Their people wear their hair bundled like a mallet and go barefoot. Some wear wooden clogs [*mulü*]. They wear [clothes made of] patterned materials with dark flowery designs[168] and lead a life of hunting and killing.

Next, to the south are the territories beyond the South River [Nanjiang][169] that link with Yong County, such as Luodian,[170] Ziqi,[171] and so on, which take their names from kingdoms. Luokong,[172]

---

165   *Hu-Tan*, 213, n. 6, argues that 滕 (which is read "teng") should instead read 程 (cheng), referring to a tribe (the Cheng Fan 程番) that had relations with China during the final years of the Northern Song.

166   Among the various tribes of Southwest Fan listed here by Fan Chengda, the Long clan was considered the most powerful. See *Songshi,* 496.14242. Cf. Zhou Qufei's list of the surnames of most dominant tribes among the Southwest Fan in *LWDD*, 1.49 (*Netolitzky*, 1.26). Beginning in the early Song, the five most important of these tribes were called the Wuxing Fan, or "Fan of the Five Surnames." Which five surnames this group comprised varies depending on which source one consults. All, however, sent tribute to the Song capital and received office appointments from the Song government. *Songshi,* 496.14241.

167   Zangge is an ancient toponym and administrative name. During the Han dynasty Zangge Commandery (established in 111 B.C.E.) occupied most of Guizhou and parts of northwestern Guangxi and eastern Yunnan. Later, however, its size and administrative status changed many times. Throughout the Tang and Song the territory of ancient Zangge fell within the jurisdiction of Qian County (Qianzhou; modern Pengshui *xian* and Qianjiang *xian*, Sichuan), which in turn fell under the administrative control of the Kui County Circuit (Kuizhou *lu*). For more specific information on the origin, meaning, and pronunciation of the place-name Zangge, see Zhou Qingquan, "Shi Zangge," 97–98, 74.

168   Fan Chengda is probably referring here to patterned cloth produced by the process described in note 125.

169   This is another name for the Right River.

170   The Kingdom of Luodian existed during the Tang and was located in what is now the southwestern part of Guizhou.

171   The Ziqi kingdom was situated on the border of modern Guangxi and Yunnan, more specifically, the northern border of modern Xilin *xian* (Guangxi) where it meets Yi *xian* (Yunnan).

172   The Luokong tribe was probably based in or near modern Luokong in Honghe *xian*, Yunnan.

Temo[dao],[173] Baiyi,[174] Jiudao,[175] and so on take their names from circuits.[176] But the territory west of E County[177] has its own separate tribal chieftain and is not subordinate to anyone. The Man of Suqi, Luozuo, Yemian,[178] Jili, Liuqiu, Wanshou, Duoling, and Awu[179] are referred to as the "Raw Man."[180] Their chieftains style themselves "grand protectors" [*taibao*]. For the most part, they are similar to the Mountain Lao, the only difference being that they have leaders. Places like Luodian have been organized into villages, and they also use written correspondence [*wenshu*] and official documents [*gongwen*] that say "under the protection of the king of the state of Luodian" [*shou Luodian guowang*].

Beyond these areas there are also large-scale Man tribes. The one in the west is called Dali;[181] the one in the east is called Jiaozhi.[182] As for Dali, this is the [former] state of Nanzhao. As for Jiaozhi, this is the Jiao County of ancient times, which ruled over Longbian[183] Town and

---

173 Located in the general area around modern Wenshan Zhuang and the Miao People's Autonomous Prefecture, Yunnan. During the Song this area was populated by the Nong clan of the Lao people.

174 This is probably a reference to the Baiyi Man, also known as the Western Cuan (Xi Cuan), who, in the tenth century, lived in the northern part of Vietnam and along the southern border of Yunnan. They wore knee-length white smocks, hence the name Baiyi, or White Clothes. Schafer, *Vermilion Bird*, 49. For additional information on the Baiyi Man see Fan Chuo, *Manshu jiaozhu*, 4.82–112 (Luce, *The Man Shu*, 33–46).

175 Jiudao is otherwise unknown.

176 All of the places mentioned in this sentence were situated along the borders of western Guangxi, southern Guizhou, and eastern Yunnan. These areas stood between the state of Dali and territory nominally under Chinese control.

177 E County (Ezhou) was a Tang bridle and halter county that continued in that capacity during the Song under the jurisdiction of Shaoqing Municipality (Shaoqing *fu*). It was probably located in the general area around modern Libo *xian* in the Qiannan Buyi and Miao Autonomous Prefecture, Guizhou.

178 *FCDBJ*, 146, reads Yemian 夜面, while *WXTK*, 328.2578, reads Yehui 夜回. *LWDD*, 1.49, follows the Yehui reading.

179 No information seems to be available on these tribes beyond what is mentioned here and repeated in *LWDD*, 1.49 (*Netolitzky*, 1.26). See *Hu-Tan*, 214, n. 8.

180 For more information on the Chinese classification system of "raw" and "cooked" barbarians, see Fiskesjö, "On the 'Raw' and 'Cooked' Barbarians."

181 On the Kingdom of Dali see note 10 in the "Treatise on Implements."

182 On Jiaozhi, see note 28 in the "Treatise on Aromatics."

183 Longbian's history dates back to the Western Han. During the Tang it served as

also served as the [site of the] Annan Protector General's Headquarters [Annan Duhu Fu].[184]

Supplementary text: In the southern quarter they are called the Man; they are also called the Southwest Fan. . . . Their tribal settlements stretch on continuously through Hu and Guang, and [eventually] join with the territory of the Western Barbarians. . . . These tribes in former times were once formally affiliated [with the Song central government].[185] A southern Qian County military headquarters was established in Rong 融 County in order to control them. Today the command in Rong County has already been abolished,[186] and all of tribes there are "beyond civilization."

Rong 融 County is south of the Yao settlements and east of the Fan Man.[187] The Fan Man sometimes emerge from the walls of the [bridle and halter] counties and towns,[188] and conduct trade in such things as honey [*mi*], jerky [*xi*],[189] herbs [*cao*],[190] and aromatics. Each year on the emperor's birthday, there are also those who come out [of the counties and settlements] and attend a feast. These people are designated

---

the administrative seat of Long County (Longzhou), a bridle and halter county under Yong County. It was located near modern Hai Phong, Vietnam. By Song times this administrative area was already defunct.

184   The Annan Protector General's Headquarters was established in 679. Sometimes called the Annan Commanding General's Headquarters (Annan Dudu Fu), it served as the command center of the regional military governor and as a focal point of Tang imperial authority. This headquarters was located near modern Hanoi.

185   *Hu-Tan*, 211–12, n. 3, presents a detailed historical outline of these relations, which go back to the early Tang and continued until the eleventh century. Judging from Fan Chengda's comments here, the formal affiliation between the tribes and the Song government had ended by the Southern Song.

186   This military headquarters, established in Rong County in 1108, was known officially as the Qian County Commanding General's Headquarters (Qianzhou Dudu Fu). It supervised some fifty bridle and halter counties, scattered throughout modern Guizhou.

187   The term Fan Man seems to be a generic designation for the various Man people who lived in northeastern Guangxi, in the general area around Guilin.

188   Cf. *Songshi*, 496.14223, which says that the Southwest Fan did not live in areas surrounded by fortified walls.

189   Reading *xi* 腊 (jerky) rather than *la* 蠟 (wax; candle). "Jerky" refers to cured meat or fish.

190   The reference here is to medicinal herbs (*caoyao*).

the Major and Minor Zhang , the Major and Minor Wang, the Long, the Shi, the Teng, and the Xie, who are referred to [collectively] as the Southwest Fan. Their territory borders Zangge. . . . They carry wooden shields [*mupai*], *biao* spears [*biaoqiang*], wooden crossbows [*munu*], and poisonous arrows [*yaojian*], and loot and plunder one another.

And west of E County there are also the Luozuo, the Yehui, the Jili, the Liuqiu, the Wanshou, the Duoling, and the Awu Man, who are referred to as "Raw Man." Their chieftains refer to themselves as grand protectors. For the most part, they are like the Mountain Lao, the only difference being that they have leaders. Their people wear their hair bundled like a mallet, which is bound with white paper. It is said this is mourning apparel for Zhuge Liang, the Martial Marquis [Zhuge Liang wuhou].[191]

As for the customs of the Southwest Fan, for the most part the differences [among them] are slight.[192] The men are very strong; the women are very clean. Husband and wife reside in different places. The place where the wife resides is deeply concealed where no one else is seen. When the husband visits his wife, he goes in only after hanging his sword on the door. Sometimes they agree to meet deep in the mountains. [This way] they do not sully or foul[193] their residence. It is said that otherwise spirits and ghosts would bring disaster on the residence. None of these various Man have ever brought harm [upon others]. Thus, we are also not able to know about their affairs in any great detail.

There are also the Chinese Man [Han Man].[194] Ten years ago, when

---

191   This custom, observed out of respect for the great statesman and strategist of the Three Kingdoms period Zhuge Liang, is also mentioned in LWDD, 3.121 (*Netolitzky*, 3.12).

192   Additional information on the customs of the Southwest Fan (or Southwest Yi) can be found in *Songshi,* 496.14223.

193   The expression "sully or foul" (*xiehui*) in this context probably means "have sexual intercourse."

194   "Chinese Man" refers to people of Chinese descent who lived among the Man. These were mainly descendents of northern Chinese who resettled in the southwest during the Six Dynasties and Tang and assimilated with the Man there. Cf. Fan Chuo, *Manshu jiaozhu,* 4.92 (Luce, *The Man Shu,* 37), which mentions a "Shang people" (Shangren; also called Hanshang Man) "who originally were Chinese." These Tang residents of the south could have

some Dali horses reached Mount Heng, these Man affiliated themselves[195] so they could come along. Their dress and attire is roughly
similar to that in China, and they are able to communicate in Chinese.
They themselves boast that they were originally descended from the
garrison troops [*shubing*] of Zhuge Liang, the Martial Marquis. I have
heard that this stock of people is extremely rare. Note: In the *Records of
the Three Kingdoms* [Sanguo zhi] nothing is said about "leaving behind
garrisons."[196] The *Tang History* [Tangshi] has a section on the Xitu Yi,
which refers to the troops of Ma [Yuan], the Subduer of Waves, who
remained behind because they could not leave. At first, their number
was limited to ten households. But by the end of the Sui, there were
three hundred households, all surnamed Ma. They went by the sobri-
quet "The Mas Who Stayed Behind" [Ma Liuren][197] and shared Tang
territory with Linyi.[198] I suspect the Chinese Man are in fact this group.

---

been the ancestors of Fan Chengda's "Chinese Man."

195 That is to say, they submitted to Chinese authority.

196 The point here is that Zhuge Liang's biography in the *Records of the Three Kingdoms* says nothing about him leaving behind Chinese troops after his pacification of the south (see Chen Shou, comp., *Sanguo zhi*, 35.911–28).

197 Fan Chengda is here paraphrasing a passage from the "Southern Man" chapter of the *Xin Tangshu*, 222*xia*.6297. As pointed out in *Hu-Tan*, 215, n. 11, this
account of "the Mas who stayed behind" is a legend. Still, it is repeated as fact
in numerous historical works. Han Zhenhua agrees that the story is a myth
but points out that the expression *ma liuren* (or *maren*) refers to the Xitu Yi, an
ancient aboriginal people who lived along the coast of central Vietnam, in an
area that was once known as Linyi (see notes 198 and 214 below). Han Zhenhua,
"Ma liuren shi shemme ren?"

198 As a result of a local rebellion against the Chinese governor, a portion of Jiaozhi Commandery in what is now central Vietnam became an independent
kingdom in 192. This kingdom, on the north-central coast in the area around
modern-day Hue, later evolved into Linyi (Vietnamese: Lâm Ap). Linyi derives
its name (lit., "Lin District") from a Han dynasty town there called Xianglin, which was the administrative center of a commandery of the same name.
The Han general Ma Yuan supposedly erected bronze pillars in Linyi. Buddhism was practiced widely there, and Linyi even had a written language that
is thought to have resembled Sanskrit, which would suggest Indian influence.
In 602, during the so-called Linyi-Champa campaign, Sui dynasty troops
invaded and took control of Linyi. Thereafter it was reduced to the status of a
Chinese tributary state. For additional details on the history of Linyi, see Maspero, *Zhanpo shi*, 31–43; Rolf Stein, "Le Lin-yi, sa localisation, sa contribution à
la formation du Champa et ses liens avec la Chine," *Han-hiue, Bulletin de Cen-*

Those places with names, located to their [the Chinese Man's] south and slightly beyond Yong County and South River, include Luodian and Ziqi, which take their names from states. Luokong, Temo, Baiyi, Jiudao, and so on take their names from circuits. All of these [tribes] and their territories are close to Nanzhao.

Luodian is west of Rong 融 and Yi Counties and northwest of Yong County. During the Huichang reign [841–847] of the Tang, Luodian's commandant [*shuai*] was made King of Luodian [Luodian Wang],[199] a hereditary title of noble rank. Each year Luodian sends horses to Mount Heng [Stockade] for trading.[200] Horses are also transferred to Yong County, designated "under protection of Luo" [*shou Luo*]. The king [of Luodian] is Luo Lü.

Those who escort the horses designate them "certified by the administrator of Wu County, order and rule commissioner, and chief of the Southwest Xie tribe" [*Xi'nan Xiefan zhi Wuzhou jiedu shi duda zhaohui*],[201] which is written in the script of the state of Luodian.[202]

---

tre d'études sinologiques de Pékin, 2 (1947): 1–335; William A. Southworth, "The Coastal States of Champa," in Ian Glover and Peter S. Bellwood, eds., *Southeast Asia: From Prehistory to History* (London and New York: Routledge and Curzon, 2004), 216–21; and especially Southworth's "The Origins of Champa in Central Vietnam: A Preliminary Review" (Ph.D. diss., University of London, School of Oriental and African Studies, 2001). Also useful are the various contributions to *New Scholarship on Champa*, edited by Bruce Lockart and Tran Ky Phuong (Singapore: Asia Research Institute, National University of Singapore, 2009); and especially Michael Vickery, "Champa Revised," ARI Working Paper No. 37, (March 2005), http://www.ari.nus.edu.sg/docs/wps/wps05_037.pdf (accessed 3 November 2007). See also the comments on Linyi in note 214 below.

199   The chieftain appointed to this position was named Apei. See *Xin Tangshu*, 222*xia*.6319.

200   These horses were not from Luodian. Traders from Luodian (and Ziqi) purchased horses from Dali and then shipped them to the Mount Heng Stockade in Yong County. All Man horses sold to the Song were from Dali. See *LWDD*, 9.348 (*Netolitzky*, 9.4).

201   The expression *duda* 都大, rendered here as "chief," is sometimes used as a prefix in Song dynasty office titles. *Hucker*, no. 7289. But here no office title follows *duda*. I suspect *duda* in this context refers to *duda tiju chama*, or supervisor-in-chief of horse trading.

202   The precise origin (and possible later development) of this written language is unknown. Hu Qiwang and Tan Guanguang speculate that it might be a precur-

Note: According to the *Tang History* [Tangshi], the Eastern Xie Man reside west of Qian County. The Xie Fan have a hereditary chieftain, who the tribes respect and fear. That being the case, the Xie tribes are probably a powerful ruling family in Luodian. We also know their territory is close to Zangge.[203]

The Ziqi people were originally Minor Man. They are especially violent and treacherous, and love to make a profit. They sell horses at the Mount Heng Stockade.[204] At the very slightest provocation they will immediately draw their knives on others. Once some of them were killed and wounded. The Yong Administration [then] killed several Man in order to make recompense, and then the matter was settled. Today its king is called Asi. He assumed the throne three years after he was born. His minister Axie held power over the state and was good at comforting its masses. A relatively large number of various Man attached themselves to him, to the extent that he amassed tens of thousands of crack cavalry. When Asi was seventeen, Axie returned the reins of government to him. Asi and the entire state still obey Axie.[205]

---

sor of the script devised by ancestors of the modern Yi people (in English sometimes called the "Lolo"). See *Hu-Tan*, 217, n. 15. This identification, however, is tentative. The origins of the written language of the Yi people are uncertain, and there has been much scholarly debate on the subject, none of it as yet conclusive. Nor has any scholar proven a connection between the Luodian people of the Tang and Song periods and the Yi people of later times and today. A useful summary of the debate concerning the origins of Yi script can be found in Stevan Harrell and Li Yongxiang, "The History of the History of the Yi: Part II," *Modern China* 29.3 (July 2003): 376–78.

203   Fan Chengda's comments here need some clarification. The Eastern Xie Man, whose territory was some 300 *li* west of Qian County (*Xin Tangshu*, 222xia.6320), should be distinguished from the powerful and feared Xie clan in Luodian. The last line of this paragraph ("We also know their territory is close to Zangge.") pertains to the Eastern Xie Man, not the Xie clan of Qian County (who lived within the territory of ancient Zangge).

204   The distance from Ziqi to the Hengshan Stockade in Yong County was approximately 16 *cheng*, or "stages." If we figure 1 *cheng* to be roughly 60 *li*, this would be a distance of 960 *li*, or about 320 miles. The usual route from Ziqi to Hengshan meant passing through territory controlled by Luodian. As a result, sometimes disputes arose (because of competition in the horse trade), and at times Ziqi horse traders had to follow an alternate route that took them to Yi County instead of Yong County. See *Hu-Tan*, 218, n. 17.

205   Fan Chengda's account here concerning the succession of Ziqi's rulers should

As for the various Man who arrive at the Yong Administration to sell horses, their customs and habits are much the same. Many of these people have deep-set eyes and lanky bodies, with dark faces and white teeth. They use damask to bundle their hair like a mallet, and wear short coarse clothing and walk barefoot. They wear wide-brimmed straw hats, drape a felt fabric over their shoulders,[206] have ear ornaments and brushed teeth. Gold bands bind their arms; on their back is a long knife. At their waist is a quiver for their crossbow arrows. Beneath their armpits they wear a leather satchel. A double length of hempen rope is tied from the chest to the waist to make it easier to ride a horse. To select a horse from the herd, they need only take a long rope and walk forward. They then lasso the horse, hitting their mark with one throw. Their knives are three *chi* in length and are very sharp. Knives from Dali are especially wondrous.[207]

By nature they are fond of cleanliness. Several people share a meal. In a single plate [of food] they plant one spoon, with a cup of water placed beside it. Young and old share the spoon as they eat. They dip the spoon into the [cup of] water, take a portion of some food and then set it [back] down [in the cup]. The food is hand-rolled on the plate, making it round and clean. Only then do they put the food onto the spoon and fling it into their mouths. The probably do this because they do not want a dirty spoon to harm others.

Each meal is extremely modest, and their drinking of wine is also limited to one cup, which they are able to drain after only a few gulps. This is probably the reason their stomachs are bound with a rope.[208] They consume salt, alum [*fan*],[209] and pepper but do not eat pork.

---

be compared with the remarks of Wu Jing in his "Lun Yongzhou huawai zhu-guo," 1.3b–4a. Wu Jing, a Chinese official who served in Yong County (after Fan Chengda), gives Axie's ascension date as 1176. Moreover, he identifies Axie as Asi's paternal uncle (not his "minister") and mentions that Axie was literate and could speak Chinese.

206 During daylight hours Man people customarily wore a piece of felt fabric over their shoulders. See the entry on Man felt in the "Treatise on Implements."

207 These are also called "Yunnan knives." See the entry in the "Treatise on Implements."

208 I understand this comment to mean that their stomachs are bound tightly with ropes to prevent them from overeating.

209 *Fan* is potassium alum or potash alum. Read, *Minerals and Stones*, no. 131.

When they finish eating, they must always brush their teeth; thus they are always sparkling white.

They hate foul smells. Whenever they defecate in the wilds, they always dig a hole and cover it up. The people in Yong County frequently use the foul smell [of feces] to deal with people whom they despise. They fling chamber pots at these people, who invariably leap onto their horses and flee in alarm.[210]

Supplementary entry: **ANNAN:** Today the territory of the state of Annan[211] adjoins the various Han [dynasty] commanderies of Jiuzhen and Rinan[212] as well as Tang counties of Huan and Ai.[213] In the south-

---

There are several varieties, distinguished by their color, which are discussed briefly in Schafer, *The Golden Peaches of Samarkand*, 217. The variety most often used in the preparation of medicines is white and is also called *baifan* or (in more recent times) *mingfan*. As far as I have been able to determine, alum is not indigenous to south China or Vietnam, nor was it used there as a food additive. Cf. Chang and Smythe, *South China in the Twelfth Century*, 40, and Chun-shu Chang's comments on 56, n. 13. In Lu You's travel diary, alum is set out on a table and seems to be used as a decoration.

210   *WXTK*, 328.2578; *FCDBJ*, 147–49.

211   This account of Annan was originally part of Fan Chengda's entry on the Man. For the sake of reference and convenience, I have made it into a separate entry. "Annan" (lit., "Secured South") is a name the Chinese gave in the seventh century to an area it administered in the northern part of modern Vietnam. During the Tang dynasty Annan (also known as "Annam" in Vietnamese, French, and English) fell under the jurisdiction of the Annan Protector General's Headquarters (Annan Duhu Fu). The administrative seat of Annan was in Jiao County (Jiaozhou), near modern Hanoi. Annan was also known as Jiaozhi, a commandery name that dates back to the Han period. During the Five Dynasties era Annan weaned itself from Chinese control and became an independent state. Sometimes it called itself Da Yue (Vietnamese: Đại Việt). Unable to control it, the Southern Song government in Lin'an followed its usual practice of buying off potential threats from border states by conferring titles and special privileges on its leaders. In 975, the leader of Annan was bestowed the title "King of Jiaozhi Commandery" (Jiaozhi Jun Wang), but in 1174 this was changed to "King of the Annan State" (Annan Guowang). Thereafter, Chinese sources consistently refer to this state as Annan.

212   The Han commandery Jiuzhen, created after the Han "pacification of the south" in 111 B.C.E., was located in what is now the northern part of Vietnam. Rinan (during the Qin dynasty known as Xiang Commandery) was south of there, in the central part of Vietnam.

213   Huan County (under the Sui known as Rinan Commandery) underwent numerous administrative and name changes during the Tang, which are

east it approaches the sea and adjoins Champa. Champa is Linyi.[214] In the east, the sea route [to and from Annan] connects with Qin and Lian Counties;[215] in the west, one gets there through the territories of the various Man [tribes]; and in the northwest one connects through Yong County. The fastest route is from the southeastern corner of Yong County to Taiping Stockade [Taiping Zhai].[216] Proceed due south from the stockade to Guanglang[217] and Huabu Towns, then cross the Fuliang[218] and Baiteng Rivers. This can be accomplished in four *cheng*. One can also proceed southeast from the stockade and go past the Danteluo

---

outlined in *Hu-Tan*, 275, n. 1. Ai County, formerly known as Jiuzhen Commandery, also experienced many name changes during the Tang. Huan and Ai Counties were both located in the general area around Qinghua (Vietnamese: Thanh Hoa) Province in north-central Vietnam.

214 Champa (Zhancheng, sometimes also called Zhanpo) is the name of an ancient kingdom that controlled central and southern Vietnam from the seventh until the nineteenth century. Most English-language sources refer to this kingdom as "Champa" and its residents as "Chams." Before the founding of Champa in the eighth century, another kingdom called Linyi (see note 198 above) existed in the same general region. As for the relationship between Linyi and Champa, this is unclear, and historians are still debating the issue. Champa reached the height of its power in the late ninth and early tenth centuries. At about the same time, the Đại Việt in northern Vietnam were asserting their independence from Chinese control, which was finalized in 968. Throughout the tenth, eleventh, and twelfth centuries, the relationship between the Đại Việt and the Chams was an uneasy one. A peace was eventually reached in 1170 that made Champa subordinate to Annan. An important secondary source on the history of Champa and Linyi is Georges Maspero's *Le royaume de Champa* (1928), which is now available in English through Walter E. J. Tips's translation.

215 Qin County was situated in what is now Qinzhou *xian*, Guangxi. Lian County corresponds to modern Lian *xian*, Guangxi.

216 According to Tan Qixiang, the Taiping Stockade was located on the north bank of the Left River, just north of modern Chongzuo *shi*, Guangxi. See Tan Qixiang et al., eds., *Zhongguo lishi ditu ji*, 6:65–66. Cf. Yang Wuquan's comments in *LWDD*, 2.62, n. 11, where he argues that the Taiping Stockade was probably downriver from there and northwest of modern Longzhou *xian*.

217 Some texts, such as *LWDD*, 2.55, and Li Tao, comp., *Xu Zizhi tongjian changbian*, 279.6832, instead read Jilang 機榔 Town.

218 Most sources identify "Fuliang" as an alternate name for the Red River (Honghe). Cf. Anderson, *The Rebel Den*, 143, which says the Fuliang (Vietnamese: Nhr Hguyệt or Cầu) River is located in modern Bắc Ninh (Chinese: Beining) Province in the Red River delta region, east of Hanoi.

Minor River,[219] and then from Liang County [Liangzhou][220] pass into Annan. This can be accomplished in six *cheng*. If you go from Wenrun Stockade [Wenrun Zhai][221] on the Right River, this is the longest route. If you go by sea from Qin County, you can reach there in one day.[222]

As for [those portions of Annan] that have served as command-eries and towns [or Chinese administrative units] throughout the successive eras, the present dynasty regards them as "beyond civi-lization." The Ding clan [Dingshi], Li clan [Lishi 黎氏], and Li clan [Lishi 李氏] have successively dominated its territory.[223] In the Xining reign [1068–1078], just after [Li] Qiande [1066?–1132; r. 1072–1127] assumed the throne,[224] a high official was in charge[225] and

---

219 This river is known today as the Ping'er River (Ping'er He). It is part of the Pearl River system and connects modern Nanning, Wuzhou, and Guangzhou with north Vietnam.

220 Liang County (Vietnamese: Lạng Châu) was a Tang dynasty administrative unit located on the lower reaches of the Left River on the Vietnamese side of the modern border between China and Vietnam.

221 This stockade was southeast of modern Jingxi *xian*, Guangxi. See LWDD, 2.64, n. 15. Fan Chengda mentions below that the Wenrun Stockade is on the Right River, but this is incorrect. It was a good distance southwest from the Right River, close to the Annan border. See Tan Qixiang et al., eds., *Zhongguo lishi ditu ji*, 6: 65–66.

222 Details of the travel itineraries described here should be compared with those outlined in LWDD, 2.55 (*Netolitzky*, 2.1). Although Zhou Qufei's itineraries are based on those in *Treatises,* there are some significant differences between the two accounts, especially concerning the distances in *cheng* between various places. See also Zhang Jinlian, "Songchao yu Annan tongdao shitan." Zhang conducts a very useful investigation of the various changes and developments in the land and sea routes between south China (mainly Guangdong and Guangxi) and Annan after the latter won independence. During the Song the major land routes to Jiaozhi began in Yong County; the major sea route was from Qin County.

223 The three clans or families mentioned here ruled over Jiaozhi (or Annan) from the tenth until the thirteenth century. Specifically, the Ding (Vietnam-ese: Đinh) clan ruled from 970 until 980, the Li 黎 (Vietnamese: Lê) clan held power from 980 until 1009, and the Li 李 (Vietnamese: Lý) clan ruled from 1010 until 1225.

224 Li Qiande was the fourth ruler of Jiaozhi (or Annan) while it was under control of the Li 李 clan. Qiande was only seven *sui* when he assumed the throne. The Jiaozhi government at that time was controlled by Li Shangjie (see text and note 225 below) and Qiande's mother, Grand Consort Yanluan (Yanluan Taifei).

225 This "high official" was Li Shangjie, who is mentioned below. His name is alter-

urged revolt [against Chinese control]. In the eighth year [1075] they invaded [Chinese territory] and pillaged, capturing Yong, Qin, and Lian Counties.[226] The imperial court commanded Guo Kui [1022–1088][227] and others to quell them. The [Annan] bandits stampeded elephants to repel Guo Kui's forces. The Song government troops then chopped at the elephants' trunks with large swords. The elephants fled in retreat, trampling their own infantry. [Song forces] took advantage of this situation, and the bandits suffered a crushing defeat. Following up on this victory, [Song troops] then took Guanglang Town.[228] The administrator of the town, who was the son-in-law of the ruler of Jiao, fled and hid in some bushes, from where he could glimpse that Song imperial troops [*wangshi*] had captured the bandits and were ripping them apart and eating them. The administrator thought the imperial troops were [sent by] the Spirit of Heaven [Tianshen].[229] He returned

---

nately given as Li Shangji, Li Changjie, Li Shangjie, and Ruan Changjie. He served as the commandant of the Annan forces that attacked and took three Song counties in late 1075 and early 1076 (see below).

226　Qin and Lian counties fell to the Vietnamese in late 1075 and early 1076. The siege of Yong County lasted for forty-two days before its commander surrendered to the Jiaozhi army. These were bloody battles. Casualties on the Chinese side alone exceeded 50,000. Li Tao, comp., *Xu Zizhi tongjian changbian*, 272.6664. This same source (280.6868–69) reports that 49,560 regular Song troops and 46,190 horses were approved for the campaign against the Vietnamese. Not counting those who died from illness or non-combat-related reasons, only 23,400 troops and 3,174 horses survived the campaign. No doubt, many of the causalities were local, non-Chinese troops recruited in the south.

227　Guo Kui was a protégé of the famous Song statesman Fan Zhongyan and achieved considerable fame as a military commander. His biography in *Song-shi*, 290.9725, along with many other later sources, mentions the major battle between Chinese and Vietnamese forces at Fuliang River in early 1076. Guo's biography also notes that more than half of his force of 300,000 soldiers died as a result of the miasmic conditions (this probably means malaria) in the south.

228　The description of the battle here is very similar to that found in Li Tao, comp., *Xu Zizhi tongjian changbian*, 279.6832. Since the latter work was completed in 1183, after Fan Chengda finished *Treatises*, it seems quite possible that Li Tao may have used Fan's text as his source.

229　The term Tianshen, rendered here as "Spirit of Heaven," is probably a reference to a local deity (with the same name) in Lei County. Zhou Qufei devotes an entry to this divine being in *LWDD*, 10.433 (*Netolitzky*, 10.38). If proper sacrifices to the god of this temple were not carried out, it had the power to withhold rainfall and send down thunderclaps. Hence, the deity was also known as the

and reported to his ruler [or father-in-law], saying: "If I can flee for my life, then my sons and grandsons will never commit crimes against the Great [Song] Dynasty [Dachao]."

The main force next moved on to the Fuliang River. Forty *li* from the Protector General's Headquarters [in Jiao County] they killed the bogus heir-apparent[230] and captured his senior generals. [Li] Qiande was now in great fear and dispatched a communication [to the Song army] begging surrender. Most of the assembled [Song] troops from the north were sick from miasma.[231] An imperial edict thereupon pardoned Jiaozhi and returned its five counties.[232] When the imperial court saw that Kui was unable to take Jiao County, he was dismissed as senior general of the Martial Guard [*Wuwei shang jiangjun*]. For this campaign, a little over 870,000 draftees [*minfu*] were deployed. Much expense and many provisions[233] were devoted to this campaign, yet so far nothing significant has been achieved.

Roughly from the Duangong [988–990] to the Jiayou [1056–1064] reign, the counties and settlements along the Two Rivers have been raided and attacked by the Man on several occasions. They covertly took these actions in order to become more outwardly aggressive.[234] Those places in Sumao, Guangyuan, and Jia settlements that fell into Jiaozhi's hands numbered sixty-two villages [*cun*]. Thus, today Jiaozhi still holds sway over the various Man.

When [Li] Qiande died, his son [Li] Yanghuan [d. 1137; r. 1127–1137][235] assumed the throne. When Yanghuan died, a posthumous son

---

"Spirit of Thunder" (Leishen). Eberhard devotes considerable attention to the various thunder gods in China, including this one. See *Local Cultures*, 253–56.

230　This "bogus" heir-apparent was Li Hongzhen. Little seems to be known about him except that he served as a Vietnamese military commander.

231　The report in Li Tao, comp., *Xu Zizhi tongjian changbian*, 279.6844, says that more than half of the Song troops had already died, and their food provisions were exhausted.

232　Among these five counties were Guangyuan, Men, Sumao, and Silang. See *Song huiyao jigao*, "Fan Yi" 4.36b.

233　Reading *jingu* 金谷 to mean 金穀 (expenses and food provisions).

234　Here I understand *waixiang* 外鄉 to mean 外向 (lit., "toward the outside").

235　Li Yanghuan assumed the throne in 1127. My dating of Li Yanghuan's death to 1137 is based on information provided in Li Xinchuan, *Jianyan yilai xinian yaolu*, 114.26a.

of Qiande who had been enjoined to Champa was summoned and put on the throne. Someone told me that there is one Li Mou, who was a member of Qiande's wife's faction. He had raised a son for the Li 李 clan. He killed the posthumous son and put this other son on the throne instead. This other son assumed the Li 李 clan's surname. His given name was Tianzuo [1136–1176; r. 1138–1176]. This actually took place in the ninth year of the Shaoxing reign [1139].[236] His countrymen still designated him "King of the Li" [Liwang].[237] In the twenty-sixth year [1156] he dispatched emissaries to the court to offer tribute. The imperial court accordingly commanded that the Li clan be granted official titles and ranks of nobility. In appearance Tianzuo is handsome and fair-skinned. He has lived thirty-nine years so far.[238] He has an older brother who once served as administrator of Liang County. He [the older brother] schemed to seize his position there. When this event became known, he was banished to Xuehe County [Xuehe *zhou*], where he shaved his head and became a Buddhist monk.[239]

As a general rule, for official communications between the

---

236 The date of Li Tianzuo's ascension to the throne should instead be the eighth year of the Shaoxing reign, or 1138. See *Hu-Tan*, 286–87, n. 8.

237 The account here about the posthumous son of Li Qiande, Li Mou's role in placing a member of the Li 黎 clan on the throne, and so on, is repeated in *LWDD*, 2.56 (Netolitzky, 2.1), and later sources. Fan's account of the succession, however, appears in no other source. This is probably because his source for this information appears to be hearsay ("Someone told me . . . "). A passage in Li Xinchuan, *Jianyan yilai xinian yaolu*, 129.16a, offers another explanation: "After Li Qiande, the 'King of Southern Peace,' died, his son by a concubine, Zhizhi, escaped to Dali, changed his family name to Zhao, and adopted the title 'Peaceful King' [Pingwang]. But when he heard that his older brother Yanghuan had died, he contended with Tianzuo for control of the [Annan] state. Dali assisted him by providing 3,000 troops." According to this account, then, there was no "posthumous son" in Zhancheng, but rather the "son of a concubine" in Dali. Zhizhi's army was eventually defeated, and Zhizhi was captured and executed.

238 Li Tianzuo was born in 1136 and assumed the throne two years later (at the age of three *sui*). If we assume that Fan Chengda wrote this line in 1175, the year he dated the preface to *Treatises*, then "thirty-nine years" makes sense here (1136 + 39 = 1175). Cf. the comments in *Hu-Tan*, 287, n. 9

239 I have not been able to find any additional information on the events described here and how they might relate to Li Tianzuo's unnamed older brother. Xuehe County is not further identified.

Guangxi Command Inspectorate and Yong County, one uses two black lacquered boards pressed and bound together to serve as a correspondence document. The message is inscribed onto the surface of the boards. These are referred to as "pressed-board documents" [*mujia wenshu*] and addressed to "Annan Protector General's Headquarters." Tianzuo does not distinguish ranks [among civil officials] but does distinguish several of his high-ranking military officers, all of whom hold improper [Chinese] office designations. There are some called grand master of the palace with golden seal and purple ribbon [*jinzi guanglu dafu*], acting vice director of the Secretariat [*shou Zhongshu shilang*], and deputy of the Protector General's Headquarters [*tongpan Duhu Fu*]. The idea here is that Protector General's Headquarters is regarded the same as the Signatory Office [Qianting][240] in the counties and commanderies. The border counties present their reports to the command inspector in writing, and they also use pressed boards.

The archivist [*zhanggu*][241] in Guilin has former cases on file from the Yuanyou [1086–1094] and Xining [1068–1078] reigns. The way people of Jiao circulated and moved [documents] was exactly the same then as it is now. The inscription on the seal reads: "Imprimatur of the State of Nanyue" [*Nanyue Guo yin*]. In recent years they have changed to using the imprimatur of the Secretariat-Chancellery [Zhongshu Menxia]. The [influence] of Chinese rule is somewhat distant and remote. Border officials, moreover, are fearful of getting in trouble, so they never ask about legal precedents, the origins of which are indeed not limited to one day!

The officials of their state are designated "king" [*wang*].[242] Patriar-

---

240   Qianting (lit., "Signatory Office") is an abbreviation for Qianshu Panguan Ting Gongshi, which actually refers to a low-ranking notary in a county or military prefecture who handles written correspondence, especially with subordinate units. *Hucker*, no. 922.

241   "Archivist" (*zhanggu*) was not an official Song dynasty office title, but clearly Fan Chengda is referring here to a government official who keeps and maintains public documents. Cf. *Qi Zhiping*, 56, n. 14.

242   I agree with Yang Wuquan's assessment that this line is corrupt, for it seems unlikely that all public officials in Annan would be designated "kings." See Yang's comments in his "*Guihai yuheng zhi jiaozhu* jiaoji zayi," 54.

chal clansmen are designated [members of the] "Ranks of the Celestial Kings" [Tianwang Ban]. Ordinary clansmen are designated "descendants" [*chengsi*]. The remainder are designated "branch descendants" [*zhisi*]. They have inner posts [*neizhi*] and outer posts [*waizhi*]. [Officials holding] inner posts govern the people [*min*] and are called bulwark and great defender of the state [*fuguo taiwei*], which is equivalent to grand councilor [*zaixiang*]. Offices above [the rank of] left and right attendants to the ministers of public works [*zuoyou lang sikong*], left and right attendants to the grand councilor [*zuoyou langxiang*],[243] left and right grand masters of remonstrance [*zuoyou jianyi dafu*], and inner attendant vice director [*neishi yuanwai lang*] are considered inner posts. The outer posts govern the military and are called military affairs commissioner [*shumi shi*], great defender of the imperial insignia [*jinwu taiwei*], senior leader of the military [*duling bing*], and leader of the military commissioner [*lingbing shi*]. There is also a judiciary official [*pan*],[244] as well as controller general of the Protector General's Headquarters in Annan [*tongpan Annan Duhu Fu*], all of which are considered outer posts. As for those who hold office, some take the civil service examination,[245] some are sons of officials, and some purchase positions.[246] Those who have taken the exams are respected the most. The sons and grandsons of skilled craftsmen and slaves and maids are not allowed to take the exams. Those who purchase a position can only serve in a clerical position [*lizhi*] but with additional payment can be appointed as gentleman of trust [*chengxin lang*] and can work their way up to administrator. Those who serve as officials receive no salary but are provided a segment of the local

---

243 This office title does not seem to have a counterpart in the Song bureaucracy.

244 Reading *pan* 判 to mean *panguan* 判官, or judiciary official.

245 During the Song civil service examinations were offered to non-Chinese candidates on the Guangnan circuits. According to *LWDD*, 4.169 (*Netolitzky*, 4.14), there was a quota of two successful candidates in the *keju* examination in the Creek Settlements along the Left and Right Rivers to be forwarded to the capital in Lin'an, where they would be eligible to take the metropolitan examination (*shengshi*) for the *jinshi* degree. See Araki, "Nung Chih-kao and the *K'o-chü* Examinations," esp. 75–81; and Anderson, *The Rebel Den*, 115–16.

246 Lit., "some enter [the ranks officials] by purchase" (*huo ru zi* 或入貲[資]).

population, so they can control[247] some tillers and fishermen to make a profit.

[The military units called] Victorious Troops [Shengbing], Imperial Dragon [Yulong],[248] Martial Victory [Wusheng], Dragon Wings [Longyi], Cicada Hall [Chandian], Gloriously Martial [Guangwu], King's Staircase [Wangjie], Supporters of the King [Pengri],[249] Ensuring Victory [Baosheng], and so on, all have left and right units. Each military unit [*jun*] is limited to two hundred men. The characters tattooed across their foreheads read: "Son of Heaven's Troops" [Tianzi Bing]. The Noble and Aspiring [Xionglüe] and the Brave and Agile [Yongjie][250] are also included among nine such military units, which are supplied with [military] commissioners like the wing regiments [*xiangjun*].[251] Soldiers [*bingshi*] serve on rotational shifts [*jian'geng*] once a month. In their spare time they till and plant or produce handicrafts to support themselves. On the seventh day of the first month, they are given three hundred cash, with each man [also] receiving one bolt of rough silk [*chou*], pongee [*juan*], and hemp cloth [*bu*], which are similar to *chougang* but are covered with damask.[252] Each

---

247 "Control" in the sense that they would be available to perform corvée labor for the official.

248 Following *LWDD*, 2.57 (*Netolitzky*, 2.1), and reading Yulong 御龍 (Imperial Dragon) rather than Xielong 卸龍.

249 Pengri, translated here as "Supporters of the King," literally means "to hold the sun in one's two hands" and, by extension, "to sustain the sun." This expression has its origin in a commentary to the biography of Cheng Yu in the *Records of the Three Kingdoms* (Chen Shou, comp., *Sanguo zhi*, 14.912). During the Tang and Song the term "Sun-Sustaining Battalion" (Pengri Ying) was applied to elite troops in the capital who guarded the imperial palaces.

250 Cf. *LWDD*, 2.57 (*Netolitzky*, 2.1), which reads *yongjian* 勇健, or "brave and vigorous."

251 "Wing regiments" refers to local military units staffed by "part-time" troops who provide corvée labor services when not on military duty. These troops are also known as corvée soldiers (*yibing*).

252 The three types of fabric mentioned here require some additional explanation. The first of these, *chou*, refers to a coarse material made from the strands of a discarded silkworm cocoon. *Juan* indicates a material (translated here as "pongee") knotted from raw silk. The quality of *juan* is superior to that of *chou*. Zhou Qufei has an entry on Annan pongee (*Annan juan*); see *LWDD*, 6.226 (*Netolitzky*, 6.26). Zhou says that Annan pongee was made from a coarse silk fabric sent from China to Annan called *shizi*. The third variety of material

month soldiers are supplied with ten bundles of grain. On New Year's Day the troops are rewarded with a plate of big-grain rice [*dahe fan*] along with several preparations of fish condiment. Their territories have plentiful amounts Champa rice,[253] so they regard the big-grain variety as precious.

On the fourth day of the first month, the chieftain fells an ox and provides a meal for his officers. On the fifth day of the seventh month, there is a great festival, where people celebrate and exchange presents. Government officials [*guanliao*] present live domestic animals [*shengkou*] to their chieftains. On the following day the chieftain holds a feast to thank them.

The chieftain resides in a building with four levels. He himself resides on the top level. As for the second level, the Yuyu, who are eunuchs [*zhongren*], reside there. As for third level, the Geli,[254] who are subordinates to the circuit general [*lingxia*], reside there.[255] As for the fourth level, military officers [*junshi*] reside there. There is also the Crystal Palace [Shuijing Gong], Celestial Prime Audience Hall [Tianyuan Dian], and other [portions of the residence] with various presumptuous names. Separate from the [main] gate is a building that still has a signboard that reads: "Annan Protector General's Headquarters." All the levels [of the building] are lacquered in vermilion. The pillars are painted with dragons, cranes, and immortal maidens.

---

mentioned here, *bu*, usually denotes clothing woven from the fibers of a hemp vine (this material is also known as *mabu*, or burlap). The practice of issuing soldiers material to make clothes (or uniforms) was a Chinese custom followed in Annan. During the Song, one bolt of cloth officially measured 42 *chi* in length and a little over 5 *chi* in width. *Songshi,* 175.4231–32.

253   Champa rice (*Zhanmi*) is quick-maturing rice that can be harvested in one growing season. Originally introduced into Champa (central and south Vietnam) from India, during the Song dynasty it spread throughout much of China. For additional details see Ho Ping-ti (He Bingdi), "Early-Ripening Rice in Chinese History," *The Economic History Review, New Series* 9.2 (1956): 200–218.

254   The precise meaning of Geli is uncertain. It may mean something like "bodyguards."

255   *Hucker,* no. 3757, says *lingxia* is the head of all regular military forces of either a circuit or a county. The character *lao* 老 in this line seems misplaced, and I have not translated it.

Natives of Jiao have no sense of the esteemed and humble; all wear their hair bundled like a mallet and go barefoot. This is also the case in the chieftain's customary residence, except that he wears gold hairpins and an upper garment of yellow and a gown of purple. All the others don clothes with twisted collars, wrap-around gowns [*siqun*], and a black upper garment, not tied at the waist but tied to the black gown beneath the upper garment. They wear silver and iron hairpins, shuffle along in leather shoes, hold crane feather fans, and wear spiral-shaped bamboo hats [*luoli*]. As for the leather shoes, the soles are made of leather, to which is fastened a small cylinder [*zhu*]. The large toe is held in place [in the cylinder] as one walks. Fans are woven with crane feathers so as to ward off snakes. The spiral-shaped bamboo hats are woven with silk splints. In shape they resemble a paddy snail [*tianluo*] and are most exquisite. Most married women are very wise [*zhe*], completely different from the men. The women are fond of wearing broad sleeves of green with a straight collar, both of which are bound [decorated] with black crane feathers [*zaoqun*]. The chieftain travels by means of a palanquin [*renman che*]. Noble officials sit on a length of cloth. Above it hangs a long bamboo pole. Two men carry it. It goes by the name *diya*.[256]

Over the course of the year, they do not provide for their ancestors; when they are sick, they do not take medicine; at night they do not light lamps. On Shangsi day,[257] young men and women assemble and gather into ranks. They join some multicolor fabrics to make a ball and then sing as they cast it about. This is referred to as the "flying

---

256　These mobile hammocks, common in Annan, Champa, and Zhenla, are also mentioned in *lwdd*, 10.428 (*Netolitzky*, 10.33). They were made of cotton cloth and carried by means of a single bamboo pole, usually borne by four men. In Annan these were called *diya*, but in other states they were known by different names. For instance, in Zhancheng they were called *ruanbudou*. See zfz, 1.8 (*Chau Ju-Kua*, 47).

257　Shangsi day fell on the third day of the third lunar month. In traditional China on this day a purification ceremony was often performed beside a river, for the purpose of doing away with the "uncleanness or evils attached to a person." See Alsace Yen, "*Shang-ssu* Festival and Its Myths in China and Japan," *Asian Folklore* 34.2 (1975): 46–85. The courtship ceremony described below, also observed on Shangsi day, is not related to this purification ceremony.

camel" [*feituo*].²⁵⁸ The men and women themselves form into ranks. If a woman catches the "camel," then her marriage to the man [who threw the ball] is set.

At the palace gate there is a large bell tower. When citizens have a complaint about a matter, they immediately ring the bell. In cases involving capital punishment [*dabi*], the guilty person is sometimes handed over to the plaintiff [*choujia*] so as to bring [the plaintiff] some satisfaction.²⁵⁹ Brigands and bandits have their fingers and toes chopped off. If they [try to] flee, their hands and feet are broken. Those who plot rebellion are buried with their heads exposed. A bamboo pole is placed next to the rebel. The bamboo pole is bent back so it fastens to his malletlike hair bun, which causes his neck to stretch. A sharp blade shears the head completely off. The head is then displayed on the end of a bamboo standard. When someone [from Annan] dies in a strange place outside his own territory, [his relatives] whip the corpse and curse loudly, regarding this as betrayal of the state.

Local products include such things as gold and silver, bronze, cinnabar, pearls, cowry [shells], rhinoceros [horn], elephant,²⁶⁰ kingfisher feathers, giant clams, and various aromatics, as well as salt, lacquer, and kapok.²⁶¹ As for fruits, they only have sweet and sour peel tanger-

---

258 This courtship ceremony, also described in *LWDD*, 10.422 (*Netolitzky*, 10.28), as well as its many later forms have been studied by scholars. See, for instance, Gu Jiegang's essay "Pao caiqiu." The ceremony described by Gu Jiegang, still observed in some parts of Guangxi, is very similar to the "flying camel" ritual mentioned here by Fan Chengda, but with one major difference: the modern version has the young man catching an embroidered ball thrown by the young woman.

259 The expression *ganxin* 甘心 (lit., "satisfied heart"), translated here as "bring some satisfaction," is drawn from the *Zuo Commentary*, where it is used specifically to refer to the satisfaction one gets when an enemy is captured and delivered up. See *Chunqiu Zuozhuan zhengyi*, 8/64/1766 (Legge, *The Chinese Classics*, 5:84).

260 *Xiang* (lit., "elephant") here probably refers to ivory (*xiangya*). Annan was also known for its tame elephants (*xunxiang*), five of which were presented as tribute to the Song court in 1156. See *LWDD*, 2.58 (*Netolitzky*, 2.1). A later incident involving the disposition of five (later ten) elephants to the Song court is described below.

261 This is only a representative list of local products from Annan. For a more complete accounting, drawn from numerous primary sources, see *Hu-Tan*, 290–91, n. 20.

ines [*ganju*], citron [*xiangyuan*],[262] betel nuts, and betel vines. As for the newer and older towns, they are separated by a single little river. Both produce aromatics.

Xin County [Xinzhou] is on the site of ancient Zhenla and was acquired [by Annan] through annexation.[263]

[The people of Annan] are unable to manufacture paper and writing brushes, so they seek these from government lands. Few of the natives communicate through the written word. Natives of Min assigned to oceangoing ships who travel to Annan must treat them lavishly and thus designate them officials [*guan*] and consult with them to settle matters. As a general rule, when written documents lead to deceit and trouble, most often this comes from traveling merchants. Tradition has it that their ancestor, [Li 李] Gongyun [974–1028; r. 1010–1028], was also a native of Min.[264]

Moreover, [in Annan] true natives of that state are extremely few. Half the people there are government subjects. Travelers to the Southern Counties entice people there to serve [in Annan] as female slaves and male bearers. But when they reach the [Man] counties and settlements, they are tied up and sold off. One slave can fetch two taels of gold. The counties and settlements then turn around and sell them in Jiaozhi, where they fetch three taels of gold. Each year no fewer than 100,000 people [are sold off as slaves]. For those with skills, the price in gold doubles. For those who are literate, the price also doubles. With hands tied behind their backs, [the slaves] are driven off. Their heads are tied and pulled backwards, so they have no idea of where they are going. By the time they leave their state, each of them knows his master [*maizhu*]. They serve as slaves their entire lives, and all are

---

262 *Xiangyuan,* also called *juyuan,* is a fragrant but inedible variety of citron (*Citris medica*).

263 Xinzhou may correspond to modern Tân Châu in Tay Ninh Province, southeastern Vietnam, but this is not certain. See Yang Bowen's comments on this place-name in ZFZ, 11, n. 3.

264 Li Gongyun (Vietnamese: Lý Công Uẩn) was the first ruler of the Li 李 dynasty. He was known posthumously as Taizu and Shenwu Huangdi. It seems likely that the source of Fan Chengda's information about Li Gongyun being a descendant of Chinese immigrants from Fujian is Shen Gua's *Mengxi bitan.* See *Mengxi bitan quanyi,* 25.822.

tattooed with four or five characters on the forehead. Adult women are tattooed from the bosom to the ribs. When taken into custody, they are treated harshly and cruelly, and if they attempt to escape, they will certainly be killed.

[In Annan] there are also budding talents [*xiucai*], Buddhists and Daoists [*sengdao*], and skilled diviners [*jishu*], as well as criminals in exile fleeing for their lives [*peili wangming*] and those who have run off.

[The people of Annan] are unable to smelt coins [*quanhuo*], so they use small copper cash from China exclusively, all of which is drained out of China by traveling merchants. Note: Trafficking in slaves, officials traveling to the border, and leaking [Chinese] coins to foreign lands—there are legal prohibitions in place against all three of these activities. But today people still engage in such evils. The pacification and comfort commissioner, director-in-chief, and Creek Settlements inspectors are probably not men of good moral character. The border administration has deteriorated and declined because of evildoers who act at the dictates of their own will. Many days and months have passed, and yet this situation has not yet improved. Since most border officials lack an established means of financial support, they exhaust every means possible to get a little miasmic territory [*litu*], where they merely live out their shameless existence until they die. As for such officials who have no time to look after border defense and matters of state, it is fitting they are distressed and angry about their situation on the border.

But the people of Jiao, after their defeat and fall during the Xining reign, do not dare to act rebellious and unruly again, and so the southern frontier has been peaceful and secure for about a hundred years.

In the twelfth year of the Shaoxing reign [1142], the sorcerer [*yaoren*] Tan Youliang slipped into Silang County, where he falsely claimed to be a diplomatic envoy and sent down orders to the counties and settlements. [Li] Tianzuo became greatly alarmed. Later, the command inspector directed that Annan subdue Youliang. Yong County also sought to entice [and capture] him with a bogus office appointment certificate. Youliang, along with twenty-some chieftains who had pledged loyalty to him, each of whom had received their copper seal, maps, and local products, paid a formal visit to the Mount

Heng Stockade. The administrator of Yong County, Zhao Yuan, tied up Youliang and took him to the command inspector, who had him hacked to death. The chieftains were all sent back to Annan, where they all died. Jiaozhi has been peaceful and secure [ever since], and no one has raised any issues [opposing these actions].

In spring of the eighth year of the Qiandao reign [1172], [Annan] sent up a memorial expressing willingness for a court audience to celebrate the Sage Master's [Shengzhu's] ascent to the throne.[265] An imperial edict was then sent to the managing and organizing inspector of Guangxi: "Tribute-bearing envoys [from Annan] who come [to the capital] may avoid appearing at court. We will accept one-tenth of the local products [they offer as tribute]." In the autumn of that same year, another imperial edict was sent down to the managing and organizing inspector: "Purchase ten tame elephants so they can serve in the honor guard procession [*lubu*] at the suburban sacrifices [*jiaosi*].[266] The managing and organizing inspector, Li Hao, *zi* Yuande [1116–1176],[267] following the usual practice of pressed-board communication,[268] informed Jiaozhi about purchasing the elephants. The Man replied that they were not willing to sell the elephants, but they would be willing to offer them as tribute. In spring of the following year [1173], after arriving at my official post [in Guilin], on several occasions I cited the former imperial edict that refused the [elephants as] tribute. The time

---

265 The Southern Song emperor (or "Sage Master") Xiaozong assumed the throne in 1162. According to the *Song huiyao jigao*, "Fan Yi" 7.51b, tribute missions from Annan to the Song court were supposed to take place once every three years but were interrupted in 1155 because "there still was no transportation network in place" to convey tribute. Since no tribute missions had been sent from Annan to the Song since that time, Annan wished to renew its status as a tributary state.

266 These sacrificial ceremonies to heaven and earth were carried out in the southern and northern suburbs of the capital.

267 The word order here is garbled. It should read Li Hao Yuande 李浩遠德. Li Hao was Fan Chengda's predecessor as chief administrative and military officer in Guilin. Fan and Li Hao met in early March 1173, when Fan was on his way to Guilin. See Fan Chengda, *Canluan lu*, 52 (Hargett, *On the Road*, 193 and 228, n. 197). Li Hao's biography in *Songshi*, 388.11903–6, says nothing about the matter concerning tribute elephants described below.

268 On government communications relayed on pressed boards, see above.

of the [suburban] sacrifices was gradually approaching, and the court urged that supervision of the elephants [matter] should move along as swiftly as a shooting star. The Man once again sought admission [into Song territory] at the border: "The six elephants and local products are about to reach the border. If they are not permitted [as tribute], then they will be sent back home. We humble Fan would never dare to engage in business with the imperial court!"[269] Since I was familiar with the matter, I conveyed a letter to the then grand councilor, which said: "My desire is to refuse their tribute. Moreover, there is nothing compulsory about the elephants! The [suburban] sacrifices rely on 'complete purity and the dual essences' [*yichun erjing*],[270] and so we should prefer to do without these elephants." Soon thereafter a gold tally [*jinzi pai*] [communication] was sent down [to me].[271] [The court ordered that I] dispatch an official with an accompanying staff to the palace.[272] At the time it was already late fall in Guilin. Ten elephants were transported via the celebrate-the-ascent-to-the-throne network, while five elephants were transported via the advance-and-offer-great-presents network.[273] The Chinese characters in Annan's congratulatory communication [*biao*] [to the Song emperor] were as tiny as the head of a fly and could barely be seen.

---

269   This line might be paraphrased as follows: "We Man would send the elephants as tribute but would never dare to sell them to the Song court."

270   This expression is drawn from the *Guoyu*, 18.20b, where it is used to describe the sacrifices carried out by the kings of antiquity. Fan Chengda's point here is that there is no need for tamed elephants at such ceremonies.

271   During the Song dynasty government correspondence couriers (*ji jiaodi*) displayed a wooden tally (*pai*) that indicated the priority and importance of the documents they were relaying. Tallies with gold writing indicated the highest priority and moved the fastest through the Song courier-post system.

272   Although Fan Chengda does not mention it, the gold tally communication he received from the capital apparently instructed him to go ahead and arrange to send the elephants to Hangzhou as tribute. The next few lines of the text indicate that fifteen elephants (rather than six) were transported to Lin'an in the fall of 1173. The official and staff mentioned here accompanied the elephants north to the capital.

273   During the Song various transportation networks (*gangyun*) were set up for the express purpose of conveying shipments of tribute items to the capital. As evidenced here, these networks sometimes had different names indicating the nature or purpose of the tribute.

Their elephants were decked out in ceremonial paraphernalia [*liwu*], which included a gold imperial *luowo* for riding elephants. A *luowo* resembles a saddle frame [*anjia*] in shape.[274] There were also elephant tusks overlaid with gold, elephant foreheads sheathed with gold, elephant hooks wrapped in gold and silver with attached knotted silk ribbons, elephant forehead [ornaments] in silver with gold inlay, vermilion-twined elephant rattan strips overlaid with silver and gold inlay,[275] elephant foot bells plated in gold and sheathed in copper, costumed elephant bronze bells with connected iron chains, embroidered imperial sitting mats for riding elephants, flowers for costuming elephants and yaks, imperial vermilion ladders for riding elephants, imperial *luowo* with attached dragon-head ribbons, and so on. As for the remaining paraphernalia, there were small gongs in gold and silver, sinking-in-water aromatic, and so on.

Their senior envoy [*dashi*] is addressed as "Yin Zisi, Grand Master for Central Security" [Zhongwei Dafu Yin Zisi];[276] their official envoy [*zhengshi*] is addressed as "Li Bangzheng, Gentleman for Discussion" [Chengyi Lang Li Bangzheng];[277] and their vice envoy [*fushi*] is "Ruan Wenxian, Loyal Assistant Gentleman" [Zhongyi Lang Ruan Wenxian].[278] Below them are staff personnel [*zhiyuan*], document drafters [*shuzhuang guan*], yamen chiefs [*duya*], reception personnel [*tongyin*],[279] military escorts [*zhike*], network supervisors [*jian'gang*],

---

274   Judging from Fan Chengda's description, a *luowo* is a frame apparatus used to convey royalty on elephants. I suspect this is a basket saddle with throne and canopy. In India they are called "howdahs."

275   The precise meaning of "elephant rattan strips" (*xiang tengtiao*) is unclear.

276   Little is known about Yin Zisi and the other members of the embassy described below. "Grand master for central security" (*zhongwei dafu*) is a Song honorific military rank, usually held by the senior-ranking military officers at a court audience.

277   Song officials holding the office "gentleman for discussion" (*chengyi lang*) usually served in the Salary Office (Jilu Guan), though clearly that is not the case here.

278   "Loyal assistant gentleman" (*zhongyi lang*) is a low-ranking prestige title that was used in the final years of the Northern Song.

279   The Song government provided its traveling officials with staff personnel from the Travelers Service (Tongyin Kesi; lit., "Receive and Guide Traveler's Service"), who assisted officials with making travel arrangements, booking overnight accommodations, and so on.

clerks [*kongmu*], squad leaders [*hangshou*],[280] menials [*yaya*], trainers [*jiaolian*], elephant masters [*xianggong*], journeymen [*changxing*],[281] and *fangshou* officers [*fangshou guan*].[282]

When these various ranks of officials had their court audience, they made slight modifications in their clothing and accoutrements. The [senior] envoy wrapped his head in a turban, carried a tablet, and wore red shoes, a gold belt, and a rhinoceros horn belt, each of which stood out because of the gold boxes used to store them. Moreover, they used fragrant oily cosmetics, [making their faces as] shiny as lacquer, and wore a carefully folded black gauze kerchief and shoes and socks on their feet. The [senior] envoy rode in a summer sedan chair [*liangjiao*].[283] Its red and black lacquered studs [*dingjiao*] were very ornate.[284] Presumably, when they reached China, they completely changed their practices of wearing their hair bundled like a mallet, going barefoot, and [riding in a] *diya*.[285]

Earlier, in the twenty-sixth year of the Shaoxing reign [1156], they once visited the court to offer tribute. [At the time] the participant in determining governmental matters [*canzhi zhengshi*], Master Shi Daren [Shigong Daren],[286] was serving as commandant of Guilin. Following the usual precedent, he used name cards [*cizi*] to announce their visit and moreover [he wanted to use] a mobile kitchen to host banquets at hostels [where the Man stayed during their journey]. I stopped this practice.

---

280   These squad leaders were probably in charge of smaller, individual military units assigned to provide security for the embassy while en route to the capital.

281   *Changxing* (lit., "go on a long journey"), translated here as "journeymen," probably refers to low-ranking military men charged with the care of the embassy's horses. On the title *changxing*, see Gong Yanming, comp., *Songdai guanzhi cidian*, 315.

282   The precise nature of this office is unclear, though *fang* 防 in the title suggests a security function.

283   The occupant compartment of a *liangjia* (lit., "cool sedan chair") typically was encased in thin silk to allow more air flow during the hot summer months.

284   Reading *chi* 飭 to mean *shi* 飾 (ornate).

285   On *diya*, see note 256.

286   According to Li Zhiliang, comp., *Song Liang Guang: Dajun shouchen yiti kao*, 294, Shi Ju, *zi* Daren, served as commandant of Jingjiang Municipality from 1156 to 1157.

The [senior Man] envoy privately addressed a low-ranking military official [*yajiao*], saying: "Participant in determining governmental matters Shi's patronage and support were most generous. Why has everything now been stopped?" I then dispatched someone to inform him of the following: "The managing and organizing commissioner and inspector and the [head of the] Annan Protector General's Headquarters are equals. The managing and organizing commissioner and the King-Who-Pacifies-the-South [Nanping Wang] stand shoulder to shoulder. The envoy is a minor official of the Protector General's Headquarters and can merely compare with a section clerk [*caoyuan*] in Guilin. The proper rules must be observed when visiting a superior at court [*tingcan*]. Otherwise, there will be no audience." The envoy yielded and thereupon [agreed to] observe [these rules] when visiting a superior at court.

As for his return home [to Guangxi], when he arrived, he was about to line up and pay obeisance [to me]. I dispatched someone to discreetly inform him: "Obeisance need not be performed." I submitted a memorial about this matter, and I also wrote it up in the register, so it would become a fixed policy.[287]

Supplementary entry: JIAOZHI: I note the following: As for the name Jiaozhi, its origins are the most ancient.[288] The "Royal Regula-

---

287   WXTK, 330.2593–94; FCDBJ, 149–55.

288   Numerous sources chronicle the fact that during the Spring and Autumn period Jiaozhi was already known in China. *Hu-Tan*, 295, n. 1, provides a useful list of these sources with citations. At times the name Jiaozhi was applied to all lands south of the Five Ranges. Down to the beginning of the Han, Jiaozhi was part of Nanyue. As discussed in the Introduction, forces sent south by the Han conquered Nanyue and divided it into nine commanderies. The area of the nine commanderies corresponds roughly to the northern and central parts of modern Vietnam. One of these commanderies, established in 111 B.C.E., was called Jiaozhi, and here also was established the seat of government for all nine commanderies. Because of this, the entire area of the nine commanderies was sometimes called Jiaozhi. From the Han to the Tang, the names Jiaozhi and Jiao County (this name dates from the late Han period) were used for at least part of the territory called Jiaozhi during the Han. In 670 Jiaozhi was absorbed into a larger administrative area called Annan (see above). After this, the name Jiaozhi was applied to the Red River delta district and most or all of northern Vietnam (Tonkin). *Chau Ju-kua*, 46, n. 1.

The *zhi* character in the name Jiaozhi has two written forms in Chinese:

tions" [Wangzhi] say: "The people in the southern quarter are called Man. Their foreheads are tattooed [*diaoti*], and their toes are crossed [*jiaozhi*]. And there are people among them who do not eat cooked food."[289] Presumably, then, [in ancient times] they tattooed their foreheads. They still do so today.

The *Grand Astrologer's History* [Taishigong shu] says: "[The Han empire] in the north extends to Youling, in the south extends to Jiaozhi, in the west extends to Longsha, and in the east extends to the Coiling Tree [Panmu]. Wherever the sun and moon may shine, there is no one who is not pacified and submissive [*dishu*]."[290] Here [in reference to Jiaozhi] he is speaking of the deepest south.

Emperor Wu of the Han was first to establish a commandery in Jiaozhi, which is 11,000 *li* from Luoyang.[291] Throughout the successive eras protectors [*shou*] have been put in place there,[292] but today

---

趾 (lit. "crossed toes") and 阯. The origin and meaning of the name Jiaozhi has been the subject of much debate among Chinese and Western scholars. Fan Chengda's discussion below of "crossed legs" exemplifies one of the possible etymologies. A useful summary of the various theories (Chinese and Western) about the etymology of the toponymn Jiaozhi appears in Vu Dinh Dinh, "Cochinchina: Reassessment of the Origin and Use of a Westernized Place Name," *The Writers Post* 9 (Jan. 2007 and July 2007), http://www.thewriterspost.net/V9I1I2_ff6_vudinhdinh.htm (accessed 25 January 2008), and Chen Jinghe, "Jiaozhi mingcheng kao." See also the comments in *Chau Ju-Kua*, 46, n. 1; *Hu-Tan*, 296–97, n. 1; Wang Dayuan, *Daoyi zhilüe jiaoshi*, 52–53; and *LWDD*, 10.410–11, n. 1.

289 These lines are quoted from the "Royal Regulations" (Wangzhi) chapter of the *Record of Rites* (Liji). See *Liji zhengyi*, 12/110/1338. The term *diaoti* (tattoo the forehead) later became a general name for tribes in the far south that tattooed their bodies.

290 *Taishigong shu* is one of the original titles of Sima Qian's *Records of the Historian* (Shiji). The lines cited here are found in *Shiji*, 1.11. In this context, "sun and moon" suggests the glories of Han civilization. Youling refers to ancient You County (Youzhou; modern Beijing, northern Hebei, and part of Liaoning), Jiaozhi is Jiao County, and Longsha (also called Liusha or "Shifting Sands") is located in the general area around Zhangye and Juyan Towns in Gansu. According to legend, the Coiling Tree is an island-mountain in the Eastern Sea.

291 As noted earlier, this commandery was established in 111 B.C.E. Fan Chengda's source for the 11,000 *li* figure is probably the ancient mathematics treatise *Zhoupi suanjing* (SKQS ed.), shang2.14a.

292 "Protectors" (*shou*) refers to Chinese officials sent to Jiaozhi to administer the region.

it functions as an independent Man land. The *Record of Rites* [Liji] says: "The people in the southern quarter are called Man. Their foreheads are tattooed, and their toes are crossed. And there are people among them who do not eat cooked food." Since the *Record of Rites* likewise speaks about tattooing the forehead, there must only be minor differences in their physical appearance.[293] The *Record of Jiao County* [Jiaozhou ji] says: "The people of Jiaozhi come out of Nanding Town [Nanding *xian*].[294] There are no joints in their foot bones, and their bodies are hairy. Those who lie down need special assistance before they can stand up."[295] The *Mountains and Seas Classic* [Shanhai jing] also mentions: "Natives of the state of Jiaojing are cross-legged [*jiaojing*]."[296] Guo Pu's [276–324] commentary says: "Their lower legs [*jiaojing*] are crooked and cross each other. Thus they call themselves the Jiaozhi."

The territory of Annan today, as it turns out, hosts [former] sites of Han and Tang commanderies and towns. The bone structure of people there is no different from that of the Chinese. As for Ai County, Jiang Gongfu of the Tang was in fact born there.[297] How, then, could there be such tales about crossed legs and so on![298]

Someone has passed down the following: In Annan there is a

---

293   Fan Chengda is distinguishing between the Man people in general and the Jiaozhi people in particular.

294   Nanding (Vietnamese: Nam Dinh) Town was established during the Jin 晉 dynasty (265–420) and was located in the Red River delta region, Vietnam. See *LWDD*, 10.410, n. 3.

295   The *Record of Jiao County*, compiled by Liu Xinqi, survives, but only in fragmentary form. According to Hao Yixing's commentary to the *Mountains and Seas Classic*, the line from the *Record of Jiao County* cited here originally appeared in the Northern Song rime dictionary *Guangyun*, but it cannot be found in surviving editions of that work.

296   Fan Chengda's quotation here does not exactly match the text of surviving editions of the *Mountains and Seas Classic*, but it is close. The same can be said for his citation of Guo Pu's commentary. See *Shanhai jing jiaozhu*, 1.195.

297   Jiang Gongfu was an important Tang dynasty official who served in several high government posts, including "Hanlin academician" (*Hanlin xueshi*). According to his biography in *Xin Tangshu*, 152.4831, he was born in Rinan, Ai County.

298   Zhou Qufei is also skeptical about such tales. See *LWDD*, 10.408 (*Netolitzky*, 10.19).

Mount Boliu [Boliu Shan], which is ringed [by other mountains] for several hundred *li*, resembling an iron enclosure [*tiewei*]. One cannot climb or scale it. Inside it there are fields, and only a single opening allows one to go in.[299] The Man themselves once blocked it off [so outsiders could not get in]. The outward appearance of the people is surprising and strange, and they have no contact with people outside. I suspect this is the site of ancient Jiaozhi. There must be someone who can resolve this question.[300]

THE LI are the Man people in the four commanderies on the island of Hainan.[301] The island is directly opposite Lei County. To ferry over from Xuwen Town[302] takes half a day.

In the center of the island are the Limu Mountains [Limu Shan].[303] Various Man people live on the four sides around them. These people are styled the Li people. The mountains are extremely high and are often shrouded in mist. The Li people themselves are rarely aware of

---

299   A portion of the description here of Mount Boliu is repeated in *LWDD*, 3.117 (*Netolitzky*, 3.10). According to *Hu-Tan*, 298, n. 2, the account of Mount Boliu being the original site of ancient Jiaozhi is an ancient myth and nothing more. Chen Jiarong et al., *Gudai Nanhai diming huishi*, 841, however, citing a Vietnamese text titled *Đạ Nam nhất thống chí* (Chinese: Da Nan yitong zhi), says Mount Boliu is another name for the Lishan Dao, which today are known as the Paracel Islands (Chinese: Xisha Qundao). These islands are off the coast of modern Da Nang. This identification, however, must remain tentative until it can be corroborated with reliable historical sources.

300   *WXTK*, 323.2544; *FCDBJ*, 155–56.

301   The four "commanderies" mentioned here are Qiong County (Qiongzhou), Dan Military District (Danjun; formerly known as Changhua Military District; renamed Nanning Military District in 1144), Wan'[an] Military District (officially abolished as a military district in 1136 and made a town under Qiong County), and Yai County (Yaizhou; officially abolished as a county in 1073; became Jiyang Military District in 1143). The numerous changes in the government-administrative organization of Hainan during the Song are outlined in *Hu-Tan*, 224, n. 1.

302   Xuwen Town was situated west of modern Xuwen *xian*, Guangdong.

303   These peaks (lit., "Mother of the Li People Mountains"), located in the very center of Hainan, are mentioned often in the history, literature, and lore of the island. For additional information, see Schafer, *Shore of Pearls*, 28. The highest peaks on Hainan, however, are the Five Finger Peaks (Wuzhi Shan), located just south of the Limu Mountains. The loftiest height among the Five Finger Peaks stands at 1,879 meters, making it the highest land point on Hainan.

the mountains' existence. When the weather has been clear for a long time, and the ocean air is deep and open, sometimes one sees blue-green [mountain] tips floating in midair, or so it is said.

The Man people all wear their hair bundled like a mallet, go barefoot, and stick silver, copper, and pewter hairpins [in their hair buns]. Married women add on copper rings and ear pendants that hang down to their shoulders. When girls reach the age of fifteen [marriageable age], they immediately have their cheeks tattooed with intricate floral patterns. These are referred to as "embroidered faces" [*xiumian*].[304] After the girl is tattooed, relatives and guests gather for a joint celebration. Only slave girls [*bihuo*] are not embroidered on the face.[305] Most people in the four commanderies have the Li surname. Presumably they are descendants of the Yi tribe [Yizu], but nowadays most Li people have the surname Wang.[306]

---

304   There are many reports of tattooing among the Man peoples of the south, and on Hainan it was especially common. The origins of the custom of tattooing the faces of young, unmarried women (young men apparently did not engage in this custom during the Song) are unclear. According to Zhou Qufei, this practice began with the purpose of making young women more beautiful. Later, however, Zhou says the purpose was to make them less beautiful so that foreigners would not steal them away. See *LWDD*, 10.419 (*Netolitzky*, 10.26). Eberhard, *Local Cultures*, 389, calls this an "artificial interpretation" that ignores the religious motivation behind tattooing (so that ancestors in the next world recognize someone as one of their own kind, and so on).

305   Slaves were in fact often tattooed in order to show proof of property. The slave girls mentioned here were probably not tattooed so as to distinguish them from young Li women with "embroidered faces." Cf. *LWDD*, 10.419 (*Netolitzky*, 10.26), where Zhou Qufei mentions that the faces of slave girls (*shinü*) in the Creek Settlements of Yong County are tattooed so they do not run away and that the tattoos on slave girls were different from those worn by Li women.

306   The origins and ethnicity of the Li 黎 people and their distinct culture is a topic of considerable dispute. Fan Chengda's comment that the Li people are "presumably descendants of the Yi tribe" is not helpful, for Yi 裔 is a very general name used for non-Chinese tribes who lived on distant borders. We do know, however, that Li people lived on Hainan before the first Chinese colonists arrived during the Han dynasty. In fact, the name "Li," presumably adopted from the Limu Mountains, was given to these people by Chinese administrators or settlers (probably) during the Tang. In the past and today, these people call themselves the "Sai" (not the "Li"). Feng Chongyi believes "they [the Li] are a mixture of the descendants of the Yue from the Chinese mainland, Malays and the South Pacific communities" ("Seeking Lost Code in the Wilderness:

Supplementary text: The people in the interior are the "Raw Li" [Sheng Li]; those on the outside [along the coast] are the "Cooked Li" [Shu Li].....[307] Sometimes one sees blue-green [mountain] tips floating in midair, but below it is still and murky and misty. Mountain streams flow down separately to the four commanderies. Those areas where the "Cooked Li" reside are already blocked and remote; the lairs of the "Raw Li" are remote and hidden. Traces of outsiders have never been left there. As for the summit of the Limu Mountains, even the "Raw Li" are unable to reach it. Tradition has it that there are people up there who take comfort and pleasure in longevity and who have never had contact with the outside world. Tigers and leopards guard its location. There are no trails by which one can clamber up there, and the people know only streams and springs, sweet and wonderful, unsurpassed and fantastic, and nothing more.[308]

The Man [on Hainan] are far away from government lands. Those who do not pay taxes or provide corvée go by the name "Raw Li." Those who till and work government land and pay taxes and provide corvée go by the name "Cooked Li." Depending on their individual proximity [to Chinese-controlled areas], [the "Raw Li"] are subordinate to one of the four commanderies.

All of them wear their hair bundled like a mallet, go barefoot, and insert silver, copper, and pewter hairpins [in their hair buns]. Their waists are wrapped with flowery cloth. They carry wooden-handled knives [*badao*][309] and long-eared bows [*changshao gong*],[310] and carry

---

The Search for a Hainanese Culture," *The China Quarterly* 160 [1999]: 1041). Cf. also the comments in Schafer, *Shore of Pearls*, 58–59.

307 On the various "raw" and "cooked" Man peoples, see Fiskesjö, "On the 'Raw' and 'Cooked' Barbarians" and the comments below.

308 Fan's description of the reclusive residents on the summit of the Limu Mountains is copied almost verbatim in *LWDD*, 1.22 (*Netolitzky*, 1.10). Yang Wuquan says that both Fan Chengda and Zhou Qufei are simply repeating a tall tale heard from other persons. See *LWDD*, 23, n. 3.

309 These are probably the same as the "Li knives" mentioned in the "Treatise on Implements." The blade of these weapons did not exceed one or two *chi*, while the handle (*ba*) measured three or four *cun* in length. See also the entry on "Settlement Knives."

310 The type of long bow described here, with extended "ears" on each end, is probably similar to the *changshao gong* mentioned in *Needham et al.*, 5.6:108. Note

long spears [*changqiang*] over their shoulders. They walk in short steps, and weapons never leave their side.

The "Cooked Li" can speak the Chinese language [Hanyu]. They change their dress and personal adornment and go to the village fairs [*xushi*] in the counties and towns. Then at nightfall, when the bugles sound, they join ranks and return home. Married women have embroidered faces and wear their hair high and bundled like a mallet, and add on copper rings and ear pendants that hang down to their shoulders. Their lower garments [*yiqun*] are all made of multicolored kapok.[311] No one wears pants and jackets [*kuru*]. They simply wrap their skirts several times around, making a style with four flounces [*wei*] sewn together. When putting them on, they do so from the feet [not from over the head] and then tie them [at the waist].

Groups of them bathe in streams. First they remove their upper outer garments and wash themselves, whereupon they wash their feet. Gradually they hoist their skirts up to their heads and file through the water. After they bathe, they lower their skirts from their heads and emerge from the water.

Embroidering faces, as it turns out, is [part of] their wedding ritual [*jili*]. When a girl is about to reach the age of fifteen, a drinking party is held with relatives and young female friends. The girls themselves prick out the patterns [of the tattoo]. The tattoo is composed of tiny insects [*chong'e*][312] and flowers, while the remaining area [on the girl's face] is covered with patterns resembling tiny grains of millet.[313] This is referred to as a "girl with an embroidered face" [*xiumian nü*]. Slave girls are denied [participation in this practice].

[Li] women are skilled at spinning and weaving. They obtain col-

---

311   The multicolored kapok (or cotton) described here was probably similar to the dyed fabric used to make Li screens and Li sheets, which were famous throughout China during the Song dynasty. See the "Treatise on Implements."

312   Reading *chong'e* 蟲蛾 to mean *chongzhi* 蟲豸, or insects. Cf. LWDD, 10.419 (Netolitzky, 10.26), which says the patterns are drawn in the shape of a moth.

313   The LWDD entry on "Embroidered Faces" (10.419; Netolitzky, 10.26) mentions that the tattoos of Li women with fair skin are colored kingfisher blue (*cuiqing*).

ored silk [*caibo*] from China, which they tear apart to get the colored silk threads. Together with kapok, this is then woven into a patterned fabric. Items such as the so-called Li damask [*Lijin*], Li sheets, and table cloths [*anda*]³¹⁴ vary in their fineness and coarseness.

Their residences consist of framed timbers with two levels. The top level is used as living quarters; the lower level is used for keeping live-stock.³¹⁵

Marriage arrangements are finalized by snapping an arrow; at [marriage] ceremonies there is dance and song accompanied by beating drums.

Upon the death of a relative, no one cries or eats rice porridge [*zhoufan*].³¹⁶ They only eat raw beef, which they regard as the ultimate way of expressing profound grief.³¹⁷ At the time for burial, they lift the coffin and start walking. One person walks in front [of the procession], casting chicken eggs [*jizi*] to the ground. The place where the chicken egg does not break is selected to serve as the grave site [*jixue*].³¹⁸

When a guest arrives, if they [the guest and the host] do not know each other, the host takes a look at him through a peephole. Only if the guest acts solemn and dignified will the host send a slave to set out a mat on the ground, where the guest will immediately sit. A short while later the host then emerges and sits down opposite the guest,

---

314 Zhou Qufei, *LWDD*, 6.228 (*Netolitzky*, 6.28), defines *anda* as a "multicolored, bright fabric that can be used to cover books and small tea tables." Zhou also notes that longer pieces of this same material are used by the Li people as wraps or skirts bound at the waist. For Li sheets see the "Treatise on Implements."

315 The *malan* homes mentioned here are described in much greater detail in note 94. *LWDD*, 2.71 (*Netolitzky*, 2.2), refers to these types of homes built by the Li as "railing houses" (*zhawu*).

316 Rice porridge (or congee) was customarily served at Chinese funerals because it was simple and plain, thereby suiting times of grief and mourning.

317 *LWDD*, 2.71 (*Netolitzy*, 2.2), mentions that when a person dies, an ox is killed as a sacrifice. See also *ZFZ*, 2.220 (*Chau Ju-Kua*, 183).

318 The practice of using chicken eggs for divination purposes is an old one in south China. For instance, the Tang author Duan Gonglu describes a practice whereby chicken eggs were boiled and, depending how the shells cracked, prognostications were made about various events. See *Beihu lu*, 2.21. This same practice is also described in *LWDD*, 10.442 (*Netolitzky*, 10.44). On the practice of divining with chicken bones, see the "Miscellaneous Items Treatise."

but does not engage in any conversation. After a brief time the host sets out some food. He first gives the guest some foul and rank food with a vile taste. If the guest eats the food without hesitation, then the host is pleased. Wine is continuously served until they are drunk, whereupon they become deeply attached to each other. Otherwise the guest is sent away, and they never again have any contact.[319]

When drinking together they never give up their knives. After three cups they invite one another to relax their guard. Although they remove their weapons and arms, these still remain in place at their sides. If either says anything inappropriate, they then get up and try to kill each other.

By nature they are fond of killing for revenge, which is referred to as "seize and destroy" [*zhuoao*]. If a relative is killed by someone, afterwards they will go to see the perpetrator's family as well as the members of his village, all of whom are taken prisoner and held in wooden fetters [*muxie*] made of lichee wood. Once [compensation] demands for cattle, wine, and silver vases are met, the prisoners are then released. This is referred to as "giving back a life" [*zengming*].

Local products include various kinds of aromatics such as sinking-in-water and Penglai.[320] Covering the mountains everywhere are betel nut and coconut trees.[321] Also produced are ponies [*xiaoma*],[322] halcyon kingfisher feathers [*cuiyu*],[323] and yellow wax

---

319   This practice of receiving guests is also described, with minor variations, in *LWDD* 2.71 (Netolitzky, 2.2).

320   See the "Treatise on Aromatics" for individual entries on these aromatics.

321   On the betel nut palm tree and the coconut palm tree and its fruit, see the "Treatise on Herbaceous Plants and Trees" and the "Treatise on Fruits, " respectively.

322   "Ponies" here likely refers to a variety of miniature horse also known as "below-the-fruit-tree horses." See the "Treatise on Quadrupeds."

323   The soft blue feathers of the halcyon kingfisher were in high demand in China, especially during the Tang and Northern Song, when they were used for fashion purposes and as head ornaments for officials. In 1107, however, the emperor Huizong issued a proclamation banning the hunting of kingfisher birds and the harvesting of their feathers, saying: "The former kings in the administration of government extended the principle of humaneness [*ren*] to plants and trees, and birds and beasts. Now halcyon kingfisher feathers are gathered and used for frivolous purposes, depriving these living creatures of their life. This was not the intent of the former kings, who sought to extend kindness

[*huangla*].[324] Local Li people trade and exchange these products with merchants from government lands.[325] The locals are very trustworthy [in business transactions] but refuse to be swindled by the traders. If the traders are trustworthy, then the locals treat them as their closest relative. If traders want credit, the locals give it to them without hesitation. The locals hope the traders will come back once each year for a visit. If a trader fails to return, the locals will frequently think of him. . . . [326]

Sometimes, if a merchant defaults on a loan by not showing up, for amounts over one cash, even if ten years have passed, someone from the merchant-debtor's commandery will be seized and held hostage [until the debt is paid]. The hostage's neck will be put in a cangue locked by a horizontal board. The lender then waits for the former debtor to come and pay up, and only then is the matter settled [and the hostage released]. The debtor is sometimes far away or has died. If an innocent person [from the debtor's commandery] is taken into custody, he will remain in captivity for consecutive years and months until he dies. Only then is the matter closed.

While the lender is waiting for payment, if someone from the debtor's commandery shows up, that person is also locked in a cangue. Family members of the prisoner will go to the family to whom the debt is owed, where they will be scolded and pressed for payment. Sometimes townsmen will raise money to pay off the debt, and only then is the prisoner released.

---

and nourish all living creatures! It is fitting that officials establish measures to prohibit this practice." *Songshi,* 153.3576 (also translated in *Chau Ju-Kua,* 236). Zhao Rukuo mentions, however, that despite the government prohibition, members of well-to-do families (*guiren jia*) still sought the feathers for adornment, which in turn led to feather smuggling activities by foreign traders. See *ZFZ,* 2.210 (*Chau Ju-Kua,* 235–36).

324   "Yellow wax" or "beeswax" was used for many different practical (candle making, as a lubricant, and so on) and medicinal purposes. According to *ZFZ,* 2.215 (*Chau Ju-Kua,* 238–39), the best beeswax came out of Sumatra (Sanfoqi), while that from Hainan was of decidedly poor quality (2.221).

325   "Government lands" here mainly refers to the four Chinese-controlled administrative areas (or "commanderies") on Hainan, mentioned earlier.

326   Tentative translation. I am not sure about the precise meaning of *nian* 念 (to think of) in this line.

As a general rule, if you owe someone one string of cash, the following year your debt will increase to two strings and will continue to so increase for ten years before it stops. If you originally owed one string, in ten years that will become a thousand strings. For this reason people do not dare to borrow even a single cash.

Sometimes, when a stranger mistakenly kills one of the Li people's chickens, drums will sound announcing to everyone that compensation is demanded, and someone will announce: "Some stranger killed one of my chickens. We should be compensated with one *dou*." One *dou* consists of a cock and a hen. One cock is worth thirty cash; one hen is worth fifty. One *dou* usually produces ten chicks, five are cocks and five are hens. In one year they produce four broods of ten chicks each. If you add the varieties together,[327] that should constitute six *dou*, and six *dou* should produce sixty chickens. Using this multiple counting method, this process would need to repeat over and over for ten years before the matter is ended. As for mistakenly killing someone's chicken, even rich merchants do not have enough money to pay off the debt. So, when a stranger goes to their homes, he dares not harm even a single hair [on a chicken].

Merchants from Min place great value on geomancy [*fengshui*]. After losing all their goods, many go into Li territory to till the land, never to return home.[328] When government officials and government subjects pass through Li villages and settlements, they will certainly spend the night in their homes, which one can depend on to be safe.

As for the territory of the "Cooked Li," at first it was the counties and towns. For the most part, the four commanderies each occupy a separate side of the island. Within these areas, the territory of the ["Cooked"] Li cannot be reached; nor is there a road connect-

---

327 "Six *dou*" here includes the original cock and hen (one *dou*) plus the five pair of male and female chicks they can produce in one brood (five *dou*).

328 The text is probably corrupt here, for the comment about geomancy does not seem to jive with the description that follows about Fujian merchants settling on Hainan and becoming farmers. Cf. zFz, 1.220–21 (*Chau Ju-Kua*, 183): "Merchants from Min are customarily blown [to Hainan] by storms and lose all their goods. Many of them then go into Li territory and till the soil to make a living."

ing through. Zhuyai is situated on the southern side of the island.[329] When one cannot find a trail to get through overland, one can instead take a small boat and head south along the coast of the island. This is the so-called twice fording the whale waves [*zaishe jingbo*].[330]

Most of the people in the four commanderies have the Li 黎 surname. This is probably because they are [descendants] of the Yi tribe. But today most of the Li people use the surname Wang. The "Raw Li," though straightforward and direct [*zhizhi*], are fierce and ferocious. They will not accept being cheated and bullied [*qichu*], are not accustomed to [accepting] civilizing influences [*wanghua*], but neither do they come out [of their territory] and bring disaster on others. The "Cooked Li" are greedy and cunning. They are fugitives [*jianmin*] from Hu, Guang, and Fujian who seek refuge by mixing in [with the local population] on Hainan. They raid and attack government lands and often bring disaster on the four commanderies.[331]

There is one Wang Erniang, who is headwoman of the "Cooked Li" in Qiong County. She has a husband, but I have never heard his name mentioned. Their family has abundant wealth, is skilled at using the multitudes, and is able to control and subdue the masses of Li. The imperial court ennobled her as "lady of suitability" [*yiren*]. The Qiong administration put out an order compelling people to be subordinate to "Lady of Suitability Wang" [Wang Yiren]. There was no one who

---

329 Zhuyai (later Yai County) is a Han dynasty commandery name that originally referred to the northernmost tip of Hainan. According to Schafer, the term *zhuyai* "had a live meaning in post-Han literature, symbolizing the barbarous southern shores of Lingnan" (*Shore of Pearls*, 9, 16–17, 22). Note that Schafer's title "shore of pearls" is a translation of the term *zhuyai*. By Southern Song times, Zhuyai was used as a general name for the southern end of the island.

330 As noted in Schafer, *Shore of Pearls*, 79, and Yang Wuquan, *LWDD*, 1.46, n. 5, this expression referred to the two-way passage by boat between the northern and southern ends of Hainan. "Whale waves" refer to the wild and dangerous waters of the Gulf of Tonkin and the South China Sea. Cf. Wang Xiangzhi, ed., *Yudi jisheng*, 127.4a, which mentions that there was a road from Qiong County (in the north) to Jiyang (in the south), but it had been "closed for eighty years."

331 Cf. *LWDD*, 2.70 (Netolitzky, 2.2), which says that among the "Raw Li" are many fugitives from Hu, Guang, and Fujian who are a "cunning, thieving, misfortune-bearing" (*jiaohan huozei*) lot who, though they pay taxes to Chinese officials, in fact collaborate with the "Raw Li" so they can plunder government lands.

failed to obey it. When Erniang dies, her daughter will be able to succeed her.[332]

As for the remaining three commanderies, they are strong in name but modest in might. In fact, they are inferior to one single village in Jiang or Zhe. In the towns and districts [of these commanderies], sometimes the government office [*tingshi*] or government seat [*zhisuo*] is seized by the Li. Only when someone is dispatched to express some kind remarks [are the offices returned].[333] This has been the experience of successive border officials, who have been fearful and have not dared to voice opposition.

In the tenth month of the first year of the Chunxi reign [1174], Wang Zhongqi—the settlement head [*dongshou*] of the "Cooked Li" at Five Fingers Mountain—led 1,820 adult males [*dingkou*] from ten[334] neighboring settlements to "submit to Chinese rule" [*guihua*].[335] Zhongqi and various settlement heads, including Wang Zhongwen and eighty-one others, paid a personal visit to the administration inspector [*guansi*] at Qiong County. The administration inspector received them, and, following precedent, the group paid a personal

---

332 According to *Songshi*, 495.14220, and *Song huiyao jigao*, "Fan Yi," 5-48.2b, in 1171 the Song court granted Wang Erniang the honorific title "lady of suitability" because she helped quell a local uprising. Since Wang Erniang was elderly at the time and had no sons, she requested that her daughter be allowed to inherit the "lady of suitability" title after her death (this happened in 1181), to which the Song court agreed. Beginning in the Zhenghe reign (1111–1118) of the Northern Song, the honorific title "lady of suitability" was sometimes granted to the wives or mothers of officials in certain classes of rank. In Wang Erniang's case, however, the title seems to have been granted outright. There are questions as to whether the family name of Erniang was Wang or Huang. See the discussion by Yang Wuquan in *LWDD*, 2.72–73, n. 3.

333 Presumably, the "kind remarks" mentioned here concern Wang Erniang and/or her daughter.

334 *LWDD*, 2.70 (*Netolitzky* 2.2), and *ZFZ*, 2.221 (*Chau Ju-Kua*, 2.184), both read "eighty."

335 The description here and following about Wang Zhongqi and others "submitting to Chinese rule" is not mentioned in the *Songshi*, *Song huiyao jigao*, or any of the other standard histories of the period. Fan's report, however, is repeated (with some variation) in *LWDD*, 2.20 (*Netolitzky*, 2.2), and *ZFZ*, 2.216 (*Chau Ju-Kua*, 2.184). The commentators to these volumes are silent about Wang Zhongqi and the other persons mentioned below, probably because they are otherwise unknown.

visit to the Illustrious Response Temple [Xianying Miao], where by rubbing an ink stone [*zhuoshi*][336] and drinking blood [*shaxue*], they swore an oath to reform and change, and never again to loot and plunder. They were rewarded with gifts and then dispatched home. The protector of Qiong County had likenesses sketched of their appearance and clothing style, and submitted these to the managing and organizing inspector [Fan Chengda]. [According to these drawings], those who wear their hair bundled like a mallet use [a piece of] scarlet silk to bind the base of the mallet. Some use multicolored silk to wrap the mallet, while others wear a small, ornamented bamboo hat [*huali*]. All of them wear two silver combs [*yinbi*] in their hair, while some of them add a pheasant tail [*zhiwei*]. They wear upper garments of ornamented embroidery and plaited skirts ornamented along the sides. All of them go barefoot. These are their grandest forms of dress.

Only Wang Juze[337] wears a blue turban [*qingbu*] and a long gown of red damask bound with a belt at the waist, along with hemp sandals [*maxie*]. He himself remarked that during the Xuanhe reign [1119–1126] his paternal grandfather received appointment as a local auxiliary official [*buguan*] for returning some land [to the Song] and was presented this damask gown [by the Chinese emperor], or so he said.[338]

THE DAN are Man people who live on the sea.[339] They make their homes on boats and gather sea products [*haiwu*] for their livelihood and, moreover, as food on which to live. They can see underwater. As for the pearls from the oysters in the Hepu Pool, only the Dan are able to submerge themselves in water and find them. The boatmen[340]

---

336   The "rubbing of an ink stone" produced the ink used to write out the oath before the ceremony was finalized by drinking blood.

337   Instead of Wang Juze, ZFZ, 2.221 (*Chau Ju-Kua*, 2.184), reads Wang Zhongqi 王仲期.

338   *WXTK*, 331.2599; *FCDBJ*, 157–60.

339   For a useful introduction in English to the Dan or Danjia (sometimes called "Tanka") boat people, see Ho Ke-en, "The Tanka or Boat People of South China," 120–23; for more detailed information on the role of the Dan people in Chinese history see Luo Xianglin, *Baiyue yuanliu yu wenhua*, 209–39. More specific information on the divers can be found in LWDD, 3115–16 (*Netolitzky*, 3.9), and ZFZ, 2.203–4 (*Chau Ju-Kua*, 229–30).

340   Here I follow Kong Fanli's emendation and read *bangren* 榜人 (boatmen)

tie a rope around the diver's waist. When he shakes the rope, he is then pulled up to the surface. Beforehand they boil a fur cloak [*cuina*] until it is extremely hot and quickly cover the diver with it when he emerges from the water. Otherwise, he would shiver to death from the cold. Sometimes divers encounter huge fish, dragons [*jiao*],[341] alligators [*tuo*],[342] or various other strange sea creatures.[343] If a diver comes in contact with a fin, it is likely that his stomach will be ripped open and his limbs snapped off. When observers see a single trail of blood floating on the surface, they know a Dan diver has died.

Supplementary text: The Dan, as it turns out, are Man people who live on the sea. They are of three varieties: the fishing Dan [Yudan], who fish; the oyster Dan [Haodan], who oyster; and the lumber Dan [Mudan], who cut down trees in the mountains. All of them, from birth to death,[344] remain inside the short awnings,[345] eating sea products to survive. In their lives they are seemingly [always] floating about, yet each of them in the border territories fulfills his corvée service to the government.[346]

Supplementary entry: DALI is the [former] state of Nanzhao.[347] It

---

rather than *pangren* 旁人. FCDBJ, 162, n. 9.

341 The term *jiao*, rendered here as "dragons," in Chinese lore usually indicates mythical flood dragons. I suspect that Fan Chengda here is referring, in a general way, to large, unusual, and scary sea creatures such as the giant squid, stingray, or shark (also pronounced *jiao* but written 鮫). Cf. the comments on *jiao* in Schafer, *Vermilion Bird*, 218–21.

342 The name *tuo* usually denotes the freshwater alligator (also called *Yangzi e; Alligator sinensis*) of the Changjiang and lake regions of Jiangnan. See Read, *Dragon and Snake Drugs*, no. 213. Fan Chengda probably has some other creature in mind, perhaps the (saltwater) man-eating, sawtooth crocodile (*eyu*) of the far south.

343 One of these dangers was the great white shark. See note 7 in the "Treatise on Insects and Fishes."

344 Here I follow Kong Fanli and read *shengsi* 生死 (from birth to death) rather than *zuosi* 坐死 (FCDBJ, 162, n. 10).

345 Here I follow Yan Pei, 147, n. 27, and read *duanpeng* 短篷 (short awnings) rather than *duanpeng* 短蓬. The term *duanpeng* 短篷 is a synecdoche for a "small boat."

346 HSRC, 67.63b–64a.

347 Originally, several non-Chinese Bai tribes inhabited the area around Erhai Lake in modern Yunnan. Each of these tribes controlled its own kingdom, which was called a *zhao*. In 649 Xinuluo, leader of the Mengshe tribe, estab-

originated from the Minor Yi during the Tang.[348] The Mengshe kingdom [Mengshe Zhao] was the southernmost[349] of its various tribes.
Hence, it is known as Nanzhao [Southern Kingdom]. From the time
Piluoge united the five kingdoms [*zhao*] into one, [the leader of Nan-
zhao] has been ennobled as the "king of Yunnan" [*Yunnan wang*]. But
since the time of Yimouxun [754–808; r. 779–808],[350] these leaders
have been ennobled as the "king of Nanzhao" [*Nanzhao wang*]. Since
the time of Qiulong[351] they have designated themselves the "Brave and
Trustworthy" [Piaoxin][352] and have adopted a reign title and designated themselves the Great Li State [Dali Guo 大禮國]. Now Dali has
contact with China and, as it turns out, is designated Great Li State
[Dali Guo 大理國]. This is a different *li* 理 character from the *li* 禮
used in the *Tang History* [Tangshi]. It is not known when this change
in characters first occurred.[353]

---

lished a kingdom in the area around Erhai Lake. Then later, in 737, with support
from the Tang dynasty, another leader of the Mengshe tribe, Piluoge, united
the six (some say eight) *zhao* and created a state called Nanzhao, or "Southern
Zhao," the capital of which was in the heart of the Erhai Valley. The Nanzhao
kingdom was overthrown in 902. In 937 Duan Siping, a military official of Bai
descent, seized power and established the Dali kingdom. Dali was crushed by
the Mongols in 1253 and a few decades later was designated with a new administrative name: Yunnan. Since that time it has remained within Chinese-controlled territory.

348 There is a wide diversity of opinion among scholars regarding the ethnography
of the Nanzhao kingdom. For a summary, see Backus, *The Nan-chao Kingdom*,
46–52. More recent scholarship favors the opinion that the Nanzhao population comprised two ethnic groups: the Bai and the Yi, both of whom were
Tibeto-Burman peoples. Fan Chengda's "Minor Yi" must refer to a subgroup
of the Yi tribe. Some historians believe that the majority of the population in
Nanzhao was Bai but that the elite was Yi.

349 Here I follow *Hu-Tan*, 258, n. 1, and read "southernmost" (*zuinan* 最南).

350 Yimouxun was the fifth ruler of Nanzhao. He was enfeoffed as "king of Nanzhao" in 794. *Xin Tangshu*, 222*shang*.6274.

351 Qiulong was the grandson of Xungequan, the seventh ruler of Nanzhao.
Xungequan was the son of Yimouxun.

352 The title "Brave and Trustworthy" was used well before Qiulong's time to
designate the rulers of various Man states in the south. See *Xin Tangshu*,
222*zhong*.6281.

353 As noted in note 33 in the "Miscellaneous Items Treatise," the names Dali 大
禮 and Dali 大理, though pronounced the same, refer to two distinct regional
political regimes that existed in Yunnan at different times: Dali 大禮 during

As for Dali, its territory is extensive and its population numerous, and its weapons and arms are excellent and superior. This is described in detail in a previous treatise.[354] The waters of the Right River in Yong County connect with the Great Pan River [Dapan Shui] in Dali. The Great Pan is located in Dali's Weichu Municipality [Weichu *fu*].[355] Temo [Temodao][356] also connects with Dali's Shanchan Municipality [Shanchan *fu*].[357] From the various Man and Lao [tribes] on the Yong-zhou Circuit to Dali is no more than 40 or 50 *cheng*.[358] Dali produces excellent horses, which can get through [overland] to Mount Heng. To the north it is blocked off by Ziqi; to the south it is blocked off by Temodao. So for a long time it was not possible to reach it. This is mentioned in the entry "Dali horses" [*Dali ma*].[359]

In the winter of the *guisi* year of the Qiandao reign [1173], some people in Dali such as Li Guanyin De, Dong Liujin Hei, Zhang Ban-ruo Shi, and others started following the practice of using three characters in their given names [*ming*].[360] Together, [they and]

---

the Five Dynasties period (beginning in 937) and Dali 大理 during the Song.

354 Fan talks about the weapons and arms of Dali in the entries on Man armor and Yunnan knives in the "Treatise on Implements."

355 Weichu Municipality corresponds with modern Chuxiong *xian*, Yunnan. The Dapan River, also known as the Nanpan River (Nanpan Jiang), does not connect with Guangxi's Right River, nor does it flow through Weichu Municipality. Fan Chengda is mistaken here. Cf. the comments in *LWDD*, 26, n. 6.

356 Temodao was located in the general area around modern Wenshan *zhou*, Yunnan. During the Song this area was populated by the Nong clan of the Lao people.

357 This municipality was situated near modern Kunming in Yunnan.

358 *Hu-Tan*, 264, n. 8, says "40 or 50 *cheng*" is an exaggeration. Hu and Tan contend that from the Mount Heng Stockade in Yong County to Dali is no more than 20 *cheng*. This tallies with the "20 *cheng*" distance provided in *LWDD*, 3.123 (*Neto-litzky*, 3.13).

359 The reference here is to the entry on "Man Horses" in the "Treatise on Quadru-peds."

360 *Hu-Tan*, 264–65, n. 10, points out that the use of three rather than four char-acters in the names of person from Dali extends back to the time of Nanzhao. As for four-character names, sometimes a Buddhist name or term will form a portion of the name. Two examples occur here in the text: Li Guanyin De 李觀音得 and Zhang Banruo Shi 張般若師. Guanyin refers to the bodhisattva Guanyin (Sanskrit: Avalokiteśvara), while Banruo (Sanskrit: *prajñā*) means "wisdom." Both Nanzhao and Dali had strong connections with Buddhism (see note 369 below).

twenty-three [other] persons reached Mount Heng to discuss the sale of horses. They produced a written document,[361] the strokes of the characters on which were somewhat standardized.[362] For the most part, their listed requirements included books such as *Literary Selections with Five Commentaries* [Wenxuan wuchen zhu],[363] *The Five Classics with Extended Commentaries* [Wujing guangzhu],[364] *Later Comments on the Spring and Autumn [Annals]* [Chunqiu houyu],[365] *The Three Histories with Added Commentary* [Sanshi jiazhu],[366] *Basic Pharmacopeia with Extended Commentaries* [Bencao guangzhu],[367] *Treatise on the Five Viscera* [Wucang lun],[368] and *Preface to the Sixteen Lessons in the Great Perfection of Wisdom Sūtra* [Da Banruo shiliu hui xu],[369] as well as the *Records for Elementary Learn-*

---

361   This document in fact was a "shopping list" for Chinese books and other things they planned to buy at the Hengshan Stockade after selling their horses.

362   "Standardized" here means that characters were written in standard or correct form rather than local or vulgar form. For some examples of vulgar characters, see the "Miscellaneous Items Treatise."

363   This well-known eighth-century commentary to the *Wenxuan* (Literary selections) in thirty *juan*, with commentaries by five different scholars, circulated widely in the Southern Song. A woodblock edition of this commentary, produced by the Chonghua Shufang in Fujian, was published in 1161.

364   The *Five Classics* (Wujing) are usually identified as the *Changes Classic* (Yijing), *Poetry Classic* (Shijing), *History Classic* (Shujing), *Record of Rites* (Liji), and *Spring and Autumn [Annals]* (Chunqiu). Numerous commentaries on these texts have been published throughout the dynasties, but I have found none bearing this particular title.

365   This work, usually attributed to Kong Yan, is extant in fragment form.

366   The *Three Histories* (Sanshi) in this title probably indicates the *Shiji*, *Hanshu*, and *Hou Hanshu*.

367   Both *Yan Pei*, 161, and *Qi Zhiping*, 48, punctuate in such a way that the two characters *duda* 都大 read as part of the book title *Basic Pharmacopeia with Extended Commentaries*. As noted earlier (see note 201), *duda* during the Song was a prefix used with office titles, meaning something like "chief." Cf. *Hu-Tan*, 257, which reads *duda* as part of the title *The Three Histories with Added Commentary*. The term *duda* seems to be misplaced here, and thus I have not translated it. As for the title *Bencao guangzhu*, I have not found any surviving edition of *The Basic Pharmacopeia* that bears this exact title.

368   This medical text, attributed to the famous Han dynasty physician Zhang Zhongjing, survives in several versions, including a manuscript copy found in Dunhuang.

369   This preface is extant. See *Taishō shinshū daizōkyō*, 55.2181. The state of Dali

ing [Chuxue ji],[370] *Zhang Meng's Rime Book* [Zhang Meng yayun],[371] *Spelling Rimes* [Qieyun],[372] *Jade Chapters* [Yupian],[373] *Experiences of the Assembled Sages* [Jisheng li],[374] and *Texts of the Hundred Schools* [Baijia shu].[375] They [further] required Fuliang porcelain [*Fuliang gangqi*] with accompanying bowls,[376] colored glass bowls and pitchers [*liuli wanhu*],[377] as well as amboyna [*zitan*],[378] sinking-in-water

---

had a strong connection to Buddhism, and it is reported that nine (some say ten) of its twenty-two rulers gave up the throne to become monks. It is not clear, however, why Dali would be interested in acquiring this particular preface.

370 This influential Tang work, compiled by Xu Jian and others, is extant.

371 *Songshi*, 202.5077, lists this title in ten *juan*, but it is not extant. The author, Zhang Meng, is otherwise unknown.

372 The *Qieyun* is an important and highly influential rime book compiled by Lu Fayan in 601. It is extant.

373 This is a dictionary compiled by Gu Yewang of the Southern Liang dynasty (502–557) sometime around 543. Originally in thirty *juan*, it survives today only in fragment form.

374 *WXTK*, 219.1780, lists a work in four *juan* bearing this title. Judging from Ma Duanlin's brief description, this text was employed to select lucky days through *yin* and *yang* correspondences.

375 This last book title is so general it is impossible to identify. According to Araki Toshikazu, "Nung Chih-kao and the *K'o-chü* Examinations," 90, the various titles on the preceding book list were intended to serve as reference works for non-Chinese students in Dali (and the bridle and halter areas) preparing for the Chinese civil service examinations.

376 Here I follow Ma Duanlin and understand *gangqi* 鋼器 to mean *ciqi* 磁[瓷]器 (porcelain; chinaware). Ma adds a note here: "I suspect this is in fact porcelain from Fuliang Town in Rao County. In their document [the representatives from Dali] wrote *liang* 量 instead of *liang* 梁" (*WXTK*, 329.2586). Ma Duanlin is probably correct. Jingde Market Town (Jingde *zhen*) in Rao County (modern Jiangxi) was the most famous production center of porcelain during the Song. Fuliang was one of six towns that fell under the jurisdiction of Rao County. It was located just north of Jingde *zhen*.

377 The term *liuli* designates colored glass, either opaque or partly translucent. For additional information see Schafer, *The Golden Peaches of Samarkand*, 235–37.

378 Also known as *qinglong mu*, amboyna (*zitan;* lit., purplish red sandalwood or sanderswood; sometimes also translated as "red sandalwood") is *Pterocarpus santalinus*. Its timber counts among the finest of the rosewoods and was often used to make red textile dye and furniture, especially cabinets. See Edward H. Schafer, "Rosewood, Dragon's Blood, and Lac," *Journal of the American Oriental Society* 77.2 (1957): 130–31. It was also used in Chinese medicine to treat sores.

aromatic,[379] licorice [root] [*gancao*],[380] abalone shell [*shijueming*],[381] well-spring stone [*jingquan shi*],[382] litharge [*mituoseng*],[383] fragrant shells [*xiangge*],[384] sea shells [*haige*],[385] and various medicines. The document was dated twelfth month, second year of the Lizhen reign[386] [1173]. Following this it read: "The ancients said: 'When scrutinizing a man's accomplishments, do not consider his reputation; when observing a man's behavior, do not ignore what he has said.'[387] People who are truly intimate friends are joyous when they meet and call upon each other. [Even if] their spoken language is not the same, their affection for each other is mutual. We have heard that Master Fu [Fuzi; that is, Confucius] said: 'The superior man is affable but not always agreeable; the inferior man is agreeable but not always affable.'[388] Now the people of the two states [China and the Dali] have come together by chance. How is it possible for us to not study the remarks of Master Fu?'" In a subsequent brief document they humbly begged for some help in making corrections [in the written document].[389] The brief document included the words

---

379   On sinking-in-water aromatic see the "Treatise on Aromatics."

380   *Gancao*, also known as *tiancao*, usually indicates licorice. CMP, no. 391. The reference here is probably to licorice root (*Glycyrrhizae radix*), which was used for various purposes in traditional Chinese medicine.

381   Abalone shell (*Haliotidis concha*) is used to treat a wide variety of conditions, especially severe headaches.

382   The precise identity of this mineral is unknown.

383   Lead oxide (sometimes called "red lead" or "litharge" in English) had many uses in traditional China, one of which was the production of cosmetics.

384   I have not been able to determine the precise identity of *xiangge*, or "fragrant shells."

385   CMP, no. 223, identifies *haige* as "venus shells." BCGM, 46.2531 (*Compendium*, 5:3688), however, points out that *haige* can refer to many different kinds of broken shells from marine bivalves.

386   Here Lizheng 利正 is a mistake for Lizhen 利貞, referring to the first reign period (1172–1176) under the last ruler of Dali, Duan Zhixing.

387   These lines are quoted from the *Lüshi chunqiu* (SKQS ed.), 16.6a. Ma Duanlin's *bu shi ci* 不識辭, or "do not ignore what he has said" (WXTK, 329.2586), should probably instead read *bu ji ci* 不譏辭 (do not ridicule what he has said). See the comments in *Qi Zhiping*, 50, n. 6.

388   These lines come from the *Analects*, 13.23. See *Lunyu zhushu*, 13/52/2508 (Legge, *The Chinese Classics*, 1-2:273). My translation is based on that of Legge.

389   The expression *fufa* 斧伐 (lit., "hew with an ax") is probably inspired by the

"Our spoken languages are not mutually comprehensible and similar, and we are separated by rivers and mountains for more than 10,000 *li*." All of them observe proper etiquette and decorum [*liyi*], and reverently recite Buddhist texts, which are written in gold and silver characters on emerald green paper. The people in Yong County have gotten hold of their *Great Compassion Sūtra* [Dabei jing],[390] which mentions that it was copied out by the official Zhao Banruo Zong[391] when he prayed for protection from eye disease. *Tanchuo, qiuwang,* and *qingping guan* are all office titles.[392] The protector of Yong County rewarded those who came [from Dali], sending them home with lavish gifts. However, the territory of Nanzhao is in the extreme southwest, and they should be considered part of the Western Rong. They are especially close to the Shu Metropolis [Chengdu] and are not a people who should be suppressed and pacified by the commandant of Gui.[393]

Supplementary entry: **FOREIGN LANDS.** Where you cross the river in Jiaozhi is in fact the Kingdom of Champa,[394] which is Linyi of the

---

opening lines of poem no. 158 in the *Poetry Classic*: "How does one hew wood to make an ax handle? / Without a second ax it simply cannot be done." *Maoshi zhengyi*, 8-3/131/399 (Legge, *The Chinese Classics*, 4:240). My translation here closely follows that of Legge.

390   This text is extant. See *Taishō shinshū daizōkyō*, 29.380. The comment that "people in Yong County have gotten hold" of this particular sūtra suggests that copies of this (and perhaps other) Buddhist texts from Dali may have been part of the commercial activity conducted between Dali and Yong County. For additional information on hand-written Buddhist texts from Dali, see Li Xiaoyou, "Nanzhao Dali de xieben Fojing," 54–56, and especially Li's essay "Nanzhao Dali xiejing shulüe."

391   The Dali official Zhao Banruo Zong is otherwise unknown. On the term *tanchuo*, rendered here as "official," see note 392 below.

392   More specific information on the Dali office titles mentioned here is provided in *Xin Tangshu*, 222*shang*.6268. Essentially, men holding the office *tanchuo* are referred to as *qingping guan*. This same source also mentions that this office is the equivalent of the Tang office *zaixiang*, or grand councilor. As for *qiuwang*, this was the equivalent in rank to a Tang dynasty examination official (*shiguan*).

393   *WXTK*, 329.2586.

394   The *HSRC* text (67.62b) reads *yishui* 一水, which is rendered here as "the river." Kong Fanli, *FCDBJ*, 160, suspects that the character *yi* 一 is corrupt, thereby suggesting that Fan Chengda had a particular river in mind, which, when crossed, would take one from Jiaozhi south into Champa. If this is the case,

Han.[395] On the river's southern bank is the mountain where Ma Yuan erected bronze pillars.[396] To the east and west is a great sea.[397] Separated by a river from Champa is Zhenla.[398] Farther on is another river [the land beyond which] is called Dengloumei.[399] To the west of these several kingdoms is a great sea that goes by the name Xilan,[400] which

---

then Fan was probably referring to the Red River.

    The description that follows, concerning places beyond China's borders, is mixed in among Fan Chengda's various passages on the Man preserved in the *Wenxian tongkao*. For the sake of reference and convenience, I have arbitrarily assigned this supplementary entry the title "Foreign Lands" (this title does not appear in the original text). Chinese geographic knowledge about the world outside China in the twelfth and thirteenth centuries was limited. What was known seems to have derived from persons knowledgeable of overseas trade, conducted mainly through Quanzhou and Guangzhou. Most of this trade was controlled by Arabs and other foreigners. This supplementary entry demonstrates that Fan Chengda's *Treatises* originally included information on foreign lands, although only a portion of the original text remains. This text was consulted, copied, and considerably expanded upon by both Zhou Qufei and Zhao Rukuo. Zhao Rukuo's information on foreign lands is especially valuable because for a time he served as maritime trade commissioner (*shibo shi*) in Fujian and thus had access to people with firsthand knowledge of overseas lands.

395   On Champa, see note 214; on Linyi, see note 198.

396   The entry on the Wen River (Wenshui) in Li Daoyuan, comp., *Shuijing zhu*, 36.22a (558), cites a passage from the *Records of Linyi* (Linyi ji) that says that in 43 C.E. Ma Yuan erected two bronze pillars on the southern border of Xianglin (or Linyi) to mark the boundary between Han territory and non-Chinese lands to the south. For additional information and references on Ma Yuan's bronze pillars, see also the supplementary entry on bronze pillars in the "Miscellaneous Items Treatise."

397   The reference here is probably to the Nanhai, or Southern Sea. If Champa is the geographic reference point (which seems to be the case), then the directional orientation of the "great sea" would be north and south rather than east and west.

398   If Fan Chengda has a particular waterway in mind here, it is probably what is known today as the Mekong River (usually called the Lancang Jiang in Chinese). As far as I know, however, the precise border between Champa and Cambodia (or Zhenla) in the twelfth century is unknown.

399   Dengloumei (or Dengliumei) is the name of ancient state that was located in southern Thailand, in and around what is now the province and city of Nakhon Sri Thammarat (formerly known as Ligor). For additional information, see note 27 in the "Treatise on Aromatics."

400   "Xilan" is a Chinese phonetic transcription of "Ceylon" (now Sri Lanka). The

marks the western borders of Jiaozhi, Dali, and Tibet.[401] To the south it adjoins a great ocean,[402] and at the mouth of this ocean is the Kingdom of Xilan. West of Xilan are the Five Indias [Wu Tianzhu].[403] To the extreme south of there is the Kingdom of Gulin.[404] Farther west is the Eastern Arabian Sea [Dong Dashi Hai]. To the west of that sea is the Kingdom of Arabia [Dashi Guo].[405] And farther west of that is the Western Arabian Sea [Xi Dashi Hai], to which foreign merchants have no access. In the Great Southern Ocean are various kingdoms, among which Sumatra [Sanfoqi] is regarded as the largest.[406] This is a

---

"Great Sea of Ceylon" probably refers in a very general sense to the various bodies of water surrounding the island of Ceylon, including what is now called the Bay of Bengal (to the east) and the Gulf of Mannar (to the west).

401 Before the 1700s, the term "Tufan" was used by the Chinese to refer to what is now Tibet.

402 Presumably, the reference here is to what we now call the Indian Ocean.

403 Chinese sources often describe the notion of "Five Indias" (Wu Tianzhu) rather than a single unified state. These are Central, Eastern, Southern, Western, and Northern India. According to Bimala Churn Law, *Historical Geography of Ancient India* (Delhi: Ess Ess Publications, 1976), p. 14, this division was borrowed directly from the Hindu Brahmanical system. On the Indian origins of the Chinese term "Five Indias," see also Tansen Sen, "Monks and Merchants: Sino-Indian Relations, 618–1281" (Ph.D. diss., University of Pennsylvania, 1996), 26–27.

404 The Chinese place-name Gulin refers to a port city (not a kingdom) on the southwestern coast of the Indian peninsula that carried on trade relations with China during the Song dynasty. Today this area is called Quilon or Kollam (Chinese: Kuilong). The state in which Gulin was located is sometimes called Qiluo (Cheras) and Jieer (Kerala) in traditional Chinese sources. For additional information, see Yang Wuquan's commentary in *LWDD*, 2.91, n. 1.

405 During the Tang and Song, "Dashi" was used as a general term for Arab states. It probably derives from the Persian word "Tāzī," meaning "Arabs." See the comments in Zhang Xinglang, *Zhong-Xi jiaotong shiliao huibian*, 4:2172, n. 3. Some modern scholars identify Dashi as the "Abbāsid Caliphate." See, for instance, Denis Twitchett and John K. Fairbank, eds., *The Cambridge History of China*, vol. 3: *Sui and T'ang China, 589–906: Part 1* (Cambridge: Cambridge University Press, 1979), 609. This caliphate, which existed from 749 to 1158, had its capital in Baghdad. During the Tang and Song it controlled large amounts of territory and numerous states or kingdoms (*guo*).

406 Most Chinese commentators associate Sanfoqi with Palembang, which during the Song was a port city (accessible by river) on the southern end of what is now the Indonesian island of Sumatra. This city served as the capital of the Srivijaya, a partly Buddhist, partly Hindu kingdom that exerted great influ-

trading center [*duhui*] for precious goods from the various Fan. To the east of Sanfoqi is the Kingdom of Java [Shepo Guo].[407] Slightly to the northeast are the Kingdom of Silla [Xinluo Guo] and the Kingdom of Goryeo [Gaoli Guo].[408] As for the distance of the various Fan [kingdoms] from China, only Champa is close by. Dashi is the most distant. To get to Dashi requires a boat journey of one year. In general, these various kingdoms are all Man and are arranged successively [as one moves away from China].[409]

---

ence throughout the Malayan Archipelago. Until the twelfth and thirteenth centuries, Srivijaya was a major economic power in Southeast Asia, controlling both the spice route traffic and local trade, and served as an trading center for Chinese, Malay, and Indian markets. Envoys from Sanfoqi traveled to and from China frequently. On the possible Javan origins of the name Sanfoqi, see Yang Wuquan's commentary in *LWDD*, 2.87, n. 1, and the commentary of Hirth and Rockhill in *Chau Ju-kua*, 63, n. 1.

407   Numerous independent kingdoms have existed on Java (Chinese: Zhuawa) throughout its long history. During the Tang and Song several kingdoms, heavily influenced by Buddhism and Hinduism from India, flourished on the island. From 1045 until 1221 Java was ruled by the Kediri kingdom, which along with Srivijaya were the two most powerful and influential kingdoms in the Southeast Asian Archipelago. The most valuable and detailed Chinese sources on Javan history during the Song are *LWDD*, 2.88 (*Netolitzky*, 2.8), and *ZFZ*, 1.54–55 (*Chau Ju-Kua*, 75–78).

408   Silla was one of the Three Kingdoms that dominated the Korean peninsula and parts of Manchuria for much of the first millennium c.e. It existed from 57 b.c.e. until 935 c.e. Silla was later replaced by the Goryeo (Chinese: Gaoli; also known as Goguryeo/ Koguryŏ; Chinese: Gaojuli) dynasty (918–1392).

409   *HSRC*, 67.62b–63a; *FCDBJ*, 160–61.

ORIGINAL CHINESE TEXT
Guihai yuheng zhi 桂海虞衡志[1]

(*Treatises of the Supervisor and Guardian of the Cinnamon Sea*)
by Fan Chengda 范成大 (1126–1193)

AUTHOR'S PREFACE 序

始予自紫微垣，出帥廣右，姻親故人張飲松江，皆以炎荒風土為
戚。予取唐人詩，考桂林之地，少陵謂之宜人，樂天謂之無瘴，退之
至以湘南江山勝於驂鸞仙去，則宦游之適，寧有踰於此者乎！　既以
解親友而遂行。

乾道八［九］年三月，既至郡，則風氣清淑，果如所聞，而巖岫之奇
絕，習俗之醇古，府治之雄勝，又有過所聞者。予既不鄙夷其民，而民
亦矜予之拙而信其誠，相戒毋欺侮。歲比稔，幙府少文書，居二年，
余心安焉。

承詔徙鎮全蜀，亟上疏固謝不能，留再閱月，辭勿獲命，乃與桂民

---

1   The source for the Chinese text of *Treatises* reproduced here is FCDBJ, 81–162.
For the most part I follow Kong Fanli's punctuation. My paragraph divisions,
however, are often different. Alternate readings followed in my English translation of the text appear in brackets [ ]. Variant forms of characters (甕 rather
than 瓮, 斮 instead of 斫, and so on) and *fanqie* 反切 readings inserted into the
text by later editors are not indicated (the *fanqie* readings for the various vulgar
characters listed in the "Miscellaneous Items Treatise" are included, however,
because these come from Fan Chengda). Supplementary text is identified as 附
文 (*fuwen*); supplementary entries are indicated as 附條 (*futiao*). For specific
information regarding alternate readings, misprints, corruptions, and other
textual matters, readers should consult the notes that accompany my English
translation.

別。民觴客於途，既出郭，又留二日，始得去。航瀟湘，絕洞庭，泝灩
澦，馳驅兩川，半年達於成都。道中無事，時念昔游，因追記其登臨
之處與風物土宜，凡方志所未載者，萃為一書，蠻陬絕徼見聞可紀
者，亦附著之，以備土訓之圖。噫，錦城以名都樂國聞天下，予幸得至
焉，然且惓惓於桂林，至為之綴緝[輯]瑣碎如此。蓋以信予之不鄙夷
其民，雖去之遠，且在名都樂國，而猶勿忘之也。淳熙二年長至日，吳
郡范成大致能書。

1. PRECIPICE-GROTTOES 志巖洞

予嘗評桂山之奇，宜為天下第一。士大夫落南者少，往往不知，而
聞者亦不能信。

予生東吳，而北撫幽、薊，南宅交、廣，西使岷峨之下，三方皆走萬
里，所至無不登覽。太行、常山、衡嶽、廬阜，皆崇高雄厚，雖有諸峰
之名，正爾魁然大山；峰云者，蓋強名之。其最號奇秀，莫如池之九
華，歙之黃山，括之仙都，溫之雁蕩，夔之巫峽，此天下同稱之者，然
皆數峰而止爾，又在荒遠僻絕之瀕，非几杖間可得。且所以能拔乎其
萃者，必因重岡複嶺之勢，盤亙而起，其發也有自來。

桂之千峰，皆旁無延緣，悉自平地崛然特立，玉筍瑤簪，森列無
際，其怪且多如此，誠當為天下第一。韓退之詩云：「水作青羅帶，山
如碧玉簪。」柳子厚《訾家洲記》云：「桂州多靈山，發地峭壁[豎]，林
立四野。」黃魯直詩云：「桂嶺環城如雁蕩，平地蒼玉忽嵯峨。」觀三
子語意，則桂山之奇，固在目中，不待予言之贅。頃嘗圖其真形，寄吳
中故人，蓋無深信者，此未易以口舌爭也。山皆中空，故峰下多佳巖
洞，有名可紀者三十餘所，皆去城不過七八里，近者二三里，一日可以
徧至。今推其尤者，記其略。

獨秀峰。直立郡治後，為桂主山，傍無坡阜，突起千丈。

讀書巖。在獨秀峰下。峰趾石屋有便房，石榻石牖，如環堵之室。
顏延年守郡時，讀書其中。

伏波巖。突然而起，且千丈。下有洞，可容二十榻。穿鑿通透，户牖
傍出。有懸石如柱，去地一綫不合。俗名馬伏波試劍石。前浸江濱，
波浪洶湧，日夜漱齧之。

疊綵巖。在八桂堂後，支徑登山，太[大]半有大洞，曲轉，穿出山
背。

白龍洞。在南溪平地半山，中龕有大石屋，由屋右壁入洞，行半
途，有小石室。

劉仙巖。在白龍洞之陽，仙人劉仲遠所居也。石室高寒，出半山間。

華景洞。高廣如十間屋，洞門亦然。

水月洞。在宜山之麓，其半枕江。天然刓刻作大洞門，透徹山背。頂高數十丈，其形正圓，望之端整如大月輪。江別派流貫洞中，踞石弄水，如坐捲蓬大橋下。

龍隱洞、龍隱巖。皆在七星山脚，没江水中。泛舟至石壁下，有大洞門，高可百丈。鼓棹而入，仰視洞頂，有龍跡夭矯，若印泥然，其長竟洞。舟行僅一箭許，別有洞門可出。巖在洞側，山半有小寺，即巖為佛堂，不復屋。

雉巖。亦江濱獨山，有小洞，洞門下臨灘江。

立魚峰。在西山後，雄偉高峻，如植立一魚。餘峰甚多，皆蒼石刻峭。

棲霞洞。在七星山。七星山者，七峯位置如北斗。又一小峯在傍，曰輔星。石洞在山半腹。入石門，下行百餘級，得平地，可坐數十人。旁有兩路。其一西行，兩壁石液凝沍，玉雪晶瑩。頂高數十丈，路闊亦三四丈，如行通衢中，頓足曳杖，彭鏗有鼓鐘聲，蓋洞之下又有洞焉。半里遇大壑，不可進。

一路北行，俯僂而入，數步則寬廣。兩旁十許丈，鍾乳垂下纍纍。凡乳牀必因石脈而出，不自頑石出也。進里餘，所見益奇。又行食頃，則多歧，游者恐迷途，不敢進，云通九疑山也。

元[玄]風洞。去棲霞傍數百步。風自洞中出，寒如冰雪。

曾公洞。舊名冷水巖。山根石門砑然，入門，石橋甚華，曾丞相子宣所作。有澗水，莫知所從來，自洞中右旋，東流橋下，復自右入，莫知所往，或謂伏流入于江也。度橋有仙田數畝。過田，路窄且濕，俯視石罅尺餘，匍匐而進，旋復高曠，可通棲霞。

屏風巖。在平地斷山峭壁之下。入洞門，上下左右皆高曠百餘丈。中有平地，可宴百客。仰視鍾乳森然，倒垂者甚多。躍石磴五十級，有石穴，通明。透穴而出，則山川城郭，恍然無際。余因其處作壺天觀，而命其洞曰空明。

隱山六洞。皆在西湖中，隱山之上。一曰朝陽，二曰夕陽，三曰南華，四曰北牖，五曰嘉蓮，六曰白雀[雀]。泛湖泊舟，自西北登山，先至南華。出洞而西，至夕陽。洞旁有石門可出，至北牖。出洞十許步，至朝陽。又西，至白雀[雀]。穴口隘狹，側身入，有穴通嘉蓮。西湖之外，既有四山繞之，碧玉千峰，倒影水面，固已奇絕，而湖心又浸隱山，諸洞之外，別有奇峰，繪畫所不及。荷花時，有泛舟故事，勝賞甲於西南。

北潛洞。在隱山之北，中有石室、石臺、石果之屬。石果作荔枝、胡桃、棗栗之形。人采取玩之，或以飣盤相問遺。

南潛洞。在西湖中，羅家山之上。

佛子巖。亦名鍾隱巖。去城十里，號最遠。一山峯起莽蒼中。山腰有上、中、下三洞，[下洞]最廣。中洞明敞，高百許丈。上洞差小，一寺就洞中結架，因石屋為堂室。

盧秀[虛秀]洞。去城差遠。大石室面平野。室左右皆有徑隧，各數十百步，穿透兩傍，亦臨平野。

以上所紀，皆附郭可日涉者。餘外邑巖洞尚多，不可皆到。興安石乳洞最奇，予罷郡時過之。上、中、下三洞。此洞與棲霞相甲乙，他洞不及也。陽朔亦有繡山、羅漢、白鶴、華蓋、明珠五洞，皆奇。又聞容州都嶠有三洞天，融州有靈巖真仙洞，世傳不下桂林，但皆在瘴地，士大夫尤罕到。

2. METALS AND STONES 志金石

本草有玉石部，專主藥物，非療病，雖重不錄。此篇亦主為方藥所須者。

生金。出西南州峒，生山谷田野沙土中，不由礦出也。峒民以淘沙為主，坏[抔]土出之，自然融結成顆。大者如麥粒，小者如麩片，便鍛作服用，但色差淡耳。欲令精好，則重鍊取足色，耗去十二三。既鍊，則是熟金。丹竈所須生金，故錄其所出。

附文：生金出溪洞沙土中，丹竈家所須，大如雞子者為金母。

丹砂。《本草》以辰砂為上，宜砂次之。今宜山人云：「出砂處與湖北犬牙，山北為辰砂，南為宜砂。地脈不殊，無甚分別。宜砂老者白色，有牆壁，如鏡，生白石床上，可入鍊，勢敵辰砂。」《本草圖經》乃云：「宜砂出土石間，非白石床所生上。」即是未識宜砂也。

別有一種色紅質嫩者，名土坑砂，乃是點，黑也。出土石間者，不堪耐火。

邕州亦有砂，大都數十百兩作塊，黑闇，少牆壁，嚼之紫黛，不堪入藥，彼人惟以燒取水銀。

《圖經》又云：「融州亦有砂。」今融州元無砂。邕、融聲相近，蓋又誤云。

水銀。以邕州溪洞朱砂末之，入爐燒取，極易成，以百兩為一銚。銚之制，以豬胞為骨，外糊厚紙數重，貯之不漏。

附文：水銀燒法，以鐵為上下釜。上釜貯砂，隔以細眼鐵板，覆之下釜之上。下釜盛水，埋地中，仰合上釜之唇，固濟周密，熾火灼之。砂化為霏霧，下墜水中，聚為水銀。

邕州取丹砂盛處椎鑿，有水銀自然流出。客販皆燒取而成者。百兩為一銚，銚以紙糊猪胞，不漏。

鍾乳。桂林接宜、融山中，洞穴至多，勝連州遠甚。余游洞親訪之，仰視石脈湧起處，即有乳牀如玉雪，石液融結所為也。乳牀下垂，如倒數峰小山，峰端漸銳，且長如冰柱。柱端輕薄中空，如鵝管。乳水滴瀝未已，且滴且凝。此乳之最精者，以竹管仰承拆取之。煉冶家又以鵝管之端尤輕明如雲母爪甲者為勝。

附文: 煉冶家又以鵝管之端，輕明如雲母爪甲，紋如蟬翼者為勝。廣東以鵝管遺人，率粗黃，蜀中所出亦枯澀。其鵝管窒塞及粗礦近床處，通謂之孽。

銅。邕州右江州峒所出，掘地數尺即有礦，故蠻人好用銅器。

綠。銅之苗也。亦出右江有銅處。生石中質如石者，名石綠。又有一種脆爛如碎土者，名泥綠，品最下，價亦賤。

附文: 淘其英華，供繪畫。次飾棟宇……

滑石。桂林屬邑及猺洞中皆出。有白、黑二種，功用相似。初出如爛泥，見風則堅，又謂之冷石。土人以石灰圬壁，及未乾時，以滑石末挑拭之，光瑩如玉。

鉛粉。桂林所作最有名，謂之桂粉，以黑鉛著糟瓮罨化之。

附文: 乾道初，始官造粉，歲得錢二萬緡。

無名異。小黑石子也。桂林山中極多，一包數百枚。

附文:價極賤。

石梅。生海中。　一叢數枝，橫斜瘦硬，形色真枯梅也。雖巧工造作，所不能及。根所附著如覆菌。或云: 本是木質，為海水所化，如石蟹、石蝦之類。

附文: 石梅、石柑。生海中，未詳，可入藥。

石柏。生海中。一幹極細，上有一葉，宛是側柏，扶疏無小異。根所附著如烏藥，大抵皆化為石矣。此與石梅雖未詳可以入藥否，然皆奇物，不可不志。

3. AROMATICS 志香

南方火行，其氣炎上，藥物所賦，皆味辛而嗅香。而沉、箋之屬世專謂之香者，又美之所種[鍾]也。

世皆云二廣出香，然廣東香乃自舶上來，廣右香廣海北者亦凡品，惟海南最勝。人士未嘗落南者，未必盡知，故著其說。

沉水香。上品出海南黎峒，亦名土沉香，少大塊。其次如蝟栗角，如附子，如芝菌，如茅竹葉者，皆佳。至輕薄如紙者，入水亦沉。

香之節因久蟄土中，滋液下向，結而為香。採時香面悉在下，其背帶木性者乃出土上。環島四郡界皆有之，悉冠諸蕃所出，又以出萬安者為最勝。說者謂萬安山在島正東，鍾朝陽之氣，香尤醖藉豐美。

大抵海南香氣皆清淑，如蓮花、梅英、鵝梨、蜜脾之類，焚一博投許氛翳彌室。翻之四面悉香，至煤爐氣亦不焦，此海南香之辨也。北人多不甚識，蓋海上亦自難得。省民以牛博之於眾黎，一牛博香一擔，歸自差擇，得沉水十不一二。中州人士但用廣州舶上占城、真臘等香，近年又貴丁[登]流眉來者。予試之，乃不及海南中、下品。舶香往往腥烈，不甚腥者，意味又短. 帶木性，尾烟必焦。其出海北者，生交趾，及交人得之海外蕃舶而聚於欽州，謂之欽香。質重實，多大塊，氣尤酷烈，不復風味，惟可入藥，南人賤之。

附文： 沉香。出海外黎洞。香木既枬，其節目久墊土中，數百年不腐，益精堅……面多在下，如山峰、怪石、怪獸、龜蛇……盡觀諸蕃所出，尤以萬安為最勝……海南香氣皆清淑……價與白金等。

蓬萊香。亦出海南。即沉水香結未成者。多成片，如小笠及大菌之狀，有徑一二尺者，極堅實，色狀皆似沉香，惟入水則浮，刓去其背帶木處，亦多沉水。

鷓鴣斑香。亦得之於海南沉水、蓬萊及絕好箋香中。槎牙輕鬆，色褐黑而有白斑，點點如鷓鴣臆上毛，氣尤清婉，似蓮花。

附文： 木性未盡，以色似名。

箋香。出海南。香如猬皮、栗蓬及漁蓑狀，蓋修治時雕鏤費工，去木留香，棘刺森然。香之精鍾於刺端，芳氣與他處箋香迥別。出海北者，聚於欽州，品極凡，與廣東舶上生、熟、速、結等香相埒。海南箋香之下，又有重[蟲]漏、生結等香，皆下色。

附文： 香木葉如冬青而圓，皮似楮皮而厚；花黃，類菜花；子，青黃類羊矢。海南人以斧斫坎，使膏液凝沍. 徐於斧痕中採以為香，如箋香之類，多出人為。

光香。與箋香同品第，出海北及交趾。亦聚於欽州，多大塊。如山石枯槎，氣粗烈如焚松檜。曾不能與海南箋香比，南人常以供日用及常程祭享。

沉[泥]香。出交趾。以諸香草合和蜜調如薰衣香。其氣溫馨，自有一種意味，然微昏鈍。

香珠。出交趾。以泥香捏成小巴豆狀，琉璃珠間之，彩絲貫之，作道人數珠。入省地賣，南中婦人好帶之。

思勞香。出日南。如乳香，歷[瀝]青黃褐色，氣如楓香，交趾人用以合和諸香。

排草。出日南。狀如白茅，香芳烈如麝香，本亦用以合香。諸草香無及之者。

檳榔苔。出西南諸島，生檳榔木上，如松身之艾蒳。單爇極臭，交
趾人用以合泥香，則能成溫馨之氣。功用如甲香。

橄欖香。橄欖木脂也，狀如黑膠飴。江東人取黃蓮木及楓木脂以
為欖香，蓋其類。出於橄欖，故獨有清烈出塵之意，品格在黃連、楓
香之上。桂林東江有此果，居人采香賣之，不能多得，以純脂不雜木
皮者為佳。

零陵香。宜、融等州多有之。土人編以為席，薦坐褥，性暖宜人。
零陵，今永州，實無此香。

附文：古零陵界甚遠。

附條：蟹殼香。出高、化州。

4. WINES 志酒

余性不能酒，士友之飲少者莫予若也，然知酒者亦莫予若也。頃
數仕於朝，游王公貴人家，未始得見名酒。使虜至燕山，得其宮中酒
號金蘭者，乃大佳。燕西有金蘭山，汲其泉以釀。及來桂林，而飲瑞
露，乃盡酒之妙，聲震湖廣，則雖金蘭之勝，未必能頡頏也。

瑞露。帥司公廚酒也。經撫廳前有井清冽，汲以釀，遂有名。今南
庫中自出一泉。近年只用庫井酒，仍佳。

古辣泉。古辣本賓、橫間墟名。以墟中泉釀酒，既熟，不煮，埋之
地中，日足取出。

附文：色淺紅，味甘，可致遠，雖行烈日中，不至壞。南州珍之。

老酒。以麥麴釀酒，密封藏之，可數年。士[土]人家尤貴重。每歲
臘中，家家造鮓，使可為卒歲計。有貴客，則設老酒，冬鮓以示勤，婚
娶以老酒為厚禮。

5. IMPLEMENTS 志器

南州風俗，猱雜蠻猺，故凡什器多詭異　；而外蠻兵甲之製，亦邊
鎮[備]之所宜知者。

竹弓。以簜[熏]竹為之。筋膠之制，一如角弓，惟揭箭不甚力。

黎弓。海南黎人所用，長弰木弓也。以藤為弦，箭長三尺，無羽，
鏃長五寸，如茨菰葉。以無羽，故射不遠三四丈，然中者必死。

蠻弩。諸峒猺及西南諸蕃，其造作略同，以硬木為弓，樁甚短，似
中國獵入射生弩，但差大耳。

猺人弩。又名編架弩。無箭槽，編架而射也。

藥箭。化外諸蠻所用。弩雖小弱，而以毒箭濡箭鋒，中者立死。藥

以蛇毒草為之。

蠻甲。惟大理國最工。甲冑皆用象皮，胸、背各一大片，如龜殼，堅厚與鐵等。又聯綴小皮片，為披膊、護項之屬，製如中國鐵甲，葉皆朱之。兜鍪及甲身內外，悉朱地間黃黑漆，作百花蟲獸之文，如世所用犀毗器，極工妙。又以小白貝纍纍絡甲縫，及裝兜鍪，疑猶傳古貝冑朱綏遺製云。

黎兜鍪。海南黎人所用，以藤織為之。

雲南刀。即大理所作。鐵青，黑沉沉，不銘。南人最貴之。以象皮為鞘，朱之，上亦畫犀毗花文。一鞘兩室，各函一刀。靶以皮條纏束，貴人以金銀絲。

峒刀。兩江州峒及諸外蠻無不帶刀者，一鞘二刀，與雲南同，但以黑漆雜皮為鞘。

黎刀。海南黎人所作。刀長不過一二尺，靶乃三四寸，纖細藤纏束之。靶端插臼角片尺許，如鷗鶒尾，以為飾。

蠻鞍。西南諸蕃所作。不用鞯，但空垂兩木鐙。鐙之狀，刻如小龕，藏足指其中，恐入榛棘傷足也。後鞦鏇木為大錢，纍纍貫數百，狀如中國騾驢鞦。

蠻鞭。刻木節節如竹根，朱墨間漆之，長纔四五寸，首小，有鐵環，貫二皮條，以策馬。

花腔腰鼓。出臨桂職田鄉。其上特宜鼓腔，村人專作窯燒之，細畫紅花紋以為飾。

銅鼓。古蠻人所用，南邊土中時有掘得者，相傳為馬伏波所遺。其製如坐墩而空其下。滿鼓皆細花紋，極工緻。四角有小蟾蜍，兩人舁行，以手拊之，其聲全似鞉鼓。

銃鼓。猺人樂。狀如腰鼓，腔長倍之。上銳下侈，亦以皮鞦植於地，坐拊之。

盧沙[蘆笙]。猺人樂。狀類簫，縱八管，橫一管貫之。

葫蘆笙。兩江峒中樂。

藤合。屈藤盤繞，成柈合狀，漆固護之。出藤、梧等郡。

雞毛筆。嶺外亦有兔，然極少。俗不能為兔毫筆，率用雞毛，其鋒跟踉不聽使。

練[練]子。出兩江州峒。大略似苧布。有花紋者謂之花練，土人亦自貴重。

附文：蜀人尤愛之。陳姚察為吏不尚書，有私門出送布一端，花練一匹。察謂之：「吾所衣止是麻布蒲服[練]。此物於吾無用。」幸不煩爾，此人遜請，察厲色而出。

緂。亦出兩江州峒。如中國綫羅，上有徧地小方勝紋。

蠻氈。出西南諸蕃，以大理為最。蠻人晝披夜臥，無貴賤，人有一番。

附文：　長或數丈，兩重夾之，故博而軟。北毯經臥，輒不能雨　；南毯且臥且披，雨不能濕，大理者為最。

黎幕。出海南黎峒。黎人得中國錦綵，拆取色絲，間木棉，挑織而成。每以四幅聯成一幕。

黎單。亦黎人所織。青紅間道，木棉布也。桂林人悉買以為臥具。

檳榔合。南人既喜食檳榔，其法，用石灰或蜆灰并扶留藤同咀則不澀。士人家至以銀錫作小合，如銀錠樣，中為三室，一貯灰，一貯藤，一貯檳榔。

鼻飲杯。南邊人習鼻飲，有陶器如杯碗，旁植一小管，若瓶嘴，以鼻就管吸酒漿，暑月以飲水，云：「水自鼻入，咽快不可言。」邕州人已如此，記之以發覽者一胡盧也。

牛角杯。海旁人截牛角令平，以飲酒，亦古兕觥一遺意。

蠻椀。以木刻，朱黑間漆之，侈腹而有足，如敦瓿之形。

竹釜。猺人所用。截大竹筒以當鐺鼎，食物熟而竹不燔，蓋物理自爾，非異也。

戲面。桂林人以木刻人面，窮極工巧，一枚或值萬錢。

6. BIRDS 志禽

南方多珍禽，非君子所問[聞]。又予以法禁采捕其急，故不能多識。偶於人家見之，及有異聞者，錄以備博物。

孔雀。生高山喬木之上，人探其雛，育之。喜臥沙中，以沙自浴，拍拍甚適。雄者尾長數尺，生三年，尾始長。歲一脫尾，夏秋復生。羽不可近目，損人。飼以猪腸及生菜，惟不食菘。

鸚鵡。近海郡尤多。民或以鸚鵡為鮓，又以孔雀為臘，皆以其易得故也。此二事，載籍所未紀，自予始志之。南人養鸚鵡者云：「此物出炎方，稍北中冷，則發瘴噤戰，如人患寒熱，以柑子飼之則愈，不然必死。」

白鸚鵡。大如小鵝，亦能言。羽毛玉雪，以手撫之，有粉黏着指掌，如蛺蝶翅。

烏鳳。如喜鵲，色紺碧，頸毛類雄雞鬃，頭有冠，尾垂二弱骨，各長一尺四五寸。其杪始有毛羽一簇，冠、尾絕異，大略如鳳。鳴聲清越，如笙簫然，度曲妙合宮商。又能為百蟲之音。生左、右江溪峒中，極難得。然書傳未之紀，當由人罕識云。

秦吉了。如鸜[鴝]鵒，紺黑色，丹咮黃距，目下連頂有深黃文，頂毛有縫，如人分髮。能人言，比鸚鵡尤慧。大抵鸚鵡聲如兒女，吉了聲則如丈夫。出邕州溪峒中。《唐書》：「林邑出結遼鳥。」林邑，今占城，去邕、欽州，但隔交趾，疑即吉了也。

錦雞。又名金雞。形如小雉，湖南、北亦有之。

山鳳凰。狀如鵝雁，嘴如鳳，巢兩江深林中。伏卵時，雄者以木枝雜桃膠封其雌於巢，獨留一竅，雄飛求食以飼之。子成，即發封；不成，則室竅殺之。此亦異物，然未之見也。

翻毛雞。翮翎皆翻生，彎彎向外，尤馴狎，不散逸。二廣皆有。

長鳴雞。高大過常雞，鳴聲甚長，終日啼號不絕。生邕州溪峒中。

翡翠。出海南、邕、賀二州，亦有臘而賣之。

灰鶴。大如鶴，通身灰慘色。去頂二寸許，毛始丹，及頸之半。亦能鳴舞。

鷓鴣。大如竹雞而差長。頭如鶉，身文亦然。惟臆前白點正圓如珠，人采食之。

水雀。蒼色，似鷓鴣。飛集庭戶，翩翩然，與燕雀為伍。

附條：　靈鵲[鶺]為人突巢穴，能禹步作法以去之。

7. QUADRAPEDS 志獸

獸莫巨於象，莫有用於馬，皆南土所宜。子治馬政，頗補苴漏隙，其說累牘所不能載，姑著其略，及畜獸稍異者，併為一篇。

象。出交趾山谷，惟雄者有兩牙。佛書云「四牙」，又云「六牙」，今無有。

附文：象出交趾象山。一軀之力皆在鼻。二廣亦有野象，盜酒害稼，目細，畏火。欽州人以機捕之，皮可為甲，或條截為杖，甚堅。

附文：　象頭不可俯，頸不可回。口隱於頤，去地尚遠，運動以鼻為用。一軀之力皆在鼻。將行，先以鼻拄地，乃移足，知其足力劣於鼻也。鼻端甚深，可以開闔取物。中有小肉夾。雖芥子亦可拾。每以鼻取食，即就爪甲擊去泥垢，而後捲以入口。飲水亦以鼻吸而捲之。足如柱，無指，而有爪甲五枚，形如大栗。登高山，下峻坂，涉深水，形臃腫而甚捷。交趾出象處曰象山。歲一捕之。山有石室，惟通一路，周圍皆石壁。先置蒭豆其中，驅一馴雌入焉。布甘蔗于道以誘野象。象來食蔗，則縱馴雌入野象羣，誘以歸石室，隨以巨石窒門。象飢，人緣石室飼馴雌，野象見雌得食，亦狎而來求飼。益狎，則鞭之。少馴則騎而制之。久則漸解人意。又為立名字，呼之則應。牧者謂之象奴，又名象公。凡制象必以鈎。象奴正跨其頸，以鐵鈎，鈎其頭，欲其左，鈎頭之右，欲右，鈎左，欲却鈎額，欲前不鈎，欲其跪伏，以鈎正案其腦。案之痛，則號鳴。人謂象能聲諸者，此也。其行列之齊，皆有鈎以前却左右之。其形雖大而不勝痛。故人得以數寸之鈎馴焉。馴之久者，象奴來則低頭，跪前左膝。人踏之以登，則奮而起行。蠻酋出入多乘象。其貢中國者，皆施鞍架御座，號羅我。象額編金鈴千數枚，行則琅琅然。及人有犯惡逆者，臥之地，使象蹴殺之。二廣亦有野象，村落小民酒熟，則尋香而來，破壁入飲。人甚苦之。所過亦害禾稼。象目細，畏火，不畏人。倉卒遇之，以長竹繫火逐之，輒退。羣象雖多，不足畏，惟獨象最可畏，蓋其強悍不容於羣，獨行無所忌，遇其肆毒，以鼻捲之，擲殺蹴其血流吸飲之。欽州人能捕象。象行觸機則刃下擊之，中其要害必死。將死，以牙觸石折之，以牙為身災也。非要害則負刃而行，肉潰則刃脫。傷其鼻亦死。鼻傷之，瘡不可合，故亦致死。殺一象，村衆飽其肉。鼻肉最美，熟而加糟，糟透臠而食之。象皮可以為甲，或條截之，硾之至乾，治[製]以為杖，甚堅。

　附條：　馬。自杞國以錦一匹博大理三馬，金鐲一兩博二馬。行十三程至四城州，又六程，至邕州。又有羅殿國及謝藩、羅孔諸部落，馬尤壯，行二十二程至四城州，與自杞等馬會，皆以十月來。經略司歲市千五百匹，尤駿者博金數十兩，官價有定數，不能致。大理去邕州橫山寨才四十餘程，自杞人爭利，不敢度自杞。而東有一路，自善闡府經時磨[特磨道]道來，其捷。時磨[特磨道]人亦貪悍，不得達。

　蠻馬。出西南諸蕃，多自毗那、自杞等國來。自杞取馬於大理，古南詔也。地連西戎，馬生尤蕃。大理馬為西南蕃之最。

　果下馬。土産小駟也。以出德慶之瀧水者為最。高不逾三尺，駿者有兩脊骨，故又號雙脊馬。健而喜[善]行。

　附文：高不逾三尺，而駿健能辛苦。以歲七月十五日會江上交易。湖南邵陽、營道等處，亦出一種低馬。

　猨。有三種：金絲者，黃；玉面者，黑；純黑者，面亦黑。金絲、玉面皆難得。或云：純黑者雄，金絲者雌。又云：雄能嘯，雌不能也。猨性不耐著地，著地輒瀉以死。煎附子汁與之，即愈。

　蠻犬。如獵狗，警而獅。

　鬱林犬。出鬱林州，極高大，垂耳拳尾，與常犬異。

　花羊。南中無白羊，多黃褐白斑，如黃牛；又有一種，深褐黑脊白斑，全似鹿。

　乳羊。本出英州。其地出仙茅，羊食茅，舉體悉化為肪，不復有血肉。食之宜人。

　綿羊。出邕州溪峒及諸蠻國，與朔方胡羊不異。

　麝香。自邕州溪峒來者名土麝，氣臊烈，不及西蕃。

　火[大]狸。狸之類不一，邕別有一種，其毛色如金錢豹，但其錢差大耳。彼人云：歲久則化為豹，其文先似之矣。

風狸。狀如黃猨，食蜘蛛，晝則拳曲如蝟，遇風則飛行空中。其溺及乳汁主治大風疾，奇效。

嫩[懶]婦。如山猪而小，喜食禾。田夫以機軸織紝之器掛田所，則不復近。安平、七源等州有之。

山猪。即毫猪。身有棘刺，能振發以射人。三二[二三]百為羣，以害禾稼，州峒中甚苦之。

石鼠。專食山豆根，賓州人以其腹乾之，治咽喉疾，效如神，謂之石鼠肚。

香鼠。至小，僅如指擘大，穴於柱中，行地中，疾如激箭。

山獺。出宜州溪峒，俗傳為補助要藥。洞人云：「獺性淫毒，山中有此物，凡牝獸悉避去。獺無偶，抱木而枯。

洞獠尤貴重，云能解藥箭毒，中箭者研其骨少許，傅治，立消。一枚直金一兩，人或求買，但得殺死者，其功力甚劣。

8. INSECTS AND FISHES 志蟲魚

蟲魚微物，外薄於海者，其類庸可既哉！錄偶見聞者萬一。

珠。出合浦海中。有珠池，蜑户没水探蚌取之。歲有豐耗，多得謂之珠熟。相傳海底有處所，如城郭大，蚌居其中，有怪物守之，不可得。蚌之細碎蔓延於外者，始得而采。

附文：　珠。有池在合浦海中孤島下，名斷望池。去岸數十里，望島如一拳。池深可十丈，四周如城郭。蚌細零溢生城郭外者，乃可採……蜑人没水采蚌，每以長繩繫竹籃攜之以没，或遇惡魚海怪則死。

硨磲。似大蚌，海人磨治其殼，為諸玩物。

附文：硨磲。大蚌之屬，殼可為荷葉杯。

蚺蛇。大者如柱，長稱之，其膽入藥。南人腊其皮，刮去鱗，以鞔鼓。蛇常出逐鹿食，寨兵善捕之。數輩滿頭插花，趨赴蛇。蛇喜花，必駐視，漸近，競拊其首，大呼紅娘子，蛇頭益俛不動，壯士大刀斷其首。衆悉奔散，遠伺之。有頃，蛇省覺，奮迅騰擲，傍小木盡拔，力竭乃斃。數十人舁之，一村飽其肉。

附文：蚺蛇。大如柱。逐麛鹿田中。南人插花呼妖，或呼紅娘子以誘之。花置蛇首，蛇俛不動，則殺之。

蠵蝐。形似龜黿輩，背甲十三片，黑白斑文，相錯鱗差，以成一背。其邊裙闌缺，齧如鋸齒。無足，而有四鬣，前兩鬣長狀如楫，後兩鬣極短，其上皆有鱗甲，以四鬣棹水而行。海人養以鹽水，飼以小鮮。

俗傳甲子、庚申日輒不食，謂之蟲蝟齋日，其說甚俚。

附文： 珇瑁。背甲……皆花紋。

蜈蚣，有極大者。

青螺。狀如田螺，其大兩拳。揩磨去粗皮，如翡翠色，雕琢為酒杯。

鸚鵡螺。狀如蝸牛殼。磨治出精采，亦雕為杯。

貝子。海旁皆有之。大者如拳，上有紫斑。小者指面大，白如玉。

附文： 世既不尚，人亦稀採。

石蟹。生海南，形真是蟹。云是海沫所化，理不可詰。又有石蝦，亦其類。

鬼蛺蝶。大如扇，四翅，好飛荔枝上。

黑蛺蝶。大如蝙蝠，橘蠹所化，北人或云玄武蟬。

嘉魚。狀如小鯽魚，多脂，味極腴美。出梧州火山。人以為鮓，以餉遠。

附文： 嘉魚。出梧州火山下丙穴……煎不假油。蜀中丙穴亦出，肥美相似。

蝦魚。出灘水。肉白而豐，味似蝦而鬆美。

竹魚。出灘水。狀如青魚，味如鱖魚。南中魚品如鯉、鯽輩皆有之，而以蝦、竹二魚為珍。

天蝦。狀如大飛蟻。秋社後，有風雨，則羣墮水中，有小翅。人候其墮，掠取之為鮓。

9. FLOWERS 志花

桂林具有諸草花木，牡丹、芍藥、桃、杏之屬，但培溉不力，存形似而已。今著其土產獨宜者，凡北州所有，皆不錄。

上元紅。深紅色，絕似紅木瓜花，不結實。以燈夕前後開，故得名。

白鶴花。如白鶴，立春開。

南山茶。葩萼大倍中州者，色微淡，葉柔薄有毛。別自有一種，如中州所出者。

紅荳蔻花。叢生，葉瘦如碧蘆。春末發。初開花，先抽一幹，有大籜包之，籜拆花見。一穗數十蕊，淡紅，鮮妍如桃、杏花色。蕊重則下垂如葡萄，又如火齊纓絡及剪綵鸞枝之狀。此花無實，不與草荳蔻同種。每蕊心有兩瓣相并，詞人託興如「比目」、「蓮理」云。

泡花。南人或名柚花。春末開，蕊圓白如大珠，既拆則似茶花。氣極清芳。與茉莉、素馨相逼。番人采以蒸香，風味超勝。

附文：　泡花。采以蒸香。法以佳沉香薄劈，着净器中，鋪半開花，與香層層相間，密封之，日一易，不待花蔫，花遇香成。番禺人吳興作心字香、瓊香，用素馨、末利，法亦然。大抵泡取其氣，未嘗炊燉。江、浙作木犀降真香，蒸湯上，非法也。

紅蕉花。葉瘦，類蘆、箬，心中[中心]抽條。條端發花，葉數層，日拆一兩葉。葉色正紅，如榴花、荔枝。其端各有一點鮮綠，尤可愛。春夏開，至歲寒猶芳。又有一種，根出土處，特肥飽如膽瓶，名膽瓶蕉。

枸那花。葉瘦長，略似楊柳。夏開淡紅花，一朵數十萼，至秋深猶有之。

史君子花。蔓生，作架植之。夏開，一簇一二十葩，輕盈似海棠。

水西花。葉如萱草，花黃，夏開。

裹梅花。即木槿。有紅、白二種，葉似蜀葵。采紅者連葉包裹黃梅，鹽漬，曝乾，以薦酒，故名。

玉脩花。粉紅色，四季開。

象蹄花。如梔子而葉小，夏開，至秋深。

素馨花。比番禺所出為少，當由風土差宜故也。

茉莉花。亦少，如番禺。以淅米漿水日溉之，則作花不絕，可耐一夏。花亦大，且多葉，倍常花。六月六日，又以治魚腥水一溉，益佳。

石榴花。南中一種，四季常開。夏中既實之後，秋深忽又大發。花且實，枝頭碩果罅裂，而其旁紅英燦然。并花實拆飣盤筵，極可玩。

添色芙蓉花。晨開，正白，午後微紅，夜深紅。歐陽公《牡丹譜》有「添色紅」者，與此意同。此花枝條經冬不枯，有高出屋者。江、浙間必宿根重茁，蜀種亦爾。

測金盞。花如小黃葵，葉似槿，歲暮開，與梅同時。

附條：　曼陀羅花。漫生原野，大葉白花，實如茄，遍生小刺。盜採花末之，置人飲食中，即昏醉。土人又以為小兒去積藥。昭州公庫取一枝挂庫中，飲者易醉。

10. FRUITS 志果

世傳南果以子名者百二十，半是山野間草木實，猿狙之所甘，人強名以為果，故予不能盡識。錄其識可食者五十七種。

荔枝。自湖南界入桂林，才百餘里，便有之，亦未甚多。昭平出櫔核、臨賀出綠色者尤勝。自此而南，諸郡皆有之，悉不宜乾，肉薄味淺，不及閩中所產。

龍眼。南州悉有之，極大者出邕州，圍如當二錢，但肉薄，不能遠過常品，為可恨。

　饅頭柑。近蒂起如饅頭尖者味香勝，可埒永嘉孔[乳]柑。

　金橘。出營道者為天下冠，出江、浙者皮甘肉酸，不逮也。

　綿李。味甘美，勝常品。擘之兩片開，如離核桃。

　石栗。圓如彈子，每顆有梗抱附之，類杓柄。肉黃白。

　甘靭[子]。似巴欖子。仁附肉，有白臕，不可食，發病。北人或呼為海胡桃。

　龍荔。殼如小荔枝，肉味如龍眼，木身，葉亦似二果，故名。可蒸食，不可生啖，令人發癇，或見鬼物。三月開小白花，與荔枝同時。

　木竹子。皮色形狀，全似大枇杷，肉甘美，秋冬間實。

　冬桃。狀如棗，深碧而光，軟爛甘酸，春夏熟。

　羅望子。殼長數寸，如肥皂，又如刀豆，[亦如橄欖，其皮七重，色正丹]，內有二三實，煨食甘美。

　人面子。如大梅李，核如人面，兩目鼻口皆具，肉甘酸，宜蜜煎。

　烏欖。如橄欖，青黑色，肉爛而甘。

　方欖。亦如橄欖，三角或四角，出兩江州峒。

　椰子。木身，葉悉類棕櫚、桄榔之屬。子生葉間，一穗數枚，枚大如五升器。果之大者，謂唯此與波羅蜜相等耳。皮中子殼可為器，子中瓤白如玉，味美如牛乳。瓤中酒，新者極清芳，久則渾濁，不堪飲。

　蕉子。芭蕉極大者，凌冬不凋，腹中抽[一]幹，長數尺，節節有花，花褪葉根有實。去皮取肉，軟爛如綠柿，極甘冷，四季實。土人或以飼小兒，云性涼去客熱。以梅汁漬，暴乾，按令褊，味甘酸，有微霜。世謂芭蕉乾者是也。又名牛蕉子，亦四季實。

　雞蕉子。小如牛蕉子，亦四季實。

　茅[芽]蕉子。小如雞蕉，尤香嫩甘美，初秋實。

　紅鹽草果。取生草荳蔻，入梅汁，鹽漬，令色紅，暴乾，以薦酒。鸚哥舌，即紅鹽草，果之珍者。實始結，即擷取，紅鹽乾之，纔如小舌。

　八角茴香。北人得之以薦酒，少許，咀嚼甚芳香。出左、右江州峒中。

　餘甘子。多販入北州，人皆識之。其木可以製器。

　附文：餘甘子。風味過橄欖，雖腐爛，猶堅脆。

　五稜子。形甚詭異，瓣五出，如田家碌碡狀。味酸，久嚼微甘，閩中謂之羊桃。

　黎曚子。如大梅，復似小橘，味極酸。

　波羅蜜。大如冬瓜，外膚礧砢，如佛髻。削其皮食之，味極甘。子練[瓣]悉如冬瓜，生大木上，秋熟。

柚子。南州名臭柚,大如瓜,人亦食之。皮甚厚,打碑者捲皮蘸墨,以代氈刷,宜墨而不損紙,極便於用。此法可傳,但北州無許大柚耳。

櫓罟子。大如半升碗。諦視之,數十房攢聚成球,每房有縫。冬生青,至夏紅,破其瓣食之,微甘。

槎[搓]擦子。如錐栗,肉甘而微澀。

地蠶。生土中,如小蠶,又似甘露子。

附文: 地蠶。。。似甘露子而不尖,以薦酒。

赤柚子。如橄欖,皮青肉赤。以下并春實。

火炭子。如烏李。

山韶子。色紅,肉如荔枝。以下八種并夏實。

山龍眼。色青,肉如龍眼。

菩提子。色黃,如石榴。

木賴子。如淡黃大李。

粘子。如指面大,褐色。

千歲子,如青黃李,味甘。

赤棗子。如酸棗,味酸。

藤韶子。大如鳧卵,蒂紅色。以下十三種并秋實。

古米子。殼黃,中有肉如米粒。

殼子。如青梅,味甘。

藤核子。生白藤上,如小蒲桃。

木連子。如胡桃,紫色。

蘿蒙子。黃大如橙柚。

毛栗。如橡栗。

特乃子。狀似榧而圓長端正。

不納子。似黃熟小梅,絕易爛,爛即皮肉腐。核可為珍珠,似菩提子。

羊矢[屎]子。色狀金[全]似羊矢[屎],味亦不佳。

日頭子。狀如櫻桃,色如蒲桃,穗生。

秋風子。色狀俱似楝子。

黃皮子。如小棗。

朱圓子。正圓深紅,狀似苦楝子。以下六種皆冬實。

匾桃。大如桃而匾,色正青。

粉骨子。皮黃,色[肉]如粉。

塔骨子。匾,如大橘,皮裏空虛。

黃肚子。如小石榴。

11. HERBACEOUS PLANTS AND TREES 草木

異草瑰木, 多生窮山荒野, 其不中醫和、匠石者, 人亦不采, 故予
所識者少; 惟竹品乃多桀異, 併附於錄。

桂。南方奇木, 上藥也。桂林以桂名, 地實不產, 而出於賓、宜州。
凡木葉心, 皆一縱理, 獨桂有兩紋, 形如圭, 製字者意或出此。葉味
辛甘, 與皮無別, 而加芳美。人喜咀嚼之。

附文: 花如海棠, 淡而葩小, 實如小橡子。取花未放者乾之。五年
可剝。以桂枝、肉桂、桂心為三等。桂枝質薄而味輕, 肉桂質厚而味
重。桂心則……剝厚桂, 以利竹卷曲, 取貼木多液處, 如經[経]帶,
味尤烈。凡木葉心皆一縱理, 獨桂有兩紋, 製字者意或出此。葉味辛
甘, 人喜咀嚼。桂之所草木不蕃。

榕。易生之木, 又易高大, 可覆數畝者甚多。根出半身, 附幹而下,
以入土, 故有「榕木倒生根」之語。禽鳥銜其子, 寄生他木上, 便蔚
茂。根下至地, 得土氣, 久則過其所寄。

附文: 葉如槐, 蔭樾可數畝。

沙木。與杉同類, 尤高大, 葉尖成叢穗, 小與杉異。

附文: 猺峒劈板博易, 舟下廣東。

桄榔木。身直如杉, 又如棕櫚, 有節似大竹, 一幹挺上, 高數丈,
開花數十穗, 綠色。

附文: 桄榔。虛心, 剖以承漏。外堅, 可為弩箭。

息欗木。生兩江州峒, 堅實, 漬鹽水中, 百年不腐。

燕脂木。堅緻, 色如臙脂, 可鏃作[器]。出融州及州峒, 桂林屬縣
亦有之。

雞桐。葉如楝, 其葉煮湯, 療足膝疾。

龍骨木。色翠青, 狀如枯骨。

風膏藥。葉如冬青, 治太陽疼, 頭目昏眩。

南漆。如稀飴, 氣如松脂, 霑霑無力。

蕩竹。葉大且密, 略如蘆葦。

澀竹。膚粗澀, 如木工所用沙紙, 可以錯磨爪甲。

附文: 澀竹。可磨以為甲。

人面竹。節密而凸, 宛如人面, 人采以為挂杖。

釣絲竹。類蕩竹, 枝極柔弱。

斑竹。中有疊暈, 江、浙間斑竹, 直一沁痕[淚痕], 無暈也。

附文: 斑竹……本出全州之清湘, 桂林亦有之。

貓頭竹。質性類筋竹。

桃枝竹。多生石上, 葉如小棕櫚, 人以大者為杖。

笏竹。刺竹也。芒棘森然。

箭竹。山中悉有。

宿根茄。茄本不凋，明年結實。

銅鼓草。其實如瓜，治瘡瘍毒。

大蒿。容、梧道中久無霜雪處年深滋長。大者可作屋柱，小亦中肩輿之扛。

石髮。出海上，纖長如絲縷。

區菜。細如荇帶，區如蓬菜，長一二尺。

都管草。一莖六葉，辟蜈蚣、蛇。

花藤。鏃以為器用，心有花紋。

胡蔓藤。毒草也，揉其草漬之水，入口即死。

附條: 修仁茶。修江，靜江府縣名。製片二寸許，上有「供神仙」三字者，上也。大片，粗淡。

附條: 檳榔。生黎峒。上春取為軟檳榔，夏秋採幹為米檳榔，小而尖為雞心檳榔。扁者為大腹子。悉能下氣，鹽漬為鹽檳榔。瓊管取其征，居歲計之半，廣州亦數萬緡。自閩至廣，以蜆灰蔞葉嚼之，先吐赤水如血，而後嚥其餘汁。廣州加丁香、桂花、三賴子，為香藥檳榔。

附條: 烏樠木。宜柁，第一。出欽州。

附條: 吉貝。如小桑，花似芙蓉，茸為席。

附條: 蛆草。辟蚊、蠅。

12. MISCELLANEOUS ITEMS 雜志

嶺南風土之異，宜錄以備博聞，而不可以部居，謂之雜志。

雪。南州多無雪霜，草木皆不改柯易葉，獨桂林歲歲得雪，或臘中三白，然終不及北州之多。靈川、興安之間，兩山蹲踞，中容一馬，謂之嚴關。朔雪至關輒止，大盛則度關至桂林城下，不復南矣。北城舊有樓曰「雪觀」，所以誇南州也。

附文: 雪。獨桂林有之。自桂林而南至海北，人不識雪。或言數十年前嘗雪，歲乃大災。蓋地氣常燠，植物柔脆，忽得雪，悉僵死。

風。廣東南海旁有颶風，西路稍北州縣悉無之。獨桂林多風，秋冬大甚，拔木飛瓦，晝夜不息。俗傳: 朝作一日止，暮七日，夜半即彌旬。去海猶千餘里，非颶也。土人自不知其說。予試論之，桂林地勢，視長沙、番禺千丈之上，高而多風，理固然也。

附文: 風……湘、灘二水，皆出靈川之海陽，行百里，分南北而下。北曰湘，下二千里至長沙，水始緩。南曰灘，過三百六十灘，又千二百里，至番禺入海。桂林獨當湘、灘之脊，在長炒、番禺千丈之上，雲物之表，高而多風，理故然也。

癸水。桂林有古記，父老傳誦之，略曰：「癸水繞東城，永不見刀兵。」癸水，灕江也。

瘴。二廣惟桂林無之，自是而南，皆瘴鄉矣。瘴者，山嵐水毒，與草莽沴氣，鬱勃蒸薰之所為也。其中人如瘧狀，治法雖多，常以附子為急須，不換金、正氣散為通用。邕州兩江，水土尤惡，一歲無時無瘴，春曰青草瘴，夏曰黃梅瘴，六七月曰新禾瘴，八九月曰黃茅瘴。土人以黃茅瘴為尤毒。

附文：瘴。乃炎方之地脈疏而氣泄，人為常燠所暵，膚理脈絡暉舒不密，又數十里無木陰、井泉、逆旅、醫藥，其病又不必皆瘴之為也。石湖《正夏堂記》極論之。

桂嶺。舊不知的實所在。城北五里，有尋丈小坡，立石其上，刻曰桂嶺。賀州自有桂嶺縣，相傳始[安]嶺在其地。今小坡非也。

俗字。邊遠俗陋，牒訴券約專用土俗書，桂林諸邑皆然。今姑記臨桂數字，雖甚鄙野，而偏傍亦有依附。

䯊音矮，不長也。

閫音穩，坐於門中，穩也。

坌亦音穩，大坐，亦穩也。

伩音嫋，小兒也。

奀音動，人瘦弱也。

歪音終，人亡絕也。

𡄢音臘，不能舉足也。

妖音大，女大及姊也。

岳音勘，山石之巖窟也。

閂音欄，門橫關也。

他不能悉記。予閱訟牒二年，習見之。

[文書。] 大理國間有文書至，南邊及商人持其國佛經，題識猶有「囝」字者。「囝」武后所作國字也。《唐書》稱大禮國，其國止用理字。

捲伴。南州法度疏略，婚姻多不正。村落強暴，竊人妻女以逃，轉移他所，安居自若，謂之捲伴，言捲以為伴侶。已而復為後人捲去，至有歷數捲未已者。其舅姑若前夫訪知所在，詣官自陳，官為追究。往往所謂前夫，亦是捲伴得之，復為後人所捲。惟其親父母兄弟及初娶者所訴，即歸始初被捲之家。

附文：捲伴。嫁娶不由禮，竊誘之名。

草子。即寒熱時疫。南中吏卒小民，不問病源，但頭痛體不佳，便謂之草子。不服藥，使人以小錐刺唇及舌尖出血，謂之挑草子。實無加損於病，必服藥乃愈。

附條:　[雞卜]。南人占法,以雄雞雛,執其兩足,焚香禱所占,撲雞殺之。拔兩股骨,净洗,線數束之。以竹筳插束處,使兩骨相背於筳端,執竹再祝。左骨為儂。儂,我也。右骨為人,人所占事也。視兩骨之側所有細竅,以細竹筳長寸餘徧插之,斜直偏正,各隨竅之自然,以定吉凶。法有十八變,大抵直而正或近骨者多吉,曲而斜或遠骨者多凶。

亦有用雞卵卜者。握卵以卜,書墨於殼,記其四維,煮熟橫截,視當墨處,辨殼中白之厚薄,以定儂人吉凶。

附條:　秦城。始皇發戍五嶺之地。

附條:　靈渠。在桂州興安縣。湘水北下湖南。又融江,牂牁下流也,南下廣西。二水遠不相謀。史祿於沙磕[磧]中壘石作鏵嘴,派湘之流,而注之融,激行六十里,置斗門三十六。舟入一斗,則復閘一斗,使水積漸進,故能循崖而上,建瓴而下。治水巧妙,無如靈渠者。

附條:　朝宗渠。浚之,則有人登科。

附條:　銅柱。馬伏波立交趾國中。人過柱下輒培石,遂成丘陵。馬總為安南都護,夷、獠為建二銅柱。又,唐何履光定南詔,復立伏波銅柱,則在大理。

附條:　僧道。無度牒而有妻子者,皆是。

附條:　月禾。無月不種。

附條:　土丁。制[製]如禁軍。

附條:　保丁。隸保正。平儂賊後所結,今困私役。

附條:　寨丁。沿溪洞所結。

附條:　洞丁。溪洞之民也。

附條:　挑生。妖術。以魚害人。在胸鬲,則服升麻吐之。在腰腹,鬱金下之。李壽翁侍郎集為雷州推官,鞫獄得此方。

附條:　蠱毒。人家無纖埃者是。

13. THE MAN 志蠻

廣西經略使,所領二十五郡,其外則西南諸蠻。蠻之區落,不可悉記。姑即其聲聞相接、帥司常有事於其地者數種,曰羈縻州洞,曰猺,曰獠,曰蠻,曰黎,曰蜑,通謂之蠻。

羈縻州洞。隸邕州左右江者為多。舊有四道儂氏,謂安平、武勒、忠[思]浪,七源四州,皆儂姓。又有四道黃氏,謂安德、歸樂、露城、田州四州,皆黃姓。又有武侯、延眾、石門、感德四鎮之民,自唐以來內附。

　　分析其種落,大者為州,小者為縣,又小者為洞。國朝開拓寖廣,州、縣、洞五十餘所,推其雄長者為首領,籍其民為壯丁。其人物獷悍,風俗荒怪,不可盡以中國教法繩治,姑羈縻之而已。

　　有知州、權州、監州、知縣、知洞,其次有同發遣、權發遣之屬,謂之主戶。餘民皆稱提陀,猶言百姓也。

　　其田計口給民,不得典賣,惟自開荒者由己,謂之祖業口分田。知州別得養印田,猶圭田也。權州以下無印記者,得蔭免田。

　　既各服屬其民,又以攻剽山獠及博買嫁娶所得生口,男女相配,給田使耕,教以武技,世世隸屬,謂之家奴,亦曰家丁。民戶強壯可教勸者,謂之田子[甲]、田丁,亦曰馬前牌,總謂之洞丁。

　　今黃姓尚多,而儂姓絕少,智高亂後,儂氏善良,許從國姓,今多姓趙氏。有舉洞純一姓者,婚姻不以為嫌。酋豪或娶數妻,皆曰媚娘。

　　宜州管下亦有羈縻州縣十餘所,其法制尤疏,幾似化外。其尤者曰南丹州,待之又與他州洞不同,特命其首領莫氏曰刺史,月支鹽料及守臣供給錢。其說以謂:宜州徼外,即唐黃家賊之地,崇建南丹,使控制之。莫氏家人亦有時相攻奪。今刺史莫延葚逐其弟延廩而自立,延廩奔朝廷,謂之出宋。凡州洞歸朝者,皆稱出宋。

　　附條:南丹在宜州西境。地產奇材異藥,惡獸毒虺。其人慓悍,以勁木為弩,聚毒傅矢,中人立死。

　　宜之高峰寨,古觀州也。與南丹接境。地勢極高。南丹對境亦高二曡矢可相及。

　　南丹日通市於高峰,少不如意,則怨毒思亂。其酋莫氏,國朝命為刺史,月支鹽料及守臣供給錢百五十千。比內部,自號莫大王。間入宜州,則禮之以列郡,來已數十年矣。其說以為,宜州徼外西原、黃洞、武陽郡小蠻,即唐黃家賊之地,崇建「南」丹,使控制之。然莫氏家人亦時自相攻剽。今刺史莫延葚逐其弟延廩而自立,延廩奔朝廷,謂之出宋。凡州洞歸朝,皆稱出宋。延葚淫酷,不能服其類。鄰永樂州玉[王]氏與為仇,歲相攻。

　　乾道丁亥,與玉[王]氏戰敗,告急於帥司,帥司遣官為和解。永樂益淬勵,有勝兵萬人,志滅莫氏。延葚乃益驕,不奉法,至私刻經略安撫司及宜州溪洞司印,效帥守花書行移,以嚇諸蕃落。

　　己丑歲,自言州去產馬蠻不遠,願與國買馬,乞於宜州置場。意欲藉朝廷任使,威制永樂。邊將常恭與交通,至為代作奏章至闕下,不經由帥司。樞密院是其說,差官置司宜州。余論奏:宜州密邇內地,無故通道諸蠻,且闊邊隙,不敢奉詔。且自行在所捕得常恭,因而劾奏其事。朝廷大悟,削籍竄之九江,永不放還。

外有省民冒法，商販入南丹受其帖牒至内地幹事者，多桂之興安人。余亦物色得其渠，送獄論如法。南丹稍讋。

附條： 安化州最鷙悍，在宜州西境。官月給生料鹽以撫之，猶日侵省地以耕，民不敢與爭，州亦不敢禁。

頃有凌、羅二將者，建炎間嘗率峒兵出勤王。賊曹成入廣西建大旗，購二人。二人遣健兵佯儒者數十輩，截髮為牧童，候成兵過，自牛背彉弩以毒矢射之，中者立死，成驚俱遁去。時盜滿四方，廣西獨晏然者，二將之力也。至今南人稱之。子孫有仕於州縣者。

附條 [Border History and Administration]： 儂智高反，朝廷討平之，因其疆域，參唐制，分析其種落，大者為州，小者為縣，又小者為洞，凡五十餘所……以藩籬内部，障防外蠻，緩急追集備禦，制如官軍。其酋皆世襲，今隸諸寨，總隸於提舉。左江四寨，二提舉。右江四寨，一提舉。寨官，民官也。知寨、主簿各一員，掌諸洞財賦。左江屯永平、太平，右江屯橫山，掌諸洞烟火民丁，以官兵盡護之。大抵人物獷悍，風俗荒怪，不可盡以中國教法繩治，姑羈縻之而已。

有知州、權州、監州、知縣、知洞，皆命於安撫若監司，給文帖朱記。其次有同發遣、權發遣之屬，謂之官典，各命於其州。每村團又推一人為長，謂之主户。餘民皆稱提陀，猶言百姓也。洞丁有爭，各訟諸酋，酋不能決；若酋自爭，則訟諸寨或提舉，又不能決，訟諸邕管，次至帥司而止。

皇祐以前，知州補授，不過都知兵馬使，僅比徽校。智高之亂，洞人立功，始有補班行者。諸洞知州不敢坐其上，視朝廷爵命，尚知尊敬。元豐以後，漸任中州官。

近歲洞酋，多寄籍内地，納粟補授，無非大小使臣。或敢詣闕陳獻利害，至借補閣職與帥守抗禮。

其為招馬官者，尤與州縣相狎。子弟有人邕州應舉者，招致游士，多設耳目，州縣文移未下，已先知之。輿騎居室服用，皆擬公侯，如安平州之李械，田州之黃諧，皆有强兵矣……

舊一州多不過五六百人，今有以千計者。元豐中嘗籍其數十餘萬，老弱不與。此籍久不修矣。

洞丁往往勁捷，能辛苦，穿皮履，上下山不頓。其械器有桶子甲、長槍、手標、偏刀、邊鐸牌、山弩、竹箭、桄榔箭之屬。其相仇殺，彼此布陣，各張兩翼，以相包裹。人多翼長者勝，無他奇。

民居苫茅，為兩重棚，謂之麻欄，上以自處，下畜牛豕。棚上編竹為棧，但有一牛皮為裀席。牛豕之穢，升聞棧罅，習慣之。亦以其地多虎狼，不爾則人畜俱不安。深廣民居，亦多如此。

洞人生理尤苟簡。冬編鵝毛木綿，夏緝蕉竹麻紵為衣，搏飯掬水以食。家具藏上窖，以備寇掠。土產生金、銀、銅、鉛、綠、丹砂、翠羽、洞緤、練布、茴香、草果諸藥，各逐其利，不困乏……

酋豪或娶數妻，皆曰媚娘。洞官之家，婚嫁以粗豪汰侈相高，聘送禮儀，多至千擔，少亦半之。婿來就親，女家於五里外結草屋百餘間與居，謂之入寮。兩家各以鼓樂迎男女至寮，女婢妾百餘，婿僮僕至數百。

成禮之夕，兩家各盛兵為備，小有言則兵刃相接。成婚後，婿常抽刃，妻之婢妾迕意即手殺之。自入寮能多殺婢，則妻黨畏之；否則謂之懦。半年而後歸夫家。

人遠出而歸者，止於三十里外。家遣巫提竹籃迓，脫歸人帖身衣貯之籃，以前導還家。言為行人收魂歸也。

親始死，被髮持瓶甖，慟哭水濱，擲銅錢、紙錢於水，汲歸浴尸，謂之買水。否則鄰里以為不孝。

此州、縣雖曰羈縻，然皆耕作省地，歲輸稅米於官。始時國家規模宏遠，以民官治理之，兵官鎮壓之，以諸洞財力養官軍，以民丁備招集驅使，上下相維，有臂指之勢。

洞酋雖號為知州、縣，多服皂白布袍，類里正、戶長。參寨官皆橫挺，自稱某州防遏盜賊。大抵見知寨，如里正之於長官，奉提舉如卒伍之於主將，視邕管如朝廷，望經略帥府則如神明。號令風靡，保障隱然。

比年不然。諸洞不供租賦，故無糧以養提舉之兵。提舉兵力單弱，故威令不行。寨官非惟惰不舉職，且日走洞官之門，握手為市。提舉官亦不復威重，與之交關通賄。其間有自愛稍欲振舉，諸洞必共污染之，使以罪去，甚則酖焉。原其始，皆邊吏冒法徇利致然，此弊固未易悉數也。

故事：安撫經略初開幕府，頒鹽、綵遍犒首領，以公文下教，謂之「委曲」。大略使固守邊界，存恤壯丁云。邕州守臣，舊不輕付。屯卒將五千人，京師遣人作司大兵城，邊備甚飭。比來邕州經費匱缺，觸事廢弛，但存羸卒數百人。城壁器械，頹壞不修。安撫都監司事體脧弱，州洞桀黠無所忌，至掠省民客旅，縛賣於交趾諸蠻。又招收省民不逞及配隸亡命者以益。田子甲反隱然平視安撫都監司，此非持久計。慶曆廣源之變，為鑒豈遠哉！

傜。本五溪槃瓠之後。其壤接廣右者，靜江之興安、義寧、古縣，融州之融水、懷遠縣界皆有之。生深山重溪中，椎髻跣足，不供征役，各以其遠近為伍。

附文：本盤瓠之後。其地山溪高深，介於巴、蜀、湖廣間，綿亙數千里。椎髻跣足，衣斑斕布褐。名為傜，而實不供征役……

以木葉覆屋，種禾、黍、粟、豆、山芋，雜以為糧，截竹筒而炊，暇則獵食山獸以續食。嶺蹬險厄，負戴者悉着背上，繩繫於額，傴而趨。

俗喜仇殺，猜忍輕死。又能忍飢行鬥，左腰長刀，右負大弩，手長槍，上下山險若飛。

兒始能行，燒鐵石烙其跟蹠，使頑木不仁，故能履棘茨根柄而不傷。兒始生，秤之以鐵如其重，漬之毒水。兒長大，煅其鋼以製刀，終身用之。試刀必斬牛，傾刃牛項下，以肩負刀，一負即殊者良刀也。

弩名偏架弩。隨跳躍中，以一足蹶張，背手傅矢，往往命中，鎗名掉鎗。長二丈餘，徒以護弩，不恃以取勝。戰則一弩一鎗，相將而前。執鎗者前却不常，以衛弩。執弩者口銜刀，而手射人。敵或冒刃逼之，鎗無所施，弩人釋弩，取口中刀，奮擊以救。度險整其行列，退去必有伏弩。土軍弓手輩與之角技藝，爭地利，往往不能決勝也。

歲首，祭盤瓠。雜揉魚肉酒飯於木槽，扣槽羣號為禮。

十月朔日各以聚落祭都貝大王。男女各成列。連袂相攜而舞，謂之「踏傜[謠]」。意相得，則男咿嗚躍之女羣，負所愛去，遂為夫婦，不由父母。其無配者，俟來歲再會。女二年無所向，父母或欲殺之，以其為人所棄云。

樂有盧沙、銃鼓、胡盧笙、竹笛之屬。其合樂時，眾音竟闋，擊竹箭以為節，團圞、跳躍、叫咏以相之。

歲暮，羣操樂入省地州縣，扣人門乞錢米酒炙，如儺然。

傜之屬桂林者，興安、靈川、臨桂、義寧、古縣諸邑，皆迫近山傜。最強者曰羅曼傜、麻園傜。其餘如黃沙、甲石、嶺屯、褒江、贈脚、黃村、赤水、藍思、巾江、竦江、定花、冷石、白面、黃意、大利、小平、灘頭、丹江、閃江等傜，不可勝數。

山谷間稻田無幾，天少雨，秬種不收，無所得食，則四出犯省地，求斗升以免死。久乃玩狎，雖豐歲，猶剽掠。

沿邊省民與傜犬牙者，風聲氣習，及筋力技藝略相當，或與通婚姻，結怨仇，往往為傜鄉導，而分鹵獲。傜既自識徑路，遂數數侵軼，邊民遂不能誰何。攻害田廬，剽穀粟牛畜，無歲無之。踉蹡篁竹，飄忽往來，州縣覺知，則已趍入巢穴。官軍不可入，但分屯路口。山多蹊，不可以遍防，加久成勞費。

又，傜人常以山貨、沙板、滑石之屬，竊與省民博鹽米。山田易旱乾，若一切閉截，無所得食，且冒死突出，為害滋烈。沿邊省民，因與交關，或侵負之，與締仇怨，則又私出相仇殺。

余既得其所以然，乾道九年夏，遣吏經理之。悉罷官軍，專用邊民，籍其可用者七千餘人，分為五十團，立之長、副，階級相制，毋得與傜通。為之器械、教習,使可悍小寇,不待報官。傜犯一團,諸團鳴鼓應之。

次告諭近傜,亦視省民相團結,毋得犯法,則通其博易之路。不然,絕之。彼見邊民已結形格勢禁,不可輕犯,幸得通博買,有鹽米之利,皆歡然聽命。

最後擇勇敢吏,將桑江歸順五十二傜頭首,深入生徑、羅曼等洞尤狠戾素不賓化者,亦以近傜利害諭之,悉從。

乃為置博易場二。一在義寧,一在融州之榮溪。天子誕節,首領得赴屬縣與犒宴。諸傜大悅,伍籍遂定,保障隱然。萬一遠傜弗率,必須先破近傜。近傜欲動,亦須先勝邊團,始能越至城郭,然亦難矣。

既數月,諸傜團長袁臺等數十人詣經略司謁謝。悉紫袍,巾裹橫梃。犒以銀碗、彩紬、鹽、酒,勞遣之。又各以誓狀來。其略云:

某等既充山職,今當鈴束男[女]。男行持棒,女行把麻,任從出入,不得生事者。上有太陽,下有地宿。其翻背者,生兒成驢,生女成豬,舉家滅絕。不得翻面說好,背面說惡。不得偷寒送暖。上山同路,下水同船。男兒帶刀同一邊,一點一齊,同殺盜賊。不用此款者,並依山例。

山例者,誅殺也。蠻語鄙陋,不欲沒其實,略志於此。

余承乏帥事二年,諸傜無一迹及省地,遂具以條約上聞,詔許遵守行之。

獠。在右江溪洞之外,俗謂之山獠。依山林而居,無酋長、版籍,蠻之荒忽無常者也。以射生、食動而活,蟲豸能蠕動者均取食。無年甲姓名,一村中惟有事力者曰郎火,餘但稱火。舊傳其類有飛頭、鑿齒、鼻飲、白衫、花面、赤褌之屬二十一種。今在右江西南一帶甚多,殆百餘種也。

附文: 歲首,以土杯十二貯水,隨辰位布列,郎火禱焉,乃集眾往觀。若寅有水而卯涸,則知正月雨,二月旱,自以不差。

諸蕃歲賣馬於官,道其境,必要取貨及鹽、牛,否則梗馬路。官亦以鹽、綵和謝之。其稍稍漸有名稱曰上下者,則入蠻類……

唐房千里《異物志》言:「獠婦生子即出。夫憊臥如乳婦,不謹則病,其妻乃無苦。」《唐志》言:「飛頭獠者,頭欲飛,周項有痕如縷,妻、子共守之。及夜如病,頭忽亡。比旦還。

又有烏武獠,地多瘴毒,中者不能飲藥,故自鑿齒。」

蠻。南方曰蠻。今郡縣之外,羈縻州洞,雖故皆蠻,地猶近省,民供稅役,故不以蠻命之。過羈縻,則謂之化外,真蠻矣!

區落連亘,接於西戎,種類殊詭,不可勝記,今志其近桂林者。

宜州有西南藩、大小張、大小王、龍、石、滕、謝諸蕃。地與牂牁接。人椎髻、跣足，或著木履，衣青花斑布，以射獵仇殺為事。

又，南連邕州南江之外者，羅殿、自杞等，以國名。羅孔、特磨、白衣、九道等，以道名。而峨州以西，別有酋長，無所統屬者：蘇綺、羅坐、夜面、計利、流求、萬壽、多嶺、阿悟等蠻，謂之生蠻。酋自謂太保。大抵與山獠相似，但有首領耳。羅殿等處，乃成聚落，亦有文書，公文稱羅殿國王。

其外又有大蠻落，西曰大理，東曰交趾。大理，南詔國也。交趾，古交州，治龍編，又為安南都護府。

附文：南方曰蠻，亦曰西南蕃......區落連亘湖、廣，接於西戎......此等前世蓋嘗內附，建黔南帥府於融州以統之。今融帥已罷，一切化外也。

融在傜洞之南，蕃蠻之東。蕃蠻時出州縣城郭，以蜜、蠟〔臘〕、草、香等貿易。每歲聖節，亦有出赴燕設者。其稱大小張、大小王、龍、石、騰、謝等，謂之西南蕃。地與牂牁接......持木牌、標槍、木弩、藥劍相鈔掠。

而峨州以西，又有羅坐、夜回、計利、流求、萬壽、多嶺、阿悟等蠻，謂之蠻酋。酋自謂太保。大抵與山獠相似，惟有首領耳。其人椎髻，以白紙繫之，云尚與諸葛武侯制服也。

西南蕃俗，大抵介別。男夫甚剛，妻女甚潔。夫婦異居，妻所居，深藏不見人，夫過其妻，掛劍於門而後入。或期於深山，不褻穢其居，謂否則鬼神禍之。此諸蠻皆未嘗為害，故其事亦不能詳知。

又有漢蠻者。十年前，大理馬至橫山，此蠻亦附以來。衣服與中國略同，能通華言，自云本諸葛武侯戍兵。聞其種人絕少。按《三國志》初無留戍事，《唐史》有西屠夷，乃馬伏波兵留不去者。初止十戶，隋末至三百戶，皆姓馬，號馬留人，與林邑分唐境。疑漢蠻即此類。

其南連邕州、南江之外稍有名稱者：羅殿、自杞，以國名；羅孔、特磨、白衣、九道等，以道名。此皆成聚落，地皆近南詔。

羅在融、宜之西，邕之西北。唐會昌中，封其帥為羅殿王，世襲爵，歲以馬至橫山互市。亦有移至邕，稱守羅。國王羅呂。

押馬者，稱西南謝蕃知武州節度使都大照會羅殿國文字。按《唐史》，東謝蠻居黔州西。謝氏世酋長，部落尊畏之。然則謝蕃蓋羅殿之巨室，又知其地近牂牁。

自杞本小蠻，尤兇狡嗜利，其賣馬於橫山，少拂意即拔刃向人，亦嘗有所殺傷，邕管亦殺數蠻以相當，事乃已。今其國王曰阿巳，生三歲而立。其臣阿謝柄國，善撫其眾，諸蠻比多附之，至有精騎萬計。阿巳年十七，阿謝乃歸國政，阿巳猶舉國以聽之。

諸蠻之至邕管賣馬者，風聲氣習，大抵略同。其人多深目長身，黑面白牙，以錦纏椎髻，短褐徒跣，戴笠荷氈，珥刷牙，金環約臂，背長刀，腰弩箭箙，腋下佩皮篋，胸至腰駢束麻索，以便乘馬。取馬於羣，但持長繩走前，擲馬首絡之，一投必中。刀長三尺，甚利，出自大理者尤奇。

性好潔，數人共飯，一杅中植一匕，置杯水其旁，少長共匕而食。探匕於水，鈔飯一哺放，搏之杅，令圓凈，始加之匕上，躍以入口，蓋不欲污匕妨他人。

每飯極少，飲酒亦止一杯，數咽始能盡。蓋腰腹束於繩故也。食鹽、礬、胡椒，不食彘肉。食已必刷齒，故常皓然。

甚惡穢氣，野次有穢，必坎而覆之。邕人每以此制其忿戾，投以穢器，輒躍馬驚走。

附條：今安南國，地接漢九真、日南諸郡，及唐驩、愛等州。東南薄海，接占城。占城，林邑也。東，海路通欽、廉；西，出諸蠻；西北，通邕州：在邕州東南隅，去左江太平寨最近。自寨正南行，至桄榔、花步，渡富良、白藤兩江，四程可至。又自寨東南行，過丹特羅小江，自諒州入，六程可至。自右江溫潤寨，則最遠。由欽州渡海，一日至。

歷代為郡縣，國朝遂在化外。丁氏、黎氏、李氏，代擅其地。熙寧間，乾德初立，其大臣用事，嗾之叛。八年，遂入寇，陷邕、欽、廉三州。朝廷命郭逵等討之。賊驅象拒戰，官軍以大刀斬象鼻，象奔却，自蹂其徒，大兵乘之，賊潰，乘勝拔桄榔縣。知縣，交主之婿，逃伏草間，窺見王師獲賊臠食之，以為天神，歸報其主，曰：「苟可逃命，子孫勿犯大朝。」

大軍次富良江，去都護府四十里，殺偽太子，擒其大將。乾德大懼，奉表乞降。會北兵多病瘴，乃詔赦交趾，還其五州。朝廷以逵不能遂取交州，黜為武衛上將軍。是役也，調民夫八十七萬有奇，金、谷[穀]稱是，迄無駿功。

大率自端拱迄嘉祐以來，兩江州洞，數為蠻所侵軼，潛舉以外鄉[向]，蘇茂、廣源、甲洞等處，入交趾者六十二村，故至今長雄諸蠻。

乾德死，子陽煥立。陽煥死，乾德有遺腹子，屬之占城，奉而立之。或云：有黎牟者，乾德妻黨也，嘗為李氏養子，殺遺腹子而立，冒姓李氏，名天祚。實紹興九年。其國人猶稱黎王。二十六年，遣使入貢，朝廷因以李氏官爵命之。天祚貌豐皙. 今生三十九年矣。有兄嘗知諒州，謀奪其位。事覺，流雪河州，髡為浮屠。

凡與廣西帥司及邕州通訊問，用二黑漆板夾繫文書，刻字於板上，謂之木夾文書。稱安南都護府天祚，不列銜，而列其將佐數人，皆僭官稱。有云金紫光禄大夫、守中書侍郎、同判都護府者，其意似以都護府如州郡簽廳也。帥司邊州報其文書，亦用木夾。

　　桂林掌故有元祐、熙寧間所藏舊案，交人行移，與今正同。印文曰「南越國印。」近年乃更用中書門下之印。中國之治略荒遠，邊吏又憚生事，例置不問，由來非一日矣！

　　其國之官稱王，宗族稱天王班，凡族稱承嗣，餘稱支嗣。有內職、外職。內職治民，曰輔國太尉，猶宰相也。左右郎司空，左右郎相，左右諫議大夫，內侍員外郎，以上為內職。外職治兵，曰樞密使、金吾太尉、都領兵、領兵使，又有判及同判安南都護府，皆為外職。外職治兵，曰樞密使、金吾太尉、都領兵、領兵使，又有判及同判安南都護府，皆為外職。仕者或科舉，或任子，或入貲[資]。科舉最貴。工技、奴婢之子孫，不許應舉。入貲[資]始為吏職，再入貲[資]補承信郎，可累遷為知州。在官者無俸給，但付一方之民，俾得以役屬耕漁以取利。

　　勝兵、卸[御]龍、武勝、龍翼、蟬殿、光武、王階、捧日、保勝等，皆有左右。每軍止二百人，橫刺字於額，曰「天子兵」。又有雄略、勇捷等九軍，充給使，如廂軍。兵士月一踐更，暇則耕種工藝自給。正月七日，人給錢三百，紬、絹、布各一匹，如紬綢，而蒙之以綿。月給禾十束。以元日犒軍，人得大禾飯一柈，魚鮓數枚。其地多占米，故以大禾為貴。

　　正月四日，酋椎牛饗其臣。七月五日為大節，人相慶遺。官僚以生口獻其酋，翌日，酋開宴酬之。

　　酋居樓四層，上以自居。第二層御宙居之，中人也。第三層箇利就居之，老鈐下之屬也。第四層軍士居之。又有水晶宮、天元殿等諸僭擬名字。門別有一樓，猶榜曰「安南都護府」。層皆朱漆，柱畫龍、鶴、仙女。

　　交人無貴賤，皆椎髻、跣足。酋平居亦然。但珥金簪，衣黃衫紫裙。餘皆服盤領四裙皁衫，不繫腰。衫下繫皁裙，珥銀鐵簪，曳皮履，執鶴羽扇，戴螺笠。皮履以皮為底，施小柱，以拇指夾之而行。扇編鶴羽，以辟蛇。螺笠，竹絲縷織，狀如田螺，最為工緻。婦人多晳，與男子絕異，好着綠寬袖直領，皆以皁裙束之。酋出入以人挽車，貴僚坐幅布上，掛大竹，兩夫舁之，名「抵鴉」。

　　歲時不供先，病不服藥，夜不燃燈。上巳日，男女集會，為行列，結五色彩為球，歌而拋之，謂之「飛駝。」男女自成列，女受駝，男婚以定。

　　宮門有大鐘樓，民訴事即撞鐘。大辟或付仇家，使甘心。盜賊斷手足指，逃亡斷手足，謀叛者埋身土中，露其頭。旁植長竿，挽竹繫其髻，使其頸伸，利鍤一劃之，其頭剗標竿杪。客死境外，鞭尸大罵，以為背國。

土産生金及銀、銅、朱砂、珠、貝、犀、象、翠羽、車渠、諸香及鹽、漆、吉貝之屬。果惟有甘橘、香圓、檳榔、扶留藤。新舊縣，隔一小江，皆出香。

新州故真臘地，侵得之。

不能造紙筆，求之省地。其人少通文墨，閩人附海舶往者，必厚遇之，因命之官，咨以決事。凡文移詭亂，多自游客出。相傳其祖公蘊，亦本閩人。

又，其國土人極少，半是省民。南州客旅，誘人作婢僕、擔夫，至州洞則縛而賣之，一人取黃金二兩。州洞轉賣入交趾，取黃金三兩。歲不下數百千人，有藝能者金倍之，知文書者又倍。面縛驅行，仰繫其首，俾不省來路。既出其國，各認買主，為奴終身，皆刺額上為四五字。婦人刺胸乳至肋。拘繫嚴酷，逃亡必殺。

又有秀才、僧、道、伎術及配隸亡命，逃奔之者甚多。

不能鼓鑄泉貨，純用中國小銅錢，皆商旅泄而出者。按：掠賣婢奴，與士人游邊，及透漏錢寶出外界，三者法禁具在，今玩弊如此，蓋安撫、都監、沿邊溪洞司不得人，邊政頹靡，奸宄肆行所致，日滋月長未艾也。及邊吏多無財用植立，窮斗升癯土，苟活待盡而已，何暇顧邊防國事者，宜痛心疾首焉。

然交人自熙寧敗降後，亦不復敢猖獗，南陲奠枕且百年。

紹興十二年，妖人譚友諒竄入思浪州，詐稱奉使，諭下州洞，天祚大恐。已而帥司檄安南捕友諒，邕州又以偽官告身招之，友諒與歸順首領二十餘人，各奉其銅印、地圖、土物詣橫山。知邕州趙願縛友諒，赴帥司斬之。首領悉送還安南，皆死。交趾安居，至今無議之者。

乾道八年春，上言願朝賀聖主登極。詔廣西經略司，貢使來者免至廷，方物受什一。其秋，復有詔下經略司，買馴象十，以備郊祀鹵簿。經略李浩遠德，用木夾事移交趾買之。蠻報不願賣，願以備貢。明年春，余至官，屢引前詔，却其貢。祀期寖近，朝命督象若星火。蠻復款塞：「六象及方物將至塞下，若不許貢，皆引歸，小蕃寧敢與朝廷為市！」余以其狀聞，且移書時相謂：「欲却其貢，并象勿須可也，祀以一純二精，寧乏此！」俄有金字牌下，差官押伴至闕。比及桂林，已秋末。以十象為賀登極綱，五象為進奉大禮綱，表字如蠅頭，僅可見。

其象飾禮物，則有金御乘象羅我，羅我如鞍架之狀，及金裝象牙、銷金象額、金銀裏象鈎連同心帶、金間銀裝象額、金銀裝朱纏象藤條、金鍍銅裝象脚鈴、裝象銅鐸、連鐵索、御乘象繡坐簟、裝象牸牛花朵、御乘象朱梯、御羅我同心龍頭帶等。餘物則有金銀鈔鑼、沉水香等。

大使稱中衛大夫尹子思，正使承議郎李邦正、副使忠翊郎阮文獻，其下有職員、書狀官、都衙、通引、知客、監綱、孔目、行首、押衙、教練、象公、長行、防授官之屬。

此等入朝，則稍更其服器。使者幞頭、靴笏、紅鞋、金帶、犀帶、每誇以金箱之。又以香膏沐髮如漆，裹細折烏紗巾，足加履襪。使者乘凉轎，釘鉸髤漆甚飭[飾]。蓋得至中國，盡變椎髻、徒跣、抵鴉之制。

先是紹興二十六年，嘗入貢，參知政事施公大任帥桂，循舊例以刺字報謁，且用行厨宴於其館。余悉罷之。

使者私謂衙校曰：「施參政惠顧厚，今奈何悉罷去？」余使人諭之，曰：「經略使司與安南都護府埒，經略使與南平王比肩，使者是都護府小官，才與桂林曹掾官比，法當廷參，不然不見也。」使者屈伏，遂廷參。

其歸也，至欲列拜，余使人掖之，曰：「免拜。」余奏其事，且著於籍，以為定制。

附條：余按交趾之名，其來最久。王制曰：「南方曰蠻，雕題交趾，有不火食者矣。」蓋涅其面額，至今猶然。

《太史公書》：「北至於幽陵，南至於交趾，西至於龍沙，東至於蟠木，日月所照，莫不砥屬。」言極南也。

漢武帝始置交趾郡，去洛陽萬一千里，歷代置守，今獨為蠻方。記曰：「南方曰蠻，雕題交趾，有不火食者矣。」記與「雕題」同言，則其人形必小異。《交州記》云：「交趾之人出南定縣，足骨無節，身有毛，卧者更扶始得起。」《山海經》亦言：「交陘國人交脛。」郭璞云：「腳脛曲戾相交，故謂之交趾。」

今安南地，乃漢、唐郡縣，其人百骸，與華無異；愛州，唐姜公輔實生之，何嘗有交脛等說！

或傳：安南有播流山，環數百里，皆如鐵圍，不可攀躋，中有土田，惟一竅可入，而常自室之，人物詭怪，不與外人通。疑此是古交趾也。必有能辯之者。

附條：黎，海南四郡郲[島]土蠻也。島直雷州，由徐聞渡，半日至。

島之中有黎母山，諸蠻環居四旁，號黎人。山極高，常在霧靄中，黎人自鮮識之。久晴，海氛清廓時，或見翠尖浮半空云。

蠻皆椎髻，跣足，插銀、銅、錫釵。婦人加銅環，耳墜垂肩。女及笄，即鯨[黥]頰為細花紋，謂之繡面。女既鯨[黥]，集親客相慶賀。惟婢獲則不繡面。四郡之人多黎姓，蓋其裔族。而今黎人乃多姓王。

附文：內為生黎，外為熟黎……或見翠尖浮半空，下猶洪濛也。

山水分流四郡。熟黎所居已阻深，生黎之巢深邃，外人不復跡。黎母之巔，則雖生黎亦不能至。相傳其上有人，壽考逸樂，不與世接，虎豹守險，無路可攀，但覺水泉甘美絕異爾。

蠻去省地遠，不供賦役者名生黎，耕作省地供賦役者，名熟黎。各以所邇，分隸四郡。

皆椎髻、跣足，插銀、銅、錫釵，腰縆花布，執長靶刀，長鞘弓，長荷槍，跬步不舍去。

熟黎能漢語，變服入州縣墟市，日晚鳴角結隊以歸。婦人繡面高髻，釵上加銅環，耳墜垂肩。衣裙皆五色吉貝，無褲襦，但繫裙數重，製四圍合縫，以足穿而繫之。

羣浴於川，先去上衣自濯，乃濯足，漸升其裙至頂，以身串入水。浴已，則裙復自頂而下，身亦出水。

繡面乃其吉禮。女年將及笄，置酒會親屬女伴，自施針筆，涅為極細蟲蛾[豸]花卉，而以淡粟紋遍其餘地，謂之繡面女。婢獲則否。

女工紡織，得中國彩帛，拆取色絲，和吉貝織花，所謂黎錦、黎單及鞍搭之類，精粗有差。

居處架木兩重，上以自居，下以畜牧。

婚媾折箭為定，集會亦椎鼓舞歌。

親死不哭，不粥飯，惟食生牛肉，以為哀痛之至。葬則舁櫬而行，令一人前行，以雞子擲地，雞子不破處即為吉穴。

客來，未相識，主人先於隙間窺之，客儼然矜莊，始遣奴布席於地，客即坐。又移時，主人乃出，對坐，不交一談。少焉置酒，先以惡臭穢味嘗客，客食不疑，則喜。繼設中酒，遂相親。否則遣客，不復與交。

會飲未嘗捨刀，三杯後各請弛備，雖解器械，猶置身傍也。一語不相能，則起而相戕。

性喜仇殺，謂之「捉拗」。所親為人所殺，後見仇家人及其洞中種類，皆擒取以荔枝木械之，要牛、酒、銀瓶，乃釋，謂之「贖命」。

土産沉水、蓬萊諸香。漫山悉檳榔、椰子木，亦産小馬、翠羽、黃蠟之屬。與省地商人博易，甚有信，而不受欺紿。商人有信，則相與如至親，借貸有所不吝。歲望其一來，不來則數數念之……

或負約不至，自一錢以上，雖數十年後，其同郡人擒之以為質，枷其項，關以橫木，俟前負者來償，乃釋。負者或遠或死，無辜被繫，累歲月至死乃已。

復伺其同郡人來，亦枷繫之。被繫家人往負債之家痛訴責償，或鄉黨率斂為償，始解。

凡負錢一緡，次年倍責兩緡，倍至十年乃止。本負一緡，十年為千緡，以故人不敢負其一錢。

客或誤殺其一雞，則鳴鼓告眾責償，曰：「某客殺我一雞，當償一闌。」一闌者，雌雄各一也。一雄為錢三十，一雌五十。一闌每生十子，五為雄，五為雌，一年四產十雞，併種當為六闌，六闌當生六十雞，以此倍計，展轉十年乃已。誤殺其一雞，雖富商亦償不足。客其家，無敢損動其一毫。

閩商值風水，蕩去其貲[資]，多入黎地耕種不歸。官吏及省民經由村洞，必舍其家，恃以安。

熟黎之地，始是州縣，大抵四郡各占島之一陲。其中黎地不可得，亦無路通。珠崖在島南陲，既不可取徑，則復桴海循島而南，所謂再涉鯨波也。

四郡之人多黎姓，蓋其裔族，而今黎人乃多姓王。生黎質直獷悍，不受欺觸，不服王化，亦不出為人患。熟黎貪狡，湖、廣、福建之姦民亡命雜焉。侵軼省界，常為四郡患。

有王二娘者，瓊州熟黎之酋，有夫而名不聞。家饒財，善用眾，能制服羣黎。朝廷封宜人。瓊管有號令，必下王宜人，無不帖然。二娘死，女能繼之。

其餘三郡，強名小壘，實不及江、浙間一村落。縣邑或為黎人據其廳事治所，遣人說謝得還。前後邊吏，懦不敢言。

淳熙元年十月，指山生黎洞首王仲期率其傍人十洞丁口千八百二十歸化。仲期與諸洞首王仲文等八十一人詣瓊管司，瓊管司受之，以例詣顯應廟研石歃血，約誓改過，不復鈔掠，犒賜遣歸。瓊守圖其形狀衣製上經略司，髻露者以絳帛約髻根，或以綵帛包髻，或戴小花笠，皆簪二銀篦，或加雉尾，衣花纈短衫，繫花襁裙，悉跣足，是其盛飾也。惟王居則青布紅錦袍束帶麻鞋，自云祖父宣和中嘗納土補官，賜錦袍云。

蜑。海上水居蠻也。以舟楫為家，采海物為生，且生食之。入水能視，合浦珠池蚌蛤，惟蜑能沒水探取。旁[榜]人以繩繫其腰，繩動搖則引而上。先煮毳衲極熱，出水急覆之，不然寒慄而死。或遇大魚、蛟、鼉諸海怪，為髯鬣所觸，往往潰腹折支，人見血一縷浮水面，知蜑死矣。

附文：蜑。乃海上水居之蠻，其種有三，漁蜑取魚，蠔蜑取蠔，木蜑伐山。皆坐[生]死短蓬[篷]間，生食海物。其生如浮，而各以疆界役於官。

附條：大理，南詔國也。本唐小夷，蒙舍詔在諸部最強[南]，故號南詔，自皮邏閣併五詔為一，受冊封雲南王。至異牟尋封南詔王，至酋龍而稱驃信，改元自稱大禮國。今其與中國接，乃稱大理國，與

《唐史》禮，理字異，未詳所始。大理地廣人庶，器械精良，前志載之詳矣。邕州右江水與大理大槃水通，大槃在大理之威楚府。而特磨道又與其善闡府者相接，自邕州道諸蠻獠至大理，不過四、五十程。産良馬可與橫山通，北梗自杞，南梗特磨，久不得至，語在大理馬條下。

乾道癸巳冬，忽有大理人李觀音得、董六斤黑、張般若師等，率以三字為名，凡二十三人，至橫山議市馬。出一文書，字畫署有法。大畧所湏《文選五臣註》、《五經廣註》、《春秋後語》、《三史加註》、《都大本草廣註》、《五藏論》、《大般若十六指序》、及《初學記》、《張孟押韻》、《切韻》、《玉篇》、《集聖歷百家書》之類、及須浮量鋼器并碗、琉璃椀壺、及紫檀、沉香水、甘草、石決明、井泉石、蜜陀僧、香蛤、海蛤等藥，稱利正［貞］二年十二月。其後云 ：「古人有云，察實者不留聲，觀行者不識詞，知己之人，幸逢相謁，言音未同，情慮相契。吾聞夫子云 ：君子和而不同，小人同而不和。今兩國之人，不期而會者，豈不習夫子之言哉。」續繼短章，伏乞斧伐。短章有「言音未會意相和，遠隔江山萬里多」之語。其人皆有禮儀。擎誦佛書，碧紙金銀字相間。邕人得其《大悲經》，稱為坦綽趙般若宗祈禳目疾而書。坦綽、酋望、清平官，皆其官名也。邕守犒來者，厚以遣歸。然南詔地極西南，當為西戎，尤邇蜀都，非桂帥所當鎮撫。

附條: Foreign Lands. 自交趾渡一水，即占城國，漢林邑也。其南浦有馬援銅柱山。東西皆大海，占城隔一水為真臘。又一水，曰登樓眉。此數國之西有大海，名細蘭，為交趾、大理、吐番之西境。南接大洋海，海口有細蘭國。其西有五天竺，極南有故臨國。又西則東大食海，海西則大食國。又西則西大食海，蕃商不通。南大洋海中諸國，以三佛齊為大，諸蕃寶貨之都會。三佛齊之東，則闍婆國。稍東北，則新羅國、髙麗國。諸蕃之去中國，惟占城最近，大食最遠。至大食，必舟行一年。凡諸國，皆蠻而遞及者也。

Abbreviations Used in
the Notes and Bibliography

BCGM	Li Shizhen, comp. *Bencao gangmu.*
Chau Ju-Kua	Hirth, Friedrich, and W. W. Rockhill, trans. *Chau Ju-Kua: His Work on the Chinese and Arab Trade in the Twelfth and Thirteenth Centuries, Entitled Chu-fan-chi.*
CMP	Read, Bernard, et al. *Chinese Medicinal Plants from the "Pen Ts'ao Gang Mu"* A.D. 1596.
Compendium	*Compendium of the Chinese Materia Medica: Bencao gangmu.* Compiled by the Committee for the Editing and Publication of the English Edition of *Compendium of Materia Medica.*
FCDBJ	*Fan Chengda biji liuzhong.* Collations and emendations by Kong Fanli.
Fourth Century Flora	Li, Hui-lin, trans. *Nan-fang ts'ao-mu chuang: A Fourth Century Flora of Southeast Asia.*
FSHJ	Fan Chengda. *Fan Shihu ji.*

HSRC	Huang Zhen. *Huangshi richao.*
Hucker	Hucker, Charles O., comp. *A Dictionary of Official Titles in Imperial China.*
Hu-Tan	*Guihai yuheng zhi jiyi jiaozhu.* Collations and annotations by Hu Qiwang and Tan Guangguang.
LWDD	Zhou Qufei. *Lingwai daida jiaozhu.* Collations and commentary by Yang Wuquan.
Needham et al.	Needham, Joseph, et al. *Science and Civilisation in China.*
Netolitzky	Netolitzky, Almut. *Das Ling-wai Tai-ta von Chou Ch'ü-fei.*
Qi Zhiping	*Guihai yuheng zhi jiaobu.* Collations and emendations by Qi Zhiping.
SKQS	Ji Yun et al., eds. *Siku quanshu.*
SSJZS	Ruan Yuan, ed. *Shisan jing zhushu.*
TPHYJ	Yue Shi, comp. *Taiping huanyu ji.*
Treatises	Fan Chengda. *Guihai yuheng zhi.*
WXTK	Ma Duanlian, ed. *Wenxian tongkao.*
Yan Pei	*Guihai yuheng zhi jiaozhu.* Collations and annotations by Yan Pei.
ZBZZCS	Bao Tingbo, comp. *Zhibuzu zhai congshu.*
ZFZ	Zhao Rukuo, comp. *Zhufan zhi jiaoshi.* Collations and commentary by Yang Bowen.

Appendix

IMPORTANT COLLECTIONS REPRINTING THE
TEXT OF *TREATISES OF THE SUPERVISOR AND
GUARDIAN OF THE CINNAMON SEA* AFTER *GUJIN
SHUOHAI* (MID-SIXTEENTH CENTURY)

SIXTEENTH CENTURY (?): GUJIN YISHI, EDITED BY WU GUAN (MING).
The modern scholar Yan Pei uses this edition as the base text for his
annotated and collated version of *Treatises*. Wu Guan's *Gujin yishi*
edition of *Treatises* is reprinted, with punctuation, in the *Congshu
jicheng xinbian* (1986; see below).

1646: SHUOFU. This "reedited" (*chongbian*) version of the *Shuofu*
collectanea, printed at Wanweishan Hall in Zhejiang, comprises 120
juan. The text of *Treatises* appears in chapter 62, reprinted in *Shuofu
sanzhong*, 6:62.2853–74. The 1646 version of the *Shuofu*, with collations by Tao Ting (*jinshi* 1610), is based on an earlier collection (now
lost), bearing the same title, traditionally ascribed to the editorship of
Tao Zongyi (fourteenth century).

1798: SIKU QUANSHU. The text of *Treatises* appears in the *Wenyuan
Ge Siku quanshu* (rpt., Taibei: Taiwan Shangwu Yinshuguan, 1983–
86), 589:367–87. In their extract the *Siku* editors say they used the edition of *Treatises* that was presented by the governor-general (*zongdu*)

of the Two Zhe (Liang Zhe).[1] No additional information on the source of this edition is provided.

1805: ZHIBUZU ZHAI CONGSHU EDITION, EDITED BY BAO TINGBO (1728–1814). This imprint of *Treatises* is based on the *Shihu jixing sanlu* edition of Fan's three travel diaries and *Treatises*, edited by Lu Xiang (*jinshi* 1523). Lu Xiang's collection is lost. His postface, dated 1527, has survived, however, and is reprinted at the end of collection 23 in the *Zhibuzu zhai congshu* (following the text of *Treatises*). Lu Xiang says nothing specific about the treatises. Bao Tingbo's editorial comments, following Lu's postface, say that Lu Xiang published printed versions of the three diaries in the Jian'an Book Ward (Jian'an Shufang) in Fujian during the Jiajing reign (1522–1567) of the Ming. Since Bao appended *Treatises* to the two diaries *Lanpei lu* and *Canluan lu*, following the "old order in which Mr. Lu published the diaries" (the *Wuchuan lu* appears separately, in collection 18), this indicates that *Treatises* was printed and published sometime in the Jiajing reign. As far as I know, no copies of this edition have survived.

LATE QING DYNASTY. There is a handwritten edition with collations by the Qing dynasty bibliophile Zhou Xingyi (1833–1904) preserved in the Beijing Library, which also cites Lu Xiang's collation notes. I have not seen this edition, but Kong Fanli has inspected it and cites Zhou and Lu's collation notes in his *Fan Chengda biji liuzhong*.

1927: SHUOFU. 100 *juan*. Edited and collated by Zhang Zongxiang (1882–1965) and published by the Commercial Press in Shanghai. This text is based on six Ming dynasty manuscript copies of the *Shuofu*. *Treatises* appears in chapter 50 of this collection, reprinted in *Shuofu sanzhong*, 2:50.792–803. Among the various "modern versions" of *Treatises*, this 1927 edition seems to have the fewest textual errors and misprints. Kong Fanli uses this version as the base text for the punctuated and collated edition of *Treatises* in *Fan Chengda biji liuzhong*, 81–161.

2002: FAN CHENGDA BIJI LIUZHONG. This is the most useful modern recension of Fan Chengda's surviving six major prose works. The text of *Treatises* appears on pp. 81–162. Kong collates the 1927 *Shuofu*

---

1   *Heyin Siku quanshu zongmu tiyao*, 14.101 (2:1525).

edition against several other surviving editions and reprints. He also cites most (but not all) of the "lost" passages preserved in the *Huang-shi richao, Wenxian tongkao,* and other collections.

In addition to the titles cited above, the text of *Treatises* also appears in the following collections. These all appear to be copies of the editions listed above, but we cannot be sure about this because the editors of these reprint collections rarely identify their textual source(s).

MING: BAICHUAN XUEHAI EDITION. The text of *Treatises* is reprinted in the Ming dynasty "reedited" (*chongji*) version of this collection (originally compiled by Zuo Gui in 1273). The anonymous editor's source for his text of *Treatises* is unknown. This edition of *Treatises* has numerous textual errors and misprints.

MING (SEVENTEENTH CENTURY): TANG SONG CONGSHU EDITION. This edition appears to have been copied directly from the *Baichuan xue-hai* version of *Treatises.*

1668, 1804: MISHU ERSHIYI ZHONG EDITION. Compiled by Wang Shi-han (seventeenth century).

1813: THIS EDITION FROM JAPAN, PUBLISHED BY THE SUISENDŌ, IS HELD IN THE TŌYŌ BUNKO. The publisher, Kuboki Sei'en, added a preface in which he praises Fan's descriptive talents but says nothing about the source(s) of his text. A Chinese translation of the preface is included in *Guihai yuheng zhi jiyi jiaozhu,* 314–15.

1831, 1920: XUEHAI LEIBIAN EDITION. Compiled by Cao Rong (1613–1677); expanded and revised by Tao Yue.

1915: SHUOKU EDITION. Edited by Wang Wenru.

1986: CONGSHU JICHENG XINBIAN (TAIBEI: XINWENFENG, 1986), 91:123-30. This modern version reproduces the edition of Wu Guan that appears in the *Gujin yishi.*

Bibliography

PREMODERN EDITIONS OF *TREATISES*
(LISTED IN APPROXIMATE CHRONOLOGICAL ORDER):

Gujin shuohai 古今說海 (The sea of talks, ancient and modern). Preface dated
1544. Lu Ji 陸楫, ed. The text of *Treatises* appears in the "Shuoxuan" 說選
section under "Pianji jia" 偏記家.

Gujin yishi 古今逸史 (Unofficial history, ancient and modern). Sixteenth century (?). Wu Guan 吳琯 (Ming), ed. *Treatises* is found in the "Yizhi" 逸志
section under "Fenzhi" 分志. Rpt. with punctuation in the *Congshu jicheng
xinbian* 叢書集成新編.

Shuofu 說郛 (Barbicans of talks). 1646. This version of the *Shuofu*, known as
the Wanweishan Tang 宛委山堂 edition, includes collations by Tao Ting
陶珽 and is based on an earlier version attributed to Tao Zongyi 陶宗儀.
Treatises is found in collection 62; rpt. in *Shuofu sanzhong*, 6:62.2853–74.

Siku quanshu 四庫全書 (Complete books of the Imperial Library). 1798. Ji
Yun 紀昀 et al., eds. The text of *Treatises* appears in the *Wenyuan Ge Siku
quanshu* 文淵閣四庫全書, 589:367–87. Rpt., Taibei: Shangwu Yinshuguan,
1983–86.

Zhibuzu zhai congshu 知不足齋叢書 (Collectaneum of the Knowledge-Is-Insufficient Studio). 1805. Bao Tingbo 鮑廷博, ed. The text of *Treatises* is included
in collection (*ji* 集) no. 23, 8:371–89. Rpt., Beijing: Zhonghua Shuju, 1999.

Shuofu 說郛 (Barbicans of talks). 1927. Zhang Zongxiang 張宗祥, ed. Shanghai:
Shangwu Yinshuguan. *Treatises* appears in chapter 50 of this collection; rpt.
in *Shuofu sanzhong*, 2:50.792–803.

MODERN PUNCTUATED AND ANNOTATED EDITIONS OF *TREATISES*

Fan Chengda biji liuzhong 范成大筆記六種 (Six examples of Fan Chengda's informal writings). Collations and emendations by Kong Fanli 孔凡禮. Beijing: Zhonghua Shuju, 2002.

Guihai yuheng zhi jiaobu 桂海虞衡志校補 (*The Treatises of the Supervisor and Guardian of the Cinnamon Sea*, with collations and emendations). Collations and emendations by Qi Zhiping 齊治平. Liuzhou: Guangxi Minzu Chubanshe, 1984.

Guihai yuheng zhi jiaozhu 桂海虞衡志校注 (*The Treatises of the Supervisor and Guardian of the Cinnamon Sea*, with collations and annotations). Collations and annotations by Yan Pei 嚴沛. Nanning: Guangxi Renmin Chubanshe, 1986.

Guihai yuheng zhi jiyi jiaozhu 桂海虞衡志輯佚校注 (*The Treatises of the Supervisor and Guardian of the Cinnamon Sea*, including lost passages, with collations and annotations). Collations and annotations by Hu Qiwang 胡起望 and Tan Guangguang 覃光廣. Chengdu: Sichuan Minzu Chubanshe, 1986.

PRIMARY SOURCES

Baibian 稗編 (The insignificant collection). *SKQS* ed.

Bao Tingbo 鮑廷博, comp. *Zhibuzu zhai congshu* 知不足齋叢書 (Collectaneum of the Knowledge-Is-Insufficient Studio). Beijing: Zhonghua Shuju, 1999.

Cai Xiang 蔡襄. *Lizhi pu* 荔枝譜 (Lichee manual). *Congshu jicheng xinbian* ed.

Cao Yin 曹寅 et al., eds. *Quan Tangshi* 全唐詩 (Complete Tang poetry). Beijing: Zhonghua Shuju, 1960.

Chao Gongwu 晁公武. *Junzhai dushu zhi* 郡齋讀書志 (Essays on reading the books in the Commandery Studio). Taibei: Shangwu Yinshuguan, 1974.

Chaoye qianzai 朝野僉載 (Note sources from court and countryside). *Congshu jicheng xinbian* ed.

Chen Shou 陳壽, comp. *Sanguo zhi* 三國志 (Records of the Three Kingdoms). Beijing: Zhonghua Shuju, 1962.

Chen Yuanlong 陳元龍. *Gezhi jingyuan* 格致鏡源 (The mirror and source of all knowledge). Rpt., Yangzhou: Yangzhou Guji Shudian, 1989.

Chen Zhensun 陳振孫. *Zhizhai shulu jieti* 直齋書錄解題 (Explanatory abstracts of books and texts in the Upright Studio). Punctuation and collation by Xu Xiaoman 徐小蠻 and Gu Meihua 顧美華. Shanghai: Shanghai Guji Chubanshe, 1987.

Cheng Minzheng 程敏政, comp. *Xin'an wenxian zhi* 新安文獻志 (Treatise of documents on Xin'an). *SKQS* ed.

Chongxiu Zhenghe jingshi zhenglei beiyong bencao 重修政和經史證類備用本草 (Revised Zhenghe reign classified and practical basic pharmacopeia [based

on material] from the classics and histories). Edited by Tang Shenwei 唐
慎微. Expanded and revised by Zhang Cunhui 張存惠. Taibei: Southern
Materials Center, 1976.

Chu Renhuo 褚人獲. *Jianhu ji* 堅瓠集 (Solid gourd collection). Hangzhou:
Zhejiang Renmin Chubanshe, 1986.

Chunqiu Zuozhuan zhengyi 春秋左傳正義 (*The Spring and Autumn [Annals]
and Zuo Commentary*, with corrected meanings). *SSJZS* ed.

Congshu jicheng xinbian 叢書集成新編 (Collected collectanea: new series).
Taibei: Xinwenfeng, 1986.

Dai Kaizhi 戴凱之. *Zhupu* 竹譜 (Bamboo manual). *Congshu jicheng xinbian* ed.

Dong Hao 董浩 et al., eds. *Quan Tangwen* 全唐文 (Complete Tang prose). Beijing: Zhonghua Shuju, 1983.

Du Guangting 杜光庭. *Dongtian fudi yuedu mingshan ji* 洞天福地嶽瀆名山
記 (Accounts of grotto-heavens, blessed sites, cardinal mounts, rivers, and
famous mountains). *Daozang* 道藏 ed.

Du Shaoling ji xiangzhu 杜少陵集詳註 (*Du Shaoling's Works*, with detailed
commentary). Hong Kong: Taiping Shuju, 1966.

Duan Chengshi 段成式. *Youyang zazu* 酉陽雜俎 (Miscellaneous morsels from
the south side of You [Mountain]). Punctuation and collations by Fang
Nansheng 方南生. Beijing: Zhonghua Shuju, 1981.

Duan Gonglu 段公路, comp. *Beihu lu* 北戶錄 (Records of a window to the
north). *Congshu jicheng xinbian* ed.

Fan Chengda 范成大. *Canluan lu* 驂鸞錄 (Diary of mounting a simurgh).
FCDBJ ed.

———. *Fan Shihu ji* 范石湖集 (Fan Shihu's collected works). Beijing: Zhonghua Shuju, 1962.

———. *Lanpei lu* 攬轡錄 (Diary of grasping the carriage reins). *FCDBJ* ed.

———. *Wuchuan lu* 吳船錄 (Diary of a boat trip to Wu). *FCDBJ* ed.

———. *Wujun zhi* 吳郡志 (Gazetteer of Wu Commandery). Nanjing: Jiangsu
Guji Chubanshe, 1999.

Fan Chuo 樊綽. *Manshu jiaozhu* 蠻書校注 (*Book on the Man*, with collations
and commentary). Collations and commentary by Xiang Da 向達. Beijing:
Zhonghua Shuju, 1962.

Fang Guoyu 方國瑜. *Zhongguo xi'nan lishi dili kaoshi* 中國西南歷史地理考釋
(Philological investigations of the historical geography of southwest China).
Beijing: Zhonghua Shuju, 1987.

Gu Zuyu 顧祖禹, comp. *Dushi fangyu jiyao* 讀史方輿紀要 (Essentials on places
and regions for reading history). Beijing: Zhonghua Shuju, 1955.

Guilin shike 桂林石刻 (Stone inscriptions of Guilin). Guilin: Guilin Wenhuaju,
1979.

Guoyu 國語 (Conversations of the states). *Sibu congkan* ed.

Han Yu. 韓愈 *Changli xiansheng ji* 昌黎先生集 (Mr. Changli's works). *Sibu
beiyao* ed.

Hanshu 漢書 (History of the [Former] Han). Ban Gu 班固 et al., eds. Beijing: Zhonghua Shuju, 1962.

Hong Chu 洪芻. *Xiang pu* 香譜 (Aromatics manual). *Congshu jicheng xinbian* ed.

Hong Kuo 洪适. *Panzhou wenji* 盤洲文集 (Coiling Islet's collected literary works). *Sibu congkan* ed.

Hong Mai 洪邁. *Yijian zhi* 夷堅志 (Accounts like those of Yijian). Beijing: Zhonghua Shuju, 1981.

Hou Hanshu 後漢書 (History of the Later Han). Fan Ye 范曄, ed. Beijing: Zhonghua Shuju, 1965.

Hu Qian 胡虔 and Zhu Yizhen 朱依真, eds. *Lingui xian zhi* 臨桂縣志 (Gazetteer of Lingui Town). 1802; rev., 1880; rpt., Taibei: Chengwen Chubanshe, 1967.

Huang Tingjian 黃庭堅. *Huang Tingjian quanji* 黃庭堅全集 (Complete works of Huang Tingjian). Chengdu: Sichuan Daxue Chubanshe, 2001.

Huang Zhen 黃震. *Huangshi richao* 黃氏日鈔 (Mr. Huang's daily transcriptions). *SKQS* ed.

Huang Zuo 黃佐 et al., eds. *Guangxi tongzhi* 廣西通志 (Comprehensive gazetteer for Guangxi). 1531; rpt., Beijing: Shumu Wenxian Chubanshe, 1988.

Ji Han 嵇含 et al. *Nanfang caomu zhuang wai shier zhong* 南方草木狀外十二種 (*Descriptions of the Herbaceous Plants and Trees in the Southern Quarter* and twelve other works). Shanghai: Shanghai Guji Chubanshe, 1993.

Jin Hong 金鉷 et al., eds. *Guangxi tongzhi* 廣西通志 (Comprehensive gazetteer for Guangxi). 1733. *SKQS* ed.

Jinshu 晉書 (History of the Jin). Fang Xuanling 房玄齡, ed. Beijing: Zhonghua Shuju, 1974.

Jiu Tangshu 舊唐書 (Old Tang history). Liu Xu 劉昫 et al., eds. Beijing: Zhonghua Shuju, 1975.

Kong Fanli 孔凡禮, comp. *Fan Chengda nianpu* 范成大年普 (Chronological biography of Fan Chengda). Ji'nan: Qi Lu Shushe, 1985.

———. *Fan Chengda yizhu jicun* 范成大佚著輯存 (Gathered remnants of Fan Chengda's lost works). Beijing: Zhonghua Shuju, 1983.

Kou Zongshi 寇宗奭, comp. *Bencao yanyi* 本草衍義 (Basic pharmacopeia, with elucidated meanings). Shanghai: Shanghai Guiji Chubanshe, 2002.

Kuang Lu 鄺露. *Chiya kaoshi* 赤雅考釋 (*Chiya*, with textual investigation and explanations). Textual investigation and explanations by Lan Hong'en 藍鴻恩. Nanning: Guangxi Renmin Chubanshe, 1995.

Li Daoyuan 酈道元, comp. *Shuijing zhu* 水經注 (Commentary on the *Waterways Classic*). 1897; rpt., Chengdu: Ba-Shu Shushe, 1985.

Li Fang 李昉 et al., comps. *Taiping guangji* 太平廣記 (Extensive records of the Taiping reign). Beijing: Renmin Wenxue Chubanshe, 1959.

———. *Taiping yulan* 太平御覽 (Imperially reviewed encyclopedia of the Taiping era). Beijing: Zhonghua Shuju, 1995.

Li Kan 李衎. *Zhupu xianglu* 竹譜詳錄 (*Bamboo Manual*, with detailed emendations). *SKQS* ed.

Li Rongdian 李榮典 and Gan Guangqiu 甘廣秋, eds. *Lingui xian zhi* 臨桂縣志 (Gazetteer for Lingui Town). Beijing: Fangzhi Chubanshe, 1996.

Li Shi 李石. *Fangzhou ji* 方舟集 (Square Boat's collected works).

Li Shizhen 李時珍, comp. *Bencao gangmu* 本草綱目 (Compendium of basic pharmacopeia). Beijing: Renmin Weisheng Chubanshe, 1977.

Li Tao 李燾, comp. *Xu Zizhi tongjian changbian* 續資治通鑑長編 (Continuation of the comprehensive mirror to aid in governing: the long draft). Beijing: Zhonghua Shuju, 1992.

Li Xinchuan 李心傳. *Jianyan yilai xinian yaolu* 建炎以來繫年要錄 (Register of essential matters during the successive years since the Jianyan reign). *SKQS* ed.

Li Yanshou 李延壽, ed. *Nanshi* 南史 (History of the Southern Dynasties). Beijing: Zhonghua Shuju, 1975.

Liji zhengyi 禮記正義 (*Record of Rites*, with corrected meanings). *SSJZS* ed.

Liu Xun 劉恂. *Lingbiao luyi* 嶺表錄異 (Records of the unusual [in areas] beyond the ranges). *Congshu jicheng xinbian* ed.

Liu Zongyuan 柳宗元. *Liu Zongyuan ji* 柳宗元集 (Liu Zongyuan's collected works). Beijing: Zhonghua Shuju, 1979.

Lou Yue 樓鑰. *Gongkui ji* 攻媿集 (Attacking Shame's collected works). *Sibu congkan* ed.

Lunyu zhushu 論語注疏 (Commentaries and subcommentaries on the *Analects*). *SSJZS* ed.

Ma Duanlin 馬端臨, ed. *Wenxian tongkao* 文獻通考 (Comprehensive investigation of texts and viewpoints). 1749; rpt., Taibei: Xinxing Shuju, 1965.

Maoshi zhengyi 毛詩正義 (*Mao's Poetry Classic*, with corrected meanings). *SSJZS* ed.

Mengzi zhushu 孟子注疏 (Commentaries and subcommentaries on the *Mencius*). *SSJZS* ed.

Mo Xiufu 莫休符. *Guilin fengtu ji* 桂林風土記 (Account of the customs and geography of Guilin). *Congshu jicheng xinbian* ed.

Ruan Yuan 阮元, ed. *Shisan jing zhushu* 十三經注疏 (Commentaries and subcommentaries on the *Thirteen Classics*). Beijing: Zhonghua Shuju, 1980.

Shangshu zhengyi 尚書正義 (*History Classic*, with corrected meanings). *SSJZS* ed.

Shanhai jing jiaozhu 山海經校注 (*Mountains and Seas Classic*, with collations and notes). Collations and notes by Yuan Ke 袁珂. Taibei: Liren Shuju, 1982.

Shao Bo 邵博, comp. *Shaoshi Wenjian houlu* 邵氏聞見後錄 (Things Mr. Shao has heard and seen: the later collection). Beijing: Zhonghua Shuju, 1983.

Shen Gua 沈括. *Mengxi bitan quanyi* 夢溪筆談全譯 (*Brush Notes from Dream Brook*: a complete translation). Notes and translations by Hu Daojing 胡道靜, Jin Liangnian 金良年, and Hu Xiaojing 胡小靜. Guiyang: Guizhou Renmin Chubanshe, 1998.

Shen Ying 沈瑩 et al., eds. *Linhai yiwu zhi* 臨海異物志 (Gazetteer of unusual products from Linhai). Beijing: Zhonghua Shuju, 1991.

Shuofu sanzhong 說郛三種 (Three versions of the *Barbicans of Talks*). Shanghai: Shanghai Guji Chubanshe, 1988.

Sima Guang 司馬光. *Zizhi tongjian* 資治通鑑 (Comprehensive mirror to aid in governing). Hong Kong: Zhonghua Shuju, 1976.

Sima Qian 司馬遷. *Shiji* 史記 (Records of the historian). Beijing: Zhonghua Shuju, 1959.

Song huiyao jigao 宋會要輯稿 (Reconstructed drafts of the assembled essentials on the Song). Xu Song 徐松, ed. Taibei: Xinwenfeng Chuban Gongsi, 1976.

Songshi 宋史 (Song History). Tuo Tuo 脫脫 [Toghto] et al., eds. Beijing: Zhonghua shuju, 1977.

Suishu 隋書 (History of the Sui). Wei Zheng 魏徵, ed. Beijing: Zhonghua Shuju, 1973.

Taishō shinshū daizōkyō 大正新修大藏經 (*The Tripiṭaka*: with major corrections and new revisions). Takakusu Junjirō 高楠順次郎 et al., eds. Tokyo: Daizō, 1924–1932.

Tan Cui 檀萃. *Dianhai yuheng zhi* 滇海虞衡志 (Treatises of the supervisor and guardian of the Yunnan Sea). *Congshu jicheng xinbian* ed.

Wang Dayuan 汪大淵. *Daoyi zhilüe jiaoshi* 島夷誌略校釋 (*Brief Treatise on the Island Barbarians*, with collations and explanations). Collations and explanations by Su Jiqing 蘇繼廎. Beijing: Zhonghua Shuju, 1981.

Wang Qinruo 王欽若 et al., eds. *Cefu yuangui* 册府元龜 (Outstanding models from the storehouse of literature). Beijing: Zhonghua Shuju, 1989.

Wang Renjun 王仁俊, comp. *Guihai yuheng zhi yiwen* 桂海虞衡志佚文 (Lost passages from the *Treatises of the Supervisor and Guardian of the Cinnamon Sea*). In *Jingji yiwen* 經籍佚文. Rpt., Shanghai: Shanghai Guji chubanshe, 2002(?).

Wang Sen 汪森, ed. *Yuexi congzai* 粵西叢載 (Miscellaneous sources on western Yue). 1705; rpt., Shanghai: Jinbu Shuju, n.d.

———. *Yuexi wenzai* 粵西文載 (Literary sources on Western Yue). *SKQS* ed.

Wang Shixing 王士性. *Guihai zhi xu* 桂海志續 (Continuation of the *Treatises of the Cinnamon Sea*). In *Wu Yue youcao* 吳岳游草, 7.111–15. Beijing: Zhonghua Shuju, 2006.

Wang Xiangzhi 王象之, ed. *Yudi jisheng* 輿地紀勝 (Chronicle of surpassing scenic spots on earth). 1849; rpt., Yangzhou: Jiangsu Guangling Guji Yinshe, 1991.

Wu Jing 吳儆. "Lun Yongzhou huawai zhuguo" 論邕州化外諸國 (On the various kingdoms beyond civilization in Yong County). In *Zhuzhou ji* 竹洲集. *SKQS* ed.

Xiao Tong 蕭統, comp. *Wenxuan* 文選 (Literary selections). Commentary by Li Shan 李善. Hong Kong: Shangwu Yinshuguan, 1973.

Xie Qikun 謝啓昆, comp. *Yuexi jinshi lüe* 粵西金石略 (Summary of inscriptions on metal and stone from western Yue). 1801; rpt., Nanjing: Jiangsu Guji Chubanshe, 1998.

Xie Qikun 謝啓昆 et al., eds. *Guangxi tongzhi* 廣西通志 (Comprehensive gazetteer for Guangxi). 1801; rpt., Taibei: Wenhai Chubanshe, 1966.

Xin Tangshu 新唐書 (New Tang History). Ouyang Xiu 歐陽修 et al., eds. Beijing: Zhonghua Shuju, 1975.

Ye Zhi 葉寘. *Tanzhai biheng* 坦齋筆衡 (Brush judgments from the level studio). *Shuofu* ed. 1927.

Yu Beishan 于北山, comp. *Fan Chengda nianpu* 范成大年譜 (Chronological biography of Fan Chengda). Shanghai: Shanghai Guji Chubanshe, 1987.

Yue Ke 岳珂. *Baozhen zhai shufa zan* 寶真齋書法贊 (Words of praise on calligraphy specimens in Precious Truth Studio). *Siku quanshu bieji* 四庫全書別集 ed.

Yue Shi 樂史, comp. *Taiping huanyu ji* 太平寰宇記 (Records encompassing the universe from the Taiping reign). Yonghe: Wenhai Chubanshe, 1963.

Zeng Zaozhuang 曾枣庄 and Liu Lin 劉琳, eds. *Quan Songwen* 全宋文 (Complete Song prose). Shanghai: Shanghai Cishu Chubanshe, 2006.

Zhan Zhi 湛之 (pseudonym for Fu Xuancong 傅璇琮), ed. *Yang Wanli Fan Chengda juan* 楊萬里范成大卷 (Documents on Yang Wanli and Fan Chengda). Beijing: Zhonghua Shuju, 1964.

Zhang Mingfeng 張鳴鳳. *Gui sheng Gui gu jiaodian* 桂勝桂故校點 (*Surpassing Sights and Ancient Matters of Guilin*, with collations and punctuation). Collations and punctuation by Qi Zhiping 齊治平. Nanning: Guangxi Renmin Chubanshe, 1988.

Zhang Shinan 張世南. *Youhuan jiwen* 游宦紀聞 (Records and experiences of a traveling official). Beijing: Zhonghua Shuju, 1997.

Zhao Rukuo 趙汝适, comp. *Zhufan zhi jiaoshi* 諸蕃志校釋 (*Treatises on the Various Man*, with collations and commentary). Collations and commentary by Yang Bowen 楊博文. Beijing: Zhonghua Shuju, 2000.

Zhou Bida. "Xianzheng dian daxueshi zeng yinqing guanglu dafu Fangong Chengda shendao bei" 賢政殿大學士贈銀青光禄大夫范公成大神道碑 (Divine way stele [epitaph] of Master Fan Chengda, senior scholarly gentleman in the Hall of Worthy Administration, conferred Great Master of Lustrous Emoluments and [Bearer of the] Silver and Azure). In Zhou Bida 周必大, *Wenzhong ji* 文忠集 (*SKQS* ed.), 61.11a–29b; rpt. with punctuation in Zhan Zhi, ed., *Yang Wanli Fan Chengda juan*, 112–122.

Zhou Hui 周揮. *Qingbo zazhi* 清波雜志 (Various notes from the Clear Waves [Gate]). Beijing: Zhonghua Shuju, 1994.

———. *Qingbo biezhi* 清波別志 (Separate notes from the Clear Waves [Gate]). *ZBZZCS* ed.

Zhou Mi 周密. *Qidong yeyu* 齊東野語 (Rustic words from east of Qi). Beijing: Zhonghua Shuju, 1983.

Zhou Qufei 周去非. *Lingwai daida jiaozhu* 嶺外代答校注 (*Vicarious Replies from Beyond the Ranges*, with collations and commentary). Collations and commentary by Yang Wuquan 楊武泉. Beijing: Zhonghua Shuju, 1999.

Zhouli zhushu 周禮注疏 (Commentaries and subcommentaries on the *Rites of Zhou*). ssjzs ed.

Zhu Mu 祝穆, comp. *Fangyu shenglan* 方輿勝覽 (Scenic sights of the world). Addenda and revisions by Zhu Zhu 祝洙. Beijing: Zhonghua Shuju, 2003.

———. *Shiwen leiju: houji* 事文類聚後集 (Classified collection of facts and texts: the later collection). skqs ed.

Zhuangzi 莊子. *Sibu beiyao* ed.

SECONDARY SOURCES AND REFERENCE WORKS

An Guolou 安國樓. *Songchao zhoubian minzu zhengce yanjiu* 宋朝周邊民族政策研究 (Study of Song dynasty policies on border nationalities). Taibei: Wenjin Chubanshe, 1997.

Anderson, James A. *The Rebel Den of Nùng Trí Cao: Loyalty and Identity Along the Sino-Vietnamese Frontier.* Seattle: University of Washington Press, 2007.

Aoyama Sadao 青山定男. *Tō Sō jidai no kōtsū to chishi chizu no kenkyū* 唐宋時代の交通と地誌地圖の研究 (Study of the communication systems of the Tang and Song and development of their topographies and maps). Tokyo: Yoshikawa Kōbun Kan, 1963.

Araki Toshikazu 荒木敏一. "Nung Chih-kao and the *K'o-chü* Examinations." *Acta Asiatica: Bulletin of the Institute of Eastern Culture* 50 (1986): 73–94.

Backus, Charles. *The Nan-chao Kingdom and T'ang China's Southwestern Frontier.* Cambridge: Cambridge University Press, 1981.

Barlow, Jeffrey. G. "The Zhuang Minority Peoples of the Sino-Vietnamese Frontier in the Song Period." *Journal of Southeast Asian Studies* 18.2 (Sept. 1987): 250–69.

Bishop, C. W. "The Elephant and Its Ivory in Ancient China." *Journal of the American Oriental Society* 41 (1921): 290–306.

Byon, Jae-Hyon. *Local Gazetteers in Southwest China: A Handbook.* Parerga: Occasional Papers on China 5. Seattle: School of International Studies, 1979.

Cao Jiaqi 曹家齊. *Songdai jiaotong guanli zhidu yanjiu* 宋代交通管理制度研究 (Study of the communication management system during the Song era). Kaifeng: Henan Daxue Chubanshe, 2002.

Carr, Michael Edward. "A Linguistic Study of the Flora and Fauna Sections of the *Erh-Ya*." Ph.D. diss., University of Arizona, 1979.

Chang, Chun-shu, and Joan Smythe, trans. *South China in the Twelfth Century: A Translation of Lu Yu's Travel Diaries, July 3–December 6, 1170.* Hong Kong: The Chinese University Press, 1981.

Chen Fenghuai 陳封懷. *Guangxi zhiwu zhi* 廣西植物志 (Atlas of the flora of Guangxi), vol. 1. Guangzhou: Guangdong Keji Chubanshe, 1991.

Chen Jiarong 陳佳榮 et al., comps. *Gudai Nanhai diming huishi* 古代南海地名匯釋 (Assembled explanations of ancient place-names of the Southern Sea). Beijing: Zhonghua Shuju, 1986.

Chen Jinghe 陳荊和. "Jiaozhi mingcheng kao" 交趾名稱考 (An investigation of the name "Jiaozhi"). *Bulletin of the College of Arts, National Taiwan University* (*Wenshizhe xuebao* 文史哲學報) 4 (1952): 79–130.

Chen Shixun 陳世訓. *Guangxi de qihou* 廣西的氣候 (The climate of Guangxi). Shanghai: Xinzhishi Chubanshe, 1956.

Chen Xin 陳新. *Lidai youji xuanyi: Songdai bufen* 歷代游記選譯: 宋代部分 (Selected translations of travel records from the successive eras: the Song era volume). Beijing: Baowentang Shudian, 1987.

Cheng Chaohuan 程超寰 and Du Hanyang 杜漢陽, eds. *Bencao yaoming huikao* 本草藥名匯考 (Glossary of herb names in the *Basic Pharmacopeia*). Shanghai: Shanghai Guji Chubanshe, 2004.

Cheng Guangyu 程光裕. "*Guihai yuheng zhi* kaolüe" 桂海虞衡志考略 (A brief investigation of the *Treatises of the Supervisor and Guardian of the Cinnamon Sea*). In *Songshi yanjiu ji* 宋史研究集 12:527–33. Taibei: Guoli Bianyiguan, 1980.

Compendium of Chinese Materia Medica: *Bencao gangmu*. Compiled by the Committee for the Editing and Publication of the English Edition of *Compendium of Materia Medica*. Beijing: Foreign Languages Press, 2003.

Csete, Mary Alice. "A Frontier Minority in the Chinese World: The Li People of Hainan Island from the Han through the High Qing." Ph.D. diss., State University of New York at Buffalo, 1995.

Cushman, Richard David. "Rebel Haunts and Lotus Huts: Problems in the Ethnohistory of the Yao." Ph.D. diss., Cornell University, 1970.

Deng Minjie 鄧敏傑. *Guangxi lishi dili tongkao* 廣西歷史地理通考 (A comprehensive investigation of the historical geography of Guangxi). Nanning: Guangxi Minzu Chubanshe, 1994.

Drake, F. S., general editor; Wolfram Eberhard, chairman of the proceedings. *Symposium on Historical, Archaeological and Linguistic Studies on Southern China, South-East Asia and the Hong Kong Region: Papers Presented at Meetings Held in September 1961 as Part of the Golden Jubilee Congress of the University of Hong Kong*. Hong Kong: Hong Kong University Press, 1967.

Eberhard, W. *The Local Cultures of South and East China*. A. Eberhard, trans. Leiden: E. J. Brill, 1968.

Erkes, Eduard. "Vogelzucht im alten China." *T'oung Pao* 37 (1944): 15–34.

Fang Jian 方健. "Jiechu de lishi dili xuejia Fan Chengda" 傑出的歷史地理學家范成大 (The outstanding historical geographer Fan Chengda). *Zhongguo lishi dili luncong* 中國歷史地理論叢 4 (1994): 207–24.

Fang Tie 方鐵. "Songchao jingying Guangxi diqu shulun" 宋朝經營廣西地區述論 (A descriptive essay on the management of the Guangxi area during the Song dynasty). *Guangxi minzu yanjiu* 廣西民族研究 2 (2001): 90–98.

Feng, H. Y., and J. K. Shryock. "The Black Magic in China Known as *Ku*." *Journal of the American Oriental Society* 55.1 (1935): 1–30.

Fiskesjö, Magnus. "On the 'Raw' and 'Cooked' Barbarians of Imperial China." *Inner Asia* 1 (1999): 139–68.

Gong Yanming 龔延明, comp. *Songdai guanzhi cidian* 宋代官制辭典 (Dictionary of the civil service system in the Song era). Beijing: Zhonghua Shuju, 1997.

Groff, George Weidman. *The Lychee and Longan*. New York: Orange Judd Company, 1921.

Gu Jiegang 顧頡剛. "Pao caiqiu" 拋綵球 (Throwing the multicolored ball). In *Shilin zashi* 史林雜識, 111–20. Beijing: Zhonghua Shuju, 1963.

Guangxi bowuguan gu taoci jingcui 廣西博物館古陶瓷精粹 (Gems of ancient ceramics in the Guangxi Museum). Beijing: Wenwu Chubanshe, 2002.

Guangxi Institute of Botany, Academia Guangxiana, eds. *Guangxi zhiwu zhi* 廣西植物誌 (*Flora of Guangxi*), vol. 1: *Zhongzi zhiwu* 種子植物 (*Spermatophyta*). Nanning: Guangxi Kexue Jishu Chubanshe, 1991.

Gudai Guilin shanshui wenxuan 古代桂林山水文選 (Literary selections from ancient eras on the landscape of Guilin). Translations and notes by Zhang Jiafan 張家璠 et al. Nanning: Lijiang Chubanshe, 1982.

Guilin Shi Wenwu Guanli Weiyuanhui 桂林市文物管理委員會. "Nan Song Guizhou chengtu jianshu" 南宋桂州城圖簡述 (A brief description of the city wall layout of Gui County during the Southern Song). *Wenwu* 文物 2 (1979): 79–82.

Guilin Zengpi yan 桂林甑皮巖. Archaeological Monograph Series, Type D, no. 69. Beijing: Wenwu Chubanshe, 2003.

Guo Jinlong 郭金龍. "Buhuan jin zhengqi san fangxiang hua shixing pi de shiyan yanjiu" 不換金正氣散芳香化濕醒脾的實驗研究 (Experimental research on using pinellia, atractylodes, and agastache formula to refresh and strengthen the spleen). *Zhongguo yiyao xuebao* 中國醫藥學報 4 (1989): 25–28.

Hagerty, Michael J. "Han Yen-chih's *Chü lu* (Monograph on the Oranges of Wen-chou, Chekiang)." *T'oung Pao* 20 (1923): 63–96.

———. "Tai K'ai-chih's *Chu-P'u*: A Fifth Century Monograph of Bamboos Written in Rhyme with Commentary." *Harvard Journal of Asiatic Studies* 11 (1948): 372–440.

Han Zhenhua 韓振華. "Ma Liuren shi shenme ren?" 馬留人是甚麼人 (Who are the Mas who stayed behind?). 1957. Reprinted in his *Zhongwai lishi guanxi yanjiu* 中外歷史關係研究, 277–85. Hong Kong: The University of Hong Kong, 1999.

Hanbury, Daniel, comp. *Notes on Chinese Materia Medica*. London: John E. Taylor, 1862.

Hanyu da cidian 漢語大詞典 (The great word dictionary of the Chinese language). Hanyu Da Cidian Bianji Weiyuanhui, ed. Shanghai: Shanghai Cishu Chubanshe, 1986.

Hargett, James M. "Boulder Lake Poems: Fan Chengda's (1126–1193) Rural Year in Suzhou Revisited." *Chinese Literature: Essays, Articles, and Reviews* 10 (1988): 109–31.

———. "Clearing the Apertures and Getting in Tune: The Hainan Exile of Su Shi (1037–1101)." *Journal of Sung-Yuan Studies* 30 (2000): 141–67.

———. "Fan Ch'eng-ta's *Lan-p'ei lu*: A Southern Sung Embassy Account." *Tsing Hua Journal of Chinese Studies,* new series 16.1–2 (Dec. 1984): 119–77.

———. *On the Road in Twelfth Century China: The Travel Diaries of Fan Chengda (1126–1193).* Stuttgart: Franz Steiner Verlag, 1989.

———. *Riding the River Home: A Complete and Annotated Translation of Fan Chengda's (1126–1193) Diary of a Boat Trip to Wu* (*Wuchuan lu* 吳船錄). Hong Kong: The Chinese University Press, 2008.

———. "Some Preliminary Remarks on the Travel Records of the Song Dynasty (960–1279)." *Chinese Literature: Essays, Articles, Reviews* 7.1–2 (July 1985): 67–93.

———. "Song Dynasty Local Gazetteers and Their Place in the History of *Difangzhi* Writing." *Harvard Journal of Asiatic Studies* 56.7 (Dec. 1996): 405–42.

———. *Stairway to Heaven: A Journey to the Summit of Mount Emei.* Albany, N.Y.: SUNY Press, 2006.

Harper, Donald. "Flowers in T'ang Poetry: Pomegranate, Sea Pomegranate, and Mountain Pomegranate." *Journal of the American Oriental Society* 106.1 (1986): 139–53.

Harrell, Stevan, ed. *Cultural Encounters on China's Ethnic Frontiers.* Seattle and London: University of Washington Press, 1995.

Hartman, Charles. "Stomping Songs: Word and Image." *Chinese Literature: Essays, Articles, Reviews* 17 (1995): 1–49.

Hervouet, Yves, ed. *A Sung Bibliography* (*Bibliographie des Sung*). Hong Kong: The Chinese University Press, 1978.

Heyin Siku quanshu zongmu tiyao ji Siku weishou shumu Jinhui shumu 合印四庫全書總目提要及四庫未收書目禁燬書目 (A joint printing of the abstracts in the *General Catalog of the Complete Books of the Imperial Library* together with the *Bibliography of Works Not Included in the Imperial Library* and the *Bibliography of Proscribed Books*). Taibei: Shangwu Yinshuguan, 1978.

Hirth, Friedrich, and W. W. Rockhill, trans. *Chau Ju-Kua: His Work on the Chinese and Arab Trade in the Twelfth and Thirteenth Centuries, Entitled Chu-fan-chi.* 1911; rpt., Taibei: Ch'eng-wen Publishing Co., 1967.

Ho Ke-en (He Geen 何格恩). "The Tanka 蜑家 or Boat People of South China." In F. S. Drake, general editor; Wolfram Eberhard, chairman of the proceedings, *Symposium on Historical, Archaeological and Linguistic Studies on Southern China, South-East Asia and the Hong Kong Region,* 120–23.

Holcombe, Charles. "Early Imperial China's Deep South: The Viet Regions through Tang Times." *T'ang Studies* 15–16 (1997–98): 125–56.

Huang Kuanchong 黃寬重. "Nan Song shidai Yongzhou de Hengshan zhai" 南宋時代邕州的橫山寨 (The Yong County Mount Heng Stockade in the Southern Song era). *Hanxue yanjiu* 漢學研究 3.2 (Dec. 1984): 507–34; rpt. in *Nan Song junzheng yu wenxian tansuo* 南宋軍政與文獻探索 (A study of Southern Song military administration and related documents), 1–49. Taibei: Xinwenfeng Chuban Gongsi, 1990.

Huang Shuguang 黃書光. *Yaozu wenxue shi* 瑤族文學史 (A literary history of the Yao nationality). Nanning: Guangxi Renmin Chubanshe, 1988.

Huang Tirong 黃體榮, ed. *Guangxi lishi dili* 廣西歷史地理 (Historical geography of Guangxi). Nanning: Guangxi Minzu Chubanshe, 1985.

Huang Xianfan 黃現璠. *Nong Zhigao* 儂智高. Nanning: Guangxi Renmin Chubanshe, 1983.

Hucker, Charles O., comp. *A Dictionary of Official Titles in Imperial China.* Stanford: Stanford University Press, 1985.

Jin Baoxiang 金寶祥. "Nan Song mazheng kao" 南宋馬政考 (An investigation of the horse administration during the Southern Song). Rpt. in Zhou Kangxie 周康燮, ed., *Song Liao Jin Yuan shi lunji* 宋遼金元史論集, 321–30. Hong Kong: Chongwen Shudian, 1971.

Kang Zhonghui 康忠慧. "Cong *Guihai yuheng zhi* jiedu Songchao dui Guangxi diqu de jingying" 從桂海虞衡志解讀宋朝對廣西地區的經營 (Song dynasty management of the Guangxi region as understood from reading the *Treatises of the Supervisor and Guardian of the Cinnamon Sea*). *Guangxi wenshi* 廣西文史 1 (2005): 31–34.

Knechtges, David R., trans. *Wen xuan or Selections of Refined Literature*, vol. 1: *Rhapsodies on Metropolises and Capitals*. Princeton: Princeton University Press, 1982.

Kohn, Livia, ed. *Daoism Handbook*. Leiden: E. J. Brill, 2000.

Laufer, Bertold. "Ivory in China." *Anthropology Leaflet*, 1–78. Chicago: Field Museum, 1925.

———. *Sino-Iranica: Chinese Contributions to the History of Civilization in Ancient Iran.* 1919; rpt., Taibei: Ch'eng Wen Publishing Company, 1978.

Legge, James, trans. *The Chinese Classics*. Second ed., revised. 1935; rpt., Taibei: Wenshizhe Chubanshe, 1971.

Li Deqing 李德清. *Zhongguo lishi diming bihui kao* 中國歷史地名避諱考 (Investigation of taboos using personal names of emperors as they relate to place names in Chinese history). Shanghai: Huadong Shifan Daxue Chubanshe, 2001.

Li Guoling 李國玲 et al., comps. *Songren zhuanji ziliao suoyin bubian* 宋人傳記資料索引補編 (Supplement to *Index to Biographical Materials of Sung Figures*). Chengdu: Sichuan Daxue Chubanshe, 1994.

Li, H. L. (Li Huilin 李惠林). *The Garden Flowers of China*. New York: Ronald Press, 1959.

————, trans. *Nan-fang ts'ao-mu chuang: A Fourth Century Flora of Southeast Asia*. Hong Kong: The Chinese University Press, 1979.

Li Tiaoyuan 李調元. *Yuedong biji* 粵東筆記 (Notes on Eastern Guangdong). In *Zhongguo fengtu zhi congkan* 中國風土志叢刊. Yangzhou: Guangling Shushe, 2003.

Li Xiaoyou 李孝友. "Nanzhao Dali de xieben Fojing" 南詔大理的寫本佛經 (Hand-copied Buddhist sūtras from Nanzhao and Dali). *Wenwu* 12 (1979): 54–56.

————. "Nanzhao Dali xiejing shulüe" 南詔大理寫經述略 (Brief description of the hand-written sūtras from Nanzhao and Dali). In Lan Jifu 藍吉富, ed., *Yunnan Dali fojiao lunwen ji* 雲南大理佛教論文集, 278–305. Gaoxiong: Foguang Chubanshe, 1991.

Li Zailong 李載龍 and Zhang Caixi 張才喜. "Woguo de dongtao ziyuan" 我國的冬桃資源 (On the natural resource "winter peaches" in our county). *Guoshu kexue* 果樹科學 (*Journal of Fruit Science*) 14 (1997): 105–9.

Li Zhiliang 李之亮, comp. *Song Liang Guang: Dajun shouchen yiti kao* 宋兩廣: 大郡守臣易替考 (Investigations into the changes in chief administrator officials in major commanderies of the Two Guang [circuits] during the Song). Chengdu: Ba Shu Shushe, 2001.

Liang Min 梁敏 and Zhang Junru 張均如. *Dong Tai yuzu gailun* 東泰語族概論 (General discussion of the Eastern Tai language family). Beijing: Zhongyang Minzu Daxue Chubanshe, 1995.

Liangqian nian Zhong-Xi li duizhao biao 兩千年中西曆對照表 (*A Sino-Western Calendar for Two Thousand Years, 1–2000 A.D.*) Taibei: Guomin Chubanshe, 1958.

Lin Ruihan 林瑞翰. "Songdai bianjun zhi mashi ji ma zhi gangyun" 宋代邊郡之馬市及馬之綱運 (Horse markets in border commanderies during the Song era and the horse transportation network). In *Songshi yanjiu ji* 宋史研究集, 11:125–45. Taibei: Guoli Bianyiguan, 1979.

Lin Tianwei 林天蔚. *Songdai xiangyao maoyi shigao* 宋代香藥貿易史稿 (Draft history of the aromatic medicine trade in the Song era). Hong Kong: Zhongguo Xueshe, 1960.

Lin Zhe 林哲. "Guilin Duxiu fengshan qian chengshi xingtai kongjian lishi yanbian" 桂林獨秀峰山前城市形態空間歷史演變 (The historical evolution of the layout of the city in front of Single Elegance Peak Hill in Guilin). *Guilin Gongxue yuan xuebao* 桂林工學院學報 (*Journal of Guilin Institute of Technology*) 24.2 (Apr. 2004): 159–64.

Liu Fusheng 劉復生. "Songdai 'Guangma' yiji xiangguan wenti" 宋代廣馬以及相關問題 (Guang horses during the Song era and related questions). *Zhongguo shi yanjiu* 中國史研究 3 (1995): 85–93.

Liu Kongfu 劉孔伏. "*Guihai yuheng zhi* chengshu qingkuang ji juanshu kaobian" 桂海虞衡志成書情況及卷數考辨 (The circumstances under which the *Treatises of the Supervisor and Guardian of the Cinnamon Sea* was completed and a critical examination of its chapter divisions). *Guangxi shiyuan xuebao* 廣西師院學報 (Zhexue Shehui Kexue Ban 哲學社會科學版) 1 (1993): 90–91, 101.

Long Qian'an 龍潛庵, comp. *Song Yuan yuyan cidian* 宋元語言詞典 (Dictionary of the language of the Song and Yuan periods). Shanghai: Shanghai Cishu Chubanshe, 1985.

Lü Mingzhong 呂名中 et al., eds. *Nanfang minzu gushi shulu* 南方民族古史書錄 (Annotated bibliography of ancient historical sources on the nationalities in the south). Chengdu: Sichuan Minzu Chubanshe, 1989.

Luce, Gordon H., trans. *The Man Shu* (*Book of the Southern Barbarians*). Data Paper Number 44. Ithaca: Cornell University, Department of Far Eastern Studies, Southeast Asia Program, 1961.

Luo Xianglin 羅香林. *Baiyue yuanliu yu wenhua* 百越源流與文化 (The origins and culture of the Hundred Yue). Taibei: Zhonghua Congshu Weiyuanhui, 1955.

Ma Tai-loi. "The Authenticity of the *Nan-fang ts'ao-mu chuang*." *T'oung Pao* 64.6–5 (1978): 218–52.

Marks, Robert B. *Tigers, Rice, Silk, and Silt: Environment and Economy in Late Imperial South China*. Cambridge: Cambridge University Press, 1998.

Maspero, Georges. *The Champa Kingdom: The History of an Extinct Vietnamese Culture*. Walter E. J. Tips, trans. Bangkok: White Lotus Press, 2002. This is an English translation of Maspero's *Le Royaume de Champa*.

———. "La géographie politique de l'Indochine aux environs de 960 a.d." *Études Asiatiques* 2 (1925): 79–126.

———. *Le Royaume de Champa*. Paris and Brussels: G. van Oest, 1928.

———. *Zhanpo shi* 占婆史. Feng Chengjun 馮承鈞, trans. Rpt., Taibei: Shangwu Yinshuguan, 1962. This is a Chinese translation of Maspero's *Le Royaume de Champa*.

Maspero, Henri. "Études d'histoire d'Annam, II: La géographie politique de l'Empire d'Annam sous les Li, les Tran et les Ho (X–XV siècles)," *Bulletin de l'École française d'Extrême-Orient* 16.1 (1916): 31–38.

Meng Yuanyao 蒙元耀. "*Guihai yuheng zhi* guoming kao" 桂海虞衡志果名考 (An Investigation of the Fruit Names in the *Treatises of the Supervisor and Guardian of the Cinnamon Sea*). *Guangxi difang zhi* 廣西地方志 5 (2004): 34–38.

———. "The Names and Classification of Common Plants in Zhuang." Ph.D. diss., University of Melbourne, 2002.

Meyer de Schauensee, Rodolphe. *The Birds of China*. Washington, D.C.: Smithsonian Institution Press, 1984.

Miles, Steven B. "Strange Encounters on the Cantonese Frontier: Region and Gender in Kuang Lu's (1604–1650) *Chiya*." *Nan Nü* 男女 8.1 (2006): 115–55.

Miyakawa Hisayuki 宮川尚志. "The Confucianization of South China." In Arthur Wright, ed., *The Confucian Persuasion*, 21–46. Stanford: Stanford University Press, 1959.

Mo Naiqun 莫乃群 et al., eds. *Guangxi fangzhi tiyao* 廣西方志提要 (Abstracts of Guangxi gazetteers). Nanning: Guangxi Renmin Chubanshe, 1988.

Needham, Joseph, et al. *Science and Civilisation in China*, vol. 4: *Physics and Physical Technology, Part III: Civil Engineering and Nautics*. Cambridge: Cambridge University Press, 1971.

———. *Science and Civilisation in China*, vol. 5: *Chemistry and Chemical Technology, Part IV: Spagyrical Discovery and Invention: Apparatus, Theories and Gifts*. Cambridge: Cambridge University Press, 1980.

———. *Science and Civilisation in China*, vol. 6: *Biology and Biological Technology, Part 1: Botany*. Cambridge: Cambridge University Press, 1986.

Needham, Joseph, and Robin Yates. *Science and Civilisation in China*, vol. 5: *Chemistry and Chemical Technology; Part VI: Military Technology: Missiles and Sieges*. Cambridge: Cambridge University Press, 1994.

Netolitzky, Almut. *Das Ling-wai Tai-ta von Chou Ch'ü-fei: Eine Landeskunde Südchinas aus dem 12, Jahrhundert*. Wiesbaden: Franz Steiner Verlag, 1977.

Ogawa Hiroshi 小川博. "Han Seidai no *Keikai gukō shi* no 'Banshi' ni tsuite" 范成大の桂海虞衡志の蛮志について (On the "Man Treatise" in Fan Chengda's *Treatises of the Supervisor and Guardian of the Cinnamon Sea*). *Chūgoku tairiku kobunka kenkyū* 中國大陸古文化研究 9 (1980): 27–29.

Okada Kōji 岡田宏二. *Zhongguo Hua'nan minzu shehui shi yanjiu* 中國華南民族社會史研究 (*Studies on the Ethnical and Social History of Southern China—Focused on the Relation with Different Racial Policy in Chinese Dynasties*). Zhao Lingzhi 趙令志 and Li Delong 李德龍, trans. Beijing: Minzu Chubanshe, 2002.

Ptak, Roderich. *Exotische Vögel: Chinesische Beschreibungen und Importe*. Wiesbaden: Harrassowitz Verlag, 2006.

Read, Bernard E., et al. *Chinese Materia Medica: Animal Drugs*. 1931; rpt., Taibei: Southern Materials Center, 1976.

———. *Chinese Materia Medica: Insect Drugs, Dragon and Snake Drugs, Fish Drugs*. 1941; rpt., Taibei: Southern Materials Center, 1982.

———. *Chinese Materia Medica: Turtle and Shellfish Drugs, Avian Drugs, Compendium of Minerals and Stones* (jointly compiled with C. Pak). 1937; rpt., Taibei: Southern Materials Center, 1982.

———. *Chinese Medicinal Plants from the "Pen Ts'ao Gang Mu" a.d. 1596: Botanical, Chemical and Pharmacological Reference List*. 1936; rpt. Taibei: Southern Materials Center, 1982.

Rudolph, Deborah Marie. "Literary Innovation and Aesthetic Tradition in Travel Writing of the Southern Sung: A Study of Fan Ch'eng-ta's *Wu-ch'uan lu*." Ph.D. diss., University at California, Berkeley, 1996.

Schafer, Edward H. *The Golden Peaches of Samarkand*. Berkeley and Los Angeles: University of California Press, 1963.

———. "Kiwi Fruit." *Sinological Papers* 3: 1–3. Berkeley, 1984.

————. *Pacing the Void: T'ang Approaches to the Stars.* Berkeley and Los Angeles: University of California Press, 1977.

————. "Parrots in Medieval China." In Søren Egerod and Else Glahn, eds., *Studia Serica Bernhard Kalgren Dedicata,* 271–82. Copenhagen: Ejnar Munksgaard, 1959.

————. "The Pearl Fisheries of Ho-p'u." *Journal of the American Oriental Society* 72.4 (1952): 155–68.

————. *Shore of Pearls.* Berkeley and Los Angeles: University of California Press, 1970.

————. *The Vermilion Bird: T'ang Images of the South.* Berkeley and Los Angeles: University of California Press, 1967.

Schafer, Edward H., and B. E. Wallacker. "Local Tribute Products of the T'ang Dynasty." *Journal of Oriental Studies* 4 (1957–58): 213–48.

Schmidt, J. D. *Stone Lake: The Poetry of Fan Chengda (1126–1193).* Cambridge: Cambridge University Press, 1992.

Shi Shenghan 石聲漢, ed. *Qimin yaoshu jinshi* 齊民要術今釋 (Modern explanations of the *Essential Arts of the Common People*). Beijing: Kexue Chubanshe, 1957–58.

Shin, Leo K. *The Making of the Chinese State: Ethnicity and Expansion on the Ming Borderlands.* Cambridge: Cambridge University Press, 2006.

Simoons, Frederick J. *Food in China: A Cultural and Historical Inquiry.* Boca Raton, Florida: CRC Press, 1991.

Smith, F. Porter, and G. A. Stuart. *Chinese Materia Medica: Vegetable Kingdom.* 1911; rpt., Taibei: Southern Materials Center, 1987.

Song Guangyu 宋光宇 et al., eds. *Hua'nan bianjiang minzu tulu* 華南邊疆民族圖錄 (Illustrated records of the borderland nationalities in southern China). Taibei: Guoli Zhongyang Tushuguan, 1991.

Song Liren 宋立人. "Gui de kaozheng" 桂的考證 (Textual research on the cinnamon cassia). *Nanjing Zhong yiyao daxue xuebao* 南京中醫藥大學學報 (*Ziran kexue ban* 自然科學版) 17.2 (March 2001): 73-75.

Stübel, Hans. "The Yao of the Province of Kwangtung." *Monumenta Serica* 3 (1938): 345–84.

Stübel, Hans, and P. Meriggi. *Die Li-Stämme der Insel Hainan: Ein Beitrag zur Volkskunde Südchinas.* Berlin: Klinkhardt & Biermann, 1937.

Su Guanchang 粟冠昌. "Tang Song Yuan Ming Qing Guangxi jimi zhouxian huo tu fuzhou xiandong sideng shezhi gaikuang" 唐宋元明清廣西羈縻州縣或土府州縣峒司等設置概況 (General survey of the bridle and halter counties and towns, and the local county, town, and settlement inspectors installed in Guangxi during the Tang, Song, Yuan, Ming, and Qing). *Guangxi minzu yanjiu* 廣西民族研究 1 (1986): 35–44.

Su Hongji 蘇洪濟 and Deng Zhuren 鄧祝仁. "Guihai yuheng zhi—Nan Song shiqi Guilin de lüyou baike quanshu" 桂海虞衡志—南宋時期桂林的旅游百科全書 (*Treatises of the Supervisor and Guardian of the Cinnamon Sea*—an encyclopedia on travel in Guilin during the Southern Song period). *Shehui kexue jia* 社會科學家 (*Social Scientist*) 5 (May 2003): 105–9.

Tan Qixiang 譚其驤 et al., eds. *Zhongguo lishi ditu ji* 中國歷史地圖集 (*The Historical Atlas of China*), 6: *Song Liao Jin shiqi* 宋遼金時期 (The Song, Liao, and Jin periods). Shanghai: Ditu Chubanshe, 1982.

Tan Xiaohang 覃曉航. *Lingnan gu Yueren mingcheng wenhua tanyuan* 嶺南古越人名稱文化探源 (A probe of the origins of name culture among the ancient Yue people of Lingnan). Beijing: Zhongyang Minzu Daxue Chubanshe, 1995.

Tan Yanhuan 覃延歡 and Liao Guoyi 廖國一, eds. *Guangxi shigao* 廣西史稿 (Draft history of Guangxi). Guilin: Guangxi Shifan Daxue Chubanshe, 1998.

Tang Zhaomin 唐兆民, comp. *Lingqu wenxian cuibian* 靈渠文獻粹編 (Essential compilation of documents on the Numinous Canal). Beijing: Zhonghua Shuju, 1982.

Took, Jennifer. "A Twelfth Century Monograph on South China: The *Guihai yuheng zhi* by Fan Chengda, a Translation and Annotation of the Chapter on the Man Peoples (*zhi man*)." Bachelor of Letters (Honours) thesis, University of Melbourne, 1996.

Ul'ianova, M. IU. *Za khrebtami, vmesto otvetov: Lin vai dai da*. Moscow: Vostochnaia Literature, 2001. A translation of *Treatises* appears on pp. 360–435.

Van Gulick, Robert Hans. *The Gibbon in China: An Essay in Chinese Animal Lore*. Leiden: E. J. Brill, 1967.

Wade, Geoff. "Champa in the *Song hui-yao*: A Draft Translation." ARI Working Paper, no. 53 (Dec. 2005). http://www.ari.nus.edu.sg/pub/wps.htm.

Wan Yingmin 萬英敏. "*Guihai yuheng zhi* de wenxian xue yanjiu" 桂海虞衡志的文獻學研究 (A philological study of the *Treatises of the Supervisor and Guardian of the Cinnamon Sea*). M.A. thesis, East China Normal University (Huadong Shifan Daxue 華東師範大學), 2005.

Wang Kaiji 王凱基 et al., eds. *Zhiwu shengwu xue cidian* 植物生物學詞典 (A dictionary of plant biology). Shanghai: Shanghai Keji Jiaoyu Chubanshe, 1998.

Wang Shuanghuai 王雙懷, chief ed. *Zhonghua rili tongdian* 中華日曆通典 (Comprehensive compendium of the Chinese calendar). Changchun: Jilin Wenshi Chubanshe, 2006.

Wang Teh-yi [Wang Deyi] 王德毅 et al., comps. *Songren zhuanji ziliao suoyin* 宋人傳記資料索引 (*Index to Biographical Materials of Sung Figures*). Taibei: Dingwen Shuju, 1974–76.

Wang Ying 王鍈, comp. *Tang Song biji yuci huishi* 唐宋筆記語辭彙釋 (Glossary of vocabulary in Tang and Song miscellanea). Revised and expanded ed. Beijing: Zhonghua Shuju, 2001.

Wei Buxuan 韋步軒. "Cong *Guihai yuheng zhi* kan Songdai Guangxi de wenhua he shehui shenghuo" 從桂海虞衡志看宋代廣西的文化和社會生

活 (Cultural and social life in Guangxi during the Song era as seen in the *Treatises of the Supervisor and Guardian of the Cinnamon Sea*). *Bianjiang jingji yu wenhua* 邊疆經濟與文化 (*The Border Economy and Culture*) 7 (2007): 94–95.

Wheatley, Paul. "Geographical Notes on Some Commodities Involved in the Sung Maritime Trade." *Journal of the Malayan Branch of the Royal Asiatic Society* 32.2 (June 1959): 1–140.

Wiens, Herold J. *China's March toward the Tropics*. Hamden, Connecticut: The Shoe String Press, 1954.

Wilkinson, Endymion, comp. *Chinese History: A Manual, Revised and Enlarged*. Cambridge and London: Harvard University Center for the Harvard-Yenching Institute, 2000.

Wright, Hope, comp. *Alphabetical List of Geographical Names in Sung China*. Paris: École practique des hautes études, Centre de recherches historiques, 1956.

Wu Yongzhang 吳永章. *Zhongguo nanfang minzu shizhi yaoji tijie* 中國南方民族史志要籍題解 (Key sources and explanatory notes on historical works concerning the nationalities of South China). Beijing: Minzu Chubanshe, 1991.

Xinbian Han-Ying Zhong yiyao fenlei cidian 新編漢英中醫藥分類辭典 (Classified Chinese-English dictionary of traditional Chinese medicine: new edition). Xie Zhufan 謝竹藩, ed. Beijing: Foreign Languages Press, 2002.

Yan Yingjun 嚴英俊. "Fan Chengda yu *Guihai yuheng zhi*" 范成大與桂海虞衡志 (Fan Chengda and the *Treatises of the Supervisor and Guardian of the Cinnamon Sea*). *Lishi jiaoyu* 歷史教育 8 (1987): 58–60.

Yang Wuquan 楊武泉. "*Guihai yuheng zhi jiaozhu* jiaoji zayi" 桂海虞衡志校注校輯雜議 (Some random opinions concerning *Treatises of the Supervisor and Guardian of the Cinnamon Sea, with collations and annotations*). *Xueshu luntan* 學術論壇 5 (1987): 52–55, 51.

Yang Zhishui 揚之水. "Songdai de chenxiang: shuichen yu Hainan chen" 宋代的沉香: 水沉與海南沉 (Sinking aromatics of the Song era: water sinking and Hainan sinking [aromatics]). *Wenhua zhishi* 文化知識 3 (2004): 28–36 (part 1).

———. "Songdai de chenxiang: zhengchen yu hexiang" 宋代的沉香: 蒸沉與合香 (Sinking aromatics of the Song era: steaming-sinking and mixed aromatics). *Wenhua zhishi* 文化知識 4 (2004): 97–102 (part 2).

Yu Guokun 余國琨 et al. *Guilin shanshui* 桂林山水 (The landscape of Guilin). Nanning: Guangxi Renmin Chubanshe, 1979.

Zeng Duhong 曾度洪 et al. *Guilin jianshi* 桂林簡史 (Brief history of Guilin). Nanning: Guangxi Renmin Chubanshe, 1984.

Zhang Jinlian 張金蓮, "Songchao yu Annan tongdao shitan" 宋朝與安南通道試探 (Preliminary probe into transportation routes in the Song Dynasty and Annan). *Dongnan Ya zongheng* 東南亞縱橫 10 (2005): 65–71.

Zhang Quanming 張全明. "*Guihai yuheng zhi* de shengtai wenhua shi tese yu jiazhi" 桂海虞衡志的生態文化史特色與價值 (The features and value of the *Treatises of the Supervisor and Guardian of the Cinnamon Sea* in ecological and cultural history). *Huazhong shifan daxue xuebao* 華中師範大學學報 (*Renwen shehui kexue ban* 人文社會科學版) 42.1 (Jan. 2003): 88–92, 97.

Zhang Xinglang 張星烺. *Zhong-Xi jiaotong shiliao huibian* 中西交通史料彙編 (Compilation of source materials on the history of communication between China and the West). Beijing: Zhonghua Shuju, 2003.

Zhang Yigui 張益桂. *Guilin.* Photographs by Feng Xiaoming 封小明. Beijing: Cultural Relics Publishing House, 1987.

———. "Nan Song 'Jingjiang fu chengchi tu' jianshu" 南宋靜江城池圖簡述 (A brief description of the Southern Song "Map of Jingjiang Municipality with Walls and Moats"). *Guangxi difang zhi* 廣西地方志 1 (2001): 43–47.

Zhao Fengyan 趙鳳燕 and Li Xiaocen 李曉岑. "Cong *Lingwai daida* kan Guangxi Songdai de kexue jishu chengjiu" 從嶺外代答看廣西宋代的科學技術成就 (Achievements in science and technology in Guangxi during the Song period as seen in *Vicarious Replies from Beyond the Ranges*). *Guangxi minzu daxue xuebao* 廣西民族大學學報 (*Ziran kexue ban* 自然科學版) 13.1 (Feb. 2007): 42–46.

Zhou Qingquan 周清泉. "Shi Zangge" 釋牂牁 (Philological explanation of the term "Zangge"). *Chengdu daxue xuebao* 成都大學學報 3 (2006): 97–98, 74.

Zhu Shangshu 祝尚書. *Songren bieji xulu* 宋人別集叙錄 (Commentaries on the individual collections of Song authors). Beijing: Zhonghua Shuju, 1999.

Glossary / Index

Page numbers in boldface type indicate Fan's main topical entries.

A